GENDER AND THE
LIFE COURSE

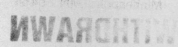

GENDER AND THE LIFE COURSE

Edited by

Alice S. Rossi
University of Massachusetts-Amherst

American Sociological Association Presidential Volume

ALDINE
Publishing Company
New York

ABOUT THE EDITOR

Alice S. Rossi is Professor of Sociology at the University of Massachusetts-Amherst. She is Past-President of the American Sociological Association. Her current research interests are in family and kinship, biosocial science, and gender and politics. Her most recent book is *Feminists in Politics: A Panel Analysis of the First National Women's Conference*. She is the editor of *The Feminist Papers: From Adams to de Beauvoir*, *Academic Women on the Move*, and *Essays on Sex Equality*.

Aldine Publishing Company
200 Saw Mill River Road
Hawthorne, New York 10532

Library of Congress Cataloging in Publication Data

Main entry under title:
Gender and the life course.
    Includes bibliographies and index.
    1. Sex—Addresses, essays, lectures. 2. Sex differences—Addresses, essays, lectures. 3. Sex role—Addresses, essays, lectures. 4. Life cycle, Human—Addresses, essays, lectures. I. Rossi, Alice S., 1922—
HQ21.G363 1984 305.3 84-12335
ISBN 0-202-30311-X
ISBN 0-202-30312-8 (pbk.)

Printed in the United States of America
10 9 8 7 6 5 4 3 2

To Pete, with gratitude
for the 35 years we have shared

CONTENTS

Contents

PREFACE

All eighteen papers in this collection were first written for presentation to the Annual Meeting of the American Sociological Association in Detroit, Michigan, in September 1983. As President of ASA and Chair of the 1983 Program Committee, it was my privilege to organize the annual meeting and to invite a variety of social scientists to prepare papers for the plenary sessions devoted to the theme: *Age and Gender: Gender Differentiation in a Life Span Framework*. The Program Committee concurred with my wish to delegate to Organizers of the Thematic Sessions the task of inviting persons of their own choice to write papers for their sessions. Six papers were given at the two Plenary Sessions, and 38 papers at the 12 Thematic Sessions. The "pool" from which I have chosen the papers in this volume, therefore, consisted of these 44 papers, supplemented by a dozen or so others given at sessions sponsored by the Section on the Sociology of Aging and the Section on Sex and Gender. All the papers that survived the initial screening have been revised, many of them extensively so, for publication in this volume. All appear here in print for the first time, with the exception of my own presidential address, which appeared in the February 1984 issue of the *American Sociological Review*, and in slightly different form, the paper by Mead Cain, which appeared in the December 1983 issue of *Population and Development Review*.

Since the Organizers of the Thematic Sessions were the people who invited many of the authors in this volume to give papers in Detroit, it is to many of these Organizers that I wish to express my appreciation and gratitude: Patricia Y. Martin, Carol M. Mueller, Orville G. Brim, Jr., William H. Form, Joan F. Huber, Jean C. Lipman-Blumen, Jessie Bernard, Valerie K. Oppenheimer, Karen O. Mason, and Gary F. Jensen. It is to the good judgment of these ten Organizers that I as editor, and you as reader, are first of all in debt.

Second, I wish to thank all 22 authors of the papers in this volume. They have worked hard, tolerated my detailed feedback and suggestions for revision, and accommodated to a tight time schedule to assure as prompt a publication as possible. It has been a pleasure to work with each and every author in this collection.

Three organizations were also critical in the help they extended to bring this project to completion. The American Sociological Association, and its executive officer, William D'Antonio, graciously encouraged the project from its inception, and extended permission to me to seek a publisher willing to produce both a hardcover and softcover edition of the book. Only by so doing, was it possible to keep down the price of a very long softcover edition, and this seemed important to assure a wide circulation of the book. I am also grateful to Aldine Publishing Company, and to Kyle Wallace, Editorial Director of Aldine, for so quickly encouraging the project in its early stages and for doing such a fine job of production. Further, I wish to express my gratitude to my colleagues and the staff at the Social and Demographic Research Institute at the University of Massachusetts, for their interest and help in all stages of manuscript preparation. A special thank you to Jeanne Reinle who handled so much of the correspondence and other paper work involved in dealing with 22 authors and 18 papers.

Lastly, my very great thanks to the University of Massachusetts, and to its Graduate Dean, Samuel Conti. It was Dean Conti's program of faculty research fellowships that provided me with the leisurely time of such a year-long fellowship to undertake this project and to bring it to a speedy completion.

Alice S. Rossi
Amherst, Massachusetts

INTRODUCTION

When the plans for the 1983 ASA annual meeting were first announced, many people asked why the theme was Age and Gender, rather than Sex and Gender. Knowing of my longstanding interest in sex and gender, they were surprised to note the linkage of gender to age. The rationale for the thematic focus provides a good introduction to this volume. Three considerations led to the thematic focus on gender differentiation in a life span framework. One was to encourage the view that theories on sex and gender are not adequate if they are limited to social, economic, and political constructs. To examine gender in a life span framework encourages an awareness that our theories must embrace biopsychological constructs as well.

The second consideration was to encourage the view that theories of aging are not adequate without a specification of gender. I had been surprised to find that gender often went unnoted in research at the two ends of the human life span: Premature low birthweight babies are rarely identified by sex in biomedical research, despite the fact that the more premature the baby, the higher the probability of maleness, since the sex ratio is approximately 124 at conception but drops to approximately 104 for full-term births. Similarly, research instruments in social gerontology typically inquire about relations with parents, children, and siblings, rather than in gender-specific terms, with mothers, fathers, sons, daughters, etc. Yet we know that across most of the life span from childhood to late middle age, social relations are structured in important ways along gender lines. To "neuter" premature infants and elderly persons seemed very strange indeed. Hence it was my hope that the dual focus on Age and Gender would alert sociologists to the importance of dealing with both constructs simultaneously.

A third consideration in linking age and gender was to encourage a concerted focus on the "maturational" dimension of age. In the past decade, life span developmental psychologists, like life course sociologists, have become enamored of cohort, historical period, and timing effects, rather than the maturational meaning of the age variable. The "in" concept in adult development research these days is "change," but the change that is of primary interest is not change as a function of growth and development but as a consequence of purposive action by individuals making life choices or the differential impact of external, historical events upon birth cohorts. The assumption is, therefore, that we are either free, purposive actors charting our own lives, or chameleons responsive to changing currents of political opinion and historical events. By calling attention to age and gender in a life-span framework, I hoped to encourage some focus on maturational processes that attend development and differentiation of a more invariant nature, i.e., those that seem to persist through time and across different societies, or that require our attention to the fact that physiological change accompanies and interacts with psychological and social change.

The underlying perspective guiding the planning of the ASA plenary sessions and many of the thematic sessions can therefore be specified as follows: The primary analytic units in sociological theory and research—roles, groups, networks, classes, nation-states—divert attention from the fact that the subject of all our scholarship is a human animal with genes, glands, bone, and flesh, occupying an ecological niche of a particular kind in a tiny fragment of time. Sex dimorphism serves the fundamental purpose of reproducing the species, and age specifies where on the biological timetable our subjects are located. Hence persistent differences between men and women, as well as many variations in the extent of these differences across the human life span, are as much a function of underlying biosocial processes of maturation and aging as they are reflections of socialization, class stratification or gender hierarchy.

Very little advance has been made as yet, in bringing together the perspectives and bodies of knowledge of the social sciences with those of human behavior to separate the body from the psyche and the social behavior of men and women. None of the papers in this volume were written by scholars whose basic training and research interests lie primarily in the biological sciences, although several papers demonstrate the relevance of biological factors for an adequate understanding and explanation of social behavior. Three such papers are by sociologists (Walter Gove, Matilda Riley, and Alice Rossi), one is by an anthropologist (Jane Lancaster), and a fifth by a clinical psychologist (Anke Ehrhardt). While present in these papers, a biosocial perspective is only one (and a minor one at that) of the several perspectives represented in the chapters in this volume.

An historical perspective is far better represented in this collection, perhaps because a concern for historical change has always been a focus within sociology. Further, the behavioral sciences have shifted from modelling themselves after the physical sciences and moved closer to the perception that they are historical disciplines. This transformation has led to significant advances and fruitful collaboration between sociologists and historians, demographers, economists, and political scientists concerned for processes of historical change.

In this volume, only one author is a professional historian (Louise Tilly), but many other authors are concerned with historical change and have used historical data in their work. This holds true for economist Michael Haines, who has analyzed 19th century surveys on the sources of household income, as it does for demographer Dennis Hogan who has done numerous historical analyses, and for demographer Mead Cain, whose work has concentrated on population changes in

developing societies. Jane Lancaster combines training in primatology with social anthropology and takes the broadest of all historical perspectives, that rooted
in evolutionary theory and cross-species comparisons. Sarah LeVine and Robert
LeVine bring their social anthropological training to bear on cultural differences
in the demographic transition taking place in Africa and Central America. Political scientist Frances Piven traces the development of political ideology among
peasants in western history and women in contemporary times.

Traditional sociological concern for social institutions is well represented in
the volume, particularly in the chapters on gender in relation to the economy and
the state. Don Treiman has focused on differences between men and women in
their job histories, James Baron and William Bielby on the differences in structural location of men and women in the American economy. Sociologist Francesca Cancian analyzes love and power in the private and public spheres in a
chapter on gender politics, while political scientist Frances Piven explores the
relationship of women to the state for its significance in bringing women not only
into the political process but the competition for political power as well.

Hence the authors in this volume come from diverse disciplines with diverse
perspectives that cut across their disciplinary origins. Of the 22 authors of the 18
chapters, one-half (11) are sociologists by training and institutional affiliation; 3
are social anthropologists; 3 are psychologists or human development specialists;
2 were trained in demography, and one each come from history, economics, and
political science. One-half the authors are women, one-half men; and they range
in age from their early thirties to their mid-seventies, a distribution on age and
gender that seems particularly appropriate to a volume on gender and the life
course.

The volume is divided into three major sections. The first focuses on gender
and the life course in broad historical perspective. Lancaster (Chap. 1) deals with
the largest historical canvas, that provided by the evolution of *Homo sapiens*
from our most closely related primate ancestors as well as the broad sweep of
human social evolution from hunter-gatherer bands to postindustrial nation-
states. The persistence of cultural differences in societies undergoing the demographic transition is depicted by the LeVines (Chap. 2) in their comparison of
Mexico and Kenya as these two agrarian societies were impacted by urbanization
and industrialization. Haines (Chap. 3) provides us with an unprecedented
opportunity to trace the changes that took place in the source of household
income of industrial workers across the life course, using a rare set of 19th
century survey data. Hogan (Chap. 4) traces temporal and gender differences in
life span transitions and poses a set of research challenges to scholars working in
this area.

The second section of the book examines gender differentiation in a variety of
institutional contexts, following a first subsection that explores the psychobiology of gender (Ehrhardt, Chap. 5), and an interesting report by Ryff (Chap. 6) of
research on how men and women subjectively experience transitions along the
life span. Walter Gove (Chap. 7) reviews sociological theories of deviance and

shows their inadequacy for explanations of why deviant behavior is a youthful phenomenon that peaks in late adolescence and declines rapidly by the late twenties. Gove then suggests alternate explanations for the cessation of deviant behavior that combine biological, psychological, and sociological constructs.

The remainder of the second section deals with the major social institutions of family, economy, and state. Cain (Chap. 8) explains why the demographic transition is quite different in many parts of Africa, Asia, and South America from the transition western societies underwent in the past, which highlights why it is that fertility has not declined very rapidly in today's developing societies despite highly effective contraceptive technology. Rossi (Chap. 9) reviews recent research on fathering and mothering and argues that sociological explanations of differences in styles of parenting shown by men and women need to be supplemented with explanations of gender differences rooted in evolutionary theory and the neurosciences.

Three chapters deal with gender and the economy. Tilly (Chap. 10) shows how rigidly occupations were structured by age and gender in early stages of industrialization in France, while Treiman (Chap. 11) and Baron and Bielby (Chap. 12) show the persistence of gender stratification in today's complex economy. Both Cancian and Piven focus on ideology in relation to gender, with Cancian (Chap. 13) contrasting concepts of love and power in family and public life, while Piven (Chap. 14) traces the impact of changes in labor force participation and ideology upon the gender gap in political values and women's search for political power.

The third section of the volume brings together four essays that deal with aspects of the aged. Neugarten (Chap. 15) argues for an interpretive social science that draws insights from diverse sources and freely uses a variety of research methods to improve our ability to describe and interpret aspects of social life among the aged. She also makes numerous suggestions for future research in the sociology of aging. Campbell, Abolafia, and Maddox (Chap. 16) provide a review of the methodology used to study changes in the aged population over time. Hess (Chap. 17) focuses on social policies affecting the aged, and shows how hidden from view it tends to be that the "aged" are predominantly not an age group but a gender group, since the overwhelming majority of the very old are women. Riley (Chap. 18) ends the book with a chapter that sketches the impact of the greatly expanded life span we now enjoy, for family and kinship relations and the quality of life of the elderly.

As this brief overview suggests, we are a long way from any integrated social science that simultaneously and conjointly deals with gender and the life course. We are even further from any integrated biopsychosocial science. The state-of-the-art in theory building is still a very modest one indeed. Hence in many chapters in this volume the predominant focus is on gender, with minimal or only implicit attention to age, while in other chapters, the reverse holds, and the focus is predominantly on age or the life course. Some chapters not only neglect age, but restrict interpretation of gender to a macroinstitutional level, while others interpret gender phenomena purely in a psychological or a sociological framework. There is excellent work in all these directions, and sufficient diversity to provide the reader with a good sampler of what is occurring in gender and age research in a number of disciplines.

Hopefully, the next time an editor puts together a volume on these core constructs of age and gender, the state-of-the-art will permit a sophisticated integration of new theory and research that is beyond our contemporary ability to provide.

LIST OF CONTRIBUTORS

Jeffery Abolafia is a doctoral student in sociology at Duke University. Current research interests: housing for the elderly, with particular focus on the patterns of housing change following retirement.

James N. Baron is Assistant Professor of Organizational Behavior, Graduate School of Business, Stanford University. Current research interest: differences in how work is structured across sectors of the economy and the impact of those differences on workers' careers.

William T. Bielby is Professor of Sociology at the University of California, Santa Barbara. Current research interests: the sociology of the employment relation and on quantitative methods.

Mead Cain is an Associate at the Center for Policy Studies, The Population Council, New York. Current research interests: the determinants and consequences of population change in developing countries, particularly South Asia.

Richard T. Campbell is Associate Professor of Sociology in the Department of Sociology and the Center for the Study of Aging and Human Development, Duke University. Current research interests: social stratification in old age, longitudinal studies, and widowhood.

Francesca Cancian is Professor of Sociology at the University of California-Irvine. Current research interests: close relationships and gender roles from a historical perspective. She is the author of *What are Norms?*

Anke A. Ehrhardt is Professor of Clinical Psychology in the Department of Psychiatry, College of Physicians and Surgeons, Columbia University, and Senior Research Scientist at the New York State Psychiatric Institute, New York. Current research interests: hormones and behavior as they relate to gender identity, gender-related behavior, and sexual orientation, particularly a study of mothers who were treated with diethylstilbestrol (DES) during pregnancy, and the potential effects on their sons and daughters in early adulthood. She is the co-author with John Money of *Man & Woman/ Boy & Girl: The Differentiation and Dimorphism of Gender Identity from Conception to Maturity*, and has co-edited two volumes on *Health Care of Women*, and *Psychosomatic Obstetrics-Gynecology*.

Walter R. Gove is Professor of Sociology at Vanderbilt University. Major research interests: deviance, with a focus on mental illness and criminology; gender roles; and the effects of living arrangements on social behavior and mental health. He is co-author of *Overcrowding in the Home: An Analysis of Its Determinants and Effects*, and *At Work and at Home: The Family's Allocation of Labor*. He is co-editor of *A Feminist Perspective in the Academy: The Difference it Makes*; *Deviance and Mental Illness*; and *The Fundamental Connection between Nature and Nurture*.

Michael R. Haines is Associate Professor of Economics, Wayne State University. Current research interests: historical fertility and mortality in the United States and Europe; differential fertility and mortality in contemporary Latin America; and historical family budget studies. His most recent book is *Fertility and Occupation: Population Patterns in Industrialization*.

xix

Beth B. Hess is Professor of Sociology at County College of Morris, Randolph, New
Jersey. Major research interests: the sociological study of gender and of age. Recent
publications include *Sociology* (2nd ed.); *Womanpower: The New Feminist Movement*;
Women and the Family: Two Decades of Change; and *Growing Old in America* (3rd
ed.).

Dennis P. Hogan is Associate Professor of Sociology and Associate Director of the
Population Research Center, University of Chicago. Current research interest: the influence of parental attitudes, family and personal characteristics, and position in the
social structure on the timing and sequencing of school completion, independent residence, full-time employment, marriage, and parenthood on young men and women. He
is the author of *Transitions and Social Change: The Early Lives of American Men*
(1981).

Jane B. Lancaster is Professor of Anthropology at the University of Oklahoma. Current
research interests: the biosocial bases of human behavior, evolutionary and cross-
cultural perspectives on human parenthood, women's lives, and the family. Her most
recent books are *Primate Behavior and the Emergence of Human Culture*, and *School-
Age Pregnancy and Parenthood: Biosocial Dimensions*.

Robert A. LeVine is Professor of Anthropology and Larsen Professor of Education and
Human Development at Harvard University. Major research interests: psychosocial
development in a variety of cultural contexts. Among his numerous books are *Nyansongo: A Gusii Community in Kenya*; *Dreams and Deeds: Achievement Motivation in
Nigeria*; *Culture, Behavior and Personality*; and *Human Potential*.

Sarah LeVine is Research Associate in the Laboratory of Human Development, Harvard
University. Major research interests: women's education in relation to fertility, infant
mortality, and maternal behavior. Her most recent publication is *Mothers and Wives*, a
study of women in East Africa.

George L. Maddox is Professor of Sociology and of Medical Sociology (Psychiatry) and
Chair, University Council on Aging and Human Development, Duke University. Current research interests: longitudinal and comparative research on health and health care
utilization in adulthood. His recent books include *Introduction to Behavioral Sciences
in Medicine*, and *Inflation and the Economic Well-Being of the Elderly*.

Bernice L. Neugarten is Professor of Education and Sociology, School of Education,
Northwestern University. Current research interests: social policies for the aging; age
norms and relations between age groups; and age and the law. Her most recent publication is *Age or Need? Public Policies for Older People*.

Frances Fox Piven is Professor of Political Science, Graduate School and University
Center of the City University of New York. Major research interests: social movements
and the development of the welfare state. She has co-authored: *Regulating the Poor:
The Functions of Public Welfare*; *Poor People's Movements: Why they Succeed, How
they Fail*; and *The New Class War: Reagan's Attack on the Welfare State and its
Consequences*.

Matilda White Riley is Associate Director for Behavior Sciences Research, National
Institute on Aging, and Emeritus Professor of Sociology, Rutgers University and Bow-
doin College. Major research interests: research methodology, communications research, and the sociology of age and of aging as a biosocial process. Her most recent
publications include *Sociological Traditions from Generation to Generation*; the 3-
volume series, *Aging and Society, Aging in Society*, and *Aging from Birth to Death*.

Alice S. Rossi is a Professor of Sociology at the University of Massachusetts-Amherst.
Current research interests: family and kinship, biosocial science, and gender and politics. Her most recent book is *Feminists in Politics: A Panel Analysis of the First
National Women's Conference*. She is the editor of *The Feminist Papers: From Adams
to de Beauvoir*, *Academic Women on the Move*, and *Essays on Sex Equality*.

Carol D. Ryff is Assistant Professor of Psychology at Fordham University. Current research interests: phenomenological and interpretive approaches to adult personality development; the impact of critical life events on personality development; and cultural and historical variations in definitions of ideal human development. Her recent book is *Social Power and Influence in Women*.

Louise A. Tilly is Professor of History and Sociology at the New School for Social Research. Current research interests: comparative historical study of family and social class in French cities, and labor force and working class in late nineteenth century Milan. She is co-author of *The Rebellious Century: 1830–1930*.

Donald J. Treiman is Professor of Sociology at the University of California-Los Angeles. Major research interests: comparative study of social mobility and status attainment; and earnings differences between women and men. His most recent book is *Women, Work, and Wages: Equal Pay for Jobs of Equal Value*.

I

GENDER AND THE LIFE COURSE IN HISTORICAL PERSPECTIVE

1

Evolutionary Perspectives on Sex Differences in the Higher Primates*

JANE B. LANCASTER
University of Oklahoma

Introduction

The past decade witnessed a period of rapid development and expansion of theory that vitalized and revolutionized the entire field of evolutionary biology and the study of the evolution of behavior. This fruition represents groundwork laid in previous decades in theoretical biology, ethology, and field work on wild animal populations, the natural laboratory for the testing of predictions based on these new hypotheses. This new body of theory represents the marriage of two separate areas of endeavor: The first drawn from Darwin's original formulation of the impact of sexual selection on species' evolution and the other drawn from population ecology. Together, these areas have brought a new series of questions to the field of primate social behavior and helped to overturn early male-oriented bias in attempts to understand the nature of primate social organization, reproductive strategies, and the factors underlying sexual dimorphisms.

---

*The stimulus for writing this chapter came from several years of planning and discussion with members of the Social Science Research Council's Committee for Biosocial Perspectives on Parenthood and Offspring Development. The support and encouragement of the Social Science Research Council is gratefully acknowledged. Partial funding for the activities of the committee was granted by the National Institute for Child Health and Human Development (Grant No. 5R13-HD11777-02) and the William T. Grant Foundation. Data on the survivorship of juveniles was developed during a Summer Research Fellowship awarded by the Faculty Research Council of the University of Oklahoma. Special thanks are due to LaDon Deatherage, Barbara King, and Wayne McGuire for their help in the collection of data and library references, to Darlene Thornton for typing the manuscript, and to Douglas Mock and Patricia Schwagmeyer for their helpful comments after reading a preliminary version.

The concepts expressed in the first section of this chapter appeared in preliminary form as an introduction to M. F. Small (Ed.), *Female Primates: Studies by Women Primatologists.* New York: A. R. Liss, 1984.

The first of these fields, sociobiology (reviewed by Daly & Wilson, 1983); focused on Darwin's original notion that competition exists between members of the same sex for mating access to the most fit or the greatest numbers of the opposite sex. Darwin successfully explained many aspects of sexual dimorphism and sex differences in behavior such as the development of weapons of male aggression to be used against members of the same sex or elaborate structures such as peacock tails for mating displays. However, it was the pivotal paper by Trivers (1972) that opened the way for a much more significant series of hypotheses based on the recognition that sexual selection interacted in subtle and complex ways with species' patterns of parental investment. Trivers noted that, in species where one sex invests much more heavily than the other in the rearing of young, the heavily investing sex becomes a limiting resource for which the opposite sex competes. This unbalanced focus of sexual selection on one sex may lead to almost run-away selection for successful competitors in promiscuous mating while the other sex remains selective or even coy in mating and puts its energy reserves into parental investment rather than mating competition. As might be expected, among mammals where females are already committed to heavy investments in each offspring in terms of ovulation, gestation, lactation, and maternal care, sexual access to females often becomes the prize for a limited number of successful male competitors in each population. An important point in Trivers' paper, which is often overlooked by its critics, is his emphasis that there is one very significant deterrent to males that bars many from an all-out pursuit of mating success and that is the degree to which it is necessaray for them to give aid to females in order that they can successfully rear young. In species where the demand for paternal investment is high, such as in many nonhuman primates, we can expect to find monogamous mating patterns, low levels of sexual dimorphism in body size and weapons of aggression, equivalent behavioral levels between the sexes in aggressiveness, territoriality, nurturance of young, sexuality, and bond formation. Males, then, are not free to pursue their own strategies but must mold them first to fit the needs of females in rearing offspring.

At the same time that sociobiological theory was developing in evolutionary biology, another area of concern was coalescing out of the experience of population biologists and field ecologists. It focused on the mesh between social systems and their ecological context, with one particular line of investigation pursuing the ways in which members of a species harvest energy from the environment and convert it into reproducing the next generation. The original formulation of the patterns of K- and r-strategies of reproduction come from this tradition and give us important insight into the selective pressures that led to the evolution of the higher primates and of humans, the most K-selected species yet described (MacArthur, 1962). An r-strategist is a creature who is a rapid, prolific breeder in an expanding population, a K-strategist focuses on restrained survival and reproduction in a population near the carrying capacity for its habitat. A K-selected pattern has tremendous impact on virtually all aspects of reproductive biology and behavior. A strategy of parental care for a small number of highly invested, high-quality offspring affects body size, growth rates, length of life, numbers of young born at once, length of lactation, interbirth interval, the behavioral development of young at birth, relations between the generations and kindred, and even courtship patterns.

For the first time, researchers in the evolution of behavior and patterns of sexual dimorphism now find a welcome body of hypotheses that can be used to formulate testable predictions using field data (Richards & Schulman, 1982). One of the most exciting applications of this theory has been in primate studies. Nonhuman primates are now probably the best studied mammalian order in terms of diversity of species, long-term study sites, diversity of geographical and ecological contexts, intraspecific variability, and variability in systems of mating, parenting, and sexual dimorphism. They are, in fact, a fertile proving ground that has provided both confirmations and surprises for the new theory. However, the one generalization that does appear to hold as more and more field experience is codified is that, for all intents and purposes, male and female primates pursue sex-specific strategies and tactics for successful reproduction through the course of the life span. The demands of sexual selection and parental investment strategies fall differently on each sex, and these patterns are highly species-specific. It is virtually impossible to generalize about what male primates do or how female primates act (Mitchell, 1979). Each species presents a complex pattern of sexual dimorphisms representing its own specific evolutionary history and current ecological context (McKenna, 1982a, 1982b).

In this chapter, I focus on the relevance of primate field studies for understanding four significant areas of sexual dimorphism: Sex differences in dominance, mating behavior and sexual assertiveness, attachment to home range and the natal group, and the ecological and social correlates of sex differences in body size. In each of these cases, field work and species comparisons among the primates have been highly instructive in redefining early, overly simple formulations and expectations, ones that failed to recognize the important impact of evolutionary pressures on the biology and behavior of females as well as males.

Sex Differences in the Higher Primates

Sex Differences in Dominance and Concern with Status Differentials

One of the earliest revelations to come from primate field studies was that among many of the Old World monkeys, dominance status was as important a concern to female primates as it was to males, even among species with males up to twice the body size of females (Small, 1984). This insight did not come from the first round of field studies but only after long-term studies had been established and representative sampling methods had become standard procedure (Altmann, 1974). Once the relations among females was studied in a number of species, it became clear that not only are female cercopithecine monkeys as potentially obsessed with status as are the males, but their rankings are clearly hierarchical and are usually inherited from the mother according to birth order (Chapais & Schulman, 1980). However, the selective value of dominance rank may be quite different for males and females. High-status males use their rank as a successful strategy to assure mating access to females around the time of ovulation (Hausfater, 1975), whereas high rank for a female guarantees her access to energy resources that she needs to bear and rear young. Under conditions where resources are scarce and concentrated, high-status females enjoy much greater reproductive success than other members of their birth cohort (Drickamer, 1974; Sugiyama & Ohsawa, 1982). They begin their reproductive lives earlier, bear more offspring, have births more closely spaced, have more infants survive, and bear earlier in the birth season. For females, the value of high status varies according to the ecosystem that the species normally occupies. Among Old World monkeys of the colobine group, females can only be roughly labeled as high or low status, and no hierarchies occur (McKenna, 1979). This is because of specializations of the digestive system of this large group of monkey species of Asia and Africa. Colobines can digest mature leaves, getting both nutrition and water from this abundant and dispersed resource for which differential access cannot be assured through competitive dominance.

Female primates have evolved to be fierce competitors, and they are obsessed with signs of status differential or disrespect when and only when it pays off in terms of access to energy resources. Males may follow a somewhat parallel policy in terms of mating competition. Among seasonal breeders, aggressive status encounters increase just before the mating season, and in some species, such as the squirrel monkey, status differentials are suspended altogether during the "off-season" because the energy expenditure demanded appears to carry too high a cost. Field work, then, indicates that concern over status is found in both male and female primates, and status attainment and security ultimately rest on the ability to aggress. However, the adaptive advantage of high status differs between the sexes: Males use status to be successful breeders, and females use status to be successful mothers.

Attachment to Home Range and the Natal Group

Popular stereotypes and some evolutionary theories predict that males can be expected to develop a wanderlust at puberty that will take them to strange territories and sexual adventure. Supposedly, this wanderlust induces the male to sample his options in terms of neighboring social groups, testing for favorable socionomic sex ratios, or an aging harem leader. Females, in contrast, have a strong attachment to their natal group and do not take the risks of wandering in strange territories or interacting with strangers. For the most part, this sex differential in gregariousness and dispersal describes the social strategies of the higher primates, but there is a growing and instructive list of species in which it is the female who is afflicted with wanderlust at puberty, as in the African red colobus monkey, the chimpanzee, and South American howler monkey. In fact, among mammals, three out of seven cases in which it is the female sex that leaves its natal group at puberty come from the primates, and one of these (the chimpanzee) is considered to be the closest living relative of humans (Greenwood, 1979; Hrdy, 1981).

Wrangham (1975, 1980) applied the insights of Wittenberger (1979) to the factors shaping bird and mammalian mating and social systems. He noted that the dispersion of female primates in space is very predictable. All else being equal, they will prefer to live alone, controlling feeding territories large enough for themselves and their offspring and permitting males to enter only for breeding. However, this ideal state cannot be realized by most species. Instead, females need to accept companions to help them control access to feeding territories and sometimes for defense against predators. When females accept companions, they often prefer their close female relatives with whom they can form long-term social attachments based on reciprocal grooming, defense, and social support. Hence, females tend to be kin-oriented, gregarious, and attached to the land and group to which they were born. The exceptions are still puzzling and poorly understood, but it appears that, among chimpanzees at least, females wander frequently during their adolescent years, visiting neighboring groups and presumably assessing the availability of resources and the relative openness of nearby social systems. Among chimpanzees, it is the males who appear to be emotionally attached to brothers and male cousins, who spend hours grooming their close kin, and support their companions in dominance interactions. So, even such time-honored stereotypes of sex differences in sexual wanderlust at puberty and in social attachment and spatial conservatism do not hold up among the nonhuman primates, and it is particularly instructive that our closest relatives, the chimpanzee and the gorilla (in which both sexes leave the natal group), represent cases that overturn the mammalian stereotypes.

Promiscuity and Sexual Assertiveness

The sexual differential in parental investment patterns common in mammals, in which females invest so heavily in gestation, lactation, and maternal care, predicts that females should be very choosy and coy in mating behavior, whereas males should be as promiscuous as the costs will permit (i.e., the energy requirements of aggressive interactions or energy diversion to paternal investment). However, one look at the behavior of most female primates in estrus suggests exactly the opposite. Not only is the length of the estrous period unusually long in the sexual cycle of many higher primates if only impregnation were its goal, but female monkeys and apes are often exceedingly promiscuous even in species that form sexual consortships (Hrdy & Williams, 1983; Stacey, 1982). Hrdy (1979) was the first to formulate an hypothesis about an adaptive value for this behavior. Evidence is accumulating that male mammals have a variety of means to assess whether there is any probability that the offspring of a particular female could be their own progeny. Such mechanisms include familiarity with the mother, having mated with her during her last estrous period, or even recognition of family traits in phenotypic characters. Hrdy suggests that female primates behave promiscuously to enmesh males into recognizing some possibility of paternity, no matter how slight. This recognition of paternity brings with it the likelihood that the male may provide some fosterage of the youngster such as carrying it, allowing it to scrounge for food scraps, or protecting it against environmental dangers. At the very least, the male might refrain from infanticide to bring the mother into estrus if that is a male reproductive strategy in his particular species or group (Hausfater & Hrdy, 1984).

Female primates may compete sexually in another way as well. They may harass other females, especially low-status ones, to such an extent that they are unable to conceive effectively, maintain gestation, or adequately lactate (Silk & Boyd, 1983; Wasser, 1983; Wasser, in press). There are also scattered reports that females may kill and cannibalize the infants of low-status females or seize them and ''aunt'' them to death. It is possible to interpret both female promiscuity and the harassment of other females as ways in which females compete to garner an investment of male energy into their own offspring and to decrease the competition from other females for access to male paternal care. Long-term field studies of monkeys such as baboons and macaques with mating systems based on male competition for access to females still show that females form special attachments to males of various statuses who get sexual preference and may also show paternal investment in the female's offspring. It is clear that among the higher primates, sexual assertiveness and promiscuity are not the prerogatives of males—even ''good'' mothers frequently show this behavior.

Sexual Dimorphism in Body Size

Nonhuman primates are not particularly noteworthy for sexual dimorphism in body size by mammalian standards, where males can be six times the size of females (Alexander, Hoogland, Howard, Noonan, & Sherman, 1979). Primates range from virtual equivalence in the gibbon and siamang to males being about twice the size of females in gorillas and baboons. Past thinking has emphasized the evolutionary forces that might lead males to being larger than females, and usually this is ascribed to the benefits in mating of enhanced aggressive potential (Alexander et al., 1979; Hamburg, 1978; McCown, 1982). Using this perspective, females equal the anatomy of the species, and males equal the species plus the anatomy of male/male aggression in terms of extra bone, muscle, and long canine teeth. However, an excellent series of papers evaluating sexual dimorphism and social systems among the primates come to the conclusion that sexual selection (i.e., differential male access to females) can only partly explain the variance in sexual dimorphism between species (Clutton-Brock, 1977; Clutton-Brock & Harvey, 1977, 1978; Clutton-Brock, Harvey, & Rudder, 1977; Harvey, Kavanagh, & Clutton-Brock, 1978). These papers, along with those of Coehlo

(1974) and Leutenegger (1982a, 1982b) and Leutenegger and Kelly (1977) suggest that at least two other important factors play a role. The first is the extent to which males need to defend the social group, perhaps especially in a terrestrial habitat—really a second measure of greater male potential for aggression but in this case one that is selected, not by mating competition, but rather in terms of male parental investment. In the latter case, large male body size is valued because of the risks males take in defending their offspring and kin.

A second set of factors, the recognition of which comes from the field of socioecology, emphasizes the extremely high energy costs of lactation (Altmann, 1980; Pond, 1977, 1978; Ralls, 1976, 1977). Field data suggest that the energy costs of being a large active male may not be so very different from the energy costs of a female nursing a large infant (Coehlo, 1974). Using this equation, the male body represents the adaptations of the species plus the anatomy of aggression, and the female's body represents the species' adaptation plus the demands of lactation. Ralls (1976), in investigating what factors led some species to evolve female body size larger than male, could find no correlates with sexual competition between females for access to males for either mating or male parental investment. Instead, she found that females are only bigger when large female body size is necessary to being a good mother. In other words, natural selection and sexual selection act quite independently on male and female body size. Sexual dimorphism in body size is the result of two independent lines of selection and development, which either diverge or stay together. For male primates, the anatomy of aggression is the key to the degree of their divergence, but this includes both aggression for male/male competition and for defense of close kin in the social group. For female primates, lactation is the overwhelming factor in determining body size. The demands of lactation can be so great that females spend as much time feeding and ingest as many calories as large males even if they are only one-half male size (Altmann, 1980; Coehlo, 1974; Post, Hausfater, & McCluskey, 1980). Again, access to energy is the foremost shaper of the biology and behavior of female primates. Their quality, K-selected, slowly maturing infants place heavy, continuous energy demands on their mothers, demands that cannot be focused on a single favorable season of the year but that continue during virtually the entire adult life of the individual female.

Summary

Studies of nonhuman primates, stimulated by major recent theoretical advances in sociobiology and socioecology, have come up with important new data sets on sexual dimorphism and sex differences in behavior. In many respects, they do not support either popular intuition about sex differences or early formulations of evolutionary theory which had a strong male-bias. Frequently, we find our semiinformed stereotypes of male and female overturned. We find that females can be fierce, dominance-oriented competitors when access to energy resources is critical to their reproductive success. They may experience wanderlust at puberty, exploring strange territories and seeking unfamiliar social groups to visit and join. Female primates are often sexually aggressive, seeking numerous sexual partners and displaying a lack of selectivity in mating that would be considered nymphomaniacal among humans. They may be similar in body size or smaller than males, but their energy requirements during lactation (that comprises most of their adult lives) are likely to be similar to males. Finally, the evolutionary factors that act on male and female primates are not the same, and even when similar patterns of behavior or body size are apparent, we cannot assume similar causal forces at play. The evolutionary task set for female primates is to rear their young effectively to adulthood, and the demands of this task shape virtually every aspect of their biology and behavior. The evolutionary task of males is to sire as many offspring as possible, but this may entail heavy demands from females for males to provide paternal energy and risk-taking in order to rear young successfully.

Human Evolution and the Division of Labor

Current scenarios for the origins of the genus *Homo* all focus on a behavioral complex that recognizes the division of labor between the sexes, paternal investment patterns subsumed under the role "husband–father," and the establishment of a long period of juvenile dependency as pivotal in the evolution of our species (Fisher, 1982; Lancaster & Lancaster, 1983; Lovejoy, 1981; Tanner, 1981; Zihlman, 1981). No matter what the differences over details in these scenarios, all recognize that among most nonhuman primates, females ultimately shoulder the major burden for the rearing of their offspring. Male monkeys and apes may contribute by defending feeding territories, protecting the group from predation, or even by carrying infants. The one thing they do not do is to forage for food for either their mates or offspring.

The Sexual Division of Labor among Humans

The human division of labor is a consequence of a dietary/ecological shift that formed the fundamental platform upon which the evolutionary history of human behavior and later elaborations of culture were built. Isaac (1978, 1981) and Isaac and Crader (1981) describe this platform as a cluster of a few simple behavioral elements that combined into a coherent pattern and fundamentally changed the relationship of the human species to its environment. The human division of labor was originally a pattern of feeding, in which the two sexes specialized in obtaining food from different levels of the food chain (Lancaster & Lancaster, 1983). Males hunt for meat, energy from high on the food chain concentrated in large "packages." Such endeavors are unpredictable and often dangerous. Females, in contrast, concentrate on gathering sources of energy from lower on the food chain,—high-grade plant food or occasional small protein packages, such as insects or small vertebrates. Their work is less dangerous, success is more predictable, and it provides a nutritional baseline adequate to sustain adults and young, even if hunting is poor for weeks on end. Among contemporary tropical hunter–gatherers, women's gathering contributes about one-half of the caloric intake of the group and perhaps 65–70% of the dietary bulk (Gaulin & Konner, 1977; Hayden, 1981). Men's contribution of meat may represent fewer calories and lesser bulk but provides essential amino acids.

In contrast to humans who regularly share food, nonhuman primates are basically individual foragers. Their diet contrasts with that of humans not so much in what is eaten but in terms of how it is obtained (Gaulin & Konner, 1977; Harding & Teleki, 1981; Teleki, 1975). Although most monkeys and apes spend their lives in social groups aiding their close relatives in mutual defense, protecting the group's territory, and socializing daily by grooming and resting together, they do not regularly share food. A sick or injured monkey can die of hunger or thirst. Even though its close relatives may show protective concern about its condition, none will respond to its need for nourishment. When food is scarce for nonhuman primates, small, weak, young, and subordinate animals suffer because of their disadvantage in finding, competing for, and processing food. The earliest humans evolved a simple, yet unique, solution to this problem. Food-sharing and the division of labor provided a kind of food insurance policy that compensates for fluctuations in individual success in the food quest at the same time that it permits regular feeding at two major levels of the food chain. When game is scarce, human omnivores do not face starvation so readily as do carnivores. In short, early humans discovered a way to eat high-quality protein regularly without taking the risks of carnivore specialists.

The Division of Labor and Feeding of Juveniles

The division of labor does not represent simply a sharing of resources collected at two different levels of the food chain and shared between males and females. Although such behavior represents a kind of feeding insurance policy for the two sexes, the division of labor is associated with a much more adaptive pattern of behavior. Unlike the young of other mammals, human juveniles do not have primary responsibility for feeding themselves once they are weaned. The division of labor takes on added significance because its feeding insurance covers not only adults but the much more vulnerable juvenile population.

It is generally agreed that the human species is characterized by prolonged juvenile dependency (Schultz, 1969; Washburn, 1981). However, even the great apes have prolonged social dependency for offspring lasting to the ages of 10 or more years. Mother monkeys and apes wean their infants after 1–5 years, depending on the species. The years of infancy and nursing are followed by an equally long period during which a juvenile enjoys the social and psychological protection of its mother and close relatives and gathers knowledge from its social group about food resources and environmental dangers. In contrast to humans, however, the juvenile monkey or ape feeds itself. The basic diet may be typical of many primates living in the tropics: Fruits, nuts, leaves, and some animal protein. The important contrast between human and nonhuman primates is not so much in what is eaten, but rather in whether each individual must forage for itself, and whether there is a collective familial responsibility for gathering and sharing food between adults and their dependents.

The demographic effects of the feeding of juveniles by adults are evident when comparing the survivorship curves of human hunter–gatherers with other mammalian species (Lancaster & Lancaster, 1983). Among group-hunting carnivores, about one in four of those born survive weaning, and only one in six survives adolescence. Monkeys and apes feed lower on the food chain than carnivores and may be somewhat less vulnerable to juvenile loss. However, Dittus (1977, 1979) found that under conditions in which the food supply fluctuated from year to year, on the average only one in eight monkeys born survived to adulthood. In the slowly developing baboon and chimpanzee, long-term field studies reveal that one in three survive to the beginning of reproductive life. The loss of offspring during early infancy appears to be relatively predictable and varies little from species to species. In contrast, the loss during late infancy and the early juvenile period varies according to environmental conditions. Dittus (1980) has fully documented why the juvenile period is so perilous: During times of poor food supply, small, weak, young, and subordinate animals suffer disproportionately because of their disadvantage in finding, and especially competing for, food. The youngest juveniles are the most disadvantaged, and life expectancy improves as juveniles age. It is worth noting that these imperiled juveniles are not necessarily the less fit in a Darwinian sense but are nevertheless forced to pass through an intense selection funnel at a tender age.

The close relationship between food supply and the survival of juveniles strengthens when a comparison is made between wild, self-feeding groups and those that are regularly provisioned by humans. When food is freely available or nearly so, juvenile primate survival is nearly double the rate of groups living in the wild. For monkeys, such a survival rate of juveniles gives an annual population growth rate of 13–35%. It is remarkable that human hunter–gatherers and horticulturalists, even without benefit of modern medicine, successfully raise to adulthood about one out of every two children born to them. Human survivorship to 5 years is 62–71%, nearly the same as survivorship to that age for primates that are freely provisioned by humans. In other words, for humans living in simple economies with occasional food scarcity, survivorship to adulthood is comparable to nonhuman primate groups with no food limitations on population growth.

The Expansion of the Juvenile Period within the Hominid Life Cycle

As a rough rule of thumb, the lengths of the periods of infancy and juvenility tend to be more or less equal in the life cycles of nonhuman primates. For example, an infant female chimpanzee may be nursed for 4–5 years and then spend an equal period living with her mother as a juvenile before she completes her physical growth and begins sexual cycles. In contrast, although human infants are usually nursed as long as 4 years in hunter–gatherer societies, it takes at least another 12 years for the completion of growth and the onset of adult reproduction (Short, 1976; Washburn, 1981). A delay in the onset of reproduction by expanding the more vulnerable juvenile period will not evolve unless it can depend on a greatly improved adult product: A more successful reproducer as a result of the investment of those extra juvenile years. In a recent review of selective costs and benefits in the evolution of learning, Johnston (1982) notes that the primary costs of learning are delayed reproductive effort and increased juvenile vulnerability, because the more an individual must rely on learning for development of adaptive behavioral skill, the more vulnerable it is during the period before necessary experience is obtained. In other words, an extension of the relative length of the juvenile period is a real gamble against future returns, because the extra vulnerability of juveniles may mean that the individual risks never reaching reproductive age at all. Johnston suggests that increased parental investment may be a selective cost of learning that evolves in concert to offset juvenile mortality due to juvenile inexperience.

According to Johnston (1982), there is a specific set of environmental factors that tends to reward learning as an adaptive strategy. The ability to learn has its primary selective benefit in that it permits adaptation to ecological factors that vary over periods of time short in comparison to the lifetime of the individual. This is especially true when populations are resource-limited and the nature and distribution of limited resources are variable. Parker and Gibson (1979) argue that the developed extractive foraging techniques associated with human food-sharing and tool-using require a long period of juvenile dependency. Extractive foraging refers to the location of food sources that are often underground or hidden from view and that may necessitate the removal of protective coverings before eating. The savannah–woodland environment typical of early hominids would seem to be a maximally demanding environment for a tropical primate because of the large proportion of encased, embedded, and hidden high-quality plant foods and the variable nature of their spatial and seasonal distribution.

Because prolonged childhood carries the dual costs of greater vulnerability to starvation and predation and the postponement of reproduction, early hominids might have evolved two major behavioral patterns that more than compensated for the high costs of learning. These were the feeding of juveniles, freeing them from the obligations of the food quest during the years when they were at a competitive disadvantage, and the creation of a protected environment in which to learn, the home base or camp. Beck (1980), in a recent review of animal tool-using behavior, gives some insight into what such a protracted, protected period of juvenile dependency might have meant to evolving hominids. Beck catalogues an impressive array of tool-using behaviors by captive species that are never known to use tools in the wild. These species, ranging from many varieties of birds and monkeys to even ungulates, had only one thing in common: Lots of leisure time in captivity, especially during the juvenile period of development. Beck argues that their seemingly more intelligent behavior compared to wild relatives is based on many opportunities to explore the properties of objects through random manipulation. Eventually, a pool of responses develops that can be fortuitously reinforced by the unexpected attainment of a food reward.

The importance of leisure time spent in a protected environment is also indicated by the work of Baldwin and Baldwin (1976, 1977) in their studies of primate play. They note the role of play as the behavioral vehicle of primate learning and how easily it is inhibited by both too much or too little environmental novelty and by time–energy budgets that demand high commitment to the food quest. They point to several studies of juvenile monkeys that were forced to reduce their play from 94 to 100% in the face of food scarcity. As Isaac (1978) recognizes, the creation of a home base for juvenile life in hunter–gatherer bands is rich with continuous opportunities for socializing with different but familiar adults and a multiage, mixed-sex playgroup in a protected environment, abundant in both objects and activities. This is exactly the kind of context that Beck (1980) would describe as optimal for the learning of complex skills and social interaction patterns.

Leisure time spent in play, object manipulation, and the development of skilled performance without a need to participate in the food quest could have led to major improvements in tool-using and tool-making and extractive foraging techniques, even before any significant expansion of size or reorganization of the human brain.

Human Sexual Dimorphism

The sexual division of labor and the feeding of juveniles by adult parents clearly played a crucial role in the establishment of our species' pattern of behavior, in which the many years spent as a juvenile were protected by adult food-sharing and the creation of a home base or camp. Such a sharing of responsibility between the male and female parent permitted the simultaneous nutritional dependence of three to four offspring at various stages of development. This contrast with nonhuman higher primates, whose females can only support one nutritionally dependent young at a time, rested both on the effectiveness of the human division of labor in exploiting two different levels of the food chain and in the capturing of male energy to provision offspring. Despite the clear success of this pattern, the biology of human females still shows a marked imprint from the demands of energy requirements of their offspring. In fact, human sexual dimorphism in body size, stature, and muscularity is relatively minor by mammalian standards, but we have one system in which sexual dimorphism is prominently developed: The storage of energy in fat deposits. The storage of energy is so important to the reproductive lives of human females that its deposition as fat affects both the sequencing of pubertal events and the establishment of fertility.

When the life cycle of the human female is viewed from the perspective of parental behavior, its major features clearly support the uniquely human pattern of high levels of long-term parental investment and the dependency of multiple young of differing ages. For a variety of reasons, most modern cultures present poor models for the female life cycle during most of human history because of their wide range of variation in women's activities, health, nutrition, numbers of children born and reared, and the use of artificial techniques to alter fertility. A real understanding of the evolutionary pressures lying behind women's reproductive biology must start with a reconstruction of how it unfolds in the hunting–gathering life-style in which it evolved, a life-style representing fully 95% of human history. Such a model, based on data drawn from the few remaining hunter–gatherers of today, is fraught with distortions but, nevertheless, has already provided us with some important insights into major evolutionary novelties in the reproductive lives of modern women. Short (1976) sketches the most striking features of women's biological legacy from the hunter–gatherer era. They include a long period of adolescent subfertility following menarche, late age for first birth, a pattern of nearly continuous nursing during the day, many years of lactation, low natural fertility, a birth spacing of 4 years between surviving siblings, a low frequency of menstrual cycling during the life course, and early menopause.

Figure 1.1 illustrates the contrasting patterns of reproductive life found in hunter–gatherers and modern women. Whereas a hunter–gatherer woman can expect nearly 15 years of lactational amenorrhea and just under 4 years each of pregnancy and menstrual cycling, the modern woman experiencing two pregnancies with little or no breast-feeding is likely to spend over 35 years in menstrual cycling, a ninefold increase. The generality of this worldwide shift from lactation amenorrhea as the usual reproductive state of adult females to menstrual cycling has been confirmed in a recent review of data from preindustrial and industrial societies (Harrell, 1981). In order to understand the evolutionary biology of women, we must begin to think about them as lactating for virtually their entire reproductive lives.

The Sequencing of Pubertal Events

Short (1976) reviews the milestones in human pubertal events and notes the interesting fact that boys and girls have very different programs. For girls, the first external sign of puberty is the development of the breast bud. This is an odd and noteworthy feature of human development, and one that is likely to go unnoticed without comparative mammalian data. The typical primate female will not begin to develop breasts until the later stages of pregnancy. The breasts of the human female are made conspicuous and stable with deposits of fat, in contrast to other primates whose breasts experience an increase in glandular tissue that resorbs again after weaning if another pregnancy does not ensue. The deposition of fat during human adolescence on the breasts and buttocks is a unique feature

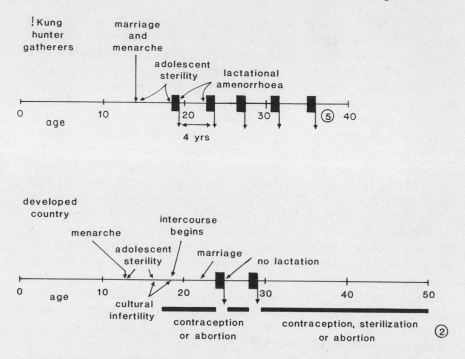

Figure 1.1 Changing patterns of human fertility. !Kung hunter–gatherers have a relatively late menarche, and adolescent infertility defers the birth of the first child until age 19. Lactational amenorrhea keeps births 4 years apart. Early menopause results in a completed family size of about 5 children, only 2–3 of which will survive into adulthood.

In developed countries, menarche occurs at age, 12–13, cultural infertility breaks down in the late teens, and intercourse before marriage requires the use of contraception or abortion. Lactation is so short that birth spacing is dependent on contraception. If the desired family size is 2, contraception, sterilization, or abortion are necessary for a further 20 years. The result of this imposed sterility is a nine-fold increase in the number of menstrual cycles (after Short, 1976, p. 16).

of human sexual dimorphism that constitutes a continuous advertisement of an ability to lactate rather than a cyclic fertility advertised by estrous swelling, as do so many other higher primates (Lancaster & Lancaster, 1983).

It is also worth noting that menarche is a relatively late event in the sequence of human pubertal changes, but that it still usually precedes the establishment of regular patterns of ovulation by several years. Menarche itself is preceded by most of the essential features of physical development indicating adult status: The adolescent growth spurt and the attainment of nearly adult values for weight and stature and the growth of breasts and pubic hair.

Another contrast in pubertal sequencing can be found when comparing the production of sex cells in boys and girls. As Short observes (1976, 1979), the onset of spermatogenesis and ejaculation for boys precedes virtually all other pubertal changes, whereas in girls, ovulation occurs very late in the sequence. As Richardson and Short (1978, p.21) put it, the boy becomes potentially fertile at the very beginning of pubertal development, passing through a phase of being a "fertile eunuch" before acquiring his male secondary sex characteristics, where-as the girl develops nearly all her secondary sex characteristics to their fullest extent before acquiring her fertility. This fact suggests some special evolutionary pressure to delay fertility for the human female, giving her time when she can function as an adult socially and sexually and accumulate energy reserves with-out assuming a maternal role.

A delay in the establishment of fertility until after the attainment of adult stature is not universal to female mammals, many of which continue to grow not only after menarche but even during their first pregnancy and lactation. Gavan and Swindler (1966) and Watts and Gavan (1982) note differences among the higher primates in the placing of menarche in the growth period. Rhesus monkey females have attained only 30% of their adult stature when they reach menarche, in contrast to humans and chimpanzees who have reached 70 and 80%, respec-tively. It is possible that this pattern of nonhuman primate female growth, which allows for conflict between maternal growth and weight gain on the one hand and fetal growth and lactation on the other, explains the poor figures for maternal success often reported for primiparous female monkeys and apes (Dazey & Erwin, 1976; Drickamer, 1974; Glander, 1980; Mori, 1979; Nadler, 1975; Taub, 1980).

The Period of Adolescent Subfertility

At least 40 years ago, there was a general recognition that adolescent female primates, whether rhesus monkey, chimpanzee, or human, are not instantly fertile at the time of menarche (Lancaster, in press; Montagu, 1979; Young & Yerkes, 1943). Data collected at that time suggested that a period of postmenar-cheal subfertility lasted for about 1 year in the rhesus and up to 2 years for the chimpanzee and human. This information fits well with observations by an-thropologists on tribal societies, indicating that, although sexual activity almost invariably followed menarche, the likelihood of pregnancy was very low for the first few years. However, it is only very recently that the mechanism behind adolescent subfertility has been outlined (Lunenfeld, Kraiem, Eshkol, & Werner-Zodrow, 1978). It appears that the rising ovarian estrogen secretion at puberty eventually triggers a reflex discharge of luteinizing hormone from the pituitary leading to ovulation. However, responsiveness to the pituitary and gonads is regulated by a progressive maturation of feedback regulatory centers in the hypothalamus. This positive feedback system takes time to mature: As Lunenfeld et al. (1978) put it, the ovary learns to ovulate. It takes nearly 1 year for this mechanism to develop in the rhesus monkey (Dierschke, Weiss, & Knobil, 1974; Robinson & Goy, 1981). In a study of 8000 Finnish girls by Widholm and Kantero (1971, cited in Ryde-Blomqvist, 1978, p.147), only 57% of the girls had established regular menstrual cycles by 1 year postmenarche and not until 6 years postmenarche were 80% cycling regularly. Similar data using basal body temperature changes to indicate ovulation suggest that not until age 18–20 are 75% of women's menstrual cycles ovulatory (Doring, 1969). What is remarkable about this data is the extremely long time it may take for fertility in the higher primates to be established after regular sexual activity is assumed. According to Richardson and Short (1978), mammals such as sheep and rats have first estrus associated with ovulation. For such species, the positive feedback mechanism regulating ovulation matures at birth, not years after puberty, so that for them, puberty equals instant fertility. One might speculate that the unusual demands placed on female primates for high levels of long-term parental investment based on experience in the social and physical environment has led to a delay in the maturation of the system regulating fertility but not in the one regulating the onset of sexual behavior.

Fat and Fertility

A crucial factor in the fertility of women relates to critical levels of fat storage. First proposed by Frisch (1978) and recently reviewed by Cohen (1980) and Huss-Ashmore (1980), the critical fatness hypothesis suggests that women will not ovulate unless adequate stores of fat have been accumulated. These fat deposits represent enough stored energy (around 150,000 calories) to permit a woman to lactate for 1 year or more without having to increase her prepregnancy caloric intake. Frisch believes that not only birth spacing but also the timing of the onsets of menarche and menopause rest on the storage of energy in fat. Cohen (1980) notes the appeal of this hypothesis for explaining the secular trend in both the earlier onset of menarche and also the loss of a long period of adolescent subfertility in modern society. Sedentism combined with high levels of caloric intake lead to early deposition of body fat in young girls and "fool" the body into early biological maturation long before cognitive and social maturity are reached.

Skeptics of the critical fatness hypothesis have tended to focus on its critical threshold aspect but do not really undercut the important relationship between fertility and fatness. Ellison (1981a, b) demonstrates that the completion of the adolescent growth spurt in stature is a much better predictor of impending menarche than is a weight gain based on fat storage. This is not surprising when it is remembered that, in terms of evolutionary priorities, growth of stature is programmed to stop virtually at menarche, whereas there should still exist something on the order of up to 2 more years before fertility during which fat can be stored. Fat deposition is a better predictor of ovulation and fecundity than it is of menarche and the onset of menstrual cycling.

Despite the criticisms of Frisch's hypothesis, there is a growing body of evidence recently published by Garn (1980) demonstrating that early-maturing girls tend to be taller earlier in life but ultimately shorter because of their earlier cessation of growth. These same girls also tend to be heavier and fatter during their entire life course. Even at age 70, nearly 55 years after menarche, heavy women report earlier menarcheal age than do lean. Children of such women tend to be faster growing but reach maturity earlier, and they are ultimately shorter as well.

It is interesting that recent studies on the link between obesity and diabetes (Kissebah, Evans, Hoffman, & Kalkhoff, 1982) suggest that there may be two routes to fat deposition in the human. One route is influenced by androgens and tends to concentrate fat around the waist and upper body in fat cells that have the capacity to expand or shrink radically. The other route is via estrogens which concentrate fat that is very resistant to loss on the lower body. When obese women diet, there is a strong tendency for weight to be lost from the upper body but not from the lower. In fact, it appears to be much harder to shrink or kill the normal-size fat cells from the lower body, so that women who are fat only in these areas find it very hard to lose weight even if they diet faithfully. If concentrations of fat on the hips, buttocks, and thighs of women is "reproductive fat," it should not be surprising that these stores might be accumulated under the influence of estrogens and buffered against weight loss (Stini, 1979).

Despite the fact that one of the most striking and uniquely developed features of human sexual dimorphism is fat deposition, very little significance has been attached to it. Reviews of sexual dimorphism in human and nonhuman primates (Alexander et al., 1979; Hamburg, 1978; Leutenegger, 1982b; McCown, 1982) tend to focus on sex differences in body size and potential for aggression and do not note the extraordinary difference between men and women in fat storage or the lack of such conspicuous dimorphism in nonhuman primates. In fact, only Bailey (1982), Hall (1982), Huss-Ashmore (1980), and Stini (1981, 1982) give fat storage in women the emphasis it deserves. Sexual dimorphism in human body fat is much greater than in muscular tissue. Approximately 15% of body weight in the young adult male and about 27% of the female is adipose tissue, whereas muscle tissue represents an average of 52% for the male and 40% for the female (Bailey, 1982). When corrections are made for the smaller body size of the human female, women are indeed a great deal fatter than calculations of average sex differences would indicate. For instance, in comparing volume of body segments corrected for frame size, Bailey (1982) found that women are 40.2% larger than men for the gluteal (buttocks) segment. Huss-Ashmore (1980) argues that the distinctiveness of fat storage in women on breasts, buttocks, and thighs advertises healthy systemic function and the ability to reproduce and rear

children successfully. As such, reproductive fat in women should be more differentially located than fat in men, localized for more dramatic display, and
closely linked to the development of other secondary sex characteristics.

Fat Reserves, Lactation, and Growth of the Human Brain

It is only very recently that evolutionary theorists have turned from such
behavioral topics as aggression and sexual behavior to lactation as a key variable
in understanding species differences (Blurton-Jones, 1972; Daly, 1979; Pond,
1977). Perhaps one reason for this delayed interest was that few recognized the
enormous interspecies variability in virtually all aspects of lactation: The constituents of milk, frequency of nursing, length of nursing bout, and duration of
lactation. Blurton-Jones (1972) and more recently Stini (1982), Stini, Weber,
Kemberling, and Vaughan (1980), and Anderson (1983) profile the unusual
features of human milk and lactation. One of the most striking of these is its
exceedingly low protein content (46% that of the cow and 15% that of the
rabbit). At the same time, it is rich with lactose and lipids with values running 22
and 42%, respectively, above those of the cow. The composition of human milk
represents a balance of numerous other constituents as well, but it is clear from
the ratios of protein, lactose, and lipids that it amply supplies the nutrients
necessary for activity and growth of the brain and provides only low levels of
nutrients necessary to develop lean muscle and tissue. This is not surprising
when it is noted that even by age 10 a human reaches only 50% of adult body size
but has reached virtually adult values for brain size by age 4 (Dobbing, 1974).

The peculiarities and uniqueness of human milk can be best understood if the
unusual program for human brain growth is taken into account. At birth, the
brain of a rhesus monkey infant is approximately 68% of the adult size, chimpanzees 45%, and humans 23%. The human infant's brain grows exceedingly rapidly after birth, but it does not reach 45% of the adult size until 6–7 months of
age, and by the end of the first year, it has completed only 65% of its total
growth. The human brain completes 93–95% of its growth in volume by the end
of the fourth year, the usual age of weaning among human hunter–gatherers.
There are other animal species that also have extensive postnatal growth of the
brain, but they are generally what zoologists have labelled as r-selected species;
that is, they tend to produce litters of small embryonic young that grow very
rapidly after birth and are weaned within a few weeks or months (Dobbing &
Sands, 1979). With the exception of the great apes and humans, most animals
with single young and large adult body size produce precocial infants with
well-developed brains, able to sense the world and locomote at birth.

Dobbing (1974) and Frisancho (1978) have reviewed the most critical and
vulnerable periods of brain growth in humans and have focused on the last
trimester of fetal life and the first postnatal year as crucial. Although the adult
number of nerve cells develops during the first trimester of pregnancy, the

energetically demanding stages for the production of the brain's packing cells (oligodendroglia, glial cells) followed by synaptic arborization of the nerve cells and by the production of insulating material (myelin), which coats the long fibers through which the nerve cells send messages, occur in the 3 months just before birth and the year following. The vulnerable nature of brain growth for such a long period postpartum may explain one recently described feature of maternal weight gain and fetal growth. According to Winick (1981), preparations for lactation are so important that if a pregnant woman is inadequately nourished, they will take place at the expense of fetal growth. The pregnant woman will continue to deposit fat during pregnancy even if it means that fetal growth in body size will be reduced below optimal levels for neonate survival. Winick recommends that women should gain at least 25 pounds during pregnancy to ensure that the fetus will not have to compete with fat storage processes for nutrients. The energetic greed of the human infant's brain is truly impressive. During the first year of life, up to 65% of its total metabolic rate is devoted to the brain and only 8% to muscle tissue (Holliday, 1978).

The timing of growth, development, and the onset of reproduction within the life cycle has always been under heavy pressure from natural selection. The result of this pressure is a special program for each species that provides a range of variation for each event that is appropriate to conditions ranging from optimal to suboptimal habitat. The evolutionary pattern for human females is one of slow growth during a prolonged period of juvenile dependency, followed by a rapid completion of growth in stature before menarche. Menarche is followed by up to several years of sexual activity with very low probability of impregnation, during which a young woman can gain experience about her social and physical environment before undertaking the demands of motherhood. During this period of adolescent subfertility, a substantial store of body fat will be deposited in the human female at the same time that her male peer is using energy surpluses to grow greater stature and lean muscle tissue. This differential in male and female growth patterns leads to the major element of human dimorphism in secondary sex characters: Fat storage. The evolutionary pressure for the development of such an unusual degree of dimorphism in nutrient reserves is the unique nutritional demands of the developing human brain, which grows two-thirds of its total size in the first 4 years of life.

Conclusion

Evolutionary theorists argue that differences between animal forms reflect a history of species' adaptations to particular strategies of both feeding and reproduction. For human beings, the fundamental platform of behavior for the genus *Homo* was the division of labor between male hunting and female gathering, which focused on a unique human pattern of parental investment—the feeding of juveniles. The importance of contributions by both the male and female parent toward juvenile survival reduced the significance of sexual selection in human reproductive strategies and emphasized parental investment and parental partnerships for the rearing of children. The improved feeding efficiency from the human division of labor between hunting and gathering, guided by human intelligence, permitted the nutritional dependency of multiple young of differing ages upon their parents. The human species represents an extreme evolutionary development of two linked patterns of behavior: Intelligence based on learning and high levels of parental investment from both sexes. Despite the evolutionary success of this adaptation, the energy requirements of nursing a slowly developing, large-brained infant have left their marks on the reproductive biology of the human female. Unlike other primates, the significant sexual dimorphism in humans is not in the anatomy of aggressive potential (bone, muscles, and canine teeth) but in the storage of fat to support nearly continuous lactation in the mature adult female.

References

Alexander, R. D., Hoogland, J., Howard, R., Noonan, K., & Sherman, P. Sexual dimorphisms and breeding systems in pinnipeds, ungulates, primates, and humans. In N. Chagnon, & W. Irons (Eds.), *Evolutionary biology and human social behavior*. North Scituate, Mass.: Duxbury Press, 1979, pp. 402–435.

Altmann, J. Observational study of behavior: Sampling methods. *Behaviour*, 1974, *49*, 227–267.

Altmann, J. *Baboon mothers and infants*. Cambridge: Harvard University Press, 1980.

Anderson, P. The reproductive role of the human breast. *Current Anthropology*, 1983, *24*, 25–46.

Bailey, S. M. Absolute and relative sex differences in body composition. In R. Hall (Ed.), *Sexual dimorphism in* Homo sapiens. New York: Praeger, 1982, pp. 363–390.

Baldwin, J. D., & Baldwin, J. I., Effects of food ecology on social play: A laboratory simulation. *Zeitschrift für Tierpsychologie*, 1976, *40*, 1–14.

Baldwin, J. D., & Baldwin, J. I. The role of learning phenomena and the ontogeny of exploration and play. In S. Chevalier-Skolnikoff & F.E. Poirier (Eds.), *Primate biosocial development*. New York: Garland, 1977, pp. 364–406.

Beck, B. B. *Animal tool behavior*. New York: Garland STPM Press, 1980.

Blurton-Jones, N. Comparative aspects of mother–child contact. In N. Blurton-Jones (Ed.), *Ethological studies of child behaviour*. Cambridge: Cambridge University Press, 1972, pp. 305–329.

Chapais, B., & Schulman, S. R. An evolutionary model of female dominance relations in primates. *Journal of Theoretical Biology*, 1980, *82*, 47–90.

Clutton-Brock, T. H. Some aspects of intraspecific variation in feeding and ranging behaviour in primates. In T. H. Clutton-Brock (Ed.), *Primate ecology*. London: Academic Press, 1977, pp. 539–556.

Clutton-Brock, T. H., & Harvey, P. H. Primate ecology and social organization. *Journal of the Zoological Society of London*, 1977, *183*, 1–39.

Clutton-Brock, T. H., & Harvey, P. H. Mammals, resources and reproductive strategies. *Nature*, 1978, *273*, 191–196.

Clutton-Brock, T. H., Harvey, P. H., & Rudder, B. Sexual dimorphism, socionomic sex ratio and bodyweight in primates. *Nature*, 1977, *269*, 797–800.

Coehlo, A. M., Jr. Socio-bioenergetics and sexual dimorphism in primates. *Primates*, 1974, *15*, 263–269.

Cohen, M. N. Speculations on the evolution of density measurement and population in *Homo sapiens*. In M. N. Cohen, R. S. Malpass, & H. G. Klein (Eds.), *Biosocial mechanisms of population regulation*. New Haven: Yale University Press, 1980, pp. 275–304.

Daly, M. Why don't male mammals lactate? *Journal of Theoretical Biology*, 1979, *78*, 325–345.

Daly, M., & Wilson, M. *Sex, evolution and behavior* (2nd ed.). North Scituate, Mass.: Duxbury Press, 1983.

Dazey, J., & Erwin, J. Infant mortality in *Macaca nemestrina*. *Theriogenology*, 1976, *5*, 267–279.

Dierschke, D. J., Weiss, G., & Knobil, E. Sexual maturation in the female rhesus monkey and the development of estrogen-induced gonadotrophic hormone release. *Endocrinology*, 1974, *94*, 198–206.

Dittus, W. P. J. The social regulation of population density and age–sex distribution in the Toque monkey. *Behaviour*, 1977, *63*, 281–322.

Dittus, W. P. J. The evolution of behaviours regulating density and age-specific sex ratios in a primate population. *Behaviour*, 1979, *69*, 265–302.

Dittus, W. P. J. The social regulation of primate populations: A synthesis. In D. Lindburg (Ed.), *The Macaques: Studies in ecology, behavior, and evolution*. New York: Van Nostrand Reinhold, 1980, pp. 263–286.

Dobbing, J. The later development of the brain and its vulnerability. In J. A. Davis & J. Dobbing (Eds.), *Scientific foundations of paediatrics*. Philadelphia: W. B. Saunders, 1974, pp. 565–577.

Dobbing, J., & Sands, J. Comparative aspects of the brain spurt. *Early Human Development*, 1979, *3*, 79–83.

Doring, G. K. The incidence of anovular cycles in women. *Journal of Reproductive Fertility, Suppl.* 1969, *6*, 77.

Drickamer, L. C. A ten-year summary of reproductive data for free-ranging *Macaca mulatta*. *Folia primatologica*, 1974, *21*, 61–80.

Ellison, P. T. Prediction of age at menarche from annual height increments. *American Journal of Physical Anthropology*, 1981, *56*, 71–75. (a)

Ellison, P. T. Threshold hypotheses, developmental age, and menstrual function. *American Journal of Physical Anthropology*, 1981, *54*, 337–340. (b)

Fisher, H. E. *The sex contract*. New York: Morrow, 1982.

Frisancho, A. R. Nutritional influences on human growth and maturation. *Yearbook of Physical Anthropology*, 1978, *21*, 174–191.

Frisch, R. Population, food intake, and fertility. *Science*, 1978, *199*, 22–30.

Garn, S. M. Continuities and change in maturational timing. In O. Brim, Jr. & J. Kagan (Eds.), *Constancy and change in human development*. Cambridge: Harvard University Press, 1980, pp. 113–162.

Gaulin, S. J., & Konner, M. J. On the natural diet of primates, including humans. In R. & J. Wurtman (Eds.), *Nutrition and the brain* (Vol. 1). New York: Raven Press, 1977, pp. 2–86.

Gavan, J. A., & Swindler, D. R. Growth rates and phylogeny in primates. *American Journal of Physical Anthropology*, 1966, *24*, 181–190.

Glander, K. Reproduction and population growth in free-ranging mantled howling monkeys. *American Journal of Physical Anthropology*, 1980, *53*, 25–36.

Greenwood, P. J. Mating systems, philopatry and dispersal in birds and mammals. *Animal Behavior*, 1979, *28*, 1140–1162.

Hall, R. L. (Ed.). *Sexual dimorphism in* Homo sapiens. New York: Praeger, 1982.

Hamburg, B. A. The biosocial bases of sex difference. In S. L. Washburn & E. R. McCown (Eds.), *Human evolution: Biosocial perspectives*. Menlo Park, Calif.: Benjamin/Cummings, 1978, pp. 155–214.

Harding, R., & Teleki, G. (Eds). *Omnivorous primates*. New York: Columbia University Press, 1981.

Harrell, B. B. Lactation and menstruation in cultural perspective. *American Anthropologist*, 1981, *83*, 796–823.

Harvey, P. H., Kavanagh, M., & Clutton-Brock, T. H. Sexual dimorphism in primate teeth. *Journal of the Zoological Society of London*, 1978, *186*, 475–485.

Hausfater, G. Dominance and reproduction in baboons (*Papio cynocephalus*): A quantitative analysis. *Contributions to primatology* (Vol. 7), Basel: Karger, 1975, 150 pp.

Hausfater, G., & Hrdy, S. B. *Infanticide: Comparative and evolutionary perspectives*. New York: Aldine, 1984.

Hayden, B. Subsistence and ecological adaptations of modern hunter/gatherers. In R. Harding & G. Teleki (Eds.), *Omnivorous primates*. New York: Columbia University Press, 1981, pp. 344–421.

Holliday, M. A. Body composition and energy needs during growth. In F. Falker & J. M. Tanner (Eds.), *Human growth* (Vol. 2). New York: Plenum, 1978, pp. 117–139.

Hrdy, S. B. Infanticide among primates: A review, classification and examination of the implications for the reproductive strategies of females. *Ethology and Sociobiology*, 1979, *1*, 13–40.

Hrdy, S. B. *The woman that never evolved*. Cambridge: Harvard University Press, 1981.

Hrdy, S. B., & Williams, G. Behavioral biology and the double standard. In S. K. Wasser (Ed.), *The social behavior of female vertebrates*. New York: Academic Press, 1983, pp. 3–18.

Huss-Ashmore, R. Fat and fertility: Demographic implications of differential fat storage. *Yearbook of Physical Anthropology*, 1980, *23*, 65–91.

Isaac, G. L. The food-sharing behavior of protohuman hominids. *Scientific American*, 1978, *238*, 90–108.

Isaac, G. L. Casting the net wide: A review of archaeological evidence for early hominid land-use and ecological relations. In L. Konigsson (Ed.), *Current argument on early man*. New York: Pergamon Press, 1981, pp. 226–251.

Isaac, G. L., & Crader, D. C. To what extent were early hominids carnivorous? In R. Harding & G. Teleki (Eds.), *Omnivorous primates*. New York: Columbia University Press, 1981, pp. 37–104.

Johnston, T. D. Selective costs and benefits in the evolution of learning. *Advances in the Study of Behavior*, 1982, *12*, 65–106.

Kissebah, A. H., Evans, D. J., Hoffman, R. G., & Kalkhoff, R. K. Relation of body fat distribution to metabolic complications of obesity. *Journal of Clinical Endocrinology and Metabolism*, 1982, *54*, 254–260.

Lancaster, J. B. Human adolescence and reproduction: An evolutionary perspective. In J. B. Lancaster & B. A. Hamburg (Eds.), *School-age pregnancy and parenthood: Biosocial dimensions*. New York: Aldine, in press.

Lancaster, J. B., & Lancaster, C. S. Parental investment: The hominid adaptation. In D. Ortner (Ed.), *How humans adapt: A biocultural odyssey*. Washington, D. C.: Smithsonian Institution Press, 1983, pp. 33–66.

Leutenegger, W. Scaling of sexual dimorphism in body weight and canine size in primates. *Folia primatologica*, 1982, *37*, 163–176. (a)

Leutenegger, W. Sexual dimorphism in nonhuman primates. In R. Hall (Ed.), *Sexual dimorphism in Homo sapiens*. New York: Praeger, 1982, pp. 11–36. (b)

Leutenegger, W., & Kelly, J. T. Relationship of sexual dimorphism in canine size, body size to social, behavioral, and ecological correlates in anthropoid primates. *Primates*, 1977, *18*, 117–136.

Lovejoy, O. The origin of man. *Science*, 1981, *211*, 341–350.

Lunenfeld, F., Kraiem, Z., Eshkol, A., & Werner-Zodrow, I. The ovary learns to ovulate. *Journal of Biosocial Science Suppl.*, 1978, *5*, 43–62.

MacArthur, R. H. Some generalized theorems of natural selection. *Proceedings of the National Academy of Sciences*, 1962, *48*, 1893–1897.

McCown, E. R. Sex differences: The female as baseline for species description. In R. Hall (Ed.), *Sexual dimorphism in* Homo sapiens. New York: Praeger, 1982, pp. 37–84.

McKenna, J. J. The evolution of allomothering behavior among Colobine monkeys: Function and opportunities in evolution. *American Anthropologist*, 1979, *8*, 818–840.

McKenna, J. J. The evolution of primate societies, reproduction and parenting. In J. Fobes & J. King (Eds.), *Primate behavior*. New York: Academic Press, 1982, pp. 87–133. (a)

McKenna, J. J. Primate field studies: The evolution of behavior and its socioecology. In J. Fobes & J. King (Eds.), *Primate behavior*. New York: Academic Press, 1982 pp. 53–83. (b)

Mitchell, G. *Behavioral sex differences in nonhuman primates*. New York: Van Nostrand Reinhold, 1979.

Montagu, M. F. A. *The reproductive development of the female: A study in the comparative physiology of the adolescent organism* (3rd ed.). Littleton, Mass.: PSG Publishing, 1979.

Mori, A. Analysis of population changes by measurement of body weight in the Koshima troop of Japanese monkeys. *Primates*, 1979, *20*, 371–399.

Nadler, R. D. Determinants of variability in maternal behavior of captive female gorillas. In S. Kondo, M. Kawai, A. Ehara, & S. Kawamura (Eds.), *Proceedings from the Symposia of the 5th International Congress of Primatology*. Tokyo: Japan Science Press, 1975, pp. 207–216.

Parker, S. T., & Gibson, K. R. A developmental model for the evolution of language and intelligence in early hominids. *The Behavioral and Brain Sciences*, 1979, *2*, 367–408.

Pond, C. M. The significance of lactation in the evolution of mammals. *Evolution*, 1977, *31*, 177–199.

Pond, C. M. Morphological aspects and the ecological consequences of fat deposition in wild vertebrates. *Annual Review of Ecology and Systematics*, 1978, *9*, 519–570.

Post, B., Hausfater, G., & McClusky, S. Feeding behavior of yellow baboons (*Papio cynocephalus*): Relationship to age, gender, and dominance rank. *Folia primatologica*, 1980, *34*, 170–195.

Ralls, K. Mammals in which females are larger than males. *Quarterly Review of Biology*, 1976, *51*, 245–276.

Ralls, K. Sexual dimorphism in mammals: Avian models and unanswered questions. *American Naturalist*, 1977, *11*, 917–938.

Richards, A. F., & Schulman, S. R. Sociobiology: Primate field studies. *Annual Reviews in Anthropology*, 1982, *11*, 231–255.

Richardson, D. W., & Short, R. V. Time of onset of sperm production in boys. *Journal of Biosocial Science Suppl.*, 1978, *5*, pp. 15–26.

Robinson, J. A., & Goy, R. W. The pubescent rhesus monkey: Characteristics of the menstrual cycle and effects of prenatal androgenization. *Biology of Reproduction*, 1981, *24*, Suppl. 1 (Abstract 90).

Ryde-Blomqvist, E. Contraception in adolescence: A review of the literature. *Journal of Biosocial Science Suppl.*, 1978, *5*, 129–158.

Schultz, A. H. *The life of primates*. London: Weidenfeld and Nicholson, 1969.

Short, R. V. The evolution of human reproduction. *Proceedings of the Royal Society*, 1976, *B195*, 3–24.

Short, R. V. Sexual selection and its component parts, somatic and genital selection, as illustrated by man and the great apes. *Advances in the Study of Behavior*, 1979, *9*, 131–158.

Silk, J. B., & Boyd, R. Cooperation, competition and mate choice in matrilineal macaque groups. In S. K. Wasser (Ed.), *Social behavior of female vertebrates*. New York: Academic Press, 1983, pp. 316–349.

Small, M. F. (Ed.). *Female primates: Studies by women primatologists*. New York: Liss, 1984.

Stacey, P. B. Female promiscuity and male reproductive success in social birds and mammals. *American Naturalist*, 1982, *120*, 51–64.

Stini, W. A. Adaptive strategies of human populations under nutritional stress. In W. A. Stini (Ed.), *Physiological and morphological adaptation and evolution*. Mouton: The Hague, 1979, pp. 387–407.

Stini, W. A. Body composition and nutrient reserves in evolutionary perspective. In D. N. Walcher & N. Kretchmer (Eds.), *Food, nutrition and evolution*. New York: Masson, 1981, pp. 107–120.

Stini, W. A. Sexual dimorphism and nutrient reserves. In R. Hall (Ed.), *Sexual dimorphism in* Homo sapiens. New York: Praeger, 1982, pp. 391–419.

Stini, W. A., Weber, C., Kemberling, S., & Vaughan, L. Lean tissue growth and disease susceptibility in bottle-fed versus breast-fed infants. In E. S. Green & F. E. Johnston (Eds.), *Social and biological predictors of nutritional status, physical growth, and neurological development*. New York: Academic Press, 1980, pp. 61–79.

Sugiyama, Y., & Ohsawa, H. Population dynamics of Japanese monkeys with special reference to the effect of artificial feeding. *Folia primatologica*, 1982, *39*, 238–263.

Tanner, N. M. *On becoming human*. New York: Cambridge University Press, 1981.

Taub, D. M. Age at first pregnancy and reproductive success among colony-born squirrel monkeys (*Saimiri sciureus*, Brazilian). *Folia primatologica*, 1980, *33*, 262–272.

Teleki, G. Primate subsistence patterns: Collector-predators and gatherer-hunters. *Journal of Human Evolution*, 1975, *4*, 125–184.

Trivers, R. L. Parental investment and sexual selection. In B. H. Campbell (Ed.), *Sexual selection and the descent of man*. Chicago: Aldine, 1972, pp. 136–179.

Washburn, S. L. Longevity in primates. In J. L. McGaugh & S. B. Kiesler (Eds.), *Aging: Biology and behavior*, New York: Academic Press, 1981, pp. 11–29.

Wasser, S. K. Reproductive competition and cooperation among female yellow baboons. In S. K. Wasser (Ed.), *Social behavior of female vertebrates*. New York: Academic Press, 1983, pp. 350–391.

Wasser, S. K. Reproductive suppression among female mammals: Implications for biomedicine and sexual selection theory. *Quarterly Review of Biology*, in press.

Watts, E. S., & Gavan, J. A. Postnatal growth of nonhuman primates: The problem of the adolescent spurt. *Human Biology*, 1982, *54*, 53–70.

Winick, M. Food and the fetus. *Natural History*, 1981, *90*, 76–81.

Wittenberger, J. F. The evolution of mating systems in birds and mammals. In P. Marler & J. Vandenbergh (Eds.), *Handbook of behavioral neurobiology* (Vol. 3). New York: Plenum, 1979, pp. 271–349.

Wrangham, R. W. On the evolution of ape social systems. *Biology and Social Life*, 1975, *18*, 335–368.

Wrangham, R. W. An ecological model of female-bonded primate groups. *Behaviour*, 1980, *75*, 262–300.

Young, W. C., & Yerkes, R. M. Factors influencing the reproductive cycle in the chimpanzee: The period of adolescent sterility and related problems. *Endocrinology*, 1943, *33*, 121–154.

Zihlman, A. L. Women as shapers of the human adaptation. In F. Dahlberg (Ed.), *Woman the gatherer*. New Haven: Yale University Press, 1981, pp. 75–120.

2

Age, Gender, and the Demographic Transition: The Life Course in Agrarian Societies

SARAH LEVINE

ROBERT A. LEVINE
Harvard University
El Colegio de Mexico

Introduction

The homogenization of the world's peoples, particularly in the structural characteristics of their social orders, is a familiar theme in sociological research. The spread of economic markets, national bureaucracies, and the Western occupational and educational systems has been documented in its structural effects throughout the globe. When we turn to demographic characteristics, however, the world's peoples are in some respects more diverse now than ever before: The birth rates of subsaharan Africa, for example, are more than four times those of Western Europe, and their infant mortality rates are fifteen times higher. Though mortality and fertility have declined in many places, the gap between rich and poor countries on indicators related to income and infant mortality has been widening. A majority of the world's families currently occupy a demographic and economic situation closer to that of the preindustrial European peasantry than to contemporary European populations. Their assumptions about life, death, and interpersonal relationships are conditioned by these proximate realities of reproduction and resources as much as by the structural impact of modernization. For them, contemporary economic and demographic conditions provide empirical support for premodern conceptions of social and moral order and of the life course possible in that order.

These realities of high fertility and mortality should not be seen simply as an outcome of a lack of medical and contraceptive technology but as aspects of human adaptation among preindustrial peoples. The agrarian societies that came to predominate several thousand years ago still constitute a majority of the world's population, and their domestic life has been organized around maximizing the number of offspring, optimizing their survival chances in infancy, and anticipating contributions of children to the family economy.

Customary beliefs and practices promoting fertility, birth spacing, and the domestic use of child labor are fundamental to the adaptive strategies by which agrarian parents maintain the family food supply and obtain both current support and long-term personal security. These agrarian imperatives of parenthood are central to the public definitions of age and gender roles in such societies and provide the structure through which women and men experience their lives as children and adults.

The aim of this chapter is first to characterize some common features of the life course in societies where birth and death rates are high and the majority of families are engaged in agriculture, and to illustrate with examples from Africa and Mexico how age and gender distinctions are structured and experienced in agrarian societies. Second, we will show that when death rates fall rapidly but birth rates remain high, the social structure of the life course is forced to change, but both the rate of change and the innovations that occur in response to demographic pressures reflect the diverse cultures of such societies.

Characteristics of Agrarian Societies

Four major features are shared in common by agricultural societies: First, gender distinctions are fundamental in determining residence, work roles, and other forms of social participation in agrarian societies and are often elaborated in their cultural ideologies. The expectancy that each woman will normally bear children over two to three decades of adulthood, according to a culturally defined natural fertility schedule, is deeply involved here, for the public positions of adult women are predominantly defined by their reproductive status. Widespread structural features such as virilocal residence and polygyny tend to further sharpen gender distinctions. Consider the contrast between women and men in a virilocal residence pattern, in which women move to their husbands' residence at the point of marriage. Such married women have moved to live among alien kin, often in distant localities from their natal homes (as in India, traditional China, and much of subsaharan Africa), whereas men continue to reside in permanent social niches with stable inherited claims on property. As girls, such women are known to be temporary residents in their natal homes, whereas their brothers are permanent residents. As a result, this contrast between male and female becomes entrenched in the way adults think about themselves, their spouses, and their children. In polygynous societies, where men take several wives and women are bound only to one husband (as in Africa and parts of the Middle East), the extreme disparity in reproductive roles tends also to enhance the contrast between men and women. A man of 70 years, for example, can take another wife and father more children at an age when his other wives are long past menopause and have assumed social positions appropriate to that reproductive status. The agrarian gender gap established by natural fertility regimes and widened by virilocality and polygyny is often interpreted as a difference in social power, but the actual power differential between men and women is extremely variable from one society to another. What is common to all agrarian societies is a sharp public distinction between the sexes, rooted in their different reproductive roles, which in turn affects their social participation and subjective experience at every phase of their lives in adulthood.

Second, agrarian societies are characterized by gender-specific age-grading. Adulthood for each gender is culturally organized as a series of hierarchical stages of maturity. Though the stages of men differ from those of women and are often based on different criteria, increasing age is positively valued for both sexes. Young adulthood is usually a position of subordination, while the later years—for those relatively few who reach them—bring more social power, public esteem, and personal choice. Each gender's age hierarchy acts as a powerful motivator for the normative performance of adults who have not yet reached the highest stage.

Third, the lifelong loyalty of children to their parents is a prominent value in agrarian societies. The centrality of this value in the Confucian tradition, translated into English as "filial piety," is the best known example of this feature, but in fact it is characteristic of most Third World societies as it was of premodern Europe. Adult children are bound to their parents by a norm of reciprocity that varies cross-culturally in its conceptual elaboration, its connections with the ownership of property, and the particular parent–child dyad most centrally involved. What is common everywhere, however, is that agrarian parents feel entitled to expect obedience from their offspring when they are children, loyalty from them when they are young adults, and increasing respect and support from them as they grow older.

Finally, interpersonal relationships based on kinship and clientage are highly salient in the social identities of agrarian adults. Regardless of their performance in work roles or their exceptional qualities in other specialized domains, adults in agrarian societies define themselves and are defined by others primarily by their locations in a specific relational order based on reciprocity and hierarchy. The concept of an entirely separate personal identity that transcends social ties and redefines relationships is rare in such societies. Thus, the structure of age and gender roles and of the parent–child relationship shapes not only how lives are led but how they are subjectively experienced through the life course. To a degree that is difficult for many Westerners to understand, agrarian men and women experience themselves as not only constrained by but motivated by the norms of age, gender, and parenthood that apply to them as individuals.

Food production is an overriding priority of agrarian peoples, and sex roles are largely determined by this constraint. The first responsibility of the men is the defense of the land and people; as warriors, they must maintain peaceful conditions so that the land can be worked in safety. They are responsible also for the care of larger domestic animals, for the clearing of woodland, for building and construction, for hunting, and for community affairs. The degree to which they participate in routine agricultural tasks varies widely and depends to a great extent upon the ploughing technique employed in a particular society. Where ploughs are drawn by animals, men take primary responsibility. Meanwhile, since food production requires intensive labor, best supplied by a large family, the essential female function is motherhood. From infancy onward, a female child is valued less for her personal qualities than for her future role as a bearer of children. Although in virilocal societies, a girl is trained for the ultimate benefit of the family into which she marries rather than of her own family, in another household another girl is being trained to become a good wife and, more important, a good mother to the children of the first girl's brother. Success as an adult woman is clear cut and quantitative: Once a girl is married, she should continue to give birth at regular intervals until menopause. The concept of ''enough'' children is irrelevant in societies where the hazards of disease, drought, and pestilence can make maternal success ephemeral. Furthermore, even if she survives her own reproductive years, a woman must continue to devote herself to the survival and maintenance of her children's children to the end of her life.

Apart from this primary maternal investment, what women do with their energy and time varies from one culture to another. In some societies, notably in many parts of Africa where ploughing is performed with a hand hoe, women are primarily responsible for food production, which often necessitates the delegation of infant care and many domestic tasks to young children. In areas in which ploughing is done largely with oxen, women's participation in agriculture is confined to sowing, weeding, and harvesting. In still other areas, women may be responsible for the processing of crops but do not go to the fields at all. This is frequently the pattern in Muslim societies in which the capacity to keep one's wives sequestered during daylight hours is a mark of high status for a man. In the Sahel, for example, while the wives of poor peasants are heavily involved in the farm, the wives of larger landowners are restricted exclusively to the performance of domestic tasks.

In some agrarian societies, women may pursue other occupations in addition to their agricultural responsibilities, such as traders or curers, or they may play a central role in religious life. But these occupations never take precedence over motherhood, and indeed they are likely to be pursued in response to reproductive failure. This is often the case among Yoruba market women and Hausa officials of the Bori or spirit possession cult.

The role of children, meanwhile, closely reflects those of adults. By age 6, they are routinely involved in the performance of domestic and agricultural tasks, and by 14, their workload is likely to equal that of an adult (Moni Nag, Peet, & White, 1977). In early childhood, boys may not be told explicitly that their future lies with war, cattle, and community affairs, or girls that their future lies with children and household management, but both sexes soon learn from observation that a deep gulf exists between the worlds of men and women as it does between the young and the old. In agrarian societies, one's standing in the community is closely equated with age: The longer one lives, the more highly is one valued. The adolescent is worth more socially and economically than the child, and the young adult commensurately more than the adolescent, while each increment in age implies an increment in status to offspring and parent alike.

The costs of raising children to the point at which they start making an economic contribution to the family are minimal. Infants are likely to stay at the breast, with nutritional supplement introduced late in the first year, until the age of 2 or older; after weaning, children take their places at the bottom of the family hierarchy, where they eat last and least. They have no special space, no special possessions, and their care involves no additional expense to their parents. They are merely absorbed into the sibling group in which, by watching older children, they are trained as contributors. The legitimacy of their labor is never questioned.

Meanwhile, in many societies, daughters enrich their parents when they marry and leave. The husband of an Ibo or Luyhia girl pays bridewealth to his parents-in-law. Whether the price agreed on is in money, cloth, blankets, livestock, or some combination, until it is paid a man may not exercise any claim to the offspring of the union. When a Hindu girl marries, she takes a large proportion of her family's moveable wealth with her as her dowry. Her parents, however, expect to be compensated for their loss in short order, for the expenditure they have made has increased their good name and reputation. Other parents will be eager to arrange their own daughters' marriages to the son in such a family. Hence, the brother of a newly married woman will have his pick of girls offering dowries at least equal in value to the one his sister took away with her.

Thus, it can scarcely be overemphasized that before the onset of the demographic transition, despite the lowly status ascribed to them in childhood, children in most agrarian societies constitute their parents' greatest asset.

The Early Stage of the Demographic Transition in Kenya and Mexico

The authors have had the opportunity to observe the early stages of the demographic transition in two countries, Kenya and Mexico. Robert LeVine first became familiar with the Gusii people of Kenya in the mid-1950s, at which point the infant mortality rate stood at about 160 per 1000 live births nationally. Twenty years later, the 1977 Kenya Fertility Survey showed that the infant mortality rate for the country as a whole stood at 87 per 1000 live births, while fertility remained unimpeded. At the same time, there was very little demand for contraceptives, which were largely unavailable in any event. The 1979 census figures showed that in Gusiiland itself, women had had an average of 8.7 live births at the end of their childbearing years, making them more fertile than the women of any other group in Kenya. Indeed, they were possibly the most fertile group of women in the world at the time.

During 1982 and 1983, we worked in Central Mexico in the state of Querétaro, where we conducted a study of the people in two communities. Their
circumstances, particularly their demographic conditions, resemble those of the
Gusii in Africa. The infant mortality rate for Mexico as a whole had fallen from
180 per 1000 live births in 1940 to 64 in 1980. The very active Family Planning
Campaign of the 1970s has resulted in a decline in the nationwide total fertility
rate from 6.7 in 1970 to 4.2 in 1980, but in the countryside, the average total
fertility rate is still over 7. In rural Querétaro, for example, the proportion of
couples using birth control remains very small. During 1982–1983, in each of
two villages (numbering 340 and 196 households, respectively), the health
authorities estimated that no more than 20 women were using contraceptives.
While a small majority of women interviewed stated that they were in favor of
limiting family size, most added a qualifier, "not until I have had enough
children," by which they meant, on average, four children. But few of the
women who had achieved this desired number had actually begun to control their
fertility.

Social Structure in Gusiiland Before the
Demographic Transition

When Robert LeVine began working in East Africa shortly before the end of
the British colonial rule, the objective of every Gusii male was the achievement
of dominance in the lineage and clan into which he had been born. While wives,
children, land, and cattle were essential indicators of status, age was equally
important. A woman's status also closely reflected age and reproductive success.
Since Gusii society was virilocal, however, the life course of females was more
problematic. A girl did not "belong" to her natal kin; she had to leave them and
marry among strangers and, as a bride, to begin the long process of acceptance
and acculturation into her husband's lineage (S. LeVine & Pfeiffer, 1982). This
obligatory separation from family of origin in adolescence encouraged the development of a sense of autonomy in girls. Furthermore, even though male and
female worlds were largely separate and the female world was subordinate to the
male, Gusii culture provided women as much as men with a path to respect and
influence (S. LeVine, 1979).

While the birth of many children was highly valued, the fact that women were
almost totally responsible for agricultural work meant they could not stay full
time with infants for long after a birth. From the first weeks of life, Gusii babies
were force-fed gruel in order to ensure an adequate weight gain, while their
mothers delegated the care of infants to surrogates, often young children, and
returned to the fields, typically within 4 or 5 months after parturition (LeVine &
LeVine, 1966). Babies continued to sleep with their mothers, and weaning was
not initiated until an average of 20 months of age, but beyond early infancy,
children rarely enjoyed any high level of maternal attention. Fathers, meanwhile,
were regarded with fear and awe; they had very little contact with young chil-

dren, since men ate and slept separately and spent most of their waking hours outside the homestead. Most verbal communication between parent and child took the form of commands by mother or father to which the child promptly complied. Shortly after weaning, children fetched and carried and made themselves useful, while in the presence of adults at other times, they were seen but not heard. Gusii children were not regarded as complete people until they "learned sense" at circumcision, which took place at the age of 8 or 9 for girls, a year or 2 later for boys. Once they had known the pain of the initiation rite, they were taken seriously as fully legitimate members of their lineage and clan. This change in status did not lead to closer parent–child relationships, however. Affective display between parents and children was at a minimum at any time, but following circumcision, the relationship became, if anything, more distant. This restraint was dictated by the need for avoidance between members of adjacent generations and between parents and children in particular. An infraction of the rules of respect constituted an abomination, requiring ritual placation of the ancestors.

After circumcision, boys entered the world of men and girls the world of women. These worlds were carefully stratified: Progress through them required an individual to achieve specific goals that could be reached only after a certain minimum of time had elapsed. Thus, although one could earn promotion later than one's peers, there was no way to achieve it earlier. Just as a child could not be regarded as a complete person until he had passed through the rite of initiation, a young man or woman could not become an adult until he or she married; furthermore, the marriage was not considered permanent until a son was born. A man had little authority within his lineage and none in the clan as a whole until he became a grandfather. Only when his eldest son became a father did a man receive acceptance into the ranks of the elders. Similarly, a woman made the final transition from her natal to her husband's kin only after she became a grandmother. One's status, then, depended first on one's age and second on the age of one's progeny. Someone who was childless or had only daughters would be ineligible for "promotion"; his or her ascent up the lineage hierarchy would be blocked. Individuals afflicted in this way did have an alternative path to status and respect: If characterologically suited to the role, Gusii men and women who experienced reproductive failures could become specialists in the religious sphere. In this way, provided they lived long enough and were "on time" (Neugarten, 1969) in relation to their peers, Gusii men and women could expect to be elevated to the highest ranks of their community.

Social Structure in Querétaro Before the Demographic Transition

No ethnographies of the Querétaro area exist and thus, in order to arrive at an understanding of the social, economic, and psychological circumstances prevailing in predemographic-transition Querétaro, we must rely primarily on the recol-

lections of informants. One hundred and fifty years ago, the population had been
Otomi-speaking people, living on common lands, but with the expansion of the
hacienda economy in the mid-nineteenth century, their lands were taken from
them and people were forced into peonage and hispanisization on the great
country estates. This estate pattern remained in existence until the agrarian
reforms of the early 1940s led to the establishment of *ejidos*.

Hence, many of our villager–informants had been children during the last
years of the *hacendados*. At that time, the worlds of men and women were as
distinctly separate as in colonial Gusiiland: Rarely did their roles and functions
overlap. At the same time, however, their separately led lives took very different
forms. In Querétaro, for example, it was men, not women, who made up the
agricultural labor force. While theoretically free to leave the estate, men in
preindustrialized Mexico had very limited alternatives to a life of toil and in-
debtedness to the *dueno* and his shop, *tienda de raya*. Although their wives
might be recruited to work in the fields at certain points in the agricultural cycle,
married women were concerned with domestic tasks most of the time. Few
women had any independent economic activity, although some women in every
community were midwives and curers, just as in Gusiiland.

Since their mothers were not heavily involved in agricultural work, Mexican
infants enjoyed a much longer period of concentrated maternal attention than
Gusii infants did. Furthermore, compared to the lack of affective display by
Gusii mothers and fathers, Querétaro fathers also showed considerable positive
affection toward their children. Mothers and fathers overtly regarded children as
a source of joy. Our informants frequently recalled their fathers playing with
them, and older women spoke about how, 40 years earlier, their husbands had
routinely helped with the youngest children. Even so, the exigencies of life in
rural Querétaro were not so different from those of East Africa, and by age 6 or
7, boys were in the fields with their fathers, while at home girls had already
assumed a heavy burden of housework. These Mexican parents, like Gusii parents, exacted the utmost obedience from their offspring, not only in childhood
but until marriage, in the case of daughters, and throughout adulthood, in the
case of sons.

Given the virtual impossibility of accumulating worldly goods, however,
respect from one's peers was earned by the fulfillment of kin and *compadrazgo*
obligations and by contributions to and participation in church festivals. While
the religious life was crucial for women, the most important source of self-
esteem for men was unsullied family honor. Men were guardians of their daughters' virginity and their wives' fidelity. If they failed in this most vital
responsibility, they failed as men.

The Demographic Transition as a Precipitant of
Social Change in Agrarian Societies

In both Gusiiland and Querétaro, infant mortality rates dropped in the course
of two generations, from around 200 per 1000 live births to below 100. As infant

mortality declined, parents started to see their children differently, especially if the mortality drop was accompanied by the introduction of universal primary education and rapid urbanization. Under these circumstances, there was a reduction in the amount of time that children were available each day to do their parents' bidding and a narrowing of the range of tasks assigned to children. Consequently, parents have been obliged to revise their notions concerning the costs and benefits of children (Caldwell, 1976, 1978; Hoffman & Hoffman, 1973). The hierarchical family organization that survived for untold generations under conditions of high fertility and high mortality now comes under pressure. Children know more than their parents; they are less compliant, less obedient, more troublesome. The young have options and alternatives to working on the land. The old social structure that had defined an individual's position almost exclusively in terms of age and gender is no longer functional. It must make way for another structure, more consistent with the new demographic reality. The rate at which change occurs, however, is by no means uniform, for the old order's resilience or vulnerability is dictated by complex cultural as well as social and economic factors.

Gusiiland

A generation after our first contact, we found that the population of Gusiiland had more than doubled, despite some outmigration, with the result that land was in very short supply. In fact, the community where we were working had reached the limit of its resources. Even so, it soon became evident that life goals had altered very little. Most Gusii men were still determined to be polygamous and to have as many children as possible, for these were still the traditional requisites for a man's dominance in the lineage and wider community. At the same time, grafted onto the traditional agrarian values, we identified a new modern set that was in sharp conflict with the old in several ways. While a mark of high status was still a successful reproductive career, the means for supporting such a career had changed. There was not enough land to acquire through inheritance; it had to be purchased from poorer neighbors. The money to buy such land had to be earned in the modern sector, through trade or government service, which required high levels of Western education. Thus, younger educated men, and in some instances women as well, were able to leapfrog their way to influence by means of wealth generated not from agriculture but employment or commerce in the urban areas. So, too, the authority of the elders, the *abagaka,* was undermined: While the elders continued to meet for the settlement of local disputes, their decisions were often impossible to enforce.

In order to contend with the continuous rise in the cost of living, a large proportion of males, whether educated or not, are now forced to seek employment in distant urban centers from which they return home once or twice a year for short periods. In their absence, their wives take total responsibility for day-to-day decisions in the running of the family and farm and for maintaining relations in the community. It is now wives, not their husbands, who deal with the coffee cooperative and the tea company and who negotiate bank loans and meet interest payments. Many women, then, have been abruptly thrust from a subordinate position in an almost exclusively female world to one of considerable autonomy in what had been a man's domain. At the same time, there are ways in which such women are less secure than in the past. For example, with the authority of the older generation undermined, women have no one to appeal to should their husbands decide to divorce them or should the husband fail to exact certain obligations from his kin.

Meanwhile, parents became acutely aware that the only chance of a reasonable economic future was through the education of their children, in the hope that they would find work off the land. Gusii culture had always permitted considerable independence to females within their own sphere; as a result, parents had few reservations about allowing their daughters, like their sons, to take advantage of new educational opportunities. Less than a generation ago, chastity had been highly valued, but owing to the decline of the bridewealth system and the predominance of love as opposed to arranged marriages, by the 1970s girls had almost complete sexual freedom. We found that girls were almost as likely to go to secondary school as boys, despite the possibility of pregnancy inherent in the coeducational boarding schools the Gusii adolescents attend.

In essence, what we were seeing in the 1970s was a rural society heavily subsidized by the cities. It is an irony that for the first time in history, the age-old objective of agrarian people to raise to adulthood large numbers of children was being achieved by the majority of parents in an era when land shortage can not absorb such high fertility. Given land shortages, the old purpose for having such large families is no longer valid. In many instances, farms had been so much reduced in size that a woman could take care of her farm virtually single-handed. Furthermore, most farms were too small to feed a family of three or four, let alone the nine or ten children that had become the rule rather than the exception. Yet, despite the costs of raising children, the overwhelming majority of adults were opposed to birth control. "If we have many children," they told us, "might not one or two of them turn out to be clever, and get educated and take their brothers and sisters after them to the city and provide for us when we are old?" The hope, if not the assumption, was that filial loyalty and the rights of parents over the fruits of their children's labor still obtained.

Querétaro

In contemporary Querétaro, 40 years after the agrarian reforms, most families are again landless. They continue to live in their ancestral villages, but nearly three-quarters of the household heads in the communities we studied were earning their living as factory workers, day laborers, and masons in nearby towns. Owing to intense population pressures, on the one hand, and inflation and increasing consumer tastes, on the other, the people can no longer survive as agriculturalists. Indeed, most do not even cultivate vegetable gardens. Yet agrarian values and practices persist. Children rarely work in the fields, but their mothers rely heavily on them for assistance; boys take care of the animals, while girls help in the house.

Querétaro villagers under 30 years of age are less likely to have been to school than their Gusii counterparts. Since independence 20 years ago, education had been the top priority of the Kenya government, but it is only since the oil boom in the late 1970s, when the Mexican government began to place a much greater emphasis on education, that the large majority of rural children have attended primary school. Moreover, Querétaro parents appear even now to have low educational aspirations for their children, their daughters in particular. In the rapidly expanding economy that Mexico enjoyed until 1982, a boy of 14 or 15 years of age cound find steady employment as a manual laborer, and literacy, let alone postprimary education, would not necessarily improve his earnings. The family honor is still closely guarded, and from puberty onward, rural parents watch their daughters carefully. After leaving school, often when she reaches menarche, a girl will stay at home until she marries. After marriage, the likelihood that she will make a direct financial contribution to her household is slight. Today, as 40 years ago, most women continue to be wholly dependent on their husbands' earnings.

In the absence of unemployment or old age insurance, rural Mexican parents, like East African parents, continue to regard their offspring as their greatest assets. Almost three-quarters of our respondents said they expected to receive support from one or more children in the future. In childhood, girls contribute more, since boys, we were told, fidget and play, but in adulthood, it is their sons to whom parents look for financial support. "What else d'you think we had them for?" they asked us.

Contemporary Age and Gender Roles in Querétaro and Gusiiland

Given the daily exodus of landless men to places of employment outside the village, the worlds of men and women in the Querétaro countryside are perhaps even more distinctly separate today than 40 years ago. Once women worked alongside their husbands at planting, weeding, and harvest time and took food out to the fields during the rest of the year; today, however, husbands and wives do not see each other from six in the morning to six at night on weekdays, while on Sundays the men are likely to spend most of the day at the village soccer game. Women are even more confined to the house than in the past. Most have never slept a night outside their village. Only the men go out into the world, and it is they, in fact not just in theory, who continue to make all major decisions affecting their families.

In contrast, Gusii women, often husbandless for the greater part of the year, lead much more independent—and harder—lives. They, too, may say they have to consult their husbands on decisions, but often this is to gain time and to avoid confrontations with kin and neighbors. Since it is women who shoulder the routine burdens of the farm as well as the household, it is women who have to make decisions on the spot, decisions that are later ratified, for appearance's sake, by their husbands.

As we have seen, many Gusii men have had to delegate their authority to their wives. Yet a majority of these new city dwellers retain very close ties with the rural area from which they come. They regard their residence in the city as a temporary expedient. They still "belong" at home in the countryside, and they return there as often as possible, bringing with them newly acquired meritocratic values and purchasing power. In the home villages, they further exacerbate endemic intergenerational hostilities. While such disputes often focus on the reluctance of parents to share their scant resources, they are symptomatic of a wider social disorder arising from the refusal of the young Gusii adults to recognize the authority of their elders. The incidence of overt physical attacks by adult Gusii sons on parents is high, and patricide and matricide are not uncommon.

This is not the case in Querétaro: Despite a preoccupation with innovation, particularly with the acquisition of consumer goods, traditional values of filial loyalty, family honor, and obligation to church and kin are largely intact. Although there are occasional incidents of overt physical attacks by sons on parents, in Querétaro, intergenerational antagonisms seem less pronounced than in Gusiiland.

Three factors seem to have diluted the challenge to the traditional social structure in Querétaro. First, there is a more mutual, less authoritarian relationship between parents and adult children, reflecting their earlier, more positively toned relationship in childhood in the Mexican case than in Gusiiland. Thus, it seems that parent–child relationships based more on affection than on power are more flexible than those based more on power than affection. Second, young people in Querétaro, especially girls, attain a much lower level of education than their Gusii counterparts. As young Mexican adults, they are thus both less alienated from their parents' values and less able to surpass their parents' material achievements. Third, Mexico is now 70% urban: For more than a generation, those who wished to escape permanent subordination to their elders have done so. Thus, for many years, the energetic and ambitious Mexicans who were resistant to parental authority have been pulling up their rural roots and transplanting themselves in urban settings. In contrast, Kenya is less than 15% urban, and much of the urban population is transient, moving back and forth between city and countryside. The great majority of Kenyan city dwellers continue to think of themselves as country people, temporarily displaced and still deeply involved with things at home.

Conclusion

We began this chapter proposing that agrarian societies before the demographic transition had much in common concerning the ways in which age and gender were culturally organized. However, our examination of the two rural settings in Mexico and Africa has shown diversity in both cultural background and the profile of sociodemographic changes. Though rural Kenyans and rural Mexicans are subject to some of the same social forces and respond in some of the same ways, their experience of the demographic transition has differed. The death rates of both countries have dropped dramatically in recent decades, but only in Mexico has there been a decline in the birth rate and a substantial migration to the city—two trends that are closely related, since fertility in rural Mexico remains very high. Despite the growth of commerce and education, Kenya is still a relatively unstratified agrarian country where all but a small proportion of the population lives in the rural areas or migrates temporarily to work in the city; fertility there is not differentiated by residence or socioeconomic status. Mexican society was more stratified and urbanized to begin with and has become more so with recent industrial development. The reduction of fertility in Mexico is strongly correlated with urban residence, education, and income level. Hence, Kenya and Mexico typify contrasting directions of change in the poor and middle-level developing countries, respectively.

What of the life course in these two settings? First, gender distinctions are publicly marked and connected with reproductive roles in the rural communities of both countries. Although the militant protection of women by male family members is part of the historic traditions of both cultures, gender roles and symbolism take different forms, with different consequences for life-course experiences. A striking contrast is the relative confinement of Mexican girls and young women to locations near home and the relative freedom of their Gusii counterparts in Kenya. The Mediterranean concept of family honor that requires women to be restricted and men to be vigilant is still alive in rural Mexico, but it has little resonance in East Africa, where each married woman forms a semi-autonomous economic and residential unit in the homestead. Gusii women are in many ways freer than their Mexican counterparts in terms of decision making and mobility; at the same time, Gusii women carry a larger burden of responsibilities with much less social support than do women in rural Mexico.

In both communities, a cultural system of age-grading and a code of filial loyalty provided hope for both mothers and fathers that their later years would bring them community respect and support from their children. While economic and demographic changes have undermined these fragile structures in both places, the disorder is more apparent in rural Kenya, in part because virtually all families are primarily located in the rural areas. In the relatively conservative Mexican villages we studied, by contrast, many entire families have left permanently for the city; the effect of such selective outmigration is that the families who remain in the countryside are characterized by considerable cohesiveness. In Mexico as well as in Kenya, mass schooling has diminished the direct labor contributions of children to the family, but child labor is still relied upon and cherished in both places. But the parent–child relationship over the life course is qualitatively different in the two settings. The Gusii father–son relationship was defined in terms of control, social distance, and respect, with little place for affection, while the relations of fathers and sons in the Mexican villages seem more intimate, warm, and reciprocal. This difference, which we are currently studying, may be particularly important in determining the extent to which the new economic participation of young men becomes translated into greater isolation or increasing support for their aging fathers.

Finally, while interpersonal ties in general, and both real and fictive kinship in particular, remain salient in the social identities of villagers in both settings, the Mexicans have well-institutionalized complementarities between the spheres of economic, kin, and community relationships which permit them to function more coherently under the varying conditions of change. Gusii adults, newcomers to modern conditions, have to improvise the integration of new employment and political roles with their kin-group membership and loyalties, a burden that causes personal stress and social disorganization in the present transitional period. Once again, different cultural and socioeconomic traditions provide different personal resources for coping with social change.

This analysis of the impact of demographic change on the life course in Third World agrarian societies suggests that demographic transition is more complex when examined closely and in detail than current theories would forecast or allow. Cultural diversity must be taken into account in theories of the demographic transition, just as cultural factors must be explored as mediators of the effects of economic and demographic pressures on the life experiences of men and women.

References

Caldwell, J. C. Toward a restatement of demographic transition theory. *Population and Development Review*, 1976, *2*, 321–366.

Caldwell, J. C. A Theory of fertility decline: From high plateau to destabilization. *Population and Development Review*, 1978, *4*, 553–557.

Hoffman, L., & Hoffman, M. The value of children to parents. In J. T. Fawcett (Ed.) *Psychological perspectives on population*. New York: Basic Books', 1973, pp. 19–76.

LeVine, R. A., & LeVine, B. *Nyansongo: A Gusii community in Kenya*. New York: Wiley, 1966.

LeVine, S. *Mothers and wives: Gusii women of East Africa*. Chicago: University of Chicago Press, 1979.

LeVine, S., & Pfeiffer, G. Separation and individuation in an African society: The developmental tasks of a Gusii married woman. *Psychiatry*, 1982, *45*, 61–75.

Moni Nag, R., Peet, C., & White, B. *Economic value of children in two peasant societies*. Paper prepared for the General Conference of the International Union of the Scientific Study of Population, Mexico City, August 1977.

Neugarten, B. L. Continuities and discontinuities of psychological issues in adult life. *Human Development*, 1969, *12*, 121–130.

3

The Life Cycle, Savings, and Demographic Adaptation: Some Historical Evidence for the United States and Europe

MICHAEL R. HAINES
Wayne State University

Introduction

A major theme of recent social science research has been the causes, nature, and effects of the family life cycle. (See, for example, Demos & Boocock, 1978; Hareven, 1978; Oppenheimer, 1982.) The emphasis is not new. Considerable prior work has related the life cycle to social and demographic phenomena (e.g., Glick, 1955; Glick & Parke, 1965; Lansing & Kish, 1957; Rodgers & Hill, 1964; Wells, 1971); historical family structural and social change (e.g., Anderson, 1971; Haines, 1979a, b; Hareven, 1974, 1978; Katz, 1975; Katz & Davy, 1978; Modell, 1978; Modell, Furstenberg, & Hershberg, 1976; Uhlenberg, 1978); and economic phenomena (Ando & Modigliani, 1963; Modigliani & Brumberg, 1954; Tobin, 1967).

One direction of this research has been explication and analysis of adaptive family strategies to cope with constraints imposed by the life course. Valerie Oppenheimer has been particularly active and has recently synthesized and extended her work in this area (Oppenheimer, 1982). She discusses three major life-cycle "squeezes;" the first one associated with marriage and the costs of household formation, the second with the failure of principal wage earner income to keep pace with desired expenditures in midlife, and the third with retirement. A number of adaptive family strategies deal with nonmarriage, age at first marriage, age at first birth, child spacing, total children ever born, migration of individuals and families, and the economic roles of husbands, wives, and children, and the timing of those roles. These strategies were proposed as possible behavioral responses to a life course constrained by the mortality and morbidity

43

environment, birth control technology, prices, child costs, norms for standard of living, labor markets (income-earning opportunities), and availability of non-wage or nonsalary income (such as government and familial transfers, wealth, retirement plans, insurance). It is a framework that holds considerable possibilities for extension and elaboration. This chapter proposes one such elaboration into the area of savings behavior.

One of the early findings in Oppenheimer's work (1974) was that blue-collar-worker families in the United States in 1960 experienced a life-cycle squeeze as husband's earnings failed to keep pace with desired expenditures later in midlife. The male age–earnings profile peaked early and was relatively flat, while child costs and other expenditure demands (partly normatively determined) created a desired late peaking age–expenditure profile. The result was the adaptive strategy of sending wives out to work later in the life cycle to augment family incomes. More recent work (Oppenheimer, 1982) has shown a similar pressure holds true for lower income white-collar husbands (clerical and sales) with responses including delayed marriage, delayed childbearing, and extensive labor-force participation of wives. In my own historical work on the 1889/1890 U.S. Commissioner of Labor Survey (Haines, 1979a, chap. 6, 1979b), I noted that a similar life-cycle squeeze affected blue-collar workers in the late nineteenth century in both the United States and Western Europe, and that the response was to rely on the earnings of children and income from boarders and lodgers later in the life cycle. Wives stayed out of the labor force in general. This was combined with early marriage and a rapid pace of childbearing at the beginning of the life cycle. This had been noted historically by others (e.g., Anderson, 1971; Modell, 1978). At that time, I paid relatively little attention to savings behavior as part of that process.

It is clear that savings behavior is intimately related to the life cycle. The two major macroeconomic hypotheses of consumption and saving, the permanent-income hypothesis (Friedman, 1957) and the life-cycle hypothesis of saving (Ando & Modigliani, 1963; Modigliani & Brumberg, 1954), rely heavily on life-course models. In simple Keynesian models of income determination, savings is regarded as a residual, simply the difference between current income and current expenditure. This actually has some reasonable basis in theory. In a microeconomic choice model of consumer behavior, expenditure is within the decision purview of the individual (or family), whereas current income is usually an exogenous factor. This led Milton Friedman (1957) to posit that consumption was based on permanent, as opposed to current, income. Current income differs from permanent income in that it contains stochastic "transitory" components and fluctuates above and below permanent income. Friedman considers expenditure on durable goods as a form of saving, with only the flow of services from the durables consumed. Savings are determined by the individual as a fairly constant fraction of permanent income (i.e., the present discounted value of long-run, expected, life-cycle earnings).

The other major hypothesis, the life-cycle model of savings, considers the motivations for savings explicitly. People dissave early in the life cycle as they set up households and purchase homes and durables (although durables may be viewed as a form of saving); they save in the middle of the life cycle, as they accumulate wealth, for retirement; and they dissave again during retirement at the end of the life cycle. Saving is an end in itself, instead of a residual. Further, during the middle of the life cycle, a major component of expenditure can be the direct cost of education of children. (In addition, there are the foregone earnings of children in school.) Viewing education as human capital (Becker, 1975; Schultz, 1981), even this portion of expenditure can be considered saving.

Considerable attention continues to be paid to aggregate savings behavior (Ferber, 1973; Mikesell & Zinser, 1973; Snyder, 1974) and, of special interest here, to demographic factors influencing savings. The work of Eizenga (1961) is a notable case. Researchers concerned with the impact of population growth on economic development have written a great deal about the effects of dependency ratios on savings rates (and hence on growth via capital accumulation). A commonly held view was that larger numbers of children per family not only would decrease savings per family but also would create additional demand for investment (e.g., Coale & Hoover, 1958). This seemed borne out by aggregate cross-section evidence (Leff, 1969). There was not always agreement on the unfavorable effects of population growth on aggregate output (Easterlin, 1967; Simon, 1977), but savings behavior was a central concern. Allen Kelley (1973, 1976, 1980) and Kelley and Williamson (1968), however, questioned both whether the *a priori* theorizing was correct and whether empirically such hypotheses could be supported. He used part of the 1889/1890 survey to estimate savings functions (Kelley, 1976) and found no clear-cut negative relationship between family size and savings. He moved away from the earlier adult equivalency models, allowed additional children to be financed, in part by reduction in consumption of other household members, allowed children to augment family income, and had family size determined endogenously with respect to economic factors. One conclusion was that the effect of children on savings was ambiguous. This was also indicated in later work with a micro sample for Kenya (Kelley, 1980). Despite frequent discussion of the life-cycle model, the usual variable to standardize for this is age of household or family head, although Lansing and Kish (1957) demonstrated substantial variation in results depending on whether one used age or life-cycle stage of the household head.

This chapter investigates more extensively the relationship of the life cycle to savings behavior in an historical setting. It is argued that savings, whether in the form of financial assets (e.g., savings accounts), real assets (e.g., homes), or human capital (e.g., children), constituted part of at least some adaptive strategies. A family might have desired to save in the form of all these assets (the exact mix depending upon tastes and preferences) but might have been constrained by low incomes, high prices for some assets (like homes), or by imperfect capital markets to invest only in children, who were initially inexpensive to produce and whose larger costs could be deferred. Further, children could have been sent to work at a relatively early age or could have been kept in school longer to accrue greater human capital and hence, presumably, to earn a larger income later (Goldin, 1981; Kaestle & Vinovskis, 1978). While the added burdens of young children early in the life cycle created hardships, or even drove some families into "poverty," the children also constituted a part of the solution to the problem by contributing at least some of their earnings to the family later on (Anderson, 1971; Haines, 1981; Oppenheimer, 1982, pp. 375–380).[1] Thus, it can be useful to view the life cycle as an accumulation process, the type of adaptive strategy chosen being conditioned by these savings (accumulation) choices or by the lack of them. In the case of blue-collar workers in the United States and Europe in 1889/1890, the early peaking male age–earnings profile, higher levels of child mortality, and availability of children's employment all induced early marriage and childbearing (i.e., investment in children over the life cycle). But many of these families were also net savers, and a number (17.7% in the United States and 6.7% in Europe) owned their own homes. Further, they made differing choices as to the extent of work versus schooling for older children. Thus, this particular historical data set, unusual in its richness of economic information, provides an opportunity for further exploration of this topic.

The Sample

Carroll Wright, first U.S. Commissioner of Labor and pioneer empirical statistician, collected demographic, income, and family budget data in 1889 and 1890 for 8544 families working in 9 industries (pig iron, bar iron, steel, bituminous coal, coke, iron ore, cotton textiles, woolens, and glass) in 24 states of the United States and in five European countries (Belgium, France, Germany, Great Britain, and Switzerland).[2] The sample has been discussed at some length elsewhere (Haines, 1979a, chap. 6, 1979b; Lees, 1980; Modell, 1978; Williamson, 1967) and appears reasonable and internally consistent. The sample method was not clear, but the data on age of family head seem to conform to age

---

[1] A recent paper by Frank Lewis (1983), using optimal control theory, notes that an important effect of using children as an asset is to shift the returns from savings to later in the life cycle. He assumes that accumulation in the form of children's human capital does not change overall lifetime savings.

[2] Not all industries were represented for all the geographic units, but all nine industries were represented for both the United States and Europe. A tabulation of industry by location may be found in Haines (1979a, pp. 206–207). Of the 8544 families, 6809 were in the United States and 1735 in Europe (of which 1024 were in Great Britain). The information coded from the original data includes: State or country of residence; industry; nationality of family head; number of children at school; number of children at home; number of children at work; presence of boarders; number of boarders and others in the household; occupation of husband; age of husband; age of wife; number of children; ages of children; sexes of each child above age 10; whether the family owned its home; income from husband, wife, children, boarders, and other sources; expenditures on food, rent, and other items; and the number of rooms in the house or apartment.

distributions by occupations of married males (Haines, 1979a). The micro data have been used by several researchers (Fishlow, 1973; Haines, 1979a, 1979b; Kelley, 1973, 1976; Lees, 1980; Modell, 1978); and the published data have furnished information for consumer budget studies (e.g., U.S. Bureau of the Census, 1975, Series G564–573). In short, although the 1889–1890 Survey might not have been representative of industries and of families within those industries, it nonetheless seems a valuable source of data on demographic and economic aspects of blue-collar family life during a period of rapid industrialization.

Adaptive Behavior, Savings, and the Life Cycle

As mentioned previously, economic studies of savings have been concerned with life-cycle events and, by extension, life-cycle strategies. One method of describing the life cycle has been to use the age of head of household as a proxy for life-cycle stage, and this has been widely used (e.g., Ando & Modigliani, 1963; Kelley, 1976), although, as Lansing and Kish (1957) pointed out, results could be different if a direct life-cycle scheme were used. This issue was approached by making all of the tabulations and analyses used here in two ways: One by age of head of household and one by life-cycle stage. This life-cycle scheme was developed to take into account family composition and age of children (Haines, 1979b; Modell, 1978). The first five stages provide one concept of the regular cycle: (1) couples with a wife in the childbearing years without children present; (2) couples with the youngest child roughly of preschool age (0–4 years); (3) couples with the youngest child roughly of school age (5–14 years); (4) couples with the youngest child old enough to be usually in the labor force (about 15 years or older); and (5) couples with the wife post-childbearing (over 45) and with no children present. The last might be called the "empty nest" stage. Two additional categories, male- and female-headed single parent households were also considered although these are outside the "normal" life cycle. Only a few (271) of the total families fell into this category, most of them in the textile industries. Of these, almost all (256) were in the United States sample. The two approaches revealed only a few notable differences between the results by age of head of household and the results of life-cycle stage. In consequence, generally only the tabulations by age of head of household will be presented, and similarities and differences with the stage categories will be noted. (An exception is Table 3.4; see later.) The single-parent households were sufficiently interesting to warrant separate consideration.

One problem with the sample is that it provides no information on "retired" individuals, since all family heads had to be employed in these industries in order to be included. Retirement in this era might have consisted largely in taking less demanding (and less well paid) or part-time work, but these cases would likely have been outside regular industrial employment represented by the sample. As a consequence, one important life-cycle stage, retirement, is absent from this analysis.

Looking first at Table 3.1, which presents family income and its composition by age of head of household, it is notable that family income peaked late in the life cycle (head's age 50–59).[3] This was also true for the life-cycle stage model, with the peak occurring at Stage four, parents with youngest child 15 and over. Husband's income peaked earlier (at head's age 30–39 or life-cycle Stage two, couples with youngest child of preschool age) and the income deficit was made up by a rising contribution of children's income to total family income. This was true both in the United States and in Europe. The percentage of total income from the husband declined steadily along the life course, while the contribution from children rose from a negligible amount to over one-third in the United States and over 40% in the European sample for families with head's age 60 and over. Again, the same was true for the life-cycle stage model. Although proportion of income from wives working outside the home declined over the life cycle, boarder income (i.e., work inside the home) increased. The latter was particularly true in the United States, where the incidence of homeownership was considerably higher (see Table 3.2 below). Thus, a clear pattern of life cycle income composition existed in the sample. Children were clearly an economic asset to the family as a whole, although it is unclear how much of the income from an individual child was redistributed within the family.

On the expenditure side, Table 3.2 presents information on total dollar expenditures, composition of expenditures, savings, and homeownership. Notably, total expenditures also peaked late in the life cycle, with head's age 50–59. This matched the age–income profile, was the same for both the United States and European samples, and was similar for the life-cycle model. Food as a proportion of total expenditure rose over the life cycle, reflecting the older average age of the children. This was an expenditure category likely subject to intrafamilial redistribution, supporting the view that children's earnings were subject to considerable reallocation. European food expenditures were a higher proportion of the total, partly reflecting the lower income and expenditures of the European families. (The share of food in total expenditures was almost always higher for lower expenditure households, a fact often known as "Engel's Law.") Rent expenditures remained relatively stable, showing small declines in proportion of total expenditure up to age group 50–59. This is, however, misleading since imputed rental payments were not reported for homeowners. Since, as may be seen in Table 3.2, the incidence of homeownership rose over the life cycle, mean rental per renting family was actually rising. The rising incidence of homeownership over the life cycle was notable as a strong indicator of real asset accumulation. There was a large difference between the United States and Europe in homeownership. It is possible that this was a matter of preference, but it was

---

[3]From this point onward, family and household will be used to describe the same thing (i.e., the unit designated as such in the survey). Also, Tables 3.1–3.3 contain fewer cases than in the total sample. This is due to missing information, such as age of the husband or female head of household, which made it impossible to classify these cases.

TABLE 3.1 Total Annual Income by Source and Age of Family Head: United States and Europe,[a] 1889–1890

Income source	Age of family head					
	20–29	30–39	40–49	50–59	60+	Total
Total income ($)						
United States	557	647	757	810	671	687
Europe	342	419	534	622	475	471
Husband's income ($)						
United States	512	577	516	454	315	518
Europe	307	367	338	330	247	337
Total income (%)						
Husband's income						
United States	91.9	89.2	68.2	56.0	46.9	75.4
Europe	89.8	87.6	63.3	53.0	52.0	71.6
Wife's income						
United States	3.2	2.3	1.3	1.0	0.6	1.9
Europe	7.6	3.8	1.7	1.0	0.0	3.0
Children's income						
United States	0.2	4.0	24.0	31.2	34.0	15.4
Europe	0.0	6.2	31.8	41.6	41.5	22.2
Boarder income						
United States	3.6	2.6	4.4	9.3	13.7	5.2
Europe	1.2	0.7	1.7	3.2	4.6	1.7
Other income						
United States	1.1	1.8	2.1	2.5	4.8	2.0
Europe	1.5	1.7	1.5	1.1	1.9	1.5
N[b]						
United States	(1297)	(2347)	(1860)	(938)	(336)	(6782)
Europe	(280)	(611)	(470)	(260)	(85)	(1707)

Source: Data from U.S. Commissioner of Labor (1890, 1891).
[a]Britain, France, Germany, Belgium, and Switzerland.
[b]The total number of cases includes family heads with ages below 20 for which no data are presented in the table.

TABLE 3.2 Annual Household Expenditures and Savings, by Age of Family Head: United States and Europe,[a] 1889–1890

Income uses	Age of family head					Total
	20–29	30–39	40–49	50–59	60+	
Total expenditure (%)						
Food						
United States	40.8	42.3	44.7	45.5	47.3	43.5
Europe	48.5	49.1	50.8	49.2	48.5	49.5
Rent						
United States	12.5	11.5	10.0	9.0	9.3	10.7
Europe	11.7	10.0	8.1	7.4	8.8	9.2
Other						
United States	46.7	46.1	45.2	45.5	43.4	45.8
Europe	39.8	40.8	41.1	43.4	42.6	41.2
Total expenditure ($)						
United States	520	590	681	712	590	618
Europe	324	399	492	541	410	434
Savings[b] ($)						
United States	37	57	76	98	81	69
Europe	18	20	42	81	65	37
Savings rate[c]						
United States	.07	.09	.10	.12	.12	.10
Europe	.05	.05	.08	.13	.14	.08
Proportion net savers						
United States	.56	.58	.62	.63	.65	.60
Europe	.59	.56	.67	.79	.74	.64
Proportion homeowners						
United States	.09	.16	.21	.25	.28	.18
Europe	.02	.05	.09	.12	.08	.07

Source: Data from U.S. Commissioner of Labor (1890, 1891). [b]Current total annual income minus current total annual expenditure.
[a]Britain, France, Germany, Belgium, and Switzerland. [c]Savings divided by current total annual income.

more likely caused by a combination of lower incomes and higher relative prices for housing in Europe compared to the United States. The lower relative and absolute expenditures for rent in Europe do not necessarily contradict this, since the housing consumed is not standardized for space and quality.

Table 3.2 also presents information on current absolute savings (current total income minus current expenditure), current savings rates (current savings divided by current income), and the proportion of families who were net savers. By all measures, savings appeared directly related to the life cycle as measured by head's age. (Results are quite similar using the five life-cycle stages.) In particular, savings rates and proportion of households who were net savers both showed a positive relationship to age of family head. The European households basically showed an upward trend in these measures over the life cycle, despite some irregularities. What were these savings used for? Largely, it appears, for housing, since payment of mortgages seems not to have been included as an expenditure. In any event, many mortgages in this era required only payment of interest with a balloon note coming due at a specified time. This promoted savings in anticipation of such a lump sum payment. Nonetheless, some financial assets were acquired, and this is confirmed by interviewer comments, which were also published with the survey and which noted that some families had bank accounts. Savings rates were not particularly different between United States and European households. European savings rates were lower earlier in the life cycle and higher later. Proportions of net savers were generally somewhat higher in Europe.

Additional dimensions of the accumulation strategies followed by these families are suggested in Table 3.3, which presents average number of surviving children present, child and wives' employment, and schooling. The percentage of wives working outside the home fell over the life cycle in both the United States and Europe, while the percentage of children working aged 10 years or older rose. The same results held true using the five life-cycle stages. The percentage of children aged 5–14 years who were in school rose in the United States to about 60% by the time the head was aged 30–39, and it remained between 70 and 80% in Europe up until the household head was above 60 years of age.

As Tables 3.1 and 3.3 indicate, wives were retained at home to engage in the accumulation process through childbearing and childrearing. Their average labor-force participation rate was low, having been only 7% overall in the United States and 10.1% overall in Europe (Table 3.3). This participation rate dropped dramatically over the life cycle as children were born.[4] Declining wives' contribution to family income was offset to a limited degree by taking in boarders

---

[4]Some evidence of this may be gleaned from the life-cycle stage model. Between Stage one, wives younger than 45 with no children present, and Stage two, youngest child 0–4, the labor force participation rate dropped from 11.5% to 6.0% in the United States sample and from 34.6% to 9.3% in the European sample.

TABLE 3.3 Wives' Employment and Schooling and Employment of Children by
Age of Family Head: United States and Europe,[a] 1889–1890

Schooling and employment	Age of family head					Total
	20–29	30–39	40–49	50–59	60+	
Average number of children						
United States	1.43	2.82	3.79	3.06	2.06	2.82
Europe	1.42	3.04	4.01	3.28	2.06	3.03
Percentage of children working, 10 or older						
United States	29.2	27.4	46.7	55.5	65.4	46.3
Europe	20.0	31.6	57.3	65.7	71.0	53.4
Percentage of children in school, 5–14 years						
United States	28.2	58.4	63.8	61.7	60.4	59.6
Europe	79.1	72.8	71.7	79.5	67.8	73.4
Percentage of wives working						
United States	10.2	7.8	5.7	4.3	3.3	7.0
Europe	20.4	11.1	9.2	5.0	0.0	10.1

Source: Data from U.S. Commissioner of Labor (1890, 1891).
[a]Britain, France, Germany, Belgium, and Switzerland.

and possibly by other income-earning activities at home (Table 3.1), but the
main strategy was to accumulate in the form of children—human capital. The
number of surviving children present rose until it peaked out at age group 40–49
for both the United States and European samples (Table 3.3). This portion of the
strategy involved both schooling and work, the realization of the investment in
children's human capital. In the United States, school attendance (as a proportion
of children roughly in the ages eligible for primary school) rose to a plateau of
about 60% by the life-cycle stage with head aged 30–39. In Europe, the level of
school enrollment was consistently higher, averaging about 73% (as opposed to
60% in the United States) and probably due to the more extensive and better
enforced compulsory schooling legislation there (Haines, 1979a, Table II-2).
Once children completed primary school (if they were permitted to attend), the
gains from earlier investment in their human capital could be realized if they
worked and made transfers of their income to their parents. This is, in fact, what
happened. Children working, as a percentage of children aged 10 and over, did
increase over the life cycle, particularly as the children aged. In regression
results reported elsewhere (Haines, 1979a, Table VI-8), the age composition of
children in the family had predictable effects on children working: Older children

and males were more likely to work than younger children and females. Life-cycle stage (as measured by age of wife) also had positive effects, even controlling for the age and sex composition of the children. (This was true both for the United States and European samples.)

Direct savings was also part of this strategy. As Table 3.2 shows, absolute savings increased with head's age up to age 50–59. Significantly, the savings rate (savings/income) did not decline for heads aged 60 and over, despite the decline in absolute dollar savings as family income fell. The course of the proportion of families who had positive net savings paralleled that of the savings rate for the United States where it reached 65% by the age group 60 and over. It did decline somewhat for the European sample, from 79% for heads aged 50–59 to 74% for heads aged 60 and over. Some of this increase in savings and savings rates was due to the rising incidence of homeownership since imputed rental income was not included as an expenditure, but a separate estimation for a sample of renters only revealed a similar increase in savings and savings rates. There is some evidence that investment in children was a substitute for financial savings (or at least a competition for resources). As Table 3.4 shows, the life-cycle stage model revealed, for both the United States and Europe, a sharp drop-off of savings, savings rates, and proportions of net savers between Stage one (no children, wife below age 45) and Stage two (youngest child 0–4) and then an increase to Stages three (youngest child 5–14) and four (youngest child 14 and over). In both the United States and Europe, the decision to have children coincided with a small increase in homeownership. Thus, the decision was often made simultaneously to acquire both more real assets and human capital. The subsequent rise in real savings is attributable to the demands of mortgage payments and the fact that children began to make increased contributions to family income (as may be seen in the last two rows of Table 3.4). When investments in children began to pay dividends (i.e., the children made substantial income contributions), savings and savings rates could be increased.

The data, then, are consistent with the view that families pursued an accumulation strategy that included children and children's education as well as acquisition of real assets and financial savings. Homeownership (a proxy for real assets) rose over the life cycle, at least until the last stage, and children were conceived and raised with an aim, it appears in part, to provide income for the family. Child labor-force participation and proportion of family income from children rose over the life cycle as children aged and children began leaving primary school (at ages 12–14). Proportions of children aged 5–14 in school were substantial and indicated the importance of human capital. The differences between the United States and Europe have already been discussed in some detail. In the European sample, there was a demonstrably lower rate of homeownership (overall, about 7%) than in the United States sample (about 18%). The lower financial savings rates for Europe seem to have been accounted for, in part, by the lower homeownership rate, although results for renter samples of both areas indicated that European renters saved less than American renters.

TABLE 3.4 Annual Household Savings Behavior, Homeownership, and Children's Income by Life-Cycle Stage: United States and Europe,[a] 1889–1890

Savings measures	Life-cycle stage				
	Wife < 45 no children	Youngest child 0–4	Youngest child 5–14	Youngest child 15+	Wife > 45 no children
Savings[b] ($)					
United States	73	45	84	134	97
Europe	38	14	51	101	30
Savings rate[c]					
United States	.13	.07	.11	.16	.18
Europe	.10	.03	.09	.17	.09
Proportion net savers					
United States	.65	.55	.63	.70	.75
Europe	.76	.53	.70	.86	.62
Proportion homeowners					
United States	.11	.16	.20	.31	.26
Europe	.05	.06	.06	.11	.06
Children's income as percentage of family income					
United States	—	9.7	22.0	28.2	—
Europe	—	11.4	31.7	45.7	—
N = United States	(634)	(3353)	(1815)	(457)	(265)
Europe	(127)	(829)	(524)	(180)	(53)

Source: Data from U.S. Commissioner of Labor (1890, 1891).
[a] Britain, France, Germany, Belgium, and Switzerland.
[b] Current total annual income minus current total annual expenditure.
[c] Savings divided by current total annual income.

The lower homeownership rates for Europe were probably due to constraints on behavior (i.e., higher housing prices and lower incomes). The expected effect would have been to shift investment strategy toward children. This is what was observed. European families kept slightly more of their surviving children at home (and this despite lower fertility rates; see Haines, 1979a, chap. 6), invested more in them through schooling (as evidenced by higher school enrollment rates), had a higher rate of child labor-force activity (among children aged 10 and over), and had a higher proportion of family income from children's earnings later in the life cycle.

Some further insight appears by examining single-parent families in the United States sample in Table 3.5. (Too few cases were available to allow meaningful comparisons to the European sample.) As judged by the relatively advanced age of the family head (48.7 years for female family heads and 50.4 years for male family heads, as compared to a sample average of 39.5 years), death of the other spouse seems the likely cause of the event of a single-parent family. In the nineteenth century, the single-parent family, particularly one headed by a woman, was a hardship perhaps greater than today.

Looking at the first column of Table 3.5, the adaptive strategy of accumulation in children demonstrated its value as insurance. For female-headed families, children's income made up 70% of total income, considerably higher than the advanced life-cycle stages in Table 3.1. For instance, for family head aged 50–59, children's income was only 31% of family income. The child labor force participation rate in female-headed families was considerably higher (84.5%) than that for any life-cycle stage in Table 3.3 (range from 27% to 65%). Similarly, the school enrollment rate in female-headed families was lower (31.1%) than for any stage in the United States sample in Table 3.3 (range from 58 to 64% for families with household heads over 30). An average of about three children per household were present, and they were much more likely to be working and less likely to be in school (given age) than at other stages. Children were a resource used to keep consumption from dropping too low.[5] These households were, despite this, less well off, as evidenced by the larger share of food expenditure (the overall average was 43.5%) and the much greater likelihood that these female household heads would work (32% as opposed to the sample average of 7% of wives working).

A similar, though less extreme, role was played by children in households headed by a male with no spouse present. Children's earnings were 40% of family income, although labor force participation of children (55.9%) and school enrollments (43.8%) were more in line with averages for later life-cycle stages

---

[5]Without making adjustment for adult equivalent consumption scales, per capita consumption expenditure by life-cycle stage was: (1) Wife < 45, no children, $238; (2) youngest child 0–4, $104; (3) youngest child 5–14, $121; (4) youngest child 15 and over, $164; (5) wife > 45, no children, $216; (6) female-headed family, $130; (7) male-headed family, no spouse, $146. The overall average was $121.

TABLE 3.5 Household Income, Expenditure, Savings, Homeownership, Family
Size, Work, and Schooling—Single-Parent Families: United States
Only, 1889–1890

Variable	Female head, no spouse	Male head, no spouse
Annual family income ($)	541	708
Total income (%)		
Husband's earnings	—	48.7
Wife's earnings	11.8	—
Children's earnings	70.4	40.0
Boarder income	15.2	9.3
Other income	2.6	2.4
Total annual expenditure ($)	526	663
Total annual expenditure (%)		
Food	47.5	47.5
Rent	11.6	9.3
Other	40.9	43.3
Savings[a] ($)	15	40
Savings rate[b]	.03	.06
Proportion net savers	.56	.57
Proportion homeowners	.09	.07
Average number of children	2.98	3.56
Percentage of children working, 10 or older	84.5	55.9
Percentage of children in school, 5–14 years	31.1	43.8
Percentage of wives working	32.0	—
Mean age of household head	48.3	51.0
$N =$	(172)	(84)

Source: Data from U.S. Commissioner of Labor (1890, 1891).
[a]Current total annual income minus current total annual expenditure.
[b]Savings divided by current total annual income.

for two-parent households. Absolute savings and savings rates for both groups
were lower than average, but the proportion of single-parent households who
were net savers was about 56%. Homeownership rates were lower for single-
parent families, although it may be that families that had had lower incomes
throughout the life cycle and were thus less capable of saving to acquire real
property, were also more likely to experience mortality of a parent. Single-parent
status is indeed likely to have been endogenous to the economic status of the

family. In any event, at the stage of single-parent status, the family was utilizing the returns from previous investments in human capital and could not afford to accumulate much in the form of financial or real capital.

Some Estimated Savings Functions

In an effort to probe more deeply into the determinants and covariates of savings behavior among the Commissioner of Labor Survey families, simple linear savings functions were estimated using ordinary least-squares (OLS) regression (Table 3.6). These functions may be characterized as empirical in that the functional form is derived on an *ad hoc* basis rather than from a theoretical utility maximization model.[6] Kelley (1976, 1980), using the empirical approach, has appropriately argued that savings, income, fertility, and child mortality are all endogenous, that is, are determined within a simultaneous equations system. Here it has indeed been hypothesized that savings, income, fertility, and (homeownership) and financial asset acquisition are all determined within a joint maximization framework. Thus, the OLS equations in Table 3.6 should be regarded as preliminary. Further, the equations must be interpreted with care. The coefficients of the endogenous variables (those for children, homeownership, income, and savings) may then be subject to statistical bias.

Given these caveats, the simple linear OLS estimates in Table 3.6 are revealing.[7] Income, by itself, explained (not unexpectedly) most of the variation in savings and savings rates (usually about 90–95% of $\bar{R}^2$). Age of family head, the life-cycle proxy, gave expected significant results for the United States sample but not for the European sample.[8] Other regressions that were run with only the life-cycle variables as independent variables only explained about 1–11% of total variation ($\bar{R}^2$ values), but the results were much more predictable. The age coefficient was positive, significant, and much larger throughout. The life-cycle states indicated the lowest savings and savings rates at Stages 1–3 and much larger at Stages 4 and 5. The results became less strong in the full equations containing other variables, confirming that head's age or life-cycle stage represent other covarying effects.

---

[6]The empirical approach has a tradition in the investigation of family expenditure (Prais & Houthakker, 1971) and savings behavior (Kelley, 1976, 1980). The theoretical approach has produced some interesting functional forms, including the linear expenditure system (Deaton & Muellbauer, 1980). Demographic variation has been explicitly introduced (Pollak & Wales, 1978), but extension to savings has been limited. (Lluch, Powell, & Williams [1977] is an exception.)

[7]The equations were estimated only for families with both husband and wife present and for which the age of the head was known.

[8]Separate regressions, using the five life-cycle stages, also gave roughly expected results—savings and savings rates having been larger (less negative or more positive) at later stages.

TABLE 3.6 Estimated Savings Functions (1889–1890): Families with Both Husband and Wife Present and With Known Ages of Husband and Wife

Variables	United States		Europe[a]	
	Coefficient/ significance Savings[b] ($)	Coefficient/ significance Savings rate[c] (× 100)	Coefficient/ significance Savings[b] ($)	Coefficient/ significance Savings rate[c] (× 100)
Dependent variable				
Independent variables				
Age of head	.9155 ***	.0986 ***	.1123 —	−.0078 —
Number of children aged				
(a) 0–4	−16.15 ***	−1.852 ***	−8.377 ***	−2.260 ***
(b) 5–9	−11.16 ***	−1.951 ***	−11.53 ***	−2.176 ***
(c) 10–14	−20.04 ***	−2.164 ***	−15.20 ***	−2.291 ***
(d) 15 +	−40.83 ***	−3.927 ***	−13.33 ***	−2.203 ***
Children in school/ children 5–14	−16.35 ***	−1.042 *	−6.966 **	−1.199 *

Children working/children 10 +	6.970	—	1.389	—	.4958	—	2.429	**
Number of boarders	-5.774	***	-.3944	**	-8.710	***	-.9234	***
Total income	.4144	***	.0327	***	.3297	***	.0376	**
Homeownership	60.90	***	7.211	***	16.74	***	-.8779	—
Native or foreign born	13.23	***	1.614	***	NI		NI	
France	NI^d		NI		5.122	—	4.973	***
Germany	NI		NI		.9516	—	1.732	—
Great Britain	NI		NI		-30.52	***	1.253	—
Constant	-205.3	NC^d	-16.44	NC	-65.16	NC	-8.274	NC
(N)	(6513)		(6513)		(1655)		(1655)	
R̄²	.516		.278		.630		.325	
F-ratio	630.932	***	228.995	***	201.938	***	57.825	***

a Britain, France, Germany, Belgium, and Switzerland.
b Current total annual income minus current total annual expenditure.
c Savings divided by current total annual income.
d NC, not calculated; NI, not included.
*$p < .10$, **$p < .05$, ***$p < .001$.

Some of these covariates are given in the full equations in Table 3.6. The presence of children had a uniformly negative (and significant) effect on savings rates through increased consumption demand. The effect rose with age after age group 5–9, as would be expected from adult equivalence consumption scales. Number of children in school, as a proportion of children aged 5–14, had a consistent and significant negative impact on savings and savings rates. Number of children working, as a proportion of children aged 10 and over, exercised a positive effect on savings through children's earnings, but only one of the four coefficients was significant. Number of boarders was negatively related to savings and the savings rate, and was significant in all but the European savings-rate equation. This represented most likely a joint relation with income—a family that had lower income was both likely to save less and to take in boarders. Homeownership was significantly and positively related to savings and savings rates for all but the European savings-rate equation, reflecting the need of homeowners to save toward mortgage payments. The effect was large, increasing savings in the United States an average of about $61 per family per year and increasing the savings rate about 7 percentage points. The European sample showed an increase in savings level due to homeownership but demonstrated no effect on savings rates.

In equations run for the total sample, residence in Europe significantly increased both savings levels and rates, holding income, life-cycle stage, and these demographic variables constant. This was an unusual finding considering that the marginal propensity to save (the coefficient of savings on income) and savings rate were both higher in the United States. But homeownership was more widespread in the United States. In an equation run for renters only in the total sample, the effect of a large, positive, and significant dummy variable for European residence was still present. Perhaps supporting this, within the United States, families with foreign-born heads were more likely to save. This confirms John Modell's (1978) finding regarding Irish immigrants to Massachusetts and the northeastern United States. In an effort to establish a foothold in American society, the foreign born saved and made an effort to acquire real property. Previous work has indicated that the foreign born were slightly more likely to own their own homes and were definitely more likely to have older children working. Finally, within Europe, the French seemed to be more frugal than the Germans who, in turn, saved more than the British. The noted ability of the French householder to save is once again confirmed.

Conclusion

Both the life-cycle tabulations and the regression results support the overall view that, in the nineteenth century, families followed life-cycle accumulation patterns that regarded children, human capital, real property, and financial assets as part of an asset portfolio strategy. Despite the fact that the data are cross-sectional and hence create "synthetic" life cycles, valid inferences can be drawn, appealing to such things as from reference-group theory to condition behavior (Oppenheimer, 1982, pp. 12–19). Income was, in 1890 as today, the major determinant of savings; but, since the income of the family head declined on average after a peak in the age group 30–39, children were used to fill the gap and to keep income, and thus expenditure, savings, and the acquisition of homes and other assets, rising. People with more income from the male family head were more likely to acquire more of all types of assets (Haines, 1979a, chap. 6), including more children and more education per child. But when head's income was lower or when choices were constrained, interesting choices were manifested. It seems probable that the relative price of housing was greater in Europe than in the United States in 1890. European working-class families had lower head's income than their United States counterparts. In consequence, they were less likely to own their own homes but compensated with greater reliance on, and investment (via schooling) in, children. Later in the life cycle, a higher proportion of older children worked, and a higher proportion of family income was derived from children's income. European savings rates were lower earlier in the life cycle but converged to United States rates later. Thus, it seems that European working-class families concentrated more on producing and educating children early in the life cycle at the expense of acquisition of real and financial assets.

The historical context of these results should not negate their generality. A number of developing countries are undergoing industrialization, have similar income levels, and have similar or better access to fertility regulation compared to the United States and Europe in 1890. Children may continue to be important family economic assets via direct labor-market earnings. Thus, working-class families in developing societies may face similar life-cycle choices and constraints to those faced by working-class families in Western industrializing societies in the late nineteenth century.

References

Anderson, M. *Family structure in nineteenth century Lancashire*. Cambridge, England: Cambridge University Press, 1971.

Ando, A., & Modigliani, F. The "life cycle" hypothesis of saving. *American Economic Review*, 1963, *53*, 55–84.

Becker, G. S. *Human capital* (2nd ed.). New York: Columbia University Press, 1975.

Coale, A. J., & Hoover, E. M. *Population growth and economic development in low-income countries*. Princeton, N. J.: Princeton University Press, 1958.

Deaton, A., & Muellbauer, J. *Economics and consumer behavior*. Cambridge, England: Cambridge University Press, 1980.

Demos, J., & Boocock, S. S. (Eds.). *Turning points: Historical and sociological essays on the family*. Chicago: University of Chicago Press, 1978.

Easterlin, R. A. The effects of population growth on the economic development of developing countries. *The Annals of the American Academy of Political and Social Science*, 1967, *364*, 98–108.

Eizenga, W. *Demographic factors and saving*. Amsterdam: North-Holland, 1961.

Ferber, R. Consumer economics: A survey. *The Journal of Economic Literature*, 1973, *9*, 1303–1342.

Fishlow, A. Comparative consumption patterns, the extent of the market, and alternative development strategies. In E. B. Ayal (Ed.), *Micro aspects of development*. New York: Praeger, 1973, pp. 41–80.

Coale, A. J., & Hoover, E. M. *Population growth and economic development in low-income countries*. Princeton, N. J.: Princeton University Press, 1958.

Glick, P. C. The life cycle of the family. *Marriage and Family Living*, 1955, *17*, 3–9.

Glick, P. C., & Parke, R., Jr. New approaches to studying the life cycle of the family. *Demography*, 1965, *2*, 187–202.

Goldin, C. Family strategies and the family economy in the late nineteenth century: The role of secondary workers. In T. Hershberg (Ed.), *Philadelphia: Work, space, family, and group experience in the nineteenth century*. New York: Oxford University Press, 1981, pp. 277–310.

Haines, M. R. *Fertility and occupation: Population patterns in industrialization*. New York: Academic Press, 1979. (a)

Haines, M. R. Industrial work and the family life cycle, 1889–1890. *Research in Economic History*, 1979, *4*, 289–356. (b)

Haines, M. R. Poverty, economic stress, and the family in a late nineteenth century American city: Whites in Philadelphia, 1880. In T. Hershberg (Ed.), *Philadelphia: Work, space, family, and group experience in the nineteenth century*. New York: Oxford University Press, 1981, pp. 240–276.

Hareven, T. K. The family as process: The historical study of the family cycle. *The Journal of Social History*, 1974, *7*, 322–329.

Hareven, T. K. (Ed.). *Transitions: The family and the life course in historical perspective*. New York: Academic Press, 1978.

Kaestle, F., & Vinovskis, M. A. From fireside to factory: School entry and school leaving in nineteenth-century Massachusetts. In T. K. Hareven (Ed.), *Transitions: The family and the life course in historical perspective*. New York: Academic Press, 1978, pp. 135–185.

Katz, M. B. *The people of Hamilton, Canada west: Family and class in a mid-nineteenth century city*. Cambridge, Mass.: Harvard University Press, 1975.

Katz, M. B., & Davy, I. Youth and early industrialization in a Canadian city. In J. Demos & S. S. Boocock (Eds.), *Turning points: Historical and sociological essays on the family*. Chicago: University of Chicago Press, 1978, pp. 581–591.

Kelley, A. C. Population growth, the dependency rate, and the pace of economic development. *Population Studies*, 1973, *27*, 406–420.

Kelley, A. C. Savings, demographic change and economic development. *Economic Development and Cultural Change*, 1976, *24*, 683–693.

Kelley, A. C. Interactions of economic and demographic household behavior. In R. A. Easterlin (Ed.), *Population and economic change in developing countries*. Chicago: University of Chicago Press, 1980, pp. 403–448.

Kelley, A. C., & Williamson, J. C. Household saving behavior in developing economies: The Indonesian case. *Economic Development and Cultural Change*, 1968, *16*, 358–402.

Lansing, J. B., & Kish, L. Family life cycle as an independent variable. *American Sociological Review*, 1957, *22*, 512–519.

Lees, L. H. Getting and spending: The family budgets of English industrial workers in 1890. In J. M. Merriman (Ed.), *Consciousness and class experience in nineteenth-century Europe*. New York: Holmes and Meier, 1980, pp. 169–186.

Leff, N. Dependency rates and savings rates. *American Economic Review*, 1969, *59*, 886–896.

Lewis, F. D. Fertility and savings in the United States: 1830–1900. *Journal of Political Economy*, 1983, *91*, 825–840.

Lluch, C., Powell, A. A., & Williams, R. A. *Patterns in household demand and saving.* New York: Oxford University Press, 1977.

Mikesell, R., & Zinser, J. The nature of the savings function in developing countries: A survey of the theoretical and empirical literature. *The Journal of Economic Literature*, 1973, *11*, 1–26.

Modell, J. Patterns of consumption, acculturation, and family income strategies in late nineteenth-century America. In T. K. Hareven & M. A. Vinovskis (Eds.), *Family and population in nineteenth-century America*. Princeton, N. J.: Princeton University Press, 1978, pp. 206–240.

Modell, J., Furstenberg, F. F., Jr., & Hershberg, T. Social change and transitions to adulthood in historical perspective. *Journal of Family History*, 1976, *1*, 7–32.

Modigliani, F., & Brumberg, R. Utility analysis and the consumption function: An interpretation of cross-section data. In K. K. Kurihara (Ed.), *Post-Keynesian economics*. New Brunswick, N. J.: Rutgers University Press, 1954.

Oppenheimer, V. K. The life-cycle squeeze: The interaction of men's occupational and family life cycles. *Demography*, 1974, *11*, 227–245.

Oppenheimer, V. K. *Work and the family: A study in social demography*. New York: Academic Press, 1982.

Pollak, R. A., & Wales, T. J. Estimation of complete demand systems from household budget data: The linear and quadratic expenditure systems. *American Economic Review*, 1978, *68*, 348–359.

Prais, S. J., & Houthakker, H. S. *The analysis of family budgets* (2nd impression). Cambridge, England: Cambridge University Press, 1971.

Rodgers, R. H., and Hill, R. The developmental approach. In H. Christensen (Ed.), *Handbook of marriage and the family*. Chicago: Rand McNally, 1964.

Schultz, T. *Investing in people: The economics of population quality*. Berkeley, Calif.: University of California Press, 1981.

Simon, J. *The economics of population growth*. Princeton, N. J.: Princeton University Press, 1977.

Snyder, D. Econometric studies of household saving behavior in developing countries: A survey. *Journal of Development Studies*, 1974, *10*, 138–151.

Tobin, J. Life cycle saving and balanced growth. In W. Fellner et al. *Ten economic studies in the tradition of Irving Fisher*. New York: Wiley, 1967.

Uhlenberg, P. Changing configurations of the life course. In T. K. Hareven (Ed.), *Transitions: The family and life course in historical perspective*. New York: Academic Press, 1978, pp. 65–97.

U.S., Bureau of the Census. *Historical statistics of the United States: Colonial times to 1970*. Washington, D.C.: U.S. Government Printing Office, 1975.

U.S. Commissioner of Labor. *Sixth Annual Report of the U.S. Commissioner of Labor*; Part III, *Cost of living*. U.S. Congress, House of Representatives, 1890, House Executive Document 265, 51st Congress, 2nd Session. Washington, D.C.: Government Printing Office.

U.S. Commissioner of Labor. *Seventh Annual Report of the U.S. Commissioner of Labor*; Part III, *Cost of living*. U.S. Congress, House of Representatives, 1891, House Executive Document 232 (Vols. 1 & 2), 52nd Congress, 1st Session. Washington, D. C.: Government Printing Office.

Wells, V. Demographic change and the life cycle of American families. *The Journal of Interdisciplinary History*, 1971, *2*, 273–282.

Williamson, G. Consumer behavior in the nineteenth century: Carroll D. Wright's Massachusetts workers in 1875. *Explorations in Entrepreneurial History*, 1967, *4*, 98–135. (Second series)

4

The Demography of Life-Span Transitions: Temporal and Gender Comparisons*

DENNIS P. HOGAN
University of Chicago

Introduction

Demographic studies of life-course transitions investigate the timing, sequencing, and number of changes in discrete demographic statuses. Relevant events include those affecting reproduction (marriage, marital dissolution, fertility), population composition (school enrollment, military service, labor force participation, household composition), and population distribution (migration). Interindividual differences in transition processes and the relationship of transitions to time (biological age, historical events, and cohort) have been of interest.

Two very different approaches have been used to study the demography of life-span transitions. The first, arising from formal demography, has used data on transitions to describe the experience of the population, and of subgroups within the population, in regard to the average timing of life-course transitions. This work has provided a basis for notions of demographic cycles, including family life cycles. Following demographic traditions, this research has focused on the experiences of females. The second approach, growing out of the interests of social demographers, concentrates on causal analyses of transition processes. This research orientation emphasizes interindividual differences in the timing and coordination of life-course transitions and directs attention to temporal changes in transition rates. This research orientation naturally leads to a consideration of nonfamilial life-span transitions and their relation to familial transitions. Such research is essential to understanding gender differences in the timing and coordination of demographic transitions over the lifetime.

*This chapter was written while the author was a Fellow at the Center for Advanced Study in the Behavioral Sciences, supported in part by a grant from the John D. and Catherine T. MacArthur Foundation.

In this chapter, I review these two approaches to the study of the demography of life-span transitions. I argue that the first approach is fundamentally misleading because: (1) the life-span transitions of individuals often are used to infer demographic life cycles for families; and (2) concentration on the average experiences of a population artifactually produce the impression of homogeneity in life-span transitions, giving rise to notions of demographic stages. These errors cause the analyst to ignore interindividual differences in the timing and coordination of demographic transitions, obscuring temporal and social structural influences on the organization of activities over the life span. Research that assumes homogeneity in demographic stages also neglects the consequences of the timing of normative and nonnormative events on subsequent life-span development. These problems are readily avoided by the adoption of a life-course perspective on the study of demographic transitions. The chapter concludes with a brief discussion of appropriate research methods for life-course studies of the timing and coordination of demographic transitions.

The Demography of Life-Span Transitions

Demographic research includes attention to the vital rates of the population (fertility and mortality); factors influencing the likelihood of childbirth (marriage, marital dissolution and remarriage, fecundability); population composition (school enrollment, military service, labor-force participation, household composition); and population distribution (residential history, migration). Although demographers sometimes deal with continuous variables (age, income, years of education), most demographic variables are categorical (e.g., alive vs. dead, single vs. ever-married) with every individual identified as belonging to exactly one of the mutually exclusive categories (states). The history of membership in these states provides a demographic profile of an individual over the life span.

In their research, demographers measure the distribution of persons across states, identify the persons exposed to the risk of moving between states, and relate the number of persons moving between states during a specified time period to the population at risk to obtain rates of movement (transition rates) between states. These central rates provide the basis for calculating transition probabilities that define the demographic survival (life) table. Such survival tables can be calculated for real cohorts of persons based on their life-span experiences but more commonly are based on the age-specific (or duration-specific) rates observed for different cohort members at a single point in time.

The usual focus of formal demography is the measurement and description of these transition processes at the population level. Age and gender are the two principal factors differentiating members of the population that are always taken into account by formal demographers. Transition rates nearly always differ by age, and it is essential to take the aging of the population into account if one is to model the experiences of a population with fixed membership over time. Nearly all demographic methods, including the life table, maintain this central focus on age. Formal demographic research on transitions over the life span ordinarily concentrates on the experiences of females. In large part, this emphasis arose because data on reproduction (collected in vital registration systems, censuses, and surveys) are for females. The biological bases of human reproduction also motivated attention to the marital and childbearing experiences of females.

On average, men marry later than females, and their mean age at parenthood is later. In formal models of population growth, the mean age at fertility is interpreted as the mean length of a generation. The sex ratio at birth typically is in the range of 102–106 males per 100 females. Thus, for any given rate of fertility, fathers have more sons than mothers do daughters. In combination, the mean age at fertility and the reproduction rate determine the growth rate of the population. Therefore, formal models of population transition project different (and inconsistent) results for population change depending on whether female or male experiences are modeled. This is referred to as the "two sex" problem in demography. Although a number of solutions for the two sex problem have been proposed, formal demographers typically have dealt with it by restricting attention to the experience of females.

Demographers interested in describing the timing of transitions during the life span have calculated the median and mean ages at transition on the basis of experiences of those persons who have completed the transitions (see Carter & Glick, 1970). Social demographers have used general linear modeling procedures to identify antecedents to the timing of transitions among those experiencing them (e.g., Hogan, 1978a; Marini, 1978; Moore & Hofferth, 1980; Zelnik, Kantner & Ford, 1981). Such techniques work reasonably well for historical analyses in which all persons who will ever experience the transition have done so. However, such techniques produce biased estimates when the last observation (date of census, survey interview, etc.) is terminated at any arbitrary point in time in relation to the transition process, a phenomenon demographers label "right censoring" (see Sørensen, 1980).

The single-decrement life table (survival table) that is the standard tool of formal demography has proved useful for summarizing the age-specific rates of a demographic transition in a population that is subject to right censoring. Survival tables can be calculated to summarize the age-specific transition experiences of a real group of persons as they age over time up to the point at which they die or are last observed. These calculations produce estimates of the age-specific probability of a transition for persons who survive to a given age without making the transition, and these age-specific rates can be used to describe the cumulative percentage of persons completing the transition by a given age. This latter information also indicates the median age of the population at the transition. The single-decrement survival table has received wide use in the study of demographic transitions (Hogan, 1981; McCarthy, 1978; Winsborough, 1978). The survival table can also be calculated based on the transition experiences of the members of the population of different ages at a single point in time (Modell, Furstenberg & Hershberg, 1976). Survival tables for such "synthetic" cohorts provide a useful way of summarizing the long-run implications of present patterns, should they be experienced by the members of an actual cohort.

In recent years, new techniques have been introduced that permit the multivariate analysis of transitions recorded in event histories. These models estimate the instantaneous rate of transition (i.e., the hazard rate, the "force of mortality" in the life table) from an origin to a destination state as log linear[1] function of the independent variables of interest. Frequently, the transition rate depends upon the duration in the origin state. The form of the nonstationarity is sometimes modeled directly but may also be treated as an unspecified source of error (see Tuma, 1982). The coefficients of such models may be estimated using either maximum or partial likelihood procedures.[2] These techniques resolve problems of bias due to right censoring, without sacrificing information produced by other types of analysis, since the hazard rate exactly determines the cumulative survivor distribution and the average waiting time until the transition.

These methods, which have proved reasonably serviceable for studies of the timing of single demographic transitions, have also been used to provide statistical profiles of demographic stages of the life span. For example, Winsborough (1978) described the joint timing (median and interquartile range) of age at school completion, beginning of first job, first marriage, and at beginning and end of military service for single-year birth cohorts of young men. Uhlenberg (1974) has described the changing configuration of nuptial and parenthood behaviors over the life span of females born over the course of this century. Modell et al. (1976) used synthetic cohort techniques to describe the changing configuration of early-life transitions among American men and women.

Perhaps the most prominent attempt to describe the coincidence of demographic transitions over the life span involves the study of the "family life cycle" (Glick, 1947, 1977; Loomis & Hamilton, 1936; Spanier & Glick, 1980). These analyses have calculated measures of the average (median or mean) age at several demographic transitions (such as age at first marriage, age at the birth of the first and last child, age at termination of the marriage, and mean number of children) to characterize the succession of critical stages through which the

---

[1]The effects of independent variables in these models are specified as the proportionate change (e.g., 10% increase, 25% decrease) in the dependent variable associated with a one-unit change in the independent variable. These models are multiplicate rather than additive (as in an ordinary least squares regression analysis). Iterative procedures are used to estimate the parameters of such models. The algorithms for iterative procedures are more tractable and the computer calculations less costly for additive models. Therefore, the multiplicative model of interest is transformed to an additive model by working with logarithms of its variables, leading to the designation of these models as "log linear."

[2]Discussions of this type of model are found in Sørensen (1980), Tuma (1982), and Tuma, Hannan, and Groeneveld (1979). See Hogan (1983a) and Teachman (1982) for a discussion of the application of these techniques to demographic studies of the timing of life-span transitions.

typical family passes during its existence. Family sociologists have linked these stages to ideas about the developmental tasks of families (Hill & Mattessich, 1979; Hill & Rodgers, 1964).

Certainly, many families pass through a set of common stages: (1) family formation when a childless couple marries; (2) the birth of the first child and the beginning of childrearing; (3) the birth of the last child and the termination of childbearing with childrearing continuing; (4) the end of the childrearing with the departure of the last child from home (the "empty nest" phase); and (5) the termination of the family through the death of the husband or wife.

However, there are a number of difficulties with the family life-cycle approach (Nock, 1979; Spanier, Sauer, & Larzelere, 1979). In the contemporary United States, some individuals do not form families, and many families do not pass through these stages (Cherlin, 1981; Hogan, 1983b; Kitagawa, 1981). By the late 1970's, age-specific rates of marriage were sufficiently low that synthetic cohort estimates of the proportion of women who would ever marry by age 44 were about 90% among whites and less than three-quarters among blacks (Thornton & Rodgers, 1983). About 10% of white and black women aged 35–44 in 1980 were childless. Some families are formed with the birth of a child to an unmarried mother, with a husband being acquired later, if at all. For example, among women who married for the first time in 1970–1974, 38% of the blacks and 6% of the whites had given birth to at least one child prior to marriage (Hogan, 1983b). A substantial proportion of marriages end through divorce, often before the last child leaves home. Of white women married in 1959, 24% were divorced by their twentieth wedding anniversary, and recent trends in divorce imply that, among women married in 1979, 38% of the whites and 48% of the blacks will be divorced within 20 years (Thornton & Rodgers, 1983). Of the divorces in 1977, 56% involved at least one child under 18. It is estimated that about 31% of the white children and 54% of the black children born from 1965 to 1967 lived in a disrupted family by age 16 (Furstenberg, Nord, Peterson & Zill, 1983). In such cases, parents may remarry to form new families while completing the childrearing tasks created in their initial families. About 62% of the white women and 40% of the black women who were born in 1940–1944 remarry within 5 years after divorcing their first husband (Cherlin & McCarthy, 1983). Among children born from 1965 to 1969 whose parental families were disrupted, 56% of the whites and 13% of the blacks were in a mother and stepfather family within 5 years (Furstenberg et al., 1983). In other cases, families have childrearing responsibilities for a grandchild that continue long after the couple's own children leave home (Hogan, 1983b).

As these examples show, the basic difficulty with the family life-cycle approach is that it fails to recognize that families are created and terminated by individual behaviors. These behaviors frequently do not occur at the usual ages or in the typical sequence assumed by the family life-cycle model. As Elder (1978a, b) has noted, the history of a family results from the intertwined life courses of its members. Families do not have lives, or stages in those lives, apart from those that are the result of individual behaviors. Thus, the transitions comprising the family life cycle, as it is usually operationalized, in fact involve the interlinked marital and childbearing transitions of a population of men and women, not a population of families. Therefore, it is inappropriate to use measures of the average age at a series of life-cycle transitions for either women or men to characterize the family life cycle since the different types of family status, and changes in family organization, do not occur in stages or cycles.

Furthermore, the technique of calculating aggregate measures of the timing of demographic transitions is not a satisfactory way to characterize the life-span of a population of individual persons. Confronted with measures of central tendency on a number of life-span transitions, the analyst will usually infer that the average age at the transition indicates when a life-cycle stage changes, and that the length of time between average age at transitions measures the duration of a particular stage (e.g., Neugarten & Datan, 1973). Implicit in such analyses is the assumption that the order of the transitions ranked from earliest to lastest indicates the sequence in which the events occur. In other words, it is assumed that all individuals pass through each of the stages in the same sequence, even though the length of time spent in those stages may differ.

This interpretation is especially likely when the stages in question are believed to result from conformity to social norms. Although the evidence is rather scattered, it appears that the age-graded regularities in life-span transitions result in a system of norms or beliefs about appropriate ages or age-ranges for specific life events, outside of which a behavior is considered too early or too late (Fallo-Mitchell & Ryff, 1982; Modell, 1980; Neugarten, Moore & Lowe, 1965). In some societies, these normative expectations are subject to formal enforcement through rites of passage which certify the age strata to which an individual belongs and the behaviors appropriate for members of those age strata (Foner & Kertzer, 1978). In the United States, the appropriate ages for events are less precisely specified, but the age-gradedness of behaviors provides evidence of statistical regularities in the timing of life events that are suggestive of underlying norms (Hogan, 1978b).

Despite these empirical regularities, many persons do not conform to these normative patterns in their life-span transitions. Uhlenberg (1978) defined a normatively expected life course for females as one that involves marrying, bearing children, and surviving to age 50 with the first marriage still intact. The proportion of women whose lives are consistent with such normative stages varies considerably between cohorts. Only 44% of the women born in 1870 who lived to reach adulthood experienced this normative pattern. This percentage increased to 60% for women born in 1930 but still remained far from a universal pattern.

Furthermore, the usual sequencing of transition events, as displayed in aggregate population data, are not always followed by members of those populations. For example, age at marriage exceeded age at school completion by more than 9 years among birth cohorts born in the early part of the twentieth century, declining to a still substantial difference of 3.2 years for the birth cohort of 1951, suggesting that the timing of school completion is substantially before marriage in the lives of twentieth-century American men. But tabulations of the sequencing of these two transitions indicated that the percentage of men marrying prior to the completion of schooling varied between 6.7 and 24.5% for the birth cohorts of 1907 to 1952, with conformity to the usual sequence of marriage and school completion depending upon social conditions and personal characteristics (Hogan, 1978b, 1981). Analysts using continuous life-history data have shown that 10% or more of the early lives of men may be spent in nonnormative combinations of activities (Featherman, Hogan & Sørensen, 1983; Featherman & Sørensen, in press). Thus, analyses that characterize demographic transitions over the life-span as a series of invariant life-cycle stages are empirically inaccurate.

This observation has caused some observers to suggest that analysts should refrain from considering the influence of social norms on the transition behavior of individuals (Marini, 1981, 1982a). Even though the data are scattered, the evidence is sufficient to document the existence of preferences about the timing and sequencing of demographic transitions in the life span. Rather than ignore what we know exists, more studies should be designed to measure interindividual differences in preferences about the demography of life-span transitions and to identify any perceived or actual sanctions that encourage conformity to those preferences. By bracketing the preferred age ranges for transitions, the analyst will be able to determine which persons are "on-time" and "off-time" in their behaviors (Neugarten et al., 1965). The causes of off-time transitions can then be identified (Hogan, 1982) as well as the consequences due to incompatibilities with other roles or as a result of normative sanctions measured (Hogan, 1980).

Family life-cycle researchers have adopted the conventions of formal demography by attempting to describe the transitions of a population by the aggregate experiences of females. There has been little effort to study the familial transitions of males. This neglect has resulted in an inaccurate picture of the changing probabilities of marriage, divorce, and remarriage among Americans since age-specific rates of these behaviors differ substantially by gender for both whites and blacks (Thornton & Rodgers, 1983), and the causal structures influencing those rates differ between males and females (Marini, 1978). Furthermore, the assumption of invariant norms about the female life course has caused family life-cycle researchers to neglect changes in nonfamilial transitions, such as the completion of education, labor force entry, rates of labor force exit in response to parenthood, and rate of labor force reentry after parenthood that impact upon rates of marriage, divorce, remarriage, and fertility. In contrast, researchers adopting a life-course perspective that emphasizes the multidimensional aspects of demographic transitions naturally direct attention to temporal changes in the life-span transitions of females (Elder, 1975, 1978a, 1978b; Featherman, 1983).

By acknowledging the multidimensional character of life-span transitions, researchers are able to identify interindividual variability in the relative timing of the transitions. Such a perspective leads the analyst to recognize the varied patterns of life-cycle transitions and to avoid the assumption of uniform demographic stages over the life span. The analyst can then direct attention to the causes of varied patterns of the timing and coordination of life-course transitions (Featherman et al., 1983; Featherman & Sørensen, in press; Hogan, 1978b; Winship, 1983). Finally, only by recognizing the different forms of demographic life histories can the researcher identify the consequences of these histories for subsequent life-span behaviors (Elder & Liker, 1982; Elder & Rockwell, 1977; Featherman & Carter, 1976; Hogan, 1980).

Most demographic transitions are age-graded, occurring during predictable times in the life span. For example, women ordinarily become mothers between ages 18 and 35. Most women live longer than their husbands and become widows at some point in their life span, usually after their mid-fifties. Most persons retire from the labor force during their sixties. These transitions are subject to varying degrees of individual discretion. Although for many they occur at an unremarkable age, sometimes these transitions occur at unexpected ages. A young husband with children may be widowed by the accidental death of his wife. A middle-level executive may be retired by his company during his early fifties, many years before his anticipated retirement date, and at an age when it is difficult to find a position elsewhere. In other cases, unexpected historical events may have major impacts on the life courses of persons of all ages (e.g., the impact of the Holocaust on the lives of European Jews). Brim and Ryff (1980) have drawn attention to these nonnormative life events as potential turning points in the life course that are particularly worthy of study. These nonnormative events pass unnoticed in analyses that assume uniform life-cycle stages but are readily identifiable in research that adopts a life-course perspective on the timing and coordination of demographic events.

Suggested Research Methods

I have argued that a life-course perspective on individual behavior provides the appropriate theoretical orientation for research on the coordination of demographic transitions. However, most empirical research has examined the timing of single demographic transitions without considering the issue of coordination of several demographic transitions. The latter type of research is essential if traditional notions of demographic life cycles are to be replaced by more sophisticated analyses of the coordination of demographic transitions over the life span. Some recent work suggests a number of appropriate directions for this research. All of these research strategies require complete histories of demographic events. Such event histories record the timing of all transitions between discrete states of interest. Event histories, therefore, provide data on both event counts and event sequences, making it possible to test alternative statistical models for continuous-time discrete state stochastic processes (Hannan & Tuma, 1979). Event history of demographic transitions naturally direct attention to temporal changes in the life-span transitions of females (Elder, 1975, 1978a, 1978b; Featherman, 1983).

A useful initial research step is the preparation of aggregate measures of person-months of time spent in every state and combinations of states at each age (Featherman et al., in press). These calculations indicate the combinations of activities that are common and those that are statistically rare. The analyst can identify temporal, gender, and socioeconomic differentials in the allocation of time to differing combinations of demographic states. By treating each person-month of time as a unit of analysis, logit models can be estimated that determine the correlates of particular combinations of demographic states (Featherman & Sørensen, in press).

Next, the analyst must investigate the sequence of different combinations of demographic states. That is, individual histories of demographic statuses over the life span are identified, and the connections between earlier and later demographic statuses must be measured. The correlates of these demographic statuses and their development over the life span can then be assessed. In cases in which the entire demographic history is known for the relevent section of the life span, the analyst can determine the sequence of the demographic transitions. Logit models can be used to determine the effects of independent variables on the demographic trajectory (Hogan, 1978b; Marini, 1982b; Moen, 1983).

Often analysts wish to investigate the coordinated timing of demographic transitions that are still underway. The continuous-time semi-Markov model for the analysis of hazard rates proposed by Tuma et al. (1979) adequately handles biases due to right censoring and provides several important ways to link transitions. The model permits the analyst to examine transitions between multiple category origin and destination states. Thus, the analyst can compare the next life-course transition for persons who are intially observed at different life-cycle statuses. Frequently, several different competing transitions would result in the change of a life-cycle status (e.g., a single, childless woman could leave that life-cycle status by marrying or by giving birth to a child). This model can handle these competing transitions by treating them as multiple possible-destination statuses. Finally, this statistical model permits the analysis of the effects of time-varying independent variables on the rate of transition from one demographic state to another. This enables the analyst to determine how characteristics on one demographic status effect the rate of transition for another demographic status, indicating the extent of linkages among demographic transitions.[3]

---

[3]In a recent paper, Winship (1983) argued that the apparent interconnectedness of life-course transitions may be due to unobserved population heterogeneity which affects the pace at which individuals age. Winship shows that a statistical model that assumes that the effects of unobserved heterogeneity are additive permits the investigator to distinguish heterogeneity and interdependence of transitions. Although Winship argues that his model is more theoretical, in the formal modeling sense favored by economists, his model

These methods of analysis should prove useful in explaining the coordinated timing of demographic transitions over the life span (and thus the movement between successive life-cycle statuses). However, they will not provide the concise summaries of the life-course experiences of real and synthetic cohort populations that the techniques of formal demography have made available for single demographic transitions. Recent innovations in formal demography have resulted in the development of life-table techniques for transitions that involve multiple origin and destination states (Keyfitz, 1980; Ledent, 1980; Rogers, 1980). As Espenshade and Braun (1982) have noted: The flexibility of these methods in characterizing the heterogeneity of individual experience over time and as individuals age makes them particularly well-suited to a study of life course transitions. (p. 1027)

One disadvantage of the multistate methods has been the necessity of assuming that the population is homogeneous (i.e., the assumption that all individuals experience the same hazard rate). This problem has been handled by estimating separate life tables for populations known to differ in their rates. For example, Espenshade (1983) considers the marriage, divorce, and remarriage experiences of black and white women separately because of the large racial differences in rates of these transitions. This technique works well with a small number of independent variables and data from the large public use samples of decennial censuses but becomes problematic when sample sizes are relatively small because of the large standard errors associated with rates based on fewer than several hundred cases (Teachman, 1982). To a large extent, this problem can be overcome by using the event-history techniques to generate sample paths of transitions for persons with different combinations of characteristics (Hannan, 1982).

---

ignores the anthropological, psychological, sociological, and economic evidence that transitions are interlinked. Instead of controlling for known sources of population heterogeneity such as educational attainment, military service experience, and birth cohort, Winship groups the effects of these variables together with the effects of other unmeasured (and unspecified) variables. The approach advocated by Winship promises to advance our knowledge about linkages among life-course transitions to the extent he is able to replace the age-stratification theory motivating other analyses with a more general theoretical model. Before such an explanation is accepted, it will be necessary to demonstrate with the analysis of longitudinal data, taking into account known sources of heterogeneity, that individuals do not try to link the various life-course transitions, and that the probability of the transitions are independent of prior transition statuses. There is substantial social scientific evidence demonstrating that the marriage market success of men is enhanced by economic sufficiency and that women have avoided motherhood prior to marriage. While these linkages might have changed over time and may differ between blacks and whites, I think it is extremely unlikely that it will be possible to convince observant social scientists that the transitions involved in these statuses are not linked.

Conclusion

I have argued that traditional methods of conceptualizing and describing the timing of demographic transitions in the life course are inadequate for analyzing the synchronization of life transitions. The life-course perspective emphasizes the interconnections between demographic transitions in the lives of individuals. All individuals experience a succession of demographic statuses over their life spans, statuses that are determined by the combinations of their characteristics in regard to reproduction, population composition, and population distribution. Since the age-graded timing and the sequencing of these component transitions differ between individuals, it is inaccurate to characterize the succession of life-cycle statuses as constituting a succession of life-cycle stages for members of the population. By abandoning false notions of demographic life-cycle stages, researchers can redirect their attention toward the sources of interindividual differences in the succession of demographic statuses over the life span. In combination with a number of new research methods, the life-course perspective offers a promising new approach to the study of demographic transitions over the life span.

References

Brim, O. G. Jr., & Ryff, C. D. On the properties of life events. In P. B. Baltes & O. G. Brim, Jr., (Eds.), *Life span development and behavior* (Vol. 3). New York: Academic Press, 1980, pp. 368–388.

Carter, H., & Glick, P. C. *Marriage and divorce: A social and economic study.* Cambridge: Harvard University Press, 1970.

Cherlin, A. J. *Marriage, divorce, remarriage.* Cambridge: Harvard University Press, 1981.

Cherlin, A. J., & McCarthy, J. *Demographic analysis of family and household structure.* Final report to National Institute of Child Health and Human Development for contract No. NO1-HD-12802, 1983.

Elder, G. H. Jr., Age differentiation and the life course. In A. Inkeles, J. Coleman & N. Smelser. (Eds.), *Annual review of sociology* (Vol. 1). Palo Alto, Calif.: Annual Reviews, 1975, pp. 165–190.

Elder, G. H. Jr., Approaches to social change and the family. *American Journal of Sociology (Suppl.)* 1978, *84*, S1-S38. (a)

Elder, G. H. Jr., Family history and the life course. In T. K. Hareven, (Ed.), *Transitions: The family and the life course in historical perspective.* New York: Academic Press, 1978, pp. 17–64. (b)

Elder, G. H. Jr., & Liker, J. K. Economic change and health in women's lives: Historical influences across forty years. *American Journal of Sociology*, 1982, *88*, pp. 241–269.

Elder, G. H. Jr., & Rockwell, R. W. Economic depression and postwar opportunity in men's lives: A study of life patterns and health. In R. G. Simmons, (Ed.), *Research in community and mental health.* Greenwich, Conn.: JAI Press, 1977, pp. 249–303.

Espenshade, T. J. *Black-white differences in marriage, separation, divorce, and remarriage*. Paper presented to the Population Association of America, Pittsburgh, 1983.

Espenshade, T. J., & Braun, R. E. Life course analysis and multistate demography: An application to marriage, divorce, and remarriage. *Journal of Marriage and the Family*, 1982, *44*, pp. 1025–1036.

Fallo-Mitchell, L., & Ryff, C. D. Preferred timing of female life events: Cohort differences. *Research on Aging*, 1982, *4*, 249–267.

Featherman, D. L. The life-span perspective in social science research. In P. B. Baltes, & O. G. Brim Jr., (Eds.), *Life span development and behavior (Vol. 5)*. New York: Academic Press, 1983, pp. 1–49.

Featherman, D. L., & Carter, T. M. Discontinuities in schooling and the socioeconomic life cycle. In W. H. Sewell, R. M. Hauser, & D. L. Featherman (Eds.), *Schooling and achievement in American society*. New York: Academic Press, 1976, pp. 133–160.

Featherman, D. L., Hogan, D. P., & Sørensen, A. B. Entry into adulthood: Profiles of young men in the 1950's. In P. B. Baltes, & O. G. Brim, Jr. (Eds.), *Life span development and behavior* (Vol. 6). New York: Academic Press, 1984, in press.

Featherman, D. L., & Sørensen, A. B. Societal transformation in Norway and change in the life course transition into adulthood. *Acta Sociologica*, in press.

Foner, A., & Kertzer, D. I. Transitions over the life-course: Lessons from age-set societies. *American Journal of Sociology*, 1978, *83*, 1081–1104.

Furstenberg, F. F. Jr., Nord, C. W., Peterson, J. L., & Zill, N. The life course of children of divorce. *American Sociological Review*, 1983, *48*, 656–668.

Glick, P. C. The family cycle. *American Journal of Sociology*, 1947, *12*, 164–174.

Glick, P. C. Updating the life cycle of the family. *Journal of Marriage and the Family*, 1977, *30*, 5–13.

Hannan, M. T., *Multistate demography and event history analysis*. Working paper 82–50 of the International Institute for Applied Systems Analysis, Laxenburg, Austria, 1982.

Hannan, M. T., & Tuma, N. B., Methods for temporal analysis. In A. Inkeles, J. Coleman, & R. H. Turner, (Eds.), *Annual review of sociology* (Vol. 5). Palo Alto, Calif.: Annual Reviews, 1979, pp. 303–328.

Hill, R., & Mattessich, P. Family development theory and life span development. In P. B. Baltes, & O. G. Brim, Jr. (Eds.), *Life span development and behavior* (Vol. 2). New York: Academic Press, 1979, pp. 162–204.

Hill, R., & Rodgers, R. H. The developmental approach. In H. T. Christensen (Ed.), *Handbook of marriage and the family*. Chicago: Rand McNally, 1964, pp. 171–211.

Hogan, D. P. The effects of demographic factors, family background, and early job achievement on age at marriage. *Demography*, 1978, *5*, 161–175. (a)

Hogan, D. P. The variable order of events in the life course. *American Sociological Review*, 1978, *43*, 573–586. (b)

Hogan, D. P. The transition to adulthood as a career contingency. *American Sociological Review*, 1980, *45*, 261–276.

Hogan, D. P. *Transitions and social change: The early lives of American men*. New York: Academic Press, 1981.

Hogan, D. P. Subgroup variations in early life transitions. In M. W. Riley, R. P. Abeles, & M. S. Teitelbaum, (Eds.), *Aging from birth to death: Sociotemporal perspectives*. Boulder, Colo.: Westview Press, 1982, pp. 87–103.

Hogan, D. P. *Cohort comparisons in the timing of life transitions*. Paper presented to the Social Science Research Council Workshop on the Family and the Life Course: Japan–United States Comparisons, New York, 1983. (a)

Hogan, D. P. *Demographic trends in human fertility and parenting across the life-span*. Paper presented at the Social Science Research Council Conference on Biosocial

Life-Span Approaches to Parental and Offspring Development, Elkridge, Maryland, 1983. (b)

Keyfitz, N. Multistate demography and its data: A comment. *Environment and Planning A*, 1980, *12*, 615–622.

Kitagawa, E. M. New life-styles: Marriage patterns, living arrangements, and fertility outside of marriage. *Annals*, American Academy of Political and Social Sciences, 1981, *453*, 1–27.

Ledent, J. Multistate life tables: Movement versus transition perspectives. *Environment and Planning A*, 1980, *12*, 533–562.

Loomis, C. P., & Hamilton, C. H. Family life cycle analysis. *Social Forces*, 1936, *15*, 225–231.

McCarthy, J. A comparison of the probabilities of the dissolution of first and second marriages. *Demography*, 1978, *15*, 345–359.

Marini, M. M. The transition to adulthood: Sex differences in educational attainment and age at marriage. *American Sociological Review*, 1978, *43*, 483–507.

Marini, M. M. *Age and sequencing norms in the transition to adulthood*. Paper presented to the American Sociological Association, Toronto, 1981.

Marini, M. M. *Determinants of the timing of adult role entry*. Paper presented to the Population Workshop of the Economic Research Center, Stanford, California. 1982. (a)

Marini, M. M. *The order of events in the transition to adulthood*. Paper presented to the American Sociological Association, San Francisco, 1982. (b)

Modell, J. Normative aspects of American marriage timing since World War II. *Journal of Family History*, 1980, *5*, 210–234.

Modell, J., Furstenberg, F., Jr. & Hershberg, T. Social change and transitions to adulthood in historical perspective. *Journal of Family History*, 1976, *1*, 7–31.

Moen, P. *Continuities and discontinuities in women's labor force activity*. Revised version of a paper presented to the Social Science Research Council Workshop on Life-Course Research with Panel Data, Elkridge, Maryland, 1983.

Moore, K. A., & Hofferth, S. L. Factors affecting early family formation: A path model. *Population and Environment*, 1980, *3*, 73–98.

Neugarten, B. L., & Datan, N. Sociological perspectives on the life cycle. In P. B. Baltes, & K. W. Schaie (Eds.), *Life span development psychology: Personality and socialization*. New York: Academic Press, 1973, pp. 53–69.

Neugarten, B. L., Moore, J. W., & Lowe, J. C. Age norms, age constraints, and adult socialization. *American Journal of Sociology*, 1965, *70*, 710–717.

Nock, S. L. The family life cycle: Empirical or conceptual tool? *Journal of Marriage and the Family*, 1979, *41*, 15–26.

Rogers, A. Introduction to multistate demography. *Environment and Planning A*, 1980, *12*, 489–498.

Sørensen, A. B. Estimating rates from retrospective questions. In D. Heise (Ed.), *Sociological methodology*. San Francisco: Jossey-Bass, 1977, pp. 209–233.

Sørensen, A. B. Analysis of change in discrete variables. In J. Clubb, & E. Scheuch (Eds.), *Historical social research*. Stuttgart: Klett-Cotta, 1980, pp. 284–299.

Spanier, G. B., & Glick, P. C. The life cycle of American families: An expanded analysis. *Journal of Family History*, 1980, *5*, 97–111.

Spanier, G. B., Sauer, W., & Larzelere, R. An empirical evaluation of the family life cycle. *Journal of Marriage and the Family*, 1979, *41*, 27–38.

Teachman, J. D. Methodological issues in the analysis of family formation and dissolution. *Journal of Marriage and the Family*, 1982, *44*, 1037–1053.

Thornton, A., & Rodgers, W. L. *Changing patterns of marriage and divorce in the United States*. Final report to the National Institute of Child Health and Human Development for contract No. NO1-HD-02850, 1983.

Tuma, N. B. Nonparametric and partially parametric approaches to event-history analysis. In K. F. Schuessler (Ed.), *Sociological methodology*. San Francisco: Jossey-Bass, 1982, pp. 1–60.

Tuma, N. B., Hannan, M. T., & Groeneveld, L. P. Dynamic analysis of event histories. *American Journal of Sociology*, 1979, *84*, 820–854.

Uhlenberg, P. Cohort variations in family life experiences of U.S. females. *Journal of Marriage and the Family*, 1974, *36*, 284–292.

Uhlenberg, P. Changing configurations of the life course. In T. K. Hareven (Ed.), *Transitions: The family and the life course in historical perspective*. New York: Academic Press, 1978, pp. 65–97.

Winsborough, H. H. Statistical histories of the life cycle of birth cohorts: The transition from school-boy to adult male. In K. E. Taeuber, L. L. Bumpass, & J. A. Sweet (Eds.), *Social demography*. New York: Academic Press, 1978, pp. 231–259.

Winship, C. *Age dependence, heterogeneity, and the interdependence of life cycle transitions*. Paper presented to the American Sociological Association, Detroit, 1983.

Zelnik, M., Kantner, J., & Ford, K. *Sex and pregnancy in adolescence*. Beverly Hills, Calif.: Sage Publications, 1981.

II

GENDER DIFFERENTIATION AND SOCIAL INSTITUTIONS

Gender and Individual Development
Chapters 5, 6

Gender, Age, and Deviance
Chapter 7

Gender and the Family
Chapters 8, 9

Gender and the Economy
Chapters 10, 11, 12

Gender and the State
Chapters 13, 14

5

The Psychobiology of Gender

ANKE A. EHRHARDT
College of Physicians and Surgeons
Columbia University

Introduction

Two changes have recently occurred in our thinking about human development. One is a change in focus from childhood and adolescence to the study of the entire life course. The other is the inclusion of biological aspects in the analysis of behavior and the exploration of the interplay between various factors—biological, sociological, psychological, and historical.To take such an interdisciplinary approach has not been popular in the past. Every discipline has perfected its argument to justify field-specific blinders. Sociologists and psychologists often shy away from biological variables out of fear of misuse: Once you consider biological aspects in the study of human behavior, the ghost of "biology is destiny" looms large. On the other hand, endocrinologists, biochemists, and geneticists are reticent to consider psychological and sociological aspects that they may consider to be imprecise and speculative. However, if progress is to be made in the comprehensive analysis of behavior, we cannot responsibly continue to hone in on the evidence presented by one discipline alone and thus neglect important new knowledge from other fields.

Models of Development

This chapter focuses on gender-related behavior, a field in which evidence of various prenatal and postnatal influences is rapidly accumulating. One of the roadblocks to progress lies in the interpretation of the data regarding the relative contribution of constitutional vs. environmental or innate vs. learned factors.

The difficulties begin with terminology. The dichotomies of nature vs. nurture, constitutional vs. acquired, and heredity vs. environment reflect outdated thinking of a bipolarity that does not exist. As John Money (1982, 504) succinctly puts it: "To polarize biology against social learning puts the latter unscientifically on a par with the occult.'' Money is referring to the fact that both kinds of influences exist in the brain, irrespective of how they gained entry— whether internally by way of genetics or externally by way of stimuli transmitted through the senses from the environment. He argues that learning and memory are just as much biology as the process of DNA replication. The bipolarity of these issues is thus a false one because social influences are not taking place outside the central nervous system.

This is important because the distinction is often drawn in order to divide the different classes of influences into immutable (i.e., biologic) and modifiable (i.e., learned) categories. This presents another false dichotomy, since *all effects* are more or less modifiable. A particular chain of events can modify conception itself. The range of hormonal variations from the mother and the fetus may also affect the development of the central nervous system which, in turn, may receive totally different stimuli postnatally during early parent–child bonding and later in sibling and peer relations, with different social reinforcers for specific behaviors.

Even without the false bipolarity of biology vs. environment, different models that help integrate all the information, prenatal or postnatal, must be considered. Three models come to mind that apply to both gender behavior and developmental disorders in general (discussed in detail in Samaroff & Chandler, 1975).

Main-Effect Model

The model most often applied is the *main-effect model*, which postulates that *one* factor determines or predominantly influences a particular behavioral outcome. A defect in the constitution, such as an abnormality in the prenatal or postnatal hormonal makeup of a person, produces a specific gender identity or gender disorder, irrespective of the social environment the individual grows up in. Conversely, a pathogenic environment will produce a disorder in gender behavior, no matter what the individual's genes, hormones, and sex organs are. This model has the advantage of being simple, practical for the researcher, and conclusive. Researchers typically hone in on one event that is taken to be the most important determinant of the behavior, and they are often ready to discard all knowledge of other relevant factors. The problem with the main-effect model is that many cases do not fit such a one-factor model. Therefore, we are particularly vulnerable to going from one new discovery to the next in the hope of finding a better explanation of the behavior under study.

Interactional Model

The second model is the *interactional model*. This model considers a variety of constitutional and social environmental factors to explain and, more importantly, to predict an individual's behavior. Basically two-dimensional, the interactional model predicts the individual's behavior outcome from any combination of two factors. As Samaroff and Chandler state, children with constitutional problems (e.g., with genetic or hormonal problems) raised in a deviant environment would be predicted to have poor outcome. Children with hormonal abnormalities with the good fortune to be raised in supportive environments and children without problems raised in deviant environments would have better outcomes. The best outcome, of course, is found among children with no hormonal or genetic problems who were raised in supportive environments. Certainly, this interactive model substantially increases the general efficiency of the main-effect model because it takes more influences into consideration. The major disadvantage of the model in this narrow version is that it presupposes the constancy of social environment and constitutional factors. The characteristics of children and their environment change, however, and, more importantly, they can modify each other at any point during development. The child can alter the response of the environment and is in turn altered by this changed world.

It is crucial then to move from a static interactional model to a more dynamic concept of development which posits a continual and progressive interplay between the organism and its environment.

Transactional Model

Such a dynamic model may be called a *transactional model*, which assumes that a variety of influences may have their source at different points in development, either in the constitution or in the outside world, exerting influence on the central nervous system. All these factors actively participate and interact with each other and are, therefore, plastic modifiers. The constants in development are not a set of genetic or hormonal traits, on the one hand, and the environmental reaction to these traits, on the other, but rather the processes by which these traits are maintained in the transactions between organism and environment. A deviant development, according to the transactional model, is not to be seen as an inborn inability to respond appropriately to a specific environment but rather a continuous malfunction in the organism–environment transaction across time that prevents the child from organizing his or her self-image and behavior adaptively. The deviant environment is not one traumatic event but rather continuous environmental responses to the child with a vulnerability that must operate throughout development. The transactional model does not assume directionality in development, that is, a greater etiological importance of one particular factor. Rather, the model stresses that the intensity of a deviant factor, be it social–environmental or constitutional, may have a *relatively* greater effect.

The outcome of development in a transactional model may consist of many different options, but regarding one aspect of psychosexual differentiation— gender identity development—there are surprisingly few possibilities. Gender identity may be unambiguously female, male, or ambiguous with no fixed anchor point in one or the other. Since the outcome is usually in accordance with expectations at birth, it appears that the human organism may produce normal developmental outcomes under seemingly all but the most adverse conditions.

Gender Identity

The definitions of gender identity vary; most of them infer a person's sense of belonging to one sex or the other, male or female. Until about 30 years ago, scientists and clinicians did not use the term *gender* but spoke of *sex*. Sex was determined by biology, and at that time biology meant the structure of the gonads, testicular or ovarian. If a person's sex was in doubt, as in babies with ambiguous genitalia, an exploratory laporotomy and a histologic examination of the gonads determined the sex of rearing. The underlying assumption was that the gonads represented the *true* sex and also determined a person's feelings of identity. Several examples exist of people with tragic lives of obscurity because they could not identify with their declared gonadal sex. Many were not allowed to get a valid birth certificate or to get married because no physician would verify their gender identity if it differed from their gonadal sex. In particular, this applied to genetic males with an extreme degree of microphallus who identified as females or to genetic females totally virilized during pre- and postnatal development who identified as males.

In 1945, Albert Ellis published a review article based on 84 cases of hermaphrodites, stating that the sex role in such cases "accords primarily not with his or her internal or external somatic characteristics, but rather with his or her masculine or feminine upbringing (p. 120)." The breakthrough, however, came in 1955 when John Money, in co-authorship with John and Joan Hampson (1955a,b) formulated a new theory of the determinants of sex, using for the first time the terms *gender role* and *gender identity*. The introduction of gender role and gender identity as new terms was critical because it meant having a term not bound to biologic sex that included other than sexual behaviors related to masculinity and femininity. The most important scientific advance of the proposed theory, though, was that sex was determined by a number of variables rather than one, including psychologic and social sex. Not until 1981 did the twenty-sixth edition of *Dorland's Illustrated Medical Dictionary* include "social sex" as one of the defining aspects under the entry on "sex."

The theory of John Money and his colleagues that the determination of sex depends on a number of variables, like links in a chain, was pioneering and may be considered a major contribution to our knowledge of psychosexual differentiation. It led to a major change in the traditional policy regarding the sex of rearing of intersex babies. Money and the Hampsons added a new criterion for sex assignment, namely, the prognosis of sexual functioning of the individual. They justified this by formulating a new theory of gender development based on their unique and rich clinical case material. Their theory stated that the best "prognosticator" of a satisfactory gender identity is the sex of assignment and rearing, and they added a critical time dimension to their model, that is, that aspects of gender identity are typically formed by two-and-a-half years of age. Money and the Hampsons had observed gender change at a later point in development but warned there was increased risk of psychopathology for the individual in such cases. Ambiguity of gender identity had been observed by them and was identified as a sequela of ambiguity in rearing. Clinicians were advised, therefore, to minimize such ambiguities by rapid decision making, counseling the parents, and surgically correcting the appearance of the external genitalia to accord with the assigned sex. Under Money and his medical collaborators and with the support of a prestigious institution such as the Johns Hopkins Hospital, sex of assignment on the basis of future social and sexual functioning became an adopted policy on a worldwide basis.

The model of gender identity development continued to be useful even when prenatal sex hormones and their effects on gender-related behavior came under study. Based on their findings, researchers generally agreed that variations of prenatal sex hormones may predispose and affect temperament in the direction of a certain pattern of sex dimorphic behavior, but they do not appear to have a major influence on the acquisition of gender identity unless coupled with a highly deviant environment (Money & Ehrhardt, 1972).

For a while, the theory that gender is determined by a number of variables interacting with each other seemed to be on solid ground. It came as a surprise, then, that the model was newly questioned and debated because of a radically different position espoused by Imperato-McGinley and co-workers beginning in 1974 based on their study of a newly diagnosed syndrome:

> It appears that the extent of androgen (i.e., testosterone) exposure of the brain in utero, during the early postnatal period and at puberty has more effect in determining male-gender identity than does sex of rearing. This experiment of nature emphasizes the importance of androgens, which act as inducers (in utero and neonatally) and as activators (at puberty) in the evolution of male-gender identity. (1979, p. 1236)

The theory has resulted in controversy, the debate is still ongoing and has had grave consequences because of its impact on clinical management of many patients with intersexuality. There is nothing wrong with a proposed new theory if it is based on new knowledge. What is startling, however, is that the Imperato-McGinley theory caused this controversy in the first place, considering the poor quality of its observational basis and what had already been learned from prior research.

The Imperato-McGinley observations are based on a group of people in the Dominican Republic who were genetic male pseudohermaphrodites due to an enzyme deficiency of 5α-reductase which decreases prenatal production of dihydrotestosterone. This results in severe ambiguity in the external genitalia in the male fetus. At birth, the subjects have a bifid scrotum which appears labia-like and a very small phallus. There is a urogenital sinus with a blind-ending vaginal pouch. The testes are in the abdomen, inguinal canal, or scrotum. In the past, these individuals were raised as girls. At puberty, under the influence of their own testosterone, these individuals undergo definite virilization with deepening of the voice, phallic growth, and masculine development. Their testes descend if they had not done so earlier. Of the original 18 subjects on which interview data exist, 17 are said to have changed their gender identity and 16 their gender role at puberty from female to male. Of the two exceptions, one kept the female gender identity and gender role, the other switched to a male gender identity but continued to dress as a female.

Most of the individuals who show this syndrome in the Dominican Republic appeared to change their gender identity during adolescence to that of a man. Before one concludes that this is due to testosterone, one needs to ask whether they really had a female gender identity in childhood and whether the rearing experience was unambiguously female. Unfortunately, the information on rearing and the concept of the parents regarding the sex of their child is very scanty in the existing publications. Some critical questions must be raised, similar to those in publications by Rubin, Reinisch, and Haskett (1981), and by Meyer-Bahlburg (1982). Perhaps the villagers and the parents of these individuals recognized some ambiguity in the children's genitalia from birth which may have given these children a special status. Imperato-McGinley suggests that after the initial observation of the pubertal change, the children became known as "penis at 12," making it likely that they were not unambiguously raised as girls. It is also likely that long before puberty, the affected individuals noted the ambiguity of their own genitalia, especially since boys play in the nude until age 7 or 8 in the Dominican village, whereas girls wear underpants after they are toilet trained. Imperato-McGinley argues that the children became slowly aware from about age 7 that their true sex was male, which certainly supports the hypothesis that the affected individuals knew themselves to be different from other girls long before puberty.

One also has to consider the specific cultural conditions in which these individuals grew up. Strict segregation of play behavior allows more freedom for boys to romp and play, whereas girls are encouraged to stay with their mothers near the house. Their prenatal androgen status might have influenced the affected individuals to have a temperamental makeup of physically energetic play behavior which would have made them happy-go-lucky tomboys in Western society. In the Dominican Republic, it might have increased their feelings of being different from other girls.

Lastly, a rural village in the Dominican Republic prescribes a dramatic status difference for men and women. To lead the life of an infertile woman with no breasts and ambiguous male genitalia probably means considerable hardship, no chance of having a normal marriage, and little possibility of supporting oneself. The gender change, on the other hand, meant joining the higher male status and attaining greater economic advantage.

Nonetheless, the example of these villagers *does* illustrate that human beings are capable of changing their gender relatively late in life under specific circumstances. That, however, was known from several earlier reports by Money and the Hampsons. In fact, Money (1968) published cases of gender change in adolescence by outlining the various roots of ambiguity in the person's development in great detail. It therefore comes as a surprise that a theory of determination of gender identity by pre- and postnatal hormones should be attractive, especially based on scanty evidence that does not explain many other existing phenomena. Women with untreated congenital adrenal hyperplasia, for instance, heavily virilized before and after birth, still usually do not want to change their gender to become male if brought up as a female. Consider the phenomenon of male transsexualism. If male gender identity is determined by prenatal androgens and pubertal hormonal activation, as Imperato-McGinley argues, shouldn't males who have normal male genitals at birth who get assigned to the male sex (even if they sometimes have ambiguous rearing experiences), and often have a totally normal male puberty, get the determining signals of testosterone to identify with the male gender? For a male child with gender ambiguity in childhood, the prognosis would be that his dilemma will definitely be solved during adolescence, and parents of effeminate boys would be reassured that everything will change in puberty, since the brain will get the message to identify with the male gender. In reality, the opposite is true—the dilemma of male transsexuals intensifies in adolescence.

Nonetheless, while the scientific debate continues, many clinicians have become insecure and now seriously suggest assigning genetic males with 5α-reductase deficiency to the male sex, despite the fact that they will grow up severely demasculinized and with ambiguous genitalia. Such clinicians believe that by puberty everything will be all right. The alternative suggested by some clinicians, to raise these children first as females and then switch them in adulthood to males, is equally naive and simple-minded considering the complexities of social events in the child's and the parents' lives.

The recent controversy on the determinants of gender identity shows how tempted researchers and clinicians are to believe in a simple truth rather than a complex interaction that may vary, be modified, and be mutable from case to case. However, simple models will not yield answers to complex pheonomena.

Sex Differences of Behavior

Gender identity, as a complex and specifically human phenomenon, may not be the most suitable aspect of gender on which to examine the interaction between biological and psychological variables. Sex-dimorphic behavior, encompassing those aspects of personality, play behavior, and temperament in which boys and girls and subsequently men and women differ, may be a more appropriate focus.

In the area of gender-related behavior, of all the constitutional variables to consider, sex hormones are of particular importance. Therefore, it is the field of behavioral endocrinology with its focus on the interplay between hormones and behavior that needs to be singled out for this discussion. Since behavioral endocrinology has made rapid advances over the past several decades, I will present a very brief discourse into some of the new knowledge that is relevant to the future study of human gender-related behavior.

Behavioral Endocrinology and Neuroendocrinology

In a recent historical overview, Frank Beach (1981) divides the field of behavioral endocrinology into three phases: The predisciplinary era (1850–1900), the formative era (1900 to the decade between 1950 and 1960), and the modern era (the post-1960 period, when the development of new methodology resulted in an increase in the amount of empirical evidence available). Within behavioral endocrinology, the research on mammalian sexual differentiation is the most exciting area for the study of human gender-related behavior. The emerging evidence is predominantly based on the study of rats, mice, guinea pigs, and nonhuman primates. The methodology of studying the relationship of hormones and behavior in nonhuman mammalian sexual differentiation has become highly sophisticated, including an increase in the number of species studied, the expansion of the type of behavioral patterns investigated, the multiplication of the types of hormones studied, and particularly the biochemical techniques for measuring and controlling endocrine variables.

In addition, there has been major progress in the area of neuroendocrinology. Over the last 100 years, it has been believed that hormonal effects have to be mediated via the central nervous system (CNS). In the modern era, our knowledge has been advanced in a number of different aspects, including the localization of structural sex differences in the brain, the identification of steroid-receptive cells, and the determination of effects of behaviorally significant hormones on neuronal metabolism. According to Beach, behavioral endocrinology is clearly on the way to an independent, mature discipline and will be established as such in the next 25 years or so.

Psychoendocrinology

Our knowledge of the psychoendocrinology of human gender-related behavior is much more fragmentary. Therefore, it is imperative that the knowledge gained on the basis of hormone-behavior relations in other species be taken as hypothesis-generating at most. Findings from such animal studies will then have to be put to a scrupulous test in human psychoendocrine studies and will most certainly have to match the sophisticated methodology used in the recent animal experimental work.

One of the important facts of psychoendocrinology is that there are distinct phases in development during which dramatic gender-specific hormonal changes occur. In the area of sexual differentiation in animals, we know most about the prenatal/neonatal phase and the time of sexual maturation, analogous to fetal development and puberty in the human life course. Animal experimentalists have paid much less attention to later phases of development; therefore, we have much less information to inspire research on the middle years or the aging process in human subjects.

The original so-called "central hypothesis" focused on the prominent role of androgens and particularly of testosterone as the most potent of all androgens. It was found that the presence of testosterone during a critical time of development is crucial for male sexual differentiation, whereas female sexual differentiation ensues in the absence of androgens. This principle was established in the study of normal animals and by hormonal modification of male and female animals: For instance, if you deprive a genetic male of androgen by castration or by treatment with an antagonist to testosterone (a so-called antiandrogen), the development of the reproductive tract proceeds along female lines. Conversely, if you provide the female fetus with androgen by injection during the critical time of differentiation, the genitals will become masculinized. Behavior differentiation has been shown to be controlled by the same principle in several subhuman species. The behaviors that have been measured in nonhuman mammals include both sexual behavior and nonreproductive behavior such as aggressive play fighting, activity, maze learning, sensitivity to taste and pain, and other sexually dimorphic behavior traits. Different sets of behavior were modified differentially so that different types of change were distinguished as "defeminization" and "masculinization." Beach, Kuehn, Sprague, and Anisko (1972) define these terms as follows:

> *Masculinization* of the female refers to the induction of anatomical, physiological or behavioral characters or traits which normally are well developed in males but lacking or poorly developed in females. *Defeminization* signifies partial or complete inhibition of traits normally well developed in females but absent or weakly developed in males. (p. 159)

The importance of distinguishing between so-called masculinization and defeminization became clear when it was found that hormones could modify different behavior sets, that is, so-called masculine behavior sets could be augmented in females by the exposure to androgens without cancelling out behavior patterns typical for females and vice versa.

The central hypothesis of organization also implies a *critical time phase* during which sex hormones can alter CNS differentiation during development. In lower mammals, this phase has been established as prenatal or neonatal, while in nonhuman primates it is limited to the prenatal developmental phase.

More recently, our knowledge has been advanced in terms of the way testosterone exerts its influence on the brain and of the importance of other sex hormones. From the work of experimental neuroendocrinologists, we now know that testosterone exerts its effects upon the developing brain in the rat through two pathways: The first is by being transformed into estrogen and by binding to specific estrogen receptors, a process called *aromatization*; the second pathway is by so-called 5 α-reductase through the reduction of testosterone to non-aromatizible androgens which bind to different androgen receptors (McEwen, 1983).

We have also learned that the modification of different behaviors is under the influence of different actions on the brain level and that the various sex hormones can antagonize each other; for instance, progesterone can act as an antiandrogen if injected at certain times in development and at certain dose levels.

While the role of sex hormones during prenatal/neonatal times has been described as *organizational* (which means they influence CNS differentiation permanently), sex hormones during adulthood have been labeled as *activational*, suggesting that they can activate behavior that was preorganized during an earlier phase of development. Sex hormones in adulthood have a facilitative effect on sex-related responses. In other words (e.g., in the rat) androgen is needed for the expression of male behavior and will occur if the normal output of testosterone from the animal's testes occurs or if castrated in adulthood and injected with androgen. However, this effect will only occur if the male fetus and neonate was not deprived of androgen at the critical time of CNS differentiation. The hormonal effect in adulthood, therefore, has been termed *temporary* and *reversible*, in contrast to the permanent and developmental action of the same hormone during fetal differentiation.

Another important principle that has been added through the study of mammalian sexual differentiation is the interactional or reciprocal aspect of hormone–environment relations. This principle encompasses the fact that environmental conditions can affect hormonal levels as seen, for instance, in the fact that testosterone decreases if a male monkey loses a dominant position in a hierarchy of social relations. This is analogous to the research on human behavior that suggests that physical or psychological stress lowers testosterone values temporarily. Another example is the well-known observation that women's menstrual cycle is affected by travel, nutrition, and even by living with other females in a dormitory situation (McClintock, 1971).

Now let us examine what is known about the application of these principles to the study of human gender-related behavior. We know that one cannot generalize from one species to the next, since rats and monkeys already differ in some important ways from each other. The question is rather whether one should include any of these established principles of hormones and behavior in nonhuman mammals as researchable hypotheses in the study of human gender-related behavior. I would suggest that one has to pay attention to hormonal variables in order to explain important developmental sequences provided, of course, that (1) one does not generalize from animal behavior but puts the observation to vigorous tests of human behavior; (2) one is not seduced by a main-effect model but applies transactional thinking; and (3) one uses the sophisticated methods developed by behavioral endocrinologists for measuring hormones in animal behavior. We also must focus on clearly defined behavior units rather than global and complex units, and we must never forget that biological markers are as modifiable as learned behavior.

What do we know so far about the roles of hormones in human sexual differentiation? Endocrine research has established that the role of sex hormones on the differentiation of reproductive and sex organs follows much the same principles as in lower mammals, that is, the male fetus is exposed to much higher levels of androgens from the output of his own testes. The basic structures of the sex organs are bipotential. If anything interferes with the action of androgens during human fetal development, a genetic male will be born with female-looking external genitalia, and if a genetic female is exposed to high levels of androgens either by maternal drugs or from her own overactive adrenal glands, she will be born with a more or less developed penis and an empty scrotum. The critical time seems to be the second trimester of pregnancy. These facts are reasonably well established.

However, the information on hormonal effects on the human CNS is speculative at this point. Up to now, all we can go by is the suggestive evidence mostly based on clinical groups of girls and boys who have a documented history of abnormal levels of sex hormones during prenatal development and whose gender-related behavior was studied at different age levels and compared with normal controls. The main findings of that research can be stated as follows (see reviews by Ehrhardt & Meyer-Bahlburg, 1981; Money & Ehrhardt, 1972): Girls who were exposed to unusually high levels of androgen during their prenatal development were found to show high levels of physically energetic outdoor play behavior and low levels of nurturant behavior in terms of parenting rehearsal. They were significantly different in these respects from matched normal controls and, in a separate study, from their endocrinologically normal sisters. The behavior was long term and could not be solely explained by the various social and environmental factors assessed. In a number of separate studies, prenatal exposure to pharmacological doses of estrogen and progesterone was assessed, and it was found that those sex hormones were associated with the expected opposite effect, namely, relatively less physically energetic play behavior and an increase in more nurturant behavior as exhibited in doll play and infant care in girls and in less aggressive play behavior in boys. This finding could be interpreted as an antiandrogenic effect of some of the estrogen/progesterone compounds, analogous to some of the actions of these hormones demonstrated in animal experiments.

The behavior differences between the samples of girls and boys exposed to abnormal levels of sex hormones during gestation and normal control groups happen to be those that are believed to be the cornerstone of so-called masculine and feminine behavior of normal females and males, as suggested in the review by Maccoby and Jacklin (1974). Therefore, it is customary to speak in terms of behavior masculinization and feminization by the exposure to androgens and other sex hormones. As is well known, the behavior of human males and females is largely overlapping, and when we refer to sex differences, we are referring to mean differences between groups. The terms *masculine* and *feminine* are unfortunate, since they are often erroneously taken to be a true dichotomy, which does not exist. The terminology is similarly misleading when we divide the major sex hormones into so-called male and female hormones. Androgens, estrogens, and progesterone occur in both sexes, albeit in different quantities and different ratios.

The behavior variation within one gender is often wider than between the genders. Therefore, it may well be that the studies on clinical populations may ultimately point to more interesting relationships between levels of sex hormones and temperamental differences *within* rather than *between* gender.

Hormonal and Social Interaction

Rather than examining in more detail the evidence on psychoendocrine relations in the development of human sex differences, we can suggest the ways in which hormones might interact with social and environmental stimuli. For instance, if high levels of prenatal androgens are indeed associated with physical, energetic, rough-and-tumble play in normal children, what conclusion can be drawn from such a contingency? It certainly does not mean that prenatal androgens *determine* this particular play behavior independent of the social environment in which a child grow up. Rather, it may mean a predisposition to learn certain behaviors more readily.

If, for instance, the child is a boy and has been exposed to relatively high levels of prenatal androgen from his own testicular production during prenatal differentiation, and if he then meets strong cultural reinforcements from his parents, peers, and school that reward physically active play behavior and athletic pursuits, the probability of the expression of that behavior is greatly increased. If the child is a girl who has a history of relatively high levels of prenatal androgens (although within the normal range for females), she may therefore have a predisposition to physically energetic play behavior, but if she grows up in a family where this kind of behavior is not reinforced or is even suppressed, she is less likely to exhibit rough-and-tumble play. Traditionally, Western society has reinforced rough-and-tumble play in boys and doll play and infant care in girls, but this socialization process may not be the most opportune for our changing society.

The model suggested by Alice Rossi (1977) regarding parenting and nurturant behavior, may also apply to physical, energetic play behavior. Rossi suggested that it might be more advantageous for a society such as ours, in which both men and women share most occupational roles, to provide equal preparation for family roles. One might even institute the opposite social reinforcement approach, namely, to expose boys more to nurturant situations than girls in a pattern Rossi calls ''compensatory learning.'' The end result might be that both sexes would be equally adept in both parental and work roles. Regarding the predisposition for physically energetic rough-and-tumble play, one may follow the same reasoning, namely, active play behavior such that sports and athletics would be more encouraged and reinforced in girls than in boys. In fact, there are more opportunities today for girls to participate in athletics and highly competitive sports than in the past, and the gap between the sexes in some areas of sports is narrowing. To continue in our developmental sequence, a predisposition toward physical, energetic play augmented by prenatal androgen and reinforced by society for participation in competitive sports has much wider implications for behavior development than just a proficiency in that particular athletic pursuit. Being part of a team, learning to compete, and having experience in both winning and losing enhances qualities that may develop competence and assertiveness in adult occupational and family roles.

Thus, a hormonal factor at one point in development is surely not the determinant of a complex behavior at a much later point in the life course. However, it may present one of the links in a long chain of events leading to the expression of a specific trait. But even if that kind of developmental sequence can be analyzed for a specific behavior set, it clearly does not mean that there is only one pathway for the expression of the same behavior. For instance, while prenatal androgen may predispose to rough-and-tumble play, it requires special social environmental reinforcement for the behavior expression to occur. The same behavior pattern may be developed in an individual with a relatively low level of prenatal androgens with a different, more strongly reinforcing social environment. The pliability of the human organism is such that *many* pathways during the life course lead to similar behavior sets.

One of the crucial developmental crossroads is puberty. At this developmental point, we do not know what the relationship is between variations in levels of prenatal hormones and pubertal hormones within the same person. For instance, it is unknown whether females with relatively high levels of prenatal androgen also secret relatively high levels of androgen in adulthood. Therefore, if a correlation between a hormonal factor and adult behavior is found, we do not know whether this relationship had hormonal precursors early in the development of that individual. Equally, we do not know whether the behavior affects the hormone levels or whether the hormonal factors precede the behavior, since the interaction between hormones and behavior is reciprocal. A good example of this point is the recent observation that testosterone is correlated with the occupational status of women. In a careful study of 55 normal females, Purifoy and Koopmans (1980) assessed their serum androstenedione, testosterone, testosterone-binding globulin, and free testosterone. These hormones are all different androgens. To measure more than one of these hormones increases the accuracy of assessment. The authors found that, independent of age, women in professional, managerial, and technical occupations had higher levels of all androgens, (i.e., androstenedione, testosterone, and free-testosterone) than women clerical workers and housewives.

Within the framework of old simple minded, now outdated, thinking, one might assume a simple cause-and-effect model stating that high levels of androgen in women determine their job status. Within a more sophisticated biosocial framework, one might instead hypothesize that the observed relationship is an indication of a complex interplay of hormones and behavior over time. For some of these women, it may reflect a developmental sequence that started in prenatal life with a relatively high level of androgen that predisposes them to learn to expend high levels of physical energy in play and sports. They may have been fortunate to live in a social environment that fostered this predisposition. Within a larger societal context, such women grew up at a time when full-time professional careers for women were permissible and socially reinforced, and they might have had a family and school environment that fostered their interest in such occupational roles. At puberty, these women might or might not have started to produce relatively high levels of androgen during their menstrual cycle, and eventually they might have excelled in a professional career. On the other hand, some or all of these women might not have had a particular hormonal pattern during prenatal or pubertal development at all but underwent a developmental sequence that was strongly influenced by social reinforcement for professional careers. Ultimately, fulfilling such an occupational status might have increased their androgen production via a feedback effect of their work upon their endocrine system. The point is that hormonal factors can play different roles in a complex interplay of many variables within a particular developmental sequence. Hence, a correlation between a specific hormone level and a particular behavior pattern has to be seen as a contingency that may signal a whole network of different transactions that vary from one individual to another.

The Purifoy and Koopmans study demonstrates several features that reflect more sophisticated thinking in human psychoendocrinology. Not only did they measure more than *one* androgen and apply up-to-date and sophisticated biochemical methodology, but their interpretation allowed for the various possibilities of transactions between hormones and behavior. Furthermore, not only did they take occupational status as *one* behavior variable, but they attempted to classify the different careers and found that different androgens seem to be associated with different types of jobs. For instance, androstenedione and free testosterone were associated with the degree of job complexity in relation to *people*, whereas testosterone significantly correlated with the degree of job complexity in relation to *things*. It is too early to draw any conclusions from this finding, but it does point to a very important rule to follow in modern psychoendocrine studies. Endocrinologists have become more and more sophisticated in breaking down the specific sex hormones they measure, but they must also be very specific regarding the behavioral units they assess.

The history of psychoendocrinology is full of dead-end investigations because the behavior under study was too complex and, therefore, different studies came up with contradictory findings. Mood changes in relation to the menstrual cycle in women is a good example. Older studies assessed mood changes in women, correlated them with the various sex hormones over their menstrual cycle, and disregarded what else went on in the lives of the women at the same time. A more sophisticated study that exemplifies the transactional approach was conducted by Alice and Peter Rossi (1977), who looked at mood patterns in relationship to two time dimensions—body time (as indexed by the female menstrual cycle) and social time (as measured by the calendar week). The complexity of their study enabled them to demonstrate individual variations of mood in relation to personality factors, phase of the menstrual cycle, and whether a specific phase of the cycle fell on week days or the weekend.

Conclusion

The study of gender requires a biosocial approach that includes knowledge from various disciplines. Behavior needs to be viewed as the end product of a complex interplay of many variables that interact with each other. Such transactional thinking may shed light on long-term developmental sequences in the areas of sex-dimorphic behavior and sexuality. It may also advance our knowledge of the etiological roots of sexual orientation and preference, and it may give us insight into change of behavior over time. If this new approach is followed, we may look forward to an exciting era in psychoendocrinology, developmental psychology, and the sociology of the life course.

References

Beach, F. A. Historical origins of modern research on hormones and behavior. *Hormones and behavior*, 1981, *15*, 325–376.

Beach, F. A., Kuehn, R. E., Sprague, R. H., & Anisko, J. J. Coital behavior in dogs—XI. Effects of androgenic stimulation during development on masculine mating responses in females. *Hormones and Behavior*, 1972, *3*, 143–168.

Ehrhardt, A. A., & Meyer-Bahlburg, H. F. L. Effects of prenatal sex hormones on gender-related behavior. *Science*, 1981, *211*, 1312–1318.

Ellis, A. The sexual psychology of human hermaphrodites. *Psychosomatic Medicine*, 1945, *7*, 108–125.

Imperato-McGinley, J., Peterson, R. E., Gautier, T., & Sturla, E. Androgens and the evolution of male-gender identity among male pseudohermaphrodites with 5α-reductase deficiency. *The New England Journal of Medicine*, 1979, *300*, 1233–1237.

McClintock, M. K. Menstrual synchrony and suppression. *Nature*, 1971, *229*, 244–245.

Maccoby, E. E., & Jacklin, C. N. *The psychology of sex differences*. Stanford: Stanford University Press, 1974.

McEwen, B. S. Gonadal steroidal influences in brain development and sexual differentiation. In R. O. Greep (Ed.), *Reproductive physiology IV, International review of physiology* (Vol. 27). Baltimore: University Park Press, 1983, pp. 99–145.

Meyer-Bahlburg, H. F. L. Hormones and psychosexual differentiation: Implications for the management of intersexuality, homosexuality and transsexuality. *Clinics in Endocrinology and Metabolism*, 1982, *11*, 681–701.

Money, J. Psychologic approach to psychosexual misidentity with elective mutism: Sex reassignment in two cases of hyperadrenocortical hermaphroditism. *Clinical Pediatrics*, 1968, *7*, 331–339.

Money, J. Search for the causes of sexual preference. *Contemporary Psychology*, 1982, *27*, 503–505.

Money, J., & Ehrhardt, A. A. *Man & woman, boy & girl.* Baltimore, Maryland: Johns Hopkins University Press, 1972.

Money, J., Hampson, J. G., & Hampson, J. L. An examination of some basic sexual concepts: The evidence of human hermaphroditism. *Bulletin of The Johns Hopkins Hospital*, 1955, *97*, 301–319. (a)

Money, J., Hampson, J. G., & Hampson, J. L. Hermaphroditism: Recommendations concerning assignment of sex, change of sex, and psychologic management. *Bulletin of The Johns Hopkins Hospital*, 1955, *97*, 284–300. (b)

Purifoy, F. E., & Koopmans, L. H. Androstenedione, T and free T concentrations in women of various occupations. *Social Biology*, 1980, *26*, 179–188.

Rossi, A. S. A biosocial perspective on parenting. *Daedalus, Journal of the American Academy of Arts and Sciences*, 1977, *106*, 1–31.

Rossi, A. S., & Rossi, P. E. Body time and social time: Mood patterns by menstrual cycle phase and day of week. *Social Science Research*, 1977, *6*, 273–308.

Rubin, R. T., Reinisch, J. M., & Haskett, R. F. Postnatal gonadal steroid effects on human behavior. *Science*, 1981, *211*, 1318–1324.

Samaroff, A. J., & Chandler, M. J. Reproductive risk and the continuum of caretaking causality. In F. D. Horowitz (Ed.), *Review of child development research* (Vol. 4). Chicago: The University of Chicago Press, 1975, pp. 187–244.

6

The Subjective Experience of
Life-Span Transitions

CAROL D. RYFF
Fordham University

Introduction

Life-span changes can be explored on many levels, including the study of externally observable status transitions, biological transformations, or internal psychological experiences. In this chapter, I focus on the latter, the "inner side" of life-span development. The emphasis is on how people think about themselves as they go through various life transitions and whether they have a personal sense of change or stability in themselves as they age. Three perspectives guide the theoretical and empirical research that is presented. First, the work has evolved within a psychological framework, meaning that the analysis has been on the level of the individual rather than the group or societal level. However, useful instruction regarding the influence of societal expectations or group norms on life-span development has been provided by sociological colleagues (Brim, 1966; Hogan, 1981; Neugarten & Hagestad, 1976). Second, the research is anchored within a phenomenological tradition. Given the multiple conceptions of phenomenology within the social sciences (Berger & Luckmann, 1967; Giorgi, 1976; Schutz, 1967; Spiegelberg, 1972; Valle & King, 1978), the significance of such an orientation is not immediately clear. In the present context, it is tied to a concern for understanding personal experience, personal choice, the meaning of experience for the individual, and the connection of experience to the everyday world, the life world. In a separate work (Ryff, in press-b), I have reviewed the history of this perspective and examined its theoretical and methodological implications for the study of personal development in adulthood and aging. Third, questions pertaining to the personal experience of change have been operationalized within the personality realm. That is, self-perceived change has been examined in terms of one's personal characteristics such as the need for achievement, social recognition, or dominance. These and other dimensions of personality have been the research variables of interest.

97

The following section provides a brief review of the adult personality literature as it relates to self-perceived changes in personal development. This literature has been criticized for its use of stage models as well as for being inappropriate to the lives of women. These criticisms are discussed. The next section summarizes our program of research and details key findings on the subjective experience of change, noting where such changes differed for men and women. The final section outlines future research directions aimed at fusing the inside experience with the outside evidence of life-span transitions.

Adult Personality Development

The literature on adult personality development reveals a number of works that have proposed developmental transitions or stages. For example, Erik Erikson (1950, 1959) formulated a psychosocial stage model that outlined the primary crises for the expanding ego from birth through old age. The ego challenge of middle age, generativity vs. stagnation, reflects a concern for establishing and guiding the next generation and emphasizes qualities such as productivity and creativity. Developmentally, the prediction is that one moves beyond the self-directed concerns of identity prominent in adolescence and the interpersonal concerns of intimacy prominent in young adulthood to the phase of sharing one's knowledge and skill with younger individuals and assuming leadership and decision-making roles. These proposed changes are largely unexplored empirically. The final stage, integrity vs. despair, is perhaps the most elusive and enticing of Erikson's stages. Many aspects of integrity have been identified: Emotional integration, accepting one's life cycle as something that had to be, adapting oneself to the triumphs and disappointments of being, possessing a love of humankind rather than self, and achieving a spiritual sense that eliminates the fear of death. According to the theory, one faces the challenge of ego integrity in old age.

Other models of personality development have paralleled or elaborated the stages proposed by Erikson. Jung (1933) wrote about the process of self-illumination in old age, which referred to a turning inward to reflect about the meaning of life. Similarly, Charlotte Buhler (1935) formulated basic life tendencies that work toward the fulfillment of life. Creative expansion, the eminent tendency of adulthood, referred to goals of advancing in the world and changing it creatively through physical or mental activities. Upholding internal order, the life tendency of old age was composed of different ordering principles that worked toward the unity of personality and behavior. Such principles are found in the integrating operations of goals, ideals, and self-assessments. Among contemporary scholars, Neugarten (1968, 1973) elaborated the personality challenges of middle age and old age. She proposed the "executive processes" of middle age that included qualities such as self-awareness, selectivity, manipulation and control of the environment, mastery, and competence. Individuals of this age viewed the environment as rewarding risk-taking and boldness. In contrast, the older person was seen as more conforming and accommodative to outer-world demands. This inward-turning was described as the process of interiority, or as the active-to-passive mastery sequence (see also Gutmann, 1977). More recently, the works of Levinson (1978), Gould (1978), and Vaillant (1977) have formulated personality transitions that individuals experience in the second half of life. A further array of popular works such as those by Sheehy (1976, 1981), Scarf (1980), and Rubin (1979) detail personality changes from the thirties to the sixties.

The above literature has been criticized from many perspectives as, for example, by those who argue that there is no essential change in personality in the second half of life (Costa & McCrae, 1980). Two other criticisms, pertinent to the present research, will be discussed in greater detail. First, the previous perspectives represent, either implicitly or explicitly, stage models. They formulate progressions of change that follow orderly, sequential patterns. Such models have generated much discussion as well as clashing of swords within the life-span developmental realm (Baltes, 1979; Brim & Kagan, 1980; Labouvie-Vief & Chandler, 1978). Essentially, stage theory has been criticized for being too rigid and restrictive, for requiring sequences of change that are undirectional, irreversible, hierarchical, universal, and so on. Such requirements were less difficult to meet as one followed the biological growth and development of the child, but when applied to adulthood and aging, the requirements flew in the face of individual differences, cohort effects, social change, and personal idiosyncracies. Thus, there ensued a period of berating stage models, accompanied by arguments that there is no overarching ground plan to adult development (Neugarten, 1979). Those who continued to endorse stage models were deemed naive and had to suffer the embarrassment of advocating theories that were uncommonly neat and tidy. However, since my graduate work I had had a fascination with the progressions of change described by Erikson, Buhler, Jung, and others. What accounted for the continued commitment to fleshing out and extending these works despite the waves of disparagement? Clearly, it was not that they were orderly, neat, and tidy. The attraction rather was that they formulated spiraling progressions of *improvement* for the individual. Each theorist had formulated ways in which the individual could continue to develop, become more differentiated, and function at a higher level. It was this quality, these spiraling progressions of improvement, that captured and sustained my interest. Admittedly, such conceptions of personal improvement are likely to be sprinkled with individual differences, cohort effects, and cultural variability, but such effects do not discount the impact these models have as guiding ideals that influence what people become and how they develop. Such images of human fulfillment (see Ryff, 1982b, in press-a) are central to understanding how we conceive of life-span development. Thus, in the study of these cultural ideals and their influence on people's self-perceptions, our current program of research has been substantially guided by stage models of adult personality development.

The above theories have also been faulted for neglecting sex differences, or more precisely, for representing male experience and a male perspective on development. Many of the preceding studies were formulated or conducted by men and were based on male samples. What, then, is their relevance for women? Barnett and Baruch (1978) argued several years ago that the works of Erikson and Levinson did not fit the experience of women. Male experience involves more emphasis on chronological age as a key variable and on continuous, uninterrupted series of events in family and occupational realms. Women's lives, in their view, involve varying role patterns not so centrally tied to chronological age. Numerous combinations of career, marriage, and children may exist, each with unique patterns of timing and commitment. Gilligan (1979, 1982) has strengthened this argument, contending that we have become accustomed to "seeing life through men's eyes" (1979, p. 432). Male life and male experience have implicitly been adopted as the norm. Women's development, in her view, is more intricately tied to human relationships. As such, women place more emphasis on attachments, intimacy, nurturance, and caring across the life cycle. Gilligan further objects to the temporal patterning of psychological changes as formulated by male theorists. Generativity, for example, is perhaps experienced by women earlier in the life cycle and sustained as a prominent concern thereafter. Useful summaries of these and other related issues are provided in Giele (1982) and Rossi (1980). Taken together, the perspectives raise numerous questions regarding the relevance of the aforementioned theories for women.

In summary, theories of adult personality development have proposed a variety of changes or transitions that people experience in the second half of life. Others have faulted these perspectives for overstating the magnitude of change, for ignoring the wide variability evident in adult behavior, and for being overly influenced by male experience. The following section will provide a brief overview of how our program of research addresses these issues.

Empirical Findings on Personality Development
Seen from the Inside

Our program of research has investigated whether people *see themselves changing* in the ways that have been described by the previous stage models. For example, do adults see themselves as being more concerned with intimacy in young adulthood, generativity in middle age, and integrity in old age? Do they see their middle years spent pursuing achievements, social status, and recognition, while their later years are a time for greater reflectiveness and searching for internal meaning in their lives? When it comes to the second half of life, one might argue that stages or transitions have their most significant, profound impact on the internal, subjective level. The history of aging research (Reinert, 1979) has repeatedly suggested that development in the adult years is more intrapsychic, concerned with self-knowledge, and self-awareness. Early aging researchers such as the Buhlers (1935) were aware of this as evidenced in their studies of reminiscence, biographies, and personal documents, though they were not working in climates receptive to such inquiry (see Baltes, Reese, & Lipsitt, 1980). Thus, subjectively experienced transitions may be powerfully important in understanding adult development. They may respond to people's needs to organize and make sense of their lives. Whether such internal patterns show nomothetic, systematic trends or are characterized by individual differences (including sex differences) is, of course, an empirical question, and one that we have tried to illuminate.

The work conducted thus far has attempted to map the descriptive content of personal experiences of change. The guiding question has been whether people see themselves changing in ways suggested by Erikson, Buhler, Jung, etc. In terms of methodology, we have used structured, self-report inventories, that is, standardized personality questionnaires. These procedures do not allow for the richness and spontaneity of unstructured interviews and may, therefore, be seen as contrary to our phenomenological orientation. We argue, however, that phenomenology does not prescribe a particular methodology, and that there are trade-offs in any choice of procedure. Standardized questionnaires make explicit the bias and preconceptions of the researcher, they minimize variability in the participants' level of articulateness, and they improve the possibilities for subsequent refutation or replication of the findings. On the other hand, such procedures do not capture the experience of change in the person's own words and may, therefore, miss important perceptions, events, or concerns. Though our first studies have utilized standardized procedures, for the reasons cited above, we are aware of their limitations. Our long-term research goals are, in fact, to utilize both quantitative and qualitative methods, thereby drawing on the unique strengths of each in furthering understanding of life-span transitions.

Self-perceived *change* has been investigated through instructional variation. That is, participants have completed the personality inventories according to varying instructions aimed at assessing how they see themselves in the present (concurrent instruction), what they recall they were like in the past (retrospective instruction), and what they anticipate they might be like in the future (prospective instruction). The comparisons among these responses are then used to provide a measure of subjective change. The data are analyzed with an analysis of variance paradigm, including the following factors: Age, sex, and temporal focus. The latter factor refers to the instructional variation, that is, participants were asked to think of themselves in the present or to focus on a past or future age period. More detailed discussions of design, sampling, and measurement procedures are provided in the published studies. For present purposes, the focus is on key questions and findings.

Self-Perceived Change in Values

A first study (Ryff & Baltes, 1976) examined self-perceived change in the domain of values. The question was whether adults perceived that their values had, or possibly would, change as they aged. The Rokeach model of values (1973), which differentiates between instrumental and terminal values, was employed. Instrumental values refer to desirable modes of conduct, such as being ambitious, capable, courageous. Terminal values refer to desirable end-states of existence, such as having a sense of accomplishment, freedom, or happiness. When considered in the context of developmental theories, particularly the description of the executive processes of middle age (Neugarten, 1968), which stressed qualities such as being active, controlling, achievement-oriented, and the old-aged literature on turning inward, becoming more reflective and contemplative (Buhler, 1935; Jung, 1933; Neugarten, 1973), we hypothesized instrumental values would be salient in middle age and terminal values would be prominent in old age. The hypothesis of subjective change was that individuals would see themselves changing in accord with this transition. Two groups of women, one middle-aged ($n = 57$, average age $= 43.1$) and one old-aged ($n = 62$; average age $= 70.4$), rated their values under various concurrent, retrospective, and prospective instructional conditions. The findings revealed that middle-aged women had a comparatively higher preference for instrumental values in the present, and they anticipated a decline in this preference in old age. The older women showed a comparatively lower preference for instrumental values in the present, though they recalled such values had been more important when they were middle-aged. As the instrument was ipsative in nature (i.e., scores on instrumental values determined scores on terminal values), the reverse change patterns were obtained for terminal value preferences. Thus, this study supported the prediction of age differences in value preferences, and moreover, it indicated that women saw themselves changing in accord with these differences.

A Replication and Extension

A second study (Ryff, 1982a) attempted to replicate the previous finding as well as examine its relevance for men. Participants were 160 individuals divided equally by age and sex. The middle-aged range extended from 40 to 55 years (average age $= 46.7$) and the old-aged participants were all over 60 years (average age $= 70.3$). As predicted, women again gave greater priority preference to instrumental values (and thereby lower preference to terminal values) during middle age than old age, and they perceived themselves changing in the same fashion. The replication was interesting given the sampling differences between the two studies, since the earlier study included highly educated groups, and the second had more representative educational levels. A similar outcome was not, however, obtained for men. Their overall priority preferences were for terminal values during both age periods. This finding was somewhat surprising given that men are stereotypically viewed as instrumental and achievement-oriented. Perhaps the stereotype does not fit with their self-perceptions. From a developmental perspective, it is possible that men shift from instrumental to terminal values at an earlier period in the life span than is true for women.

The above study also investigated subjective change in the personality realm. To identify aspects of personality that might change in the middle-to old-age transition, the relevant personality theories were again reviewed. Descriptions of middle age emphasized traits such as being independent, bold, active, achievement-oriented, energetic, controlled, and powerful. The description of old age emphasized characteristics such as being reflective, philosophical, contemplative, accepting, accommodating, hedonistic, and nonwork oriented. Following from these summaries, personality inventories were sought that could operationalize the characteristics of interest. For example, the scales of achievement, dominance, social recognition, and play were selected from the Personality Research Form (Jackson, 1967). The former three were predicted to be most salient in self-descriptions focused on middle age, while the latter (play) was predicted to be more salient in old age. Because these scales were predicted to show perceived changes, they were jointly referred to as Developmental Scales. To differentiate personality characteristics showing subjective change from those showing perceived stability, four Control Scales were also administered. These included measures of abasement, defendence, impulsivity, and order—qualities that had not been emphasized in the previous theoretical descriptions. The prediction was that participants would not see themselves changing on these dimensions in the middle- to old-age transition.

The expected outcomes for the Developmental Scales were obtained but only for middle-aged men. Their current scores on achievement, dominance, and social recognition were higher than the ratings of older men, and they anticipated that these qualities would become less salient to them in old age. Also as predicted, the play scale showed the reverse pattern with scores being lower in middle age than old age. The older cohort of men, in contrast, did not see themselves changing on these qualities over time. Their scores on the Developmental Scales were low during both age periods. The outcomes for women were in the predicted direction but were not significant. That is, they had higher scores on achievement, dominance, and social recognition (while lower on play) for the middle-aged temporal focus than for the old-aged temporal focus. Finally, the Control Scales of abasement, defendence, impulsivity, and order showed no subjective change processes. As predicted, people did not see themselves changing on these dimensions as they aged.

Following a similar research design, Ryff and Migdal (1984) investigated self-perceived personality change in the transition from young adulthood to middle age. Theoretical guidance was provided by Erikson's description of intimacy as the psychosocial task of young adulthood and generativity as the psychosocial task of middle age. According to Erikson, intimacy refers to interpersonal relationships where close friendships, affiliations, sexual unions, and self-disclosure with significant others are salient. Generativity, as noted earlier, describes the transition to a broader social orientation, an interest in teaching and guiding younger generations, and a concern with improving the nature of society. As with the preceding studies, these constructs were operationalized with structured personality scales (Jackson, 1967, 1976). Intimacy was measured by scales of affiliation, interpersonal affect (valuing close emotional ties), and succorance (the ability to confide in and seek the support of others). Generativity was measured by scales of breadth of interest, dominance, and innovation (having productive and creative goals). Four Control Scales (abasement, anxiety, organization, risk-taking) were also administered with the aim of showing perceived stability. The usual concurrent, retrospective, and prospective instructions were employed, and the sample consisted of 100 women divided equally among young adulthood (18–30) and middle age (40–55).

As predicted, women of both age groups saw intimacy as being more salient in their self-assessments during young adulthood than during middle age. Thus, young adult women saw intimacy as more prominent in their present self-perceptions than they anticipated it would be when they reached middle age, while middle-aged women recalled that intimacy was more salient during young adulthood than at present. For the generativity scales, the middle-aged women rated themselves higher in the present than they recalled being in young adulthood, thereby supporting the hypothesis. The young adult women, however, showed the reverse pattern in which they saw generativity as more important to them in the present than they anticipated it would be in the future. Finally, the Control Scales supported the prediction of no systematic change in self-perceptions from young adulthood to middle age.

Taken together, the pattern of findings from these preliminary studies was rather mixed. The predicted subjective changes were obtained for some measures, some age groups, and occasionally for only one sex. Such outcomes might have reflected inherent variability in subjective change processes. While adults may see personal change in themselves over time, the experience may not be systematically organized by age or by personality dimension. It may be more idiographic in nature. Another interpretation is that the guiding developmental theories may not tap the key experiences of change. Perhaps more open-ended, exploratory procedures are necessary to identify the salient dimensions of change. A third explanation for the mixed findings was that the studies had not utilized assessment procedures that were good measures of the underlying theory. The scales employed had been developed for other purposes and populations and were, therefore, only approximations of the developmental processes of interest. Thus, the problem might have been one of operationalization. This third possibility served as a basis for the next study (Ryff & Heincke, 1983), which attempted a more direct empirical translation of the developmental dimensions guiding the research.

Subjective Change on Developmental Dimensions of Personality

Four dimensions of personality were selected as targets for scale construction. Two, generativity and integrity, came from Erikson's (1950) psychosocial stage theory of development. As noted before, generativity referred to having a concern for guiding the next generation and a sense of responsibility to those younger in age. Integrity was defined as adapting to the triumphs and disappointments of being and to viewing one's past life as inevitable, appropriate, and meaningful. The third dimension, complexity, was derived from Neugarten's (1968) discussion of the "executive processes" of personality in adulthood. It referred to being actively engaged in a complex environment and to selectively manipulating and controlling activities in multiple spheres. Interiority, the final dimension, described the "turning inward" that had been addressed by several theorists (Buhler, 1935; Jung, 1933; Neugarten, 1973). It referred to one who was freely relinquishing signs of external status and becoming more reflective, comtemplative, and individuated. The scale construction process is detailed in Ryff and Heincke (1983).

The predictions were that generativity and complexity would be prominent dimensions of personality in middle age, while integrity and interiority would be salient in old age. The sample consisted of 270 individuals divided by sex and age (i.e., young adulthood, 20–35; middle age, 40–55; old age, 65+). The young adults were included for comparative purposes. The measures were completed according to the usual concurrent, retrospective, and prospective instructions. The four Control Scales used previously (Ryff, 1982a) were also administered.

The predicted changes for the measures of generativity and integrity were supported. Participants rated themselves higher on generativity when focusing on middle age than on any other period. Thus, young adults anticipated becoming more generative in middle age, old-aged individuals recalled being more generative in middle age, and middle-aged persons scored higher on generativity in the present than they recalled being in young adulthood or anticipated being in old age. The integrity scores, in contrast, were highest for self-perceptions focused on old age. The finding meant that old persons currently rated themselves higher on integrity than they recalled being in the past, and that young adults and middle-aged individuals anticipated having more of the qualities of integrity in old age than they saw themselves having in the present.

The complexity scale revealed the highest scores among the middle-aged individuals as had been predicted, but the three age groups did not see themselves changing on this dimension over time. This outcome is perhaps related to the cohort issue (Baltes, Cornelius, & Nesselroade, 1978; Elder, 1981). Perhaps the juggling of multiple demands and responsibilities growing out of changing sex-role norms has left current middle-aged individuals, those caught between old and new role expectations, with a strong sense of complexity in themselves that appears to be stable over time. Interiority, the final scale, produced a wide range of individual differences. There seemed to be little consensus regarding the inevitability or desirability of becoming more inward in the later years. Finally, three of the four Control Scales replicated the earlier finding of perceived stability.

Summary and Implications of Previous Research

The preceding studies provide evidence that adults do have a subjective sense of change in themselves with age, and that these processes can be diffcrentiated from personality dimensions on which adults do not see change. Women in two studies (Ryff, 1982a; Ryff & Baltes, 1976) showed perceived change in values from an instrumental to a terminal orientation in the middle to old-age transition. Using existing, nondevelopmental inventories, two studies (Ryff, 1982a; Ryff & Migdal, in press) provided partial support for perceived change in the personality realm as well as support for perceived stability on Control Scales. A final study (Ryff & Heincke, 1983) constructed personality scales on the basis of developmental theory and using these measures found clear patterns of subjective change for the Eriksonian dimensions of generativity and integrity. The outcomes for the complexity and interiority scales were less clear, while the majority of Control Scales replicated the previous finding of perceived stability.

What do the above findings mean in light of the theoretical questions that opened this chapter—namely, what is the utility of stage theories of adult personality development, and what is the relevance of current research for women? With regard to the stage question, as we have examined it on the phenomenological level, the findings perhaps bolster all sides. There was evidence of systematic perceived change on certain theory-derived dimensions, including instrumental to terminal values and personality scales of intimacy, generativity, and integrity. These outcomes indicated that people do see themselves changing in ways proposed by developmental theories. On the other hand, a measure of complexity suggested cohort rather than an aging process, and the scale of interiority produced such wide individual differences as to imply idiosyncratic organization. Thus, all was not neat and tidy nor was there total lack of systematic variation. We are left, then, with data that do not allow for impassioned vindication or refutation of stage theory. The call rather is for moderation and an attentiveness to sorting out what aspects of stage theory do apply, when, and for whom? As noted earlier, our concern is as much with the question of human betterment, how it is conceptualized and assessed, as with the controversy surrounding stage theory.

Finally, the question of sex differences in adult personality processes also produced mixed findings. Initial studies found that men and women differed in terms of their perceived value changes and on certain personality dimensions. However, as we moved closer to developmental scales, that is, those constructed on the basis of developmental theory, sex differences dropped out of the findings. The patterns described in the final study did not differ by sex. Such outcomes suggest that certain aspects of Eriksonian theory may characterize the subjective experiences of both men and women. As with the stage theory issue, there is need to move beyond either/or posturing to more precise questions of which parts of what theories are or are not appropriate for men and for women? We would argue that equally important questions pertain to the significance of such changes for men and women. Are their transitions, whether experienced jointly or separately, adaptive? Do they represent improved functioning? In what domains of life? Are there maladaptive consequences for certain changes? Our data provide no answers to these questions. What we can say is that in the progression toward improved developmental measures, we saw sex differences disappear from the data. The processes of subjective change appeared to be organized around life stage rather than sex.

Future Research Directions

One might examine the above research on adults' recollections and anticipations about themselves and ask whether they matter? Do such changing self-perceptions have an impact, and if so, how? We have argued that past memories and future expectations say much about who one is and what one will become. The recalling of past selves may be a component of self-evaluation related to the general question of "am I getting better or worse?" As such, present adjustment may be influenced by subjective comparison with recalled selves. One can further distinguish between adaptive and maladaptive reconstructions (i.e., those that influence present feelings, motivations, and cognitions) in ways that are beneficial from those that have detrimental effects. These issues and others relate to the recent work on narratives of the self (Cohler, 1982; Gergen & Gergen, in press). In a similar vein, Peskin and Livson (1981) have studied the role of the past in adult psychological health and have discussed the process of discontinuous recoveries from the past.

There is also the question of impact with regard to future expectations. Looking ahead, or anticipating what one will be like in the future as obtained through prospective reports, may be related to the process of anticipatory socialization. Whether drawing on aging stereotypes or ideal types, the projection of oneself into the future may indicate a preparation or readiness for change and, as such, may be a partial determinant or what one becomes. Bandura (1977, 1982), for example, has shown that people's beliefs in or expectations about their own effectiveness influence their behavior on several levels including their choice of activities, the effort expended, and their persistence. When examined in a larger time frame, Sears (1981) has examined the role of expectancy in adaptation to aging, focusing on such topics as intellectual performance, family relations, and achievement motivation. Considered from these perspectives, retrospective and prospective reports provide insight as to how one maximally structures and uses the past as well as prepares for the future. Self-perceived change thus becomes not just a chronicling of subjective experience but a source of information about present and future functioning.

The above comments address the relevance of studying subjective change in and of itself. When the connection between subjective change and objective change is considered, the link between the outside and the inside realm of life transitions, additional avenues for research emerge. To begin with, one could examine the relationship between discrete, readily defined status transitions such as marriage, parenthood, and first job (see Hogan, 1981) and the subjective changes in personality we have investigated. Such research would examine how one's sense of personal change related to one's actual life experiences. To pursue such questions, we have looked at the personality changes adults report after experiencing particular life events such as parenthood. Fathers, for example, saw themselves as becoming more nurturant, less impulsive, more generative, and having a greater purpose in life after parenthood (Zeren & Ryff, 1983). We are currently conducting a similar study with women. Another study (Ryff & Dunn, 1983) has investigated the relationship between cumulative ratings of life events and personality development. Briefly, it was found that men's personality development scores are better predicted by their life-event ratings than women's. Perhaps, as Gilligan (1982) has suggested, women's development is more tied to human relationships than particular life events or status transitions. In combination, the above studies illustrate our interest in examining the connections between adults' life events and their changing perceptions of self.

A further line of research joining these two realms might be in the study of *discrepancies* between what occurs on the outside and what one feels on the inside. To simplify, the individual can have a sense of change or stability in self, and similarly, the social structure in terms of observable status transitions can evidence change or stability. When the two are coordinated, both showing either change or stability, we observe standard transitions or periods of tranquillity. However, when society sees the person as changing, going through a status transition, and yet the person feels no change, an interesting discrepancy occurs. Such instances probably point to life events that are overrated in terms of their psychological impact on the person. Menopause, empty nest, or certain career promotions may be such events where there are noticeable external changes, but their internal impact for certain individuals is of minimal significance. The other case of discrepancy occurs when the social order (one's social group, family, or community) sees stability and yet the person has an internal sense of change. In this instance, much is going on internally, though there are no obvious outside markers. The ubiquitous midlife crisis comes to mind, though it has received so much attention in recent years, one is hesitant to describe it as an invisible transition. These "hidden events" (see Brim & Ryff, 1980) often await the perceptive novelist to provide shape and form to the unseen transformation that has no external explanation or cultural label. Though such discrepancies carry a tone of trauma or turmoil for the individual, there may be more lighthearted examples by which people quietly mark their own aging process. One might reflect nostalgically, "yes, that was the era when we ate quiche, took vitamins, listened to Joan Baez, and drove the old beetle." These personal markers, though not the substance of typical social/psychological variables, may nonetheless be central to people's internal sense of change. Thus, subjective change may not always jibe with social structural change, and when it does not, we are in a position to learn about the emergence of new events and about the creation of personal, private transition markers.

The study of cohort effects in subjective processes is a kind of automatic question for life-span developmentalists. Rossi (1980) has persuasively criticized all of the previous literature on adult personality development for suffering from "cohort particularity." The findings from nearly all leading studies were based on people born between the 1920s and 1930s. Thus, generalizations are being drawn from the lives of individuals who grew up during the Depression, spent early adulthood in war, parented large families, were pioneers in suburbia, and so on. The knowledge of life-span development these studies provide may be based on a unique and distinctive cohort of men and women. Attending to the subjective side of cohort effects may, however, raise additional questions. Hareven (1983), for example, has written of changing perceptions of the life course. She has found that cohorts vary in how they segment the life course and what they view as key transitions. Older cohorts in her research were less conscious of stages, seeing only the transitions of marriage and first child or their emigration experience. Younger cohorts, on the other hand, were more conscious of timing, transition, and the segmentation of the life course. They relied more on the popular culture, such as the talk of midlife crisis and empty nest, to influence their timing perceptions. A related topic that we have pursued is cohort differences in the preferred timing of life transitions (Fallo-Mitchell & Ryff, 1982). Younger cohorts of women were found to prefer earlier ages for educational/occupational events and later ages for family events than older cohorts of women.

Further direction for historical analysis of subjective processes addresses our very definitions of personal development—how they evolve and are transformed over time (Ryff, in press-a). Conceptions of what it means to be fully developed, mature, fulfilled are inevitably time and culture bound; they are images of the ideal that are transformed over time. For example, current descriptions of personal growth and development as evident in the writings of Maslow (1968), Rogers (1961), and Allport (1961) emphasize such qualities as self-acceptance, self-knowledge, and openness to experience. These contrast markedly with ideal images from other eras (see Coan, 1977), such as in Christian writings from the Middle Ages in which the ultimate human qualities were saintliness, close contact with the divine, a concern for the welfare of others, a life of poverty, and unselfish love. Similarly, the contrast between Western and Eastern conceptions of human fulfillment shows an emphasis on individualism and rationality, in the one, and on intuition and the unity of the individual with nature, on the other. Apart from these surface comparisons are trends and countertrends in contemporary conceptions of human development. For example, competing ideologies of individualism and interdependence are much a part of current attempts to define ultimate human goals (Waterman, 1981). In response to the views of Maslow, Rogers, and other contributors to the human potential movement comes the argument that our era has become one of intense subjectivity in which individuals are preoccupied with self-development, realization of potential, sexual and psychological fulfillment (Etzioni, 1982; Lasch, 1978; Nisbet, 1982). Such preoccupations are seen as crippling the family and our social institutions. What is needed, from this perspective, are human ideals of cooperative interdependence, commitment, and an ability to delay gratification. Thus, even present conceptions of human fulfillment are in flux, changing, and evolving as a function of prevailing ideologies. Despite their changing character, these images are ideals toward which individuals strive as they progress through their lives and, as such, take on profound importance. Kenneth Boulding, in his book *The Image* (1956), captured the need for studying such topics. In his words, "it is the fall of the ideal image that leads to the collapse of empires and the decay of cultures" (p. 145). Whether examined on the level of the individual, as we have done here, or of the society, as in changing views of utopias (e.g., Morawski, 1982), the ideal image tells much of who we are and where we are going.

To summarize, future research in this area might usefully combine questions of subjectively experienced developmental change with studies of the actual events or critical experiences in people's lives so as to illuminate where outside changes are producing inside changes, and, alternatively, where inside changes are leading to external transitions. In addition, research on possible discrepancies between these two realms will advance understanding of transitional events that have minimal significance for the individual as well as identify emergent, culturally unlabeled events and the private markers people use to identify their own transitions. Finally, thoughtful historical analysis of change and transformation in guiding developmental ideals will elucidate the larger cultural images that set many of these processes in motion. In pursuing such research, knowledge of life-span development will be advanced both with regard to its external contours and in terms of its internal meaning for the individual.

References

Allport, G. W. *Pattern and growth in personality*. New York: Holt, Rinehart & Winston, 1961.

Baltes, P. B. Life-span developmental psychology: Some converging observations on history and theory. In P. B. Baltes & O. G. Brim, Jr. (Eds.), *Life-span development and behavior* (Vol. 2). New York: Academic Press, 1979, pp. 256–279.

Baltes, P. B., Cornelius, S. W., & Nesselroade, J. R. Cohort effects in behavioral development: Theoretical and methodological perspectives. In W. A. Collins (Ed.), *Minnesota symposium on child psychology* (Vol. 11). Hillsdale, N. J.: Erlbaum, 1978, pp. 256–279.

Baltes, P. B., Reese, H. W., & Lipsitt, L. P. Life-span developmental psychology, *Annual Review of Psychology*, 1980, *31*, 65–110.

Bandura, A. Self-efficacy: Toward a unifying theory of behavioral change. *Psychological Review*, 1977, *84*, 191–215.

Bandura, A. Self-efficacy mechanism in human agency. *American Psychologist*, 1982, *37*, 122–147.

Barnett, R. C., & Baruch, G. K. Women in the middle years: A critique of research and theory. *Psychology of Women Quarterly*, 1978, *3*, 187–197.

Berger, P. L., & Luckmann, T. *The social construction of reality*. New York: Anchor Books, 1967.

Boulding, K. *The image: Knowledge in life and society*. Ann Arbor, Michigan: University of Michigan Press, 1956.

Brim, O. G., Jr. Socialization through the life cycle. In O. G. Brim, Jr. & S. Wheeler (Eds.), *Socialization after childhood: Two essays*. New York: Wiley, 1966, pp. 1–49.

Brim, O. G., Jr., & Kagan, J. (Eds.). *Constancy and change in human development*. Cambridge, Mass.: Harvard University Press, 1980.

Brim, O. G., Jr., & Ryff, C. D. On the properties of life events. In P. B. Baltes & O. G. Brim, Jr. (Eds.), *Life-span development and behavior* (Vol. 3). New York: Academic Press, 1980, pp. 367–388.

Buhler, C. The curve of life as studied in biographies. *Journal of Applied Psychology*, 1935, *19*, 405–409.

Coan, R. W. *Hero, artist, sage or saint?* New York: Columbia University Press, 1977.

Cohler, B. J. Personal narrative and life course. In P. B. Baltes & O. G. Brim, Jr. (Eds.), *Life-span development and behavior* (Vol. 4). New York: Academic Press, 1982, pp. 205–241.

Costa, P. T., & McCrae, R. R. Still stable after all these years: Personality as a key to some issues in aging. In P. B. Baltes & O. G. Brim, Jr. (Eds.), *Life-span development and behavior* (Vol. 3). New York: Academic Press, 1980, pp. 65–102.

Elder, G. H., Jr. Social history and life experience. In D. H. Eichorn, J. A. Clausen, N. Haan, M. P. Honzik, & P. H. Mussen (Eds.), *Present and past in middle life*. New York: Academic Press, 1981, pp. 3–31.

Erikson, E. *Childhood and society*. New York: W. W. Norton & Co., 1950.

Erikson, E. Identity and the life cycle. *Psychological Issues*, 1959, *1*, 18–164.

Etzioni, A. *An immodest agenda: Rebuilding America before the 21st century*. New York: McGraw-Hill, 1982.

Fallo–Mitchell, L., & Ryff, C. D. Preferred timing of female life events: Cohort differences. *Research on Aging*, 1982, *4*, 249–267.

Gergen, K. J., & Gergen, M. M. Narratives of the self. In T. Sarbin & K. Scheibe (Eds.), *Studies in social identity*. New York: Praeger, in press.

Giele, J. Z. (Ed.). *Women in the middle years: Current knowledge and directions for research and policy*. New York: Wiley, 1982.

Gilligan, C. Woman's place in man's life cycle. *Harvard Educational Review*, 1979, *49*, 431–446.

Gilligan, C. *In a different voice: Psychological theory and women's development*. Cambridge, Mass.: Harvard University Press, 1982.

Giorgi, A. Phenomenology and the foundations of psychology. In J. K. Cole & W. J. Arnold (Eds.), *1975 Nebraska Symposium on motivation*. Lincoln, Nebr.: University of Nebraska Press, 1976, pp. 281–348.

Gould, R. *Transformations*. New York: Simon & Schuster, 1978.

Gutmann, D. The cross-cultural perspective: Notes toward a comparative psychology of aging. In J. E. Birren & K. W. Schaie (Eds.), *Handbook of the psychology of aging*. New York: Van Nostrand Reinhold, 1977, pp. 302–326.

Hareven, T. K. *Historical changes in the timing of life-course transitions: A phenomenological perspective*. Paper presented at the International Society for the Study of Behavioral Development, Munich, Germany, August 1983.

Hogan, D. P. *Transitions and social change: The early lives of American men*. New York: Academic Press, 1981.

Jackson, D. N. *Personality research from manual*. Goshen, N. Y.: Research Psychologists Press, 1967.

Jackson, D. N. *Jackson personality inventory manual*. Goshen, N. Y.: Research Psychologists Press, 1976.

Jung, C. G. *Modern man in search of a soul*. New York: Harcourt, Brace, & World, 1933.

Labouvie-Vief, G., & Chandler, M. J. Cognitive development and life-span developmental theory: Idealistic versus contextual perspectives. In P. B. Baltes (Ed.), *Life-span development and behavior* (Vol. 1). New York: Academic Press, 1978, pp. 181–210.

Lasch, C. *The culture of narcissism*. New York: W. W. Norton & Co., 1978.

Levinson, D. J. *The seasons of a man's life*. New York: Alfred A. Knopf, 1978.

Maslow, A. H. *Toward a psychology of being* (2nd ed.). New York: D. Van Nostrand, 1968.

Morawski, J. G. Assessing psychology's moral heritage through our neglected utopias. *American Psychologist*, 1982, *37*, 1082–1095.

Neugarten, B. L. The awareness of middle age. In B. L. Neugarten (Ed.), *Middle age and aging*. Chicago: University of Chicago Press, 1968, pp. 93–98.

Neugarten, B. L. Personality change in late life: A developmental perspective. In C. Eisdorfer & M. P. Lawton (Eds.), *The psychology of adult development and aging*. Washington, D. C.: American Psychological Association, 1973, pp. 311–335.

Neugarten, B. L. Time, age, and the life cycle. *American Journal of Psychiatry*, 1979, *136*, 887–894.

Neugarten, B. L., & Hagestad, G. O. Age and the life course. In R. H. Binstock & E. Shanas (Eds.), *Handbook of aging and the social sciences*. New York: Van Nostrand Reinhold, 1976, pp. 35–55.

Nisbet, R. *Prejudices: A philosophical dictionary*. Cambridge, Mass.: Harvard University Press, 1982.

Peskin, H., & Livson, N. Uses of the past in adult psychological health. In D. H. Eichorn, J. A. Clausen, N. Haan, M. P. Honzik, & P. H. Mussen (Eds.), *Present and past in middle life*. New York: Academic Press, 1981, pp. 153–181.

Reinert, G. Prolegomena to a history of life-span development psychology. In P. B. Baltes & O. G. Brim, Jr. (Eds.), *Life-span development and behavior* (Vol. 2). New York: Academic Press, 1979, pp. 205–254.

Rogers, C. R. *On becoming a person*. Boston: Houghton Mifflin, 1961.

Rokeach, M. *The nature of human values*. New York: The Free Press, 1973.

Rossi, A. S. Life-span theories and women's lives. *Signs: Journal of Women in Culture and Society*, 1980, *6*, 4–32.

Rubin, L. B. *Women of a certain age: The midlife search for self*. New York: Harper & Row, 1979.

Ryff, C. D. Self-perceived personality change in adulthood and aging. *Journal of Personality and Social Psychology*, 1982, *42*, 108–115. (a)

Ryff, C. D. Successful aging: A developmental approach. *The Gerontologist*, 1982, *22*, 209–214. (b)

Ryff, C. D. Adult personality development and the motivation for personal growth. In D. A. Kleiber & M. L. Maehr (Eds.), *Motivation in adulthood*. Greenwich, Conn.: JAI Press, in press. (a)

Ryff, C. D. Personality development from the inside: The subjective experience of change in adulthood and aging. In P. B. Baltes & O. G. Brim, Jr. (Eds.), *Life-span development and behavior* (Vol. 6). New York: Academic Press, 1984, pp. 243–279. (b)

Ryff, C. D., & Baltes, P. B. Value transitions and adult development in women: The instrumentality–terminality sequence hypothesis. *Developmental Psychology*, 1976, *12*, 567–568.

Ryff, C. D., & Dunn, D. D. *Life stresses and personality development: A life-span developmental inquiry*. Paper presented to the Gerontological Society Meetings, San Francisco, November 20, 1983.

Ryff, C. D., & Heincke, S. G. The subjective organization of personality in adulthood and aging. *Journal of Personality and Social Psychology*, 1983, *44*, 807–816.

Ryff, C. D. & Migdal, S. Intimacy and generativity: Self-perceived transitions. *Signs: Journal of Women in Culture and Society*, 1984, *9*, 974–983.

Scarf, M. *Unfinished business: Pressure points in the lives of women*. Garden City, N.Y.: Doubleday, 1980.

Schutz, A. *The phenomenology of the social world*. Evanston, Illinois: Northwestern University Press, 1967.

Sears, R. R. The role of expectancy in adaptation to aging. In S. B. Kiesler, J. N. Morgan, & V. K. Oppenheimer (Eds.), *Social change*. New York: Academic Press, 1981, pp. 407–430.

Sheehy, G. *Passages: Predictable crises of adult life*. New York: Dutton, 1976.

Sheehy, G. *Pathfinders*. New York: William Morrow, 1981.

Spiegelberg, H. *Phenomenology in psychology and psychiatry: An historical introduction*. Evanston, Illinois: Northwestern University Press, 1972.

Vaillant, G. E. *Adaptation to life*. Boston: Little, Brown, 1977

Valle, R. S., & King, M. (Eds.). *Existential-phenomenological alternatives for psychology*. New York: Oxford University Press, 1978.

Waterman, A. S. Individualism and interdependence. *American Psychologist*, 1981, *36*, 762–773.

Zeren, A., & Ryff, C. D. *The experience of fatherhood: Its impact on a man's growth and development*. Unpublished manuscript, Fordham University, Bronx, N.Y., 1983.

7

The Effect of Age and Gender on Deviant Behavior: A Biopsychosocial Perspective*

WALTER R. GOVE
Vanderbilt University

Introduction

Age is by far the most powerful predictor of the cessation of those forms of deviant behavior that involve substantial risk and/or physically demanding behavior. As Robins states: "All common forms of deviance (drug use, theft, drinking, sexual promiscuity, fighting) seem to drop off with age, whether or not they have been labelled and whether or not being labelled eventuated in the form of treatment or punishment" (1980, p.37). In this chapter, I make several points. First, virtually all forms of deviance that involve substantial risk and/or physically demanding behavior occur mainly among young persons, and the rates of such deviance decline sharply by the late twenties and early thirties. Second, although the relationship with age holds for both males and females, such deviance is primarily a male phenomenon. Third, the cessation of deviance with age is not predicted by sociological theories of deviance; in fact, it tends to be inconsistent with such theories. Fourth, sociological theories of aging are of little help in explaining why such forms of deviance tend to cease at a relatively early age while an adult psychological development perspective provides some useful insights. Fifth, sociologists have no good explanation for why deviance is primarily a male phenomenon. Finally, the incorporation of biological, psychological, and societal variables suggests an explanation of the cessation of these forms of deviance that makes intuitive sense, is consistent with existing evidence, and at least partially explains why males have much higher rates than females.

*I would like to thank Jack Gibbs, Debra Umberson, and particularly Alice Rossi for their comments on earlier drafts of this chapter. The special effort by Cindy Miller in typing this chapter is particularly appreciated.

115

Empirical Evidence on the Relationship of Age, Gender, and Deviant Behavior

That deviant behavior involving substantial risk and/or physically demanding behavior is primarily a youthful phenomenon is vividly shown in national data on arrests as reported in the uniform crime reports. As Steffensmeier and Terry (1983) have shown, for *serious property crime* (robbery, burglary, receiving stolen property), *minor property crime* (larceny, fraud, forgery), and *criminal mischief* (auto theft, arson, and vandalism), the age group with the highest crime rate is 13–17 years. For these crimes, there is a drop in the arrest rate among persons 18–24 years and a sharp drop for persons 25–30 years old. The arrest rate is very low among persons 40 and over. The arrest rate for *violent crimes* (murder, rape, aggravated assault, other assaults, carrying weapons) and *disturbance of the public order* (disorderly conduct, vagrancy, suspicion) is the highest among persons 18–24 years old. For these crimes, the second highest arrest rate is found among persons 13–17 years old, while the third highest arrest rate is found among persons 25–30 years old; after 30, there is a gradual decline in the rates. The pattern with age is virtually identical for males and females for each type of crime, although the rates are much lower for females (for a similar analysis see Cline, 1980).

This same age profile is found in other empirical evidence on deviant behavior. For example, data from self-reports show a sharp decline in crime with age (e.g., Rowe and Tittle, 1977). Similarly, rates of alcoholism drop sharply with age (Gove, 1980a; Robins, 1980) as do rates of drug addiction (McAuliffe, 1980). If one ignores the issue of addiction and looks simply at the issue of use and amount of use, one finds that tobacco, alcohol, marijuana, and stimulants are much more heavily used by young adults and their use sharply declines with age (Crutchfield, 1980; Mellinger, Balter, Manheim, Cisin & Parry, 1978). Survey data indicate that extramarital sex is limited almost exclusively to young adults (Booth & Edwards, 1977). So too, survey data show that high levels of psychiatric distress (e.g., Brocki, 1979; Gaitz & Scott, 1972; Gove & Style, 1983) and reports of having experienced a nervous breakdown in the past 6 months (Thomas, 1983) are much higher among young adults and decline steadily with age. The evidence also consistently indicates that suicide attempts decline sharply with age (Jarvis, Ferrence, Johnson, & Whitehead, 1976). Furthermore, there is strong evidence that persons with an antisocial personality (also referred to as *sociopaths* or *psychopaths*), who tend to perform a vast array of deviant acts, lose the characteristics of an antisocial personality by age 40 (American Psychiatric Association, 1980).

Robins (1980) notes that in the area of deviance, the relationships, such as the sharp decline with age, have been consistent regardless of the conceptual perspective of the investigator, the degree of methodological sophistication, the indices used, or the social setting of the research, and that the relationship holds across a variety of cultures. Hirschi and Gottfredson (1983) look at the relationship between age and crime across a wide variety of cultures and find a pattern identical to the age profile summarized here. They conclude that the age distribution of crime is invariant across social and cultural conditions (also see Steffensmeier & Terry, 1983).

Furthermore, the relationship between age and poor mental health is quite consistent over time (e.g., Gurin, Veroff & Feld, 1960; Veroff, Douvan & Kulka, 1981) as are reports of happiness (e.g., Whitt, Lowe, Peck & Curry, 1980). That is, the same pattern is found in studies widely separated in the years they were conducted. Hence, there is every reason to believe that the relationship between age and deviance is not attributable to cohort effects but involves some maturational effects. This is true despite the fact that different cohorts may show clear differences in their rates of deviant behavior (e.g. Hirschi & Gottfredson, 1983).

With the growth of the women's movement, the general emphasis on equality between the sexes, and the increased labor force participation of women, there has been considerable speculation that the behavior of women generally would become more similar to that of men and that this would include most types of behavior (e.g., Adler, 1976; Deming, 1977). The evidence does provide some support for this assumption, but it tends to be specific to certain types of crime (e.g., Simon, 1975; Steffensmeier & Cobb, 1981; Steffensmeier & Terry, 1983).

Data on arrest (Steffensmeier & Terry, 1983) provide a good illustration of what has happened. Throughout the period studied (1960–1980), arrest rates of men have been much higher than the arrest rates for women, with the exception of prostitution, where the arrest rate of women has been consistently higher than that of men. From 1960 to 1980, there was a clear monotonic decline in the sex differentials in the arrest rates. Between 1960 and 1961, and 1970 and 1971, there was a substantial increase in the number of women arrested compared to the number of men arrested, while after 1970 and 1971, the relative increase is quite modest.[1]

However, the increased arrest rate of females relative to that of males has not occurred across all crimes. The female arrest rate for violent crime has not increased. The arrest rate of males compared to females has remained relatively constant over time for prostitution, disorderly conduct, drugs, drunkenness, other liquor violations, gambling, family offenses, vagrancy, other sex offenses, and drunken driving.[2] All property crimes in contrast show a relatively increased

---

[1]The Uniform Crime Reports prior to 1960 suffered from nonreporting and inconsistencies in reporting procedures. Nevertheless, the data are suggestive. In 1940, there were 10.8 males arrested for every female, while in 1947, the rate had dropped to 9.0 males arrested for every female. Thus, overall, the data suggest that prior to World War II, compared to females, males were particularly likely to be arrested, and that in the period after World War II, the relative arrest rate of females had increased. This is consistent with the position taken by Gove and Tudor (1973) that World War II marked a change in the roles of women.

[2]For "other sex offenses," the relative arrest rate of women actually decreased, whereas for drunken driving it slightly increased. In 1980–1981, there were still 9.8 men arrested for drunken driving for every woman.

arrest rate among women as compared to men.[3] However, only for larceny, fraud, and forgery has the arrest rate of women shown a dramatic increase, and the rate of arrests among women is relatively high (also see Steffensmeier & Cobb, 1981).[4] Thus, the increased arrest rate of women is limited to the crimes of larceny, fraud, and forgery. These are crimes where the risk of being caught is low, severity of punishment is mild, the risk of bodily harm is minimal, the crimes require minor physical exertion, and they do not require confronting a victim or being in a place where one does not have a right to be (Steffensmeier, 1981).

To summarize, the forms of deviant behavior that involve substantial risk and/or physically demanding behavior are primarily committed by males during late adolescence and early adulthood, and the commission of such crimes (whether by males or females) drops off sharply as persons move into their late twenties and early thirties.[5] In the remainder of this chapter, deviant behavior will be used to refer only to deviant acts involving substantial risk and/or physical exertion.

Sociological Explanations of Deviance: Their Inability to Explain the Relationship with Age

Sociological theories of deviant behavior would not predict these negative relationships between age and deviance. The theoretical perspectives to be considered here are labelling theory, conflict theory, differential association, control theory, Merton's (1957) theory of anomie, and the functional theory of deviance. (Durkheim's conception of anomie will be considered later.) All of these theoretical perspectives either explicitly or implicitly suggest that deviant behavior is an amplifying process that leads to further and more serious deviance. Thus,

---

[3]For robbery, burglary, auto theft, and stolen property in 1960–61 (or even 1947), there was a very modest increase in the arrest rate of women as compared to men; however, the data on arrests suggest these crimes are still committed primarily by males. (For 1980–1981, the ratio of male arrests to female arrests was 14.7 for robbery, 16.9 for burglary, 10.9 for auto theft, and 8.8 for stolen property.)

[4]For 1980–1981, the ratio of male arrests to female arrests was 2.6 for larceny, 1.5 for fraud, and 2.3 for forgery.

[5]There would appear to be three exceptions to this generalization: (1) In our society, women appear to have higher rates of mental illness than men (Gove & Tudor, 1973; Gove, 1978); (2) women are more likely to attempt suicide (e.g., Jarvis et al., 1976; Kessler & McRae, 1983); and (3) for males, the likelihood of committing suicide increases with age. However, these expectations would not appear to be really inconsistent with the assertion noted above. First, mental illness is nonvolitional, and the evidence from survey data on psychological distress and from suicide attempts indicates that for both males and females the level of psychiatric distress is highest in late adolescence and early adulthood and declines rapidly with age. Second, most suicide attempts do not reflect a commitment to deviant life-styles; typically, they are a cry for help. Third, most persons who commit suicide actually intend to do so, and it is clearly inappropriate to view them as reflecting a commitment to a deviant life-style.

although these perspectives rarely explicitly discuss the link between age and deviance, they imply that with age people become increasingly locked into a deviant career. This is clearly inconsistent with the empirical facts reviewed above.

Labelling Theory

During the past two decades, labelling theory has been the most popular perspective in the area of deviance (e.g., Cole, 1975; Gibbs, 1981; Gove, 1980b). Labelling theorists do not attach much significance to the etiological factors that cause an individual to commit a deviant act; rather, they are concerned with societal reaction to an individual's initial acts of deviance (primary deviance). According to labelling theory, societal reaction to primary deviance is the major reason persons turn to or adopt a deviant career (secondary deviance). If an individual is reacted to and labelled as a deviant, it is assumed that the deviant status then becomes permanent.

According to labelling theory, the most crucial step in the development of a stable pattern of deviant behavior is the experience of being caught and publicly labelled deviant. As Erikson puts it: "The community's decision to bring deviant sanctions against the individual . . . is a sharp rite of transition at once moving him out of his normal position in society and transferring him into a distinctive deviant role" (1962, p. 311). Erikson suggests, furthermore, that such transitions are "Irreversible." Labelling theorists consider the status of deviant a master status that overrides all other statuses in determining how others will act toward such a person (Becker, 1963). Once a person is stigmatized by being labelled a deviant, a self-fulfilling prophecy is initiated, with others perceiving and responding to the person as a deviant (Becker, 1963; Erikson, 1962). Furthermore, once persons are publicly processed as deviants, they are typically forced into a deviant group (often by being placed in an institution). As Becker notes (1963), the one thing such groups have in common is their deviance. Sharing a common fate, they face the same problems and develop a deviant subculture.

Labelling theorists believe it is extremely difficult for a person to break out of a deviant status: "Once deviance becomes a way of life, the personal issue often becomes the cost of making a change rather than the higher status to be gained through rehabilitation or reform. Such costs are calculated in terms of the time, energy and distress seen as necessary for change" (Lemert, 1967, p. 55). The deviant has learned to perform deviant activities with a minimum of trouble (Becker, 1963). Such individuals have already failed in the normal world, suggesting to themselves and others an inability to make it even when things are relatively normal; now they face the world as stigmatized persons.

It is clear that labelling theorists consider the reaction to deviance to involve an amplifying process that leads to an increase in the deviant behavior. Labelling theory has been attacked for not paying enough attention to etiological factors and for deemphasizing the degree to which acts of deviance play a role in determining the action of others. Labelling theory has also been attacked for overemphasizing the degree to which the stigmatization of those labelled deviant impairs their ability to adopt the behavior and status of a normal individual (e.g., see Gove, 1980b). However, labelling theorists are in fact pointing to real processes. Few would deny that being labelled a deviant does not make it more difficult to adapt to a normal role or that the more involved one is in a career of deviance the more difficult it is to give up that role. Both labelling theorists and their critics agree that the process they point to exists; the major point of disagreement is in the *importance* of these processes and their adequacy as a general explanation of deviant behavior.

Conflict Theory

Some conflict theorists explicitly identify themselves as Marxists and others do not. One of the earliest proponents of this perspective was Bonger (1936), and some of the more prominent recent proponents are Chambliss (1969), Greenberg (1981), Quinney (1970), and Taylor, Walton, and Young (1973). All conflict theorists accept the following propositions: (1) In complex industrial societies, there is an unequal distribution of wealth, status, and power; (2) persons who are at an advantage in terms of wealth, status, and power will want to improve their position; thus, there is always conflict between those who are advantaged and those who are disadvantaged; (3) persons who are advantaged make the laws of society and control the criminal justice system; hence, the laws of society and the way the criminal justice system works benefit those who are in a position of advantage and work against those who are in a position of disadvantage; (4) because of their limited opportunities and/or because of their opposition to the established social order, the disadvantaged are likely to commit crimes, and because of their disadvantaged position, they are particularly likely to be severely punished for those crimes; (5) the advantaged will benefit if the disadvantaged are perceived as receiving severe punishment when they oppose the social order, and the advantaged will make it difficult for the disadvantaged to (re)establish themselves as acceptable members of society. Although conflict theorists have not focused on the issue of the relationship between age and deviance, their theoretical formulation implies that deviance would not only persist with age, but a deviant life-style would become increasingly structured as a prominent part of deviant individuals' ways of behaving as they grow older.

The Functional Theory of Deviance

Most sociologists see what is socially appropriate or inappropriate almost entirely as a matter of social definition. What is deviant is therefore virtually always perceived in relative terms. Thus, textbooks on deviant behavior not only do not use the term *pathology* but pointedly do not do so, typically noting that sociology has advanced to the point where conceptions such as *social pathology* (which created the image of something being intrinsically wrong) is now recognized as an outdated notion rooted in an ethnocentric conception of the world. Functional theorists consider the social fabric to be fragile, in need of constant reaffirmation. Durkheim (1951, 1964) argued that it was functional for society to define certain acts as deviant and to punish those individuals who committed those acts because punishment clearly delineates the normative boundaries of what is acceptable in society. Kai Erikson (1966) used this perspective to explain the Salem witch trials.[6] He argued that at the time of the Salem witch trials, the Puritans were losing their control over the Massachusetts Bay Colony, and the trials served both to label the transgressors as unacceptable and to highlight the values of the Puritans. Gusfield (1963) has used this formulation to explain prohibition, and Goode has used it to explain the criminalization of drug use (1970) and what is defined as sexual deviance (1974). According to this formulation, it benefits the established order to define and punish persons on the margins of society who commit acts that run counter to the values of those who maintain and control society. It follows that the more "heinous" the act and the more frequently a person performs such acts, the more important it is that such persons be punished. By making life harder for persons who have violated the social order, members of society will recognize how undesirable it is to be labelled a deviant. Again, there is nothing in this formulation to suggest that persons labelled deviant would cease their deviant behavior as they age. The assumption is that such persons will be stigmatized, isolated, and defined as socially unacceptable; as a consequence, they will tend to persist in their deviance.

Social Control or Containment Theory

Social control or containment theory starts by asking why some persons do *not* commit deviant acts. This perspective has focused on the relationship between the family environment and juvenile delinquency. It was a very popular perspective during the 1920s and 1930s (e.g., see Aichhorn, 1935); it then waned in popularity but has recently reemerged as a respectable perspective in sociology (e.g., Gove and Crutchfield, 1982; Hirschi, 1969). This theory argues that in an effective home environment children will become attached to their parents and through this bond they will develop appropriate societal values.

Implicit in this formulation is the view that the greater the involvement of juveniles with delinquent peers, the greater the likelihood of conflict with their families. Such involvement should lead to a decrease in the attachment to one's family and an increase in attachment to delinquent peers that, in turn, leads to an increase in delinquent behavior. Thus, the process is essentially a reciprocal one

---

[6]For a very different explanation of the Salem witch trials, which suggests the symptoms of witchcraft were produced by ergotism and describes the behavior of the village members in Salem very differently, see Caporael (1982).

that, once started, leads to an ever increasing involvement in delinquent behavior. This perspective suggests that as individuals become increasingly involved in a delinquent life-style, they will increasingly adopt values that are consistent with their deviant behavior and in conflict with society. Hence, this perspective implies that deviant behavior acts as an amplifying process that results in an increase in deviant behavior and greater involvement in a deviant life-style. Again, there is nothing in this theory to predict a decline in deviance with age.

Differential Association

Differential association is essentially a theory of socialization. It suggests that if persons are brought up in an environment where the dominant message is that deviant behavior is acceptable and appropriate, they will accept this view and commit deviant acts. This perspective, first articulated by Sutherland in 1924, has undergone a number of revisions over the years, many in collaboration with Cressey (most recently, Sutherland & Cressey, 1978). Ronald Akers (1977) has taken Sutherland and Cressey's relatively loose theoretical formulation and developed a more precise formulation, applying the principles of learning theory (i.e., operant theory) to a variety of deviant behaviors. This theory focuses on interpersonal association, the rewards and punishments obtained from these associations, and how they shape the individual's subsequent behavior. The theory suggests that if individuals perform delinquent acts, they will be punished by persons who conform to society's values and rewarded by persons who have a deviant life-style. Thus, this theory implies that over time, persons who perform deviant acts with some regularity would shift their allegiance to persons who had a deviant life-style and increasingly associate with such persons. Like other theories we have considered, the theory of differential association suggests deviant behavior is an amplifying process. There is nothing in the theory to suggest decline in deviant behavior with age; this is particularly true for institutionalized forms of punishment, such as imprisonment, which are not believed to have any specific deterrence effect (e.g., Blumstein, 1983).

Merton's Version of the Relationship between Anomie and Deviance

Merton (1957) has developed an explanation for why certain groups in society commit deviant acts and others do not. In his formulation, the focus is on the institutional goals and the institutional means to achieve those goals. Many members of society can readily achieve the institutionalized goals through institutional means, and such persons will tend to conform to the values of society, while other members of society (particularly members of the lower class and disadvantaged ethnic and racial groups) will not be able to use the institutionalized means because they will not be available to them. Under these conditions, such persons will resort to deviant behavior. Some of these individuals (labelled *innovators* by Merton) will resort to illegitimate means to achieve institutional goals; an example are persons who commit crime for profit (i.e., crooks). Other individuals for whom institutionalized means are blocked will not attempt to achieve institutionalized goals but will tend to withdraw and to seek psychological comfort in disvalued ways. Merton refers to such persons as *retreatists*; in more common parlance, such persons are labelled drug addicts or alcoholics. Treated as a dynamic process, Merton's theory seems inconsistent with the empirical relationship between age and deviance. In particular, if persons whose institutionalized means are limited turn to deviant behavior, their involvement in crime, drugs, alcohol, and other socially disapproved forms of behavior would have the consequence of further limiting their access to socially approved institutionalized means. Thus, like the other theories we have considered, Merton's formulation of deviance implies an amplifying process that would result in an increase in deviance over time and not a decrease.

Overview

In sum, none of the six theoretical perspectives we have sketched would predict the sharp decline in deviance that occurs with age. In fact, they would predict an *increase* in deviance as the development of a deviant life-style becomes more clearly delineated and entrenched over the years. This is particularly true of labelling theory, conflict theory, and, to a slightly lesser extent, control theory, functional theory, and the theory of differential association.

This summation must be qualified in one respect. The drop in deviance rates that has been noted has started by the mid-twenties. At least up until early adulthood, there appears to be an increase in deviant behavior. Indeed, the idea that deviance leads to more deviance is well supported in the literature. Holding in mind that the behavior sequence refers to childhood through early adulthood, Robins' (1980) summary of longitudinal studies is relevant:

> the best predictor of any specific later deviant act always seems to be earlier deviant behavior, and the specific *nature* of that earlier deviant behavior seems uniformly to be relatively unimportant. Being a late adolescent or young male adult and having parents with a history of deviance—again the specific nature of that deviance is not important—are the next best predictors of later deviance. (p. 36)

Such studies of the etiology of antisocial behavior (Robins, 1978, 1980; Robins & Wish, 1977) show that all types of antisocial behavior in children predict high levels of antisocial behavior in adulthood; virtually all antisocial adults were antisocial as children; the *number* of antisocial behaviors committed during childhood is a better predictor of adult antisocial behavior than is any particular childhood antisocial behavior. Nonetheless, most antisocial children do not become antisocial as adults. These results on the proximate continuity of deviant behavior in the first few decades of the life span make all the more puzzling why there is a sharp drop in such behavior by the third decade of life. But none of the six theoretical perspectives reviewed above offers any explanatory illumination of this social pattern.

Hirschi and Gottfredson (1983, pp. 552–554) concur with this assessment. They indicate that when attention shifts to interpreting the relationship between age and crime, "it easily qualifies as the most difficult fact in the field. Efforts to discern the meaning of the large amount of research on the topic in terms supplied by those doing the research have turned out to be futile, . . . as have efforts to explain the relationship in statistical terms." Hirshi and Gottfredson conclude that "the age distribution of crime cannot be accounted for by any variable or combination of variables currently available to criminology."

Sociological Explanations of Deviance and the Issue of Gender

Turning to the issue of gender difference in deviant behavior, one finds that no sociological theory of deviance explains why deviant behavior is primarily a male phenomenon. There is nothing in labelling theory, conflict theory, the functional theory of deviance, or in Merton's theory of anomie that explains why women have such low rates of deviant behavior. Schur (1984), in fact, has argued that labelling processes produce female deviance. It could be argued by conflict theorists (or possibly even from Merton's formulation) that the exclusion of women from essential socioeconomic processes is such that they lack opportunity to commit deviant acts and, given their subordinate position and submissive behavior, there is no need for others to react to women who commit deviant acts or to place them in a stigmatized role. However, given the changes that have occurred in the role of women in developed societies, these theories would predict a sharp increase in the deviant behavior of women relative to men across a vast array of deviant behaviors, not that the increase would be limited to larceny, fraud, and forgery.

Although neither control theory nor learning theory (i.e., differential association) have been specifically used to explain the relatively low rates of deviance among females, from what is known about sex and gender role socialization one could readily argue that girls are much more likely to develop close family attachments and adopt socially conforming behavior. But the blurring of gender distinctions in childrearing and greater involvement of adult women in nonfamily roles would predict a sharp increase in the general rate of deviant behavior among women since World War II. Yet we have seen that the increase is limited to relatively nonserious property crimes. In short, as with age, to explain the relationship between gender and deviant behavior, we need to look elsewhere.

In my view, an understanding of why rates of deviant behavior peak at late adolescence and early adulthood and drop sharply thereafter for both males and females, and why males have much higher rates of deviant behavior than females, must be sought by examining age and gender as reflections of the interaction of biological, psychological, and social factors.

Explaining the Age-Deviant Behavior Link:
The Issue of Social Roles

Society structures the life course of the individual by specifying the sequential stages through which an individual moves (Foner and Kertzer, 1978; Gordon, 1972). This appears to be a common characteristic across societies, although there are cultural differences in the timing, duration, and rigidity of these stages and in the extent to which they are marked by sharp transition points. In American society, one's family and school largely structure one's life from infancy through early adolescence. During these early years, one's autonomy is relatively low, and one's size, strength, and limited opportunities impose constraints on behavior in a variety of ways. The period from adolescence to adulthood is one of transition that is marked by several important characteristics: (1) a high level of uncertainty over the particular roles one will occupy as an adult; (2) a great many new experiences that may initially provoke anxiety and frustration; (3) the occupancy of roles that provide little intrinsic satisfaction and little sense of their relevance to subsequent adult roles; (4) a social expectation that young people will experiment with a variety of accepted and unaccepted behaviors that are generally forbidden to adults, coupled with the expectation that young people will settle down as they age; (5) limited opportunities to carry responsibilities for other people; and (6) having relatively high levels of autonomy and freedom of choice as a consequence of low responsibility and adult tolerance for youthful experimentation. Furthermore, since adolescent roles do not tend to give a sense of meaning and purpose to one's life, adolescents and young adults are attracted to highly stimulating behaviors because such stimulation gives one an acute sense of self. Seeking gratification through stimulation can easily lead to the use of alcohol or drugs to alleviate frustration or boredom. And, of course, by lowering one's inhibitions, alcohol and drugs bolster one's courage to undertake acts that have substantial risk and are highly stimulating.

One general sociological explanation of deviance appears compatible with the above formulation and also suggests that deviant behavior would be common in adolescence and early adulthood but would tend to cease by the time the person reaches the mid- to late twenties. This is an explanation that draws upon Durkheim's conception of *anomie*.

Durkheim's Theory of Anomie and Its Relationship to Deviance

One of Durkheim's major concerns was the issue of social integration and how the nature of social integration changed with the transition from an agrarian to an industrial society. Durkheim argued that the shift to urban industrial society was accompanied by a breakdown in traditional norms and values, an increase in both the complexity and segmentation of roles, a decline in social regulation, and an increase in autonomy. Durkheim suggested that this profile of characteristics created a societal situation of anomie or normlessness where many individuals

were apt to find their lives empty of meaning. There would be a lack of normative guidance and a breakdown in the external forms of social control due to the
high level of autonomy. Durkheim argued and empirically explored the idea that
anomie would be related to the suicide rate. In the years since his work, a large
number of sociologists have argued that Durkheim's concept of anomie would be
related to a variety of forms of deviant behavior.

If the concept of anomie is applied to the human life course, then the period of
late adolescence and early adulthood can be seen as having the least social
structure and normative guidance. The lack of any firm responsibilities coupled
with social expectations that young people will experiment can readily trigger the
experience of normlessness that is similar to Durkheim's concept of anomie.
This anomic state is accompanied not only by a rise in suicidal behavior but the
whole range of deviant behaviors that peak in late adolescence and early adulthood. A decided advantage of using the concept of anomie as a partial explanation of deviant behavior is that, unlike other theories, it carries no assumption of
the persistence of deviant behavior. If social roles change and life takes on
structure and meaning, then deviance should decline accordingly. Indirect evidence of anomie can be seen in a variety of social psychological studies that
reveal heightened states of stress and lowered psychological well-being in
adolescence and early adulthood. It is to such studies that we now turn.

The Relationship between Psychological Well-Being and Age

Campbell (1981) has provided an overview of the five national probability
surveys that have focused on the issue of psychological well-being. People under
30 are the most likely to describe their lives as hard rather than easy, to feel
themselves tied down rather than free, to worry about financial and other difficulties, and to be concerned that they might have a nervous breakdown. In all but
one of the domains of life studied, people under 30 were the least satisfied: They
expressed more dissatisfaction than older persons with regard to their education,
their work, their marriage, their family life, friendships, standard of living,
savings, housing, their community and neighborhood, and the country as a
whole. Only in their satisfaction with their health were they substantially more
positive than people in the older age groups (Campbell, 1981, pp. 176–177).

Gove and Ortega (1984), using a national probability sample of 2258 respondents designed to study the relationship of gender and marital status to mental
health, also found (after appropriate controls) that life satisfaction and happiness
increased with age. In this survey, the respondents' disenchantment with their
life was measured by a scale using four items.[7] Persons 18–25 reported the most
disenchantment, there was a very sharp monotonic decline with age, and age was
by far the most powerful predictor. Persons 15–25 were also found to have the

---

[7]The questions were: (1) I feel as if my life just isn't complete; (2) I often feel
trapped; (3) I wish I could change my life; (4) I often feel as if I've missed something.

lowest self-esteem. A measure of psychological distress that contained items indicative of depression, anxiety, and paranoia showed a very strong negative association with age.[8] Indeed, age was five times more powerful in terms of explained variance than the next demographic predictor, education. Persons between 18–25 had especially high scores (Gove & Style, 1983).[9]

Campbell (1981, p. 178) discusses a number of possible explanations for why young people are the least satisfied with their jobs, housing, standard of living, education, and other domains of their life, except for health.[10] He notes that "It is difficult to separate these social life style effects from those associated with aging" (Campbell, 1981, p. 202); however, he focuses on finding one's niche in society.

The Niche-Finding Process

In a relatively fluid, complex, industrial society such as our own, there is great uncertainty in the process whereby young people discover the particular complex set of niches they are going to occupy. High school youths are uncertain as to whether they will marry, whom they will marry, when they will marry, and whether they will have children. They are uncertain about the processes of schooling (potentially up through graduate school or professional school), about getting launched into a job or career, and how successful that job or career will be. In short, the process of finding out who one is going to be involves waiting, effort, and change; it is a process that involves both painful and pleasant feedback, often requiring changes in goals and expectations. It seems likely that it is increased knowledge of self and the world, together with the formation of more realistic expectations, that explains the increase of satisfaction with age. Campbell, Converse, and Rodgers (1976) suggest that it is through this process that young people develop increasing skills with regard to learning how to perform and with regard to knowing what to expect. After a review of the evidence from their study as well as from the work of others, Campbell et al. (1976) conclude that there seem to be "important psychological mechanisms operative such that beyond a certain initial point of familiarity, *satisfaction with a situation increases as one becomes increasingly accommodated to it*" (p. 163).

---

[8]Studies using self-reports of psychiatric symptoms show a very mixed relationship with age; however, this appears to be due to scales containing a number of psychophysiologic symptoms that reflect poor physical health as well as psychological distress (Gove & Hughes, 1979).

[9]It is important to note that the relationship found between age and psychological well-being is very stable (e.g., see Campbell, 1981; Veroff et al., 1981; Whitt et al., 1980).

[10]Campbell asserts: "The early years of adult life are characterized by strong affective experience; many pleasant and unpleasant events punctuate the lives of adult people. As people grow older, these events are less common and less intense; life is more bland" (1981, p. 202). Also see Brim (1968) and Pressey and Kuhlen (1957).

The strong patterning of the relationship between youthful age and low points in psychological well-being, life disenchantment, anxiety, and depression provide some empirical support for applying the Durkheimian concept of anomie to the transition adolescents and young adults are undergoing. As they move out of unattached statuses and take on adult responsibilities in work and family roles, they accommodate to the niche they have carved out for themselves in society. Among the experimental and highly stimulating experiences they give up are the deviant behaviors we suggest are associated with the anomic circumstances affecting the young during their transition to a mature and settled adulthood.

Explaining the Age-Deviant Behavior Link: Adult Psychological Maturation[11]

Erikson (1963, 1968, 1977) views adolescence as a time for experimentation and testing that is followed in turn by a concern with achievement (the stage of young adulthood), a concern for others (the stage of generativity), and finally a concern for understanding life in general and attempting to come to terms with one's own life and making it meaningful (the stage of maturity). This theoretical framework is consistent with the one articulated by Jung (1963, 1964) and is generally consistent with the perspective of Levinson (1978, 1980) and Gould (1978). According to this perspective, as persons make the transition from adolescence to adulthood and move through the life cycle, (1) they will shift from self-absorption to concern for others; (2) they will increasingly accept societal values and behave in socially appropriate ways; (3) they will become more comfortable with social relations; (4) their activities will increasingly reflect a concern for others in their community; and (5) they will become increasingly concerned with the issue of the meaning of life.

---

[11]I have chosen to use the phrase "psychological maturation" in order to emphasize that I do not share some of the assumptions made by sociologists, demographers, and historians doing work on the life course (e.g., Davis & van den Oever, 1982; Elder, 1974; Elder & Liker, 1982; Hareven, 1982) and developmental psychologists doing work on the life span. As Rossi (1980) notes, some developmental psychologists have taken a "normative-crisis model" which assumes an inherent ground plan to all human development (e.g., Gould, 1978; Levinson, 1978; Vaillant, 1977) and others a "timing-of-events model" where stress is a consequence of asynchrony in the timing of life events (e.g., Butler & Lewis, 1977; Neugarten, 1968, 1979). As Rossi (1980) indicates, whether social scientists take a life-course perspective, a normative-crisis perspective, or a timing-of-events perspective they have cut the link to biology. The phrase "adult pyschological maturation" is used to suggest an association with the ontogenetic framework found in Jung (1963, 1964) and Erikson (1963, 1968, 1977), which suggests that over the life course, there is an unfolding set of problems to be dealt with but assumes that these problems are a normal part of adult development and do not necessarily result in a "crisis."

Changes in Self-Concept with Age

Ortega and Gove (1981) and Gove and Ortega (1984) describe in detail the changes in self-image that occur with age. Their data were drawn from a national sample described above. Respondents were given a checklist and asked to identify adjectives that they believed described the type of person they were. Persons 18–25 were particularly apt to describe themselves as emotional and nervous and as behaving in an uncooperative fashion. The younger respondents reported that they were somewhat less likely to be instrumental or to be supportive of others. Younger respondents also described themselves as more competitive. With age, there was a sharp monotonic decline in the degree to which persons perceived themselves as emotional, nervous, uncooperative, and (to a lesser extent) competitive; there was a monotonic increase with age in persons perceiving themselves as instrumental and supportive of others. These changes in the self-concept suggest that as one ages, one becomes less self-absorbed, more cooperative and attentive to others, and that one functions more effectively and becomes more content and less emotional.

Age and Inclination to Behave in a Socially Appropriate Fashion

There is a large body of evidence indicating that as persons age they are more inclined to conform to social norms (Gove & Style, 1983; Riley, Foner & Johnson, 1968a). The evidence is strong that with increasing age, people show a need for approval,[12] and behave in a socially appropriate fashion. In the national probability sample cited above, young respondents were much more likely to indicate that they would act in a socially inappropriate fashion than older respondents, who generally indicated that they would act in socially appropriate ways. The relationship with age is strong and monotonic. In terms of explained variance, age is six times more powerful than the next most powerful predictor, education (Gove & Style, 1983). This finding is consistent with other surveys using the same or similar scales (e.g., Campbell et al., 1976; Gove, McCorkel,

---

[12]The actual questions were: (1) Before voting I thoroughly investigate the qualifications of all candidates; (2) I never hesitate to go out of the way to help someone in trouble; (3) on occasion I have had doubts about my ability to succeed in life; (4) if I could get into a movie without paying and be sure I was not seen I probably would do it; (5) there have been times when I felt like rebelling against people in authority even though I know they were right; (6) no matter who I'm talking to, I'm always a good listener; (7) at times I have really insisted on having things my own way; (8) I never resent being asked to return a favor; (9) I have never been irked when persons expressed ideas very different from my own; (10) I sometimes try to get even, rather than forgive and forget. These items are drawn from the Crowne Marlow scale which was designed to measure need for approval. However, recent research shows that persons scoring high on this scale are much more likely to behave in a socially appropriate fashion.

Fain & Hughes, 1976). In short, these and other data suggest that the young are particularly willing to violate social norms.

Age and How One Relates to Others

Gove and Style (1983), using both the national survey referred to above and a large survey conducted in Chicago (see Gove, Hughes & Galle, 1979), looked at a scale of four questions designed to discover if persons saw others as being generally friendly and considerate.[13] In both surveys, they found that the young respondents perceived other people to be unfriendly and uncaring while older respondents perceived others as friendly and considerate. In both data sets, the relationships were monotonic and, in terms of variance explained, age was more than 5 times stronger than education. In both surveys, there was a strong positive relationship between age and being socially integrated into one's neighborhood, with the level of social integration of persons 18–25 being particularly low (Gove & Style, 1983). The study in Chicago also collected data on whether or not persons had serious arguments and whether such arguments led to physical blows. Having arguments, particularly ones that led to physical blows, occurred almost exclusively among the young (Gove & Style, 1983). In summary, the young tend to be distrustful of others and likely to get into arguments and fights.

Having a General Concern for One's Community

There are at least three very clear indicators that aging is associated with the development of a general concern for one's community. First, studies show that age is positively associated with political behavior in general and with voting in particular. The most notable findings for our purposes are the very low rates of voting among persons under 30 years of age and particularly among persons under 25 years of age (e.g., see Gove & Style, 1983; Riley et al., 1968a). Second, making charitable contributions, (with controls for per capita income), strongly increases with age. Persons under 25 are particularly unlikely to make such contributions (Gove & Style, 1983). Third, rates of participation in voluntary organizations are very low among the young (under 25 or under 30 depending on the study), and there is a sharp increase at a relatively constant rate until about age 65[14] (Gove & Style, 1983; Riley et al., 1968a).

---

[13]The actual questions were: (1) Most people really *do* care what happens to the next fellow; (2) most people are just naturally friendly and helpful; and (3) I hardly ever feel awkward or out of place.

[14]Much of the increase in participation in community activities by age 30 is probably due to the fact that parenthood leads to community involvement (O'Donnell, 1983).

Concern with the Meaning of Life

It is commonly assumed that religious involvement reflects a concern with the meaning of life. Looking at the role religion plays in an individual's life, we find that older persons are more likely (1) to say that religion is very important to them; (2) to express a strong interest in worship and religion; (3) to regard themselves as religious; (4) to say they turn to God for help; and (5) to indicate that religion comforts them[15] (Campbell et al., 1976; Gove & Style, 1983; Riley et al., 1968b; Veroff et al., 1981). For our purposes, it is particularly important to note that young adults do not perceive themselves as particularly religious and rarely turn to religion and/or God for guidance and help. In short, religion plays a relatively minor role in the lives of young individuals and takes on increasing significance as persons age.

Overview

Young adults are self-absorbed, relatively uncooperative, and emotional and tense. They tend to be willing to behave in socially unacceptable ways, to distrust others, to have arguments and fights, to show little concern for their community, and to have little religious involvement. The evidence indicates that as persons age, they become more concerned with others, more trusting, more socially integrated, more concerned with the general welfare of the community, and more concerned with religious issues. This evidence supports the human development perspective of psychological maturation outlined above. It should be noted that this perspective has a number of similarities with many Eastern religions. Nor should we ignore the fact that this perspective grew out of a psychoanalytic tradition that views adult personality development as a process involving a number of characteristics that are not culturally specific. The fact that this perspective is supported from a variety of data that are not culture specific suggests a link to evolutionary processes.[16]

Cline (1980) has correctly noted that criminal behavior has rarely been studied from a life-span perspective. However, as Hirschi and Gottfredson (1983) note, the cessation of crime is typically attributed to some vaguely identified maturational process (also see Robins & Wish, 1977). The data reviewed above, originally analyzed to look at psychological maturation, have a direct bearing on the age-deviance link. Since young persons tend to be self-absorbed, un-cooperative, distrustful, unconcerned for the community, and willing to behave

---

[15]Church attendance also conforms to this general pattern, but there are some significant deviations (e.g., Riley, Foner & Johnson, 1968b).

[16]Levinson (1980), for example, indicates that these processes can only be explained by an evolutionary perspective.

in socially unacceptable ways, one would expect them to be willing to commit deviant acts. This is particularly true when it is combined with the fact that compared to older adults, young persons tend to be in poor mental health, disenchanted with their life, occupy a role that has a high level of autonomy, have little normative guidance, and are at a stage in their lives where deviant acts typically have few consequences for their future career. On the other hand, the data on deviance suggests a *sharp* drop in deviant behavior with age, whereas the data we have reviewed suggests a *more gradual* decline. Hence, to explain the *sharpness* of the age-deviance decline we need to look elsewhere.

Explaining the Age-Deviant Behavior Link: A Consideration of Biological Factors

Physical strength. Quetelet (1969) pointed out, as early as 1835, that there was a close correlation between the development of physical strength and the age at which violent crimes occurred (also see Hirschi & Gottfredson, 1983). These qualities are also important in lives that revolve around the heavy use of drugs and alcohol. Consider the life-style reported by a heroin addict (Tardola, 1970, p. 60):

> [It was] the worst period of my life. I found myself wandering around the streets of New York filthy all the time. I had no place to stay. I slept on rooftops, in hallways, in damp cellars, any available place and always with one eye open. I felt that everyone was my enemy, and I thought everybody was a stoolie. I was really low then, not eating, using dirty "works" [i.e., drug paraphernalia] and cold all the time.

Similar accounts are routinely presented at meetings of Alcoholics Anonymous. Clearly, such a life-style is physically very demanding.

For normal adults, physical strength peaks in the early twenties and then undergoes a fairly steady decline (Finch & Heyflick, 1973; Riley & Foner, 1968, pp. 221–274; Spirluso, 1980). Many aspects of body functions start to deteriorate in the very early twenties, while the remainder start to deteriorate in the late twenties. Obviously, any average peak in physical strength involves an interaction of a biological process with social behavior, such as diet and physical training. Athletes and those committed to vigorous participation in fitness regimens would show a long plateau of peak physical condition compared to the average adult.

Strength is only one physical characteristic that enhances a person's ability to undertake very strenuous activities and/or lead a physically demanding life-style. Other major components are (a) physical energy, (b) psychological drive, and (c) the need for stimulation.

Physical Energy. Physical energy involves two interrelated components. One is *staying power*, the ability to persist and perform a physically demanding activity over a substantial period of time. Persons who are out-of-shape may show a high level of physical strength for a brief period but with time will quickly collapse. Thus, a boxer who underestimates an opponent and does not train, may hold up for a few rounds and then fall apart. Conditioning through training clearly affects staying power, but staying power is also age-related. Sports vary in the overall demands they place on the biological system and hence show variations in the age at which professional players are forced to retire.

The second component of physical energy is the ability to *rebound*, namely, the time it takes to get in shape or to recuperate. After the early twenties, it takes an ever increasing amount of time for almost any part of one's body to mend after an injury (Goodson & Hunt, 1979; Linn, 1980), and with age it takes an ever increasing period of time to get in shape.

Psychological Drive. Psychological drive in many respects parallels the staying power component of physical energy in that it affects the degree to which one persists in performing a strenuous activity. While staying power has to do with one's ability to persist, psychological drive has to do with one's willingness and desire to persist.

For many years, students of crime and delinquency, frustrated by the inability of sociological theories to explain the deviant behavior of adolescents, have attributed such behavior to "psychic energy" or "psychological drive" (cf. Jensen, 1977). Recent developments in endocrinology are beginning to provide a base for such a notion. From early adolescence to early adulthood, the amount of plasma testosterone increases sharply; however, a substantial decline does not occur until age 50 (Ellis, 1982; Gregerman & Bieman, 1981). There is evidence that high levels of testosterone in adolescence lead to assertive behavior[17] (e.g., Doering, Brodie, Kramer, Moos, Becker & Hamburg, 1975; Persky, Smith, & Basu, 1971; Sands, 1954), whereas high levels of testosterone in adults do not appear to be related to assertive (or aggressive) behavior, at least as measured by psychological tests (Kreuz & Rose, 1972; Persky et al., 1971; Schiavi, Theilgaard, Owen, & White, 1984). These findings have a parallel in animal studies, which show that testosterone is related to aggression at puberty but not later[18] in development (see the review in Hoyenga and Hoyenga, 1979).

Testosterone, in combination with the adolescent role and peer pressure, should greatly increase one's willingness to take risks and participate in strenuous physical activity. The physical and psychological stress of such activities

---

[17]I have chosen to use the term *assertive behavior* instead of *aggressive behavior* because the effects of testosterone appear to have a general energizing effect that only sometimes leads to overt physical aggression.

[18]Why testosterone should be related to assertive (aggressive) behavior at adolescence in humans or other animals but not during adulthood is not clear. Persky et al. (1971), and Rossi (1984) suggest it is due to social maturation which permits greater impulse control. The fact that the same pattern occurs with other animals suggests that it may be produced by conditioning; acting on an assertive impulse is paired with the experience of pain (see the following section).

produce adrenaline and endorphins (Liddle, 1981). Adrenaline gives one a physiological "high" which mobilizes one's physical and psychological state (Liddle, 1981). Endorphins[19] are opiate-like substances which, like morphine, minimize the extent one feels pain (e.g., Davis et al., 1982). Thus, among adolescents, the level of one's testosterone should have a substantial impact on one's psychological drive. Due to the fact that the effects of testosterone on assertive behavior decline as one moves into adulthood, one would anticipate a concomitant decline in one's psychological drive. Thus, many sportsmen, such as mountain-climbers, report that as they age they are no longer willing to put up with the physical pain and intense cold, and they are not able to muster the constant physical push that is required in so strenuous a sport.

The Need for Stimulation. We have already noted that many adolescents find their roles lacking in intrinsic rewards and turn to sensate activities to achieve a sense of self. Furthermore, the increased testosterone levels in adolescence should lead to increased risk taking. The fact that adolescents take substantially more risks than older adults is well documented by data on motor vehicle accidents (e.g., New York State, 1979). Such risks will result in an adrenalin high. In many social contexts, such highs will be extremely pleasurable (Gordon, 1981; Hochschild, 1979), and one's adolescent peers are apt to provide such a context. In short, adolescents and young adults will frequently find the high from adrenaline (or its equivalent) very rewarding. With age, having the experience of such a "high" may shift from desirable to undesirable. Many persons involved in high-risk sports, such as mountaineering, "burn out." Persons give up serious mountaineering because the risks become intolerable. It does not appear to be a matter of increased concern for social responsibilities, but rather that they no longer find the adrenaline rush produced by risk taking pleasurable. Instead, it has become an unpleasant experience they wish to avoid. Research has consistently found that elevated emotional status can be experienced as unpleasurable as well as pleasurable (Gordon, 1981; Hochschild, 1979). Adrenaline highs are paired with substantial risk and thus anxiety, and it is not surprising that with time persons come to experience them as undesirable.[20]

The desire of late adolescent and early adult *males* for a strong sensate experience is well illustrated by a very intense sex drive that tends to be relatively detached from a need for intimate social relations (e.g., Gove & Style, 1983). Again, there is a strong endocrine component to this sex drive. Furthermore, if

---

[19]It is interesting to note the reason for the search for endorphins. As Davis, Buchsbaum, and Bunney (1982, p. 41) state, the search was undertaken "as no one believed that evolution has endowed a man with an opiate receptor in order that drugs could be administered, for example, to suppress pain. Instead, it was assumed "that the body must synthesize (opiate-like) substances."

[20]While stress substantially increases secretion levels of adrenaline and endorphins it leads to a substantial decrease in testosterone. The constant pairing of stress with anxiety and a lowering of the level of testosterone may help explain why high levels of testosterone are not associated with assertive behavior in adults.

persons find the desirability of psychophysiologic highs to decline with age and the undesirability of psychophysiologic lows to increase with age, one would predict a decline in affect intensity with age, a prediction that receives considerable empirical support (Back & Gergen, 1966; Brocki, 1979; Campbell et al., 1976; Cumming & Henry, 1961; Gaitz & Scott, 1972; Gove & Style, 1983).

The discussion of the relationship between biology and deviant behavior has focused on levels of testosterone. While this discussion has been somewhat speculative, it is noteworthy that studies of prisoners have consistently found a correlation between elevated testosterone levels and a record of violent or aggressive behavior, particularly during their adolescence (Ehrenkranz, Bliss and Sheard, 1974; Kreuz & Rose, 1972; Mattson, Schilling, Olweus, Low & Stevenson, 1980; Rada, Laws & Kellner, 1976). Furthermore, the community study by Schiavi et al. (1984), which paired persons with a criminal record with persons with no record, found that persons with a criminal record had significantly higher levels of testosterone, and this was particularly true of persons who had committed violent crimes. Most of these studies did not find a relationship between high levels of testosterone and measures of aggression that were derived from interviews or psychological tests.

The Interaction of Social and Biological Variables

The types of deviant behavior covered in this chapter virtually all require high levels of physical and psychic energy and drive. Some of them require physical strength, and the desire for a high would be a major source of motivation. If these characteristics decline rapidly with age, then the benefits experienced by the persons committing the deviant acts will *tend* to rapidly decrease and the physical and psychological costs experienced will *tend* to rapidly increase. There are two reasons to emphasize the word *tend*: First, there is substantial variation in the degree to which individuals are endowed with physical strength and energy, psychological drive, and the need for an adrenaline high. Second, successful and other committed deviants, just like successful athletes, will be much more likely to persist in their deviant behaviors for a longer period of time.

Studies of drug addicts and alcoholics often point to severe physical and social hardship. When drug addicts and alcoholics find such hardship too great, they are said to have "bottomed out." In a description of the bottoming out process, McAuliffe (1980) describes how heroin addicts, as a consequence of their behavior, experience a form of social bankruptcy where they are distrusted by everyone, including other drug addicts, and become very isolated. McAuliffe (1980) argues that the social processes described by labelling theorists are magnified by the addicts' own deviant behavior, with the result that life becomes so miserable they eventually decide to quit their deviant behavior. A similar process explains why most alcoholics eventually quit abusing alcohol (e.g., see Armor, Polich & Stombul 1978; Gove, 1980a). Most forms of deviant behavior would appear to lead to a form of social bankruptcy resulting in a life that is strenuous,

unpleasant, and painful. Age-related processes of physiological changes in tolerance to pain and hardship are therefore strongly implicated in the turning away
by older persons from a deviant life-style. The societal reaction described by
labelling theory may apply to the early stages of commitment to deviant life-
styles, but biological and psychological factors appear to play a critical role in
the termination of deviant behavior.

Gender Differences in Deviant Behavior

As the statistics presented in the introductory section show, deviant behavior
as defined in this chapter is primarily a male phenomenon. Earlier, we noted that
sociological theories of deviant behavior were unable to account for this male/
female difference. The inadequacy of sociological explanations of the gender
difference in deviant behavior is highlighted by the fact that most sociologists
concerned with the issue had anticipated that the changes in the roles of women
would be reflected in changes in the rates of deviant behavior relative to the rates
of males, a prediction that has not been upheld to date. In fact, the gender
difference in deviant behavior seems to be sufficiently stable across time and
place that it can not be explained by the structure of society or by sex-role
socialization. This suggests that biological differences between males and
females may contribute to their different rates of deviant behavior.

We should also note that the low rates of deviant behavior among women
cannot be attributed to low rates of psychological distress. The evidence clearly
indicates that young boys experience more psychological distress than young
girls, but by late adolescence, females are more likely to experience psychological distress than males, distress associated with the nature of adolescent female
roles (Gove & Herb, 1974; Locksley & Douvan, 1979). Furthermore, adult
females experience higher rates of psychological distress than adult males in our
society, and this also seems to be due to the nature of their roles in our society
(e.g., Gove, 1978; Gove & Tudor, 1973).

There is one similarity between the rates of deviant behavior of males and
females, namely, the rates tend to peak at the same age, although the peak is less
sharp for females (Hirschi & Gottfredson, 1983). This, however, makes sense in
terms of the combined influence of social, psychological, and biological factors.
For females, as with males, late adolescence and early adulthood is marked by a
lack of social structure, normative guidance, and clear responsibilities. The
psychological well-being of both males and females is at a low point during
adolescence and early adulthood. Young females are more self-absorbed, uncooperative, distrustful, and willing to act in socially unacceptable ways than
older females, although the difference with age is not nearly so sharp for females
as for males (Gove & Ortega, 1984; Gove & Style, 1983). Furthermore, physical
strength and energy tend to peak at approximately the same age for males and
females.

Basic Personality Differences between Males and Females

There is a growing literature that demonstrates that males and females interpret and relate to their environment differently. Males tend to have greater agentic characteristics that are manifest in terms of self-protection, self-assertion, and self-expression. They tend to be more focused, to be more future-oriented, and to be more objective. They have a greater urge to master. Females tend to be affiliative, are more concerned with social contact, and with being cooperative and open to others (e.g., Bakan, 1966; Gutmann, 1965). Gilligan (1982) using TAT story-telling protocols, found women perceived danger and projected violence into interpersonal achievement situations, whereas men perceived danger and projected violence into close personal situations. According to Gilligan (1982, p. 171), "women's sense of integrity appears to be entwined with the ethic of care, so that to see themselves as women is to see themselves in a relationship connection." The affiliative orientation of females and their concern for the impact of their behavior on others should significantly limit their interest, desire, and/or willingness to commit deviant acts. In contrast, the independent, assertive personality of males is much more compatible with a willingness to be involved in deviant behavior.

Social scientists tend to attribute such personality characteristics to socialization, although their ubiquitous nature would suggest a biological base. Rossi, Chapter 9, this volume, has outlined the basic biological processes involved. Language skills are dominant in the left hemisphere of the brain whereas in the right hemisphere, visual–spatial relationships are dominant. Human males show a more rigid separation in the functioning of the two brain hemispheres, with the right hemisphere tending to be dominant. There is less rigid lateralization of hemispheres in human females, suggesting a greater ease and frequency of communication. This gender difference in brain lateralization is in place in the late stages of fetal development. These neurological developments occur largely during the last trimester of pregnancy when the brain is undergoing rapid development and differentiation. Hormonal influences play a critical role in this stage of development. The evidence suggests that the gender differences in brain lateralization and hemisphere development lead to the use of different ways of processing information and play a substantial role in the dominant agentic trait in males and the dominant affiliative trait in females (also see Durden-Smith & DeSimone, 1983; Ellis, 1982; Goy & McEwen, 1980; Hoyenga & Hoyenga, 1979; McGlone, 1980; Parsons, 1982).

Physique and Assertiveness

A higher proportion of males than females have a physique that is associated with deviant behavior. Males are bigger, have more muscle mass, higher metabolism rates, and have a higher proportion of red blood corpuscles (Parsons, 1982). Perhaps at least as important, males are much more likely than females to have a mesomorphic body type (as measured by indicators other than strength) (e.g. Cortés, 1982; Cortés & Gatti, 1972; Sheldon, 1940), which is related to a number of traits (including personality traits) that tend to be found among persons who have been officially labelled deviant. Furthermore, males have consistently been found to be more aggressive than females, although many of the studies may be more properly interpreted as indicating males are simply more active and assertive than females (e.g. Hoyenga & Hoyenga, 1979; Maccoby & Jacklin, 1974; Parsons, 1982). The greater aggressiveness or assertiveness of males appears to be largely due to their increased exposure to androgens,[21] although the nature of the relationship is not so clear as one might wish (Hoyenga & Hoyenga, 1979; Parsons, 1982; Petersen, 1980).

In summary, it would appear that the low rate of deviant behavior among females is due largely to their affiliative nature, their physique, and to their lack of assertiveness, all of which have a biological base. It is likely that the same attributes also account for some of the differences in the typical athletic performances of males and females.

The Age–Deviant Link: A Summary Statement

Late adolescence and early adulthood represent a life stage characterized by stressful life choices, high autonomy coupled with low responsibility, and a social expectation that most young people who engage in socially disapproved behavior will settle down with time. The evidence on the relationship between psychological well-being and psychological maturation with age clearly indicates that persons 18–25 years old are the most self-absorbed and the most dissatisfied with their lives, which suggests they would be the most prone to deviant behavior. The social expectation that young people will "settle down" may contribute to the observed tendency for deviance to decline with age, although this runs directly counter to the general sociological view that deviance is an amplifying process. However, while social roles, psychological well-being, and psychological maturation are all compatible with the notion that deviance should peak at an early age and then decline, by themselves they cannot account for the *rapidity* of both the rise and fall of deviant behavior as one ages. To explain the rapidity of the decline in deviant behavior with age, we need to look at physical strength, energy, psychological drive, and the reinforcement effect of an adrenaline high. We have pointed out that these variables peak at the same time deviant behavior peaks and suggest that their rapid decline is a major contribution to the rapid decline in deviant behavior. If this argument is correct, it would tend to explain why the age–deviance relationship seems to be universal across societies and historic time (Hirschi & Gottfredson, 1983; Robins, 1980).

---

[21]The increased exposure involves both a direct activation mode, such as occurs during adolescence, and an inductive mode that, as discussed in the preceding section, leads to the development of a "male brain" (Parsons, 1982).

If the biological component of age is critical, one should find parallels to the age–deviance pattern in a variety of other activities that are physically demanding and often involve a type of commitment that makes it difficult to lead a normal life. Physically demanding sports are a case in point. One supportive piece of evidence is that most criminals and most athletes tend to have similar physiques, that is, to have a mesomorphic development. (See Herrnstein, 1983, for a review of the evidence on physiques and criminals).[22] Also supportive is the fact that both the age of Olympic participants and winners is very similar to the age pattern found with deviant behavior. The majority of gold medal Olympic winners and of felons are young adults who withdraw from the field as they age.

References

Adler, F. *Sisters in crime*. New York: McGraw–Hill, 1976.

Aichhorn, A. *Wayward youth*. New York: Viking, 1935.

Akers, R. *Deviant behavior: A social learning approach* (2nd ed.). Belmont, Calif.: Wadsworth, 1977.

American Psychiatric Association. *Diagnostic and statistical manual of mental disorders* (2nd ed.) (DSM III). Washington, D.C.: American Psychiatric Association, 1980.

Armor, D., Polich, J. M., & Stombul, H. B. *Alcoholism and treatment*. New York: Wiley, 1978.

Back, K., & Gergen, K. U. Cognitive and motivational factors in aging and disengagement. In I. Simpson & J. McKinney (Eds.), *Social aspects of aging*. Durham: Duke University Press, 1966, pp. 289–295.

Bakan, D. *The duality of human existence*. Chicago: Rand McNally, 1966.

Becker, H. *Outsiders: Studies in the sociology of deviance*. New York: The Free Press, 1963.

Blumstein, A. Prisons: Population, capacity and alternatives. In J. G. Wilson (Ed.), *Crime and public policy*. San Francisco: ICS Press, 1983, pp. 229–250.

Bonger, W. *An introduction to criminology*. London: Methuen, 1936.

Booth, A., & Edwards, J. Crowding and human sexual behavior. *Social Forces*, 1977, 55, 791–807.

Brim, O. G., Jr. Adult socialization. In J. Clauson (Ed.), *Socialization and society*. Boston: Little, Brown, 1968, pp. 182–226.

Brocki, S. *Marital status, sex and mental well-being*. Unpublished doctoral dissertation, Vanderbilt University, 1979.

Butler, R. N., & Lewis, M. I. *Aging and mental health*. St. Louis: C. V. Mosby, 1977.

Campbell, A. *The sense of well-being in America*. New York: McGraw-Hill, 1981.

---

[22]As Herrnstein (1983) notes, social scientists have discounted the evidence of Glueck and Glueck (1950, 1956, 1968), Sheldon (1940, 1949), Cortés and Gatti (1972), and Cortés (1982) on the relationship between physique and crime, but that evidence is quite compelling. For a discussion of how the properties associated with mesomorph physique increase the likelihood of involvement in deviant behavior, see Cortés (1982). The process linking a mesomorph physique to demanding athletic activities is virtually identical.

Campbell, A., Converse, P. E., & Rodgers, W. *The quality of American life: Perceptions, evaluations and satisfactions.* New York: Russell Sage Foundation, 1976.

Caporael, L. Ergotism: The satan loosed in Salem? In W. Gove & G. R. Carpenter (Eds.), *The fundamental connection between nature and nurture.* Lexington, Mass.: Lexington Books, 1982, pp. 265–270.

Chambliss, W. *Crime and the legal process.* New York: McGraw–Hill, 1969.

Cline, H. Criminal behavior over the life span. In O. G. Brim, Jr. & J. Kagan (Eds.), *Consistency and change in human development.* Cambridge: Harvard University Press, 1980, pp. 641–674.

Cole, S. The growth of scientific knowledge: Theories of deviance as a case study. In L. Coser (Ed.), *The idea of social structure: Papers in honor of Robert K. Merton.* New York: Harcourt, Brace, Jovanovich, 1975, pp. 175–220.

Cortés, J. Delinquency and crime: A biopsychosocial theory. In W. Gove & G. R. Carpenter (Eds.), *The fundamental connection between nature and nurture.* Lexington, Massachusetts: Lexington Books, 1982, pp. 191–229.

Cortés, J., & Gatti, F. M. *Delinquency and crime: A biopsychological approach.* New York: Academic, 1972.

Crutchfield, R. *An examination of the demographic, mental health, and social role correlates of adult drug use.* Unpublished doctoral dissertation, Vanderbilt University, 1980.

Cumming, E., & Henry, W. *Growing old: The process of disengagement.* New York: Basic Books, 1961.

Davis, G. C., Buchsbaum, M. S., & Bunney, W. E. Endorphins: Endogenous control of the perception of pain. In W. Gove & G. R. Carpenter (Eds.), *The fundamental connection between nature and nurture.* Lexington, Mass.: Lexington Books, 1982, pp. 41–56.

Davis, K., & van den Oever, P. Demographic foundations of new sex roles. *Population and Human Development Review*, 1982, *8*, 495–511.

Deming, R. *Women: The new criminals.* Nashville: Thomas Nelson, 1977.

Doering, C., Brodie, H., Kramer, H., Moos, R. H., Becker, H., & Hamburg, D. Negative affect and plasma testosterone: A longitudinal human study. *Psychosomatic Medicine*, 1975, *37*, 484–491.

Durden-Smith, J., & DeSimone, D. *Sex and brain.* New York: Basic Books, 1983.

Durkheim, E. *Suicide.* New York: The Free Press, 1951.

Durkheim, E. *The division of labor in society.* New York: The Free Press, 1964.

Ehrenkranz, J., Bliss, E., & Sheard, M. H. Correlation of aggressive behavior and social dominance in man. *Psychosomatic Medicine*, 1974, *36*, 469–475.

Elder, G. H., Jr. *Children of the great depression.* Chicago: University of Chicago Press, 1974.

Elder, G. H., Jr. & Liker, J. K. Hard times in women's lives: Historical influences across forty years. *American Journal of Sociology*, 1982, *88*, 241–269.

Ellis, L. Developmental androgen fluctuations and the five dimensions of mammalian sex (with emphasis upon the behavioral dimension and the human species). *Ethology and Sociobiology*, 1982, *3*, 171–197.

Erikson, E. *Childhood and society.* New York: Norton, 1963.

Erikson, E. *Identity: Youth and crisis.* New York: Norton, 1968.

Erikson, E. *Adulthood and world views.* Paper presented at the American Academy Conference on Love and Work in Adulthood, Palo Alto, May 6–7, 1977.

Erikson, K. Notes on the sociology of deviance. *Social Problems*, 1962, *9*, 307–314.

Erikson, K. *Wayward Puritans: A study of the sociology of deviance.* New York: Wiley, 1966.

Finch, C., & Heyflick, L. *Handbook of the biology of aging*. New York: Van Nostrand, 1973.

Foner, A., & Kertzer, D. I. Transition over the life course: Lessons from ageset societies. *American Journal of Sociology*, 1978, *83*, 1081–1104.

Gaitz, C., & Scott, J. Age and the measurement of mental health. *Journal of Health and Social Behavior*, 1972, *13*, 55–67.

Gibbs, J. P. *Norms, deviance and social control: Conceptual matters*. New York: Elsevier, 1981.

Gilligan, C. *In a different voice: Psychological theory and women's development*. Cambridge: Harvard University Press, 1982.

Glueck, S., & Glueck, E. *Unraveling juvenile delinquency*. Cambridge: Harvard University Press, 1950.

Glueck, S., & Glueck, E. *Physique and delinquency*. New York: Harper, 1956.

Glueck, S., & Glueck, E. *Delinquents and nondelinquents in perspective*. Cambridge: Harvard University Press, 1968.

Goode, E. *The marijuana smokers*. New York: Basic Books, 1970.

Goode, E. *Sexual deviance*. New York: Morrow, 1974.

Goodson, W., & Hunt, T. Wound healing and aging. *Journal of Investigative Dermatology*, 1979, *73*, 88–91.

Gordon, C. Role and value development across the life cycle. In J. A. Jackson (Ed.), *Role*. Cambridge: Cambridge University Press, 1972, pp. 65–106.

Gordon, S. L. The sociology of sentiments and emotions. In M. Rosenberg & R. Turner (Eds.), *Social psychology: Sociological perspectives*. New York: Basic Books, 1981, pp. 562–592.

Gould, R. *Transformations: Growth and change in adult life*. New York: Simon & Schuster, 1978.

Gould, R. Transformations during early and middle adult years. In N. Smelser & E. Erikson (Eds.), *Themes of love and work in adulthood*. Cambridge: Harvard University Press, 1980, pp. 213–237.

Gove, W. Sex differences in mental illness among adult men and women: An examination of four questions raised regarding whether or not women actually have higher rates. *Social Science and Medicine*, 1978, *12*, 187–198.

Gove, W. Postscript to alcoholism and labelling theory. In W. Gove (Ed.), *The labelling of deviance* (2nd ed.). Beverly Hills, Calif.: Sage, 1980, pp. 47–51. (a)

Gove, W. (Ed.). *The labelling of deviance* (2nd ed.). Beverly Hills, Calif.: Sage, 1980. (b)

Gove, W., & Carpenter, G. R. (Eds.). *The fundamental connection between nature and nurture: A review of the evidence*. Lexington, Mass.: Lexington Books, 1982.

Gove, W., & Crutchfield, R. The family and delinquency. *The Sociological Quarterly*, 1982, *23*, 301–319.

Gove, W., & Herb, T. Stress and mental illness among the young: A comparison of the sexes. *Social Forces*, 1974, *53*, 256–265.

Gove, W., & Hughes, M. Possible causes of the apparent sex differences in physical health: An empirical investigation. *American Sociological Review*, 1979, *44*, 126–146.

Gove, W., Hughes, M., & Galle, O. Overcrowding in the home: An empirical evaluation of possible pathological consequences. *American Sociological Review*, 1979, *44*, 59–80.

Gove, W., McCorkel, J., Fain, T., & Hughes, M. Response bias in community surveys of mental health: Systematic bias or random noise? *Social Science and Medicine*, 1976, *10*, 407–502.

Gove, W., & Ortega, S. *The stability and changes in the self-concept and self-evaluation of adult men and women across the life span.* Paper presented at the International Interdisciplinary Conference on Self and Identify, Cardiff, Wales, July 1984.

Gove, W., & Style, C. B. The effects of aging during the adult years: An empirical examination, 1983. (Mimeographed)

Gove, W., & Tudor, J. Adult sex roles and mental illness. *American Journal of Sociology*, 1973, *77*, 812–835.

Goy, R. W., & McEwen, B. S. *Sexual differentiation of the brain.* Cambridge: MIT Press, 1980.

Greenberg, D. (Ed.). *Crime and capitalism: Readings in Marxist criminology.* Palo Alto, Calif.: Mayfield, 1981.

Gregerman, R., & Bieman, E. Aging and hormones. In R. Williams (Ed.), *Textbook of endocrinology.* Philadelphia: Saunders, 1981, p. 1192.

Gurin, G., Veroff, J., & Feld, S. *Americans view their mental health.* New York: Basic Books, 1960.

Gusfield, J. *Symbolic crusade: Status politics and the American temperance movement.* Urbana, Illinois: University of Illinois Press, 1963.

Gutmann, D. Women and the concept of ego strength. *Merrill-Palmer Quarterly*, 1965, *11*, 229–240.

Hareven, T. K. (Ed.). *Patterns of aging.* New York: Guilford, 1982.

Herrnstein, R. J. Some criminogenetic traits of offenders. In J. Q. Wilson (Ed.), *Crime and public policy.* San Francisco, Calif.: ICS Press, 1983.

Hirschi, T. *Causes of delinquency.* Berkeley: University of California Press, 1969.

Hirschi, T., & Gottfredson, M. Age and the explanation of crime. *American Journal of Sociology*, 1983, *89*, 552–584.

Hochschild, A. R. Emotion work, feeling rules, and social structure. *American Journal of Sociology*, 1979, *85*, 551–575.

Hoyenga, K. B., & Hoyenga, K. T. *The question of sex differences: Psychological, cultural and biological issues.* Boston: Little, Brown, 1979.

Jarvis, G., Ferrence, R., Johnson, F. G., & Whitehead, P. Sexual patterns of self-injury. *Journal of Health and Social Behavior*, 1976, *17*, 146–155.

Jensen, G. Age and rule-breaking in prison: A test of socio-cultural interpretation. *Criminology*, 1977, *14*, 555–568.

Jung, C. G. *Memories, dreams, reflections.* New York: Pantheon, 1963.

Jung, C. G. *Man and his symbols.* Garden City, N. J.: Doubleday, 1964.

Kessler, R., & McRae, J. Trends in the relationship between sex and attempted suicide. *Journal of Health and Social Behavior*, 1983, *24*, 98–111.

Kreuz, L. E., & Rose, R. M. Assessment of aggressive behavior and plasma testosterone in a young criminal population. *Psychosomatic Medicine*, 1972, *34*, 321–322.

Lemert, E. *Human deviance, social problems, and social control.* Englewood Cliffs, N. J.: Prentice-Hall, 1967.

Levinson, D. J. *The seasons of a man's life.* New York: Knopf, 1978.

Levinson, D. J. Toward a conception of the life course. In N. Smelser & E. Erikson (Eds.), *Themes of work and love in adulthood.* Cambridge: Harvard University Press, 1980, pp. 265–290.

Liddle, G. The adrenals. In R. Williams (Ed.), *Textbook of endocrinology.* Philadelphia: Saunders, 1981, pp. 249–292.

Linn, B. Age differences in the severity and outcomes of burns. *Journal of American Geriatric Society*, 1980, *28*, 118–123.

Locksley, A., & Douvan, E. Problem behavior in adolescents. In E. Gomberg & V. Franks (Eds.), *Gender and disordered behavior: Sex differences in psychopathology.* New York: Brunner/Mazel, 1979, pp. 71–100.

McAuliffe, W. Beyond secondary deviance: Negative labelling and its effects on the heroin addict. In W. Gove (Ed.), *The labelling of deviance* (2nd ed.). Beverly Hills, Calif.: Sage, 1980, pp. 303–340.

Maccoby, E. E., & Jacklin, C. N. *The psychology of sex differences*. Stanford, California: Stanford University Press, 1974.

McGlone, J. Sex differences in human brain asymmetry: A critical survey. *Behavioral and Brain Science*, 1980, *3*, 215–227.

Mattson, A. D., Schilling, D., Olweus, D., Low, H., & Stevenson, J. Plasma testosterone, aggressive behavior and personality dimensions in young male delinquents. *Journal of the American Academy of Child Psychiatry*, 1980, *19*, 476–490.

Mellinger, G., Balter, M., Manheim, D., Cisin, I., & Parry, H. Psychic distress, life crises and the use of psychotherapeutic medications: National household survey data. *Archives of General Psychiatry*, 1978, *33*, 1045–1052.

Merton, R. K. Social structure and anomie. In R. K. Merton (Ed.), *Social Theory and Social Structure*. New York: The Free Press, 1957, pp. 161–194.

Neugarten, B. L. The awareness of middle age. In B. L. Neugarten (Ed.), *Middle age and aging: A reader in social psychology*. Chicago, Illinois: University of Chicago Press, 1968, pp. 93–98.

Neugarten, B. L. Timing, age and the life cycle. *American Journal of Psychiatry*, 1979, *136*, 887–894.

New York State. *New York State statistical yearbook* (1979–1980 ed.). Albany: Division of the Budget, 1979.

O'Donnell, L. The social world of parents. *Marriage and Family Review*, 1983, *5*, 9–36.

Ortega, S., & Gove, W. *Age and gender differences in the cognitive and evaluative components of self*, Paper presented at the Annual Meeting of the American Sociological Association, Toronto, August 1981.

Parsons, J. E. Biology, experience and sex dimorphic behaviors. In W. Gove & G. R. Carpenter (Eds.), *The fundamental connection between nature and nurture*. Lexington, Mass.: Lexington Books, 1982, pp. 137–170.

Persky, H., Smith, K. D., & Basu, G. K. Relationship of psychological measures of aggression and hostility to testosterone production in man. *Psychosomatic Medicine*, 1971, *33*, 265–277.

Petersen, A. C. Biopsychosocial processes in the development of sex related differences. In J. E. Parsons (Ed.), *The psychology of sex differences and sex roles*. Washington, D. C.: Hemisphere, 1980, pp. 31–56.

Pressey, S., & Kuhlen, R. *Psychological development through the life span*. New York: Harper, 1957.

Quetelet, L. *A treatise on man*. Gainesville, Fla.: Scholars' Facsimilies and Reprints, 1969.

Quinney, R. *The social reality of crime*. Boston, Mass.: Little, Brown, 1970.

Rada, R. T., Laws, D. R., & Kellner, R. Plasma testosterone levels in the rapist. *Psychosomatic Medicine*, 1976, *38*, 257–268.

Riley, M. W., & Foner, A. In M. Riley & A. Foner (Eds.), *Aging and society: An inventory of research findings* (Vol. 1). New York: Russell Sage Foundation, 1968.

Riley, M. W., Foner, A., & Johnson, M. E. Political roles. In M. Riley & A. Foner (Eds.), *Aging and society*, (Vol. 1). *An inventory of research findings*. New York: Russell Sage Foundation, 1968, pp. 463–482. (a)

Riley, M. W., Foner, A., & Johnson, M. E. Religious roles. In M. Riley & A. Foner (Eds.), *Aging and society: An inventory of research findings* (Vol. 1). New York: Russell Sage Foundation, 1968, pp. 483–500. (b)

Robins, L. Sturdy childhood predictors of adult antisocial behavior: Replications from longitudinal studies. *Psychological Medicine*, 1978, *8*, 611–622.

Robins, L. Alcoholism and labelling theory. In W. Gove (Ed.), *The labelling of deviance* (2nd ed.). Beverly Hills, Calif.: Sage, 1980, pp. 35–47.

Robins, L., & Wish, E. Childhood deviance as a developmental pattern process: A study of 233 urban black men from birth to 18. *Social Forces*, 1977, *56*, 488–498.

Rossi, A. S. Life-span theories and women's lives. *Signs: A Journal of Women in Society and Culture*, 1980, *6*, 4–32.

Rossi, A. S. Gender and parenthood. In A. Rossi (Ed.), *Gender and the life course*. Hawthorne, N. Y.: Aldine, 1984.

Rowe, A., & Tittle, C. Life cycle changes and criminal propensity. *The Sociological Quarterly*, 1977, *18*, 223–236.

Sands, D. E. Further studies on endocrine treatment in adolescence and early adult life. *Journal of Mental Science*, 1954, *100*, 211–219.

Schiavi, R. C., Theilgaard, A., Owen, D. R., & White, D. Sex chromosome anomalies, hormones and aggressivity. *Archives of General Psychiatry*, 1984, *41*, 93–99.

Schur, E. *Labelling women deviant: Gender, stigma and social control*. New York: Random House, 1984.

Sheldon, W. H. *The varieties of human physique*. New York: Harper, 1940.

Sheldon, W. H. *Varieties of delinquent youth*. New York: Harper, 1949.

Simon, R. *Women and crime*. Lexington, Mass.: D. C. Heath, 1975.

Spirluso, W. Physical fitness, aging and psychomotor speed: A review. *Journal of Gerontology*, 1980, *35*, 840–865.

Steffensmeier, D. Patterns of female property crime, 1960–1978: A postscript. In L. H. Bowker (Ed.), *Women and crime in America*. New York: Macmillan, 1981, pp. 209–219.

Steffensmeier, D., & Cobb, M. Sex differences in urban arrest patterns, 1934–1979. *Social Forces*, 1981, *29*, 37–50.

Steffensmeier, D., & Terry, R. Age and sex in crime: Theoretical synthesis and new directions. Paper presented at the annual meeting of the American Sociological Association, Detroit, September 1983.

Sutherland, E., & Cressey, D. *Criminology* (10th ed.). Philadelphia, Pa.: Lippincott, 1978.

Tardola, H. The needle scene. In G. Jacobs (Ed.), *The participant observer: Encounters with social reality*. New York: George Braziller, 1970, pp. 48–63.

Taylor, I., Walton, P., & Young, J. (Eds.). *Critical criminology*. London: Routledge and Kegan Paul, 1973.

Thomas, R. The mental patient career: Alternative coping techniques. Unpublished doctoral dissertation, Vanderbilt University, 1983.

Vaillant, G. E. *Adaptation to life*. Boston: Little, Brown, 1977.

Veroff, J., Douvan, E., & Kulka, R. *The inner American: A self-portrait from 1957 to 1976*. New York: Basic Books, 1981.

Whitt, D., Lowe, G., Peck, C., & Curry, E. The changing association between age and happiness: Emerging trend or methodological artifact. *Social Forces*, 1980, *58*, 1302–1307.

8

Fertility as an Adjustment to Risk*

MEAD CAIN
Population Council

Introduction

A curious myopia characterizes recent research on the value of children and its relation to fertility levels and trends in rural areas of developing countries. By this I mean that disproportionate theoretical and empirical attention is devoted to the costs and benefits of children to parents while the children are young. The underlying presumption is that positive discount rates pertain (giving greater weight to near term costs and benefits than to more distant streams). Attention is directed to the time and commodity costs of child care and the labor contributions of young children to their parents' household. Change in these parameters dominates scholarly perceptions of change in the demand for children over the course of economic development. This myopia is evident in the recent National Academy of Sciences report on the determinants of fertility in developing countries (Bulatao & Lee, 1983). Consider, for example, the following passage from the summary chapter on demand for children by Lee and Bulatao:

> In the course of economic development, the relative [child] cost measure first falls (that is, children's net value rises) as wage rates rise. Then, as various influences of development reduce child labor services and render women's work less compatible with childcare . . . children cease to be net suppliers of labor. From that point on, higher wages render the relative and absolute costs of children greater, and the Mincer–Becker–Willis model becomes more appropriate. This increase in relative costs is reinforced by the declining price of luxuries relative to staples as development proceeds, and perhaps by an increase in women's wage rates relative to children's as women's skill levels increase. (1983, p. 199)[1]

---

*This is a slightly revised version of a paper with the same title that appeared in *Population and Development Review*, 1983, 9, 688–702.
[1]The "relative cost measure" referred to in this passage is the index developed by Peter Lindert, to be discussed presently.

Preoccupation with the more immediate costs and benefits of children leads to the neglect of another major class of potential economic benefits—the value of children as insurance against the risk of income insufficiency in parents' old age and in a variety of other circumstances. The value of children as security assets presents a number of analytical problems for which the methodology and theory that have been developed to study the time and commodity costs of children, and their relation to reproductive behavior, are not well adapted.

The Value of Children: Accounting Procedures

Conventional wisdom regarding the cost accounting of children is well represented by the work of Peter Lindert. He developed a formula for estimating the relative cost of an additional child in the course of his research on fertility transition in the United States (Lindert, 1978). Subsequently, he applied his concept of *relative child cost* to developing country settings (Lindert, 1980, 1983).

According to Lindert, the relative cost of an additional child may be expressed as the ratio of an index of child input prices to an index of input prices for alternative home activities. In influencing parental demand for children, it is change in the price of children relative to other forms of expenditure, rather than absolute child cost, that is significant. The index of child input prices is calculated from a formula that yields the absolute discounted cost of a child, net of the child's economic contribution, over the parents' expected lifetime (Lindert, 1983, p. 402).

As Lindert notes, his accounting framework incorporates several factors generally ignored in previous work on the value of children. Among these refinements are an allowance for child survival probabilities and an exhaustive accounting of the time costs to all family members. Regardless of what is gained on a conceptual level by these refinements (and ignoring the formidable measurement problems they raise), it remains to be emphasized that the estimate of net present value yielded by this formula is highly sensitive to the discount rate that is applied. The relative weight of the security asset value of children in the calculation is particularly sensitive to the chosen discount rate because of the timing of such benefits over the parents' life cycle. On the choice of a discount rate, Lindert recommends applying the rates of return on "such risky human investments as schooling" (1983, p. 402). In applications of his framework to the rural Philippines (for 1975) and the urban United States, he uses a 13% discount rate. If only time and commodity transfers from children to elderly parents are considered, a 13% discount rate renders the present value of such transfers negligible, absolutely and in comparison to more immediate time and commodity costs and benefits. Lindert, moreover, is openly skeptical about the actual (undiscounted) size of such transfers (both historically and at present in developing societies) and their relevance to reproductive decisions. For example, he says:

It is traditional to argue that, in underdeveloped countries, parents expect and receive significant economic support from their surviving children, especially sons, in their old age. The subsequent decline in this reliance on children is traditionally thought to be one of the main ways in which economic development reduces fertility. The evidence for this view comes in three forms, each of which can be challenged. (Lindert, 1983, p. 410).[2]

In empirical applications of his framework, Lindert does not bother to consider the economic costs and returns of children past the age of 19, and it is on the basis of such truncated analyses as these that he concludes: "When . . . likely empirical biases are recognized, and when the more remunerative later years of childhood have been deflated by appropriate survival and discount rates, it seems likely that children are a net economic cost even in the least developed settings" (1983, p. 408).

This conclusion, and the analysis that supports it, have become the received wisdom. For example, although Lee and Bulatao (1983) point out the frailty of the assumptions underlying the concept of relative cost and the associated discounting procedures under certain circumstances, they nevertheless gravitate toward Lindert's general conclusions: that children everywhere (or with very few exceptions) have a negative asset value; That the major factors influencing the demand for children are captured by the ingredients of relative child cost in the first two decades of a child's life; and that the major factors influencing change in demand are these same ingredients.

Suppose, however, that parents do, in fact, place a high value on children as security assets and that they do so both because they value their own future security and because there are no real alternatives to children as sources of security. If this is the case (and I believe it is for much of the developing world), then clearly there is something wrong with conventional cost accounting procedures and the conclusions they yield.

Welfare Institutions in Comparative Perspective

In those parts of South Asia that I have studied, all indications—whether from individual responses to such questions as why sterilization is delayed until a particular parity and child-sex composition have been achieved; from instances of misfortune befalling aging parents who do not have a surviving son to depend

---

[2]He then proceeds to challenge each of these. The three kinds of evidence that he cites are residential patterns that show elderly parents living with children, responses to "value of children" survey questions indicating that old-age security is an important perceived benefit of children, and cross-national regression analyses of the effects of social security programs on fertility. Lindert's challenges are not particularly convincing. In reference to residence patterns, for example, he suggests that one cannot tell from such data who is supporting whom. With respect to survey responses, he suggests that "it is cheap for interview respondents to say they feel old age support from children is one of the most salient advantages of having children" (1983: 410).

on; or from evidence of the insecurity of property rights, widespread failure of financial and insurance markets, and absence of important extrafamilial welfare institutions—point to the salience of parental security concerns for reproductive strategies (Cain, 1978, 1981, 1982). Perhaps it is because my view of the developing world is primarily informed by my experience in South Asia that I find the dismissal of security concerns as a motivational force so odd. Similarly, I suspect that the general skepticism of Lindert and others regarding the relevance of security concerns for reproductive behavior may in large part be a product of the irrelevance of such concerns in the societies with which such scholars are most familiar.

One of the more distinctive features of certain Western cultures is the relative unimportance of lineal kin (i.e., children and grandchildren) in societal solutions to the problem of providing care and economic support to those among the elderly no longer able to support themselves. It is important to note, moreover, that this feature is not of recent origin. As a characteristic of society in England, for example, it would appear to predate both the Industrial Revolution and the Reformation.[3] From a very early period in English history, it seems, risk devolution (in Lesthaeghe's terminology) and poor relief have been centered on the community rather than the family. While particular institutional arrangements have varied over time—with the source of relief, for example, shifting from manor and guild to parish and then to the state—there has nevertheless been a remarkable consistency in the extrafamilial locus of welfare institutions. Although less well-documented, a similar orientation toward poor relief seems to characterize much of eighteenth- and nineteenth-century American society. Lindert (1980, pp. 51–53) is only one of several historians to have suggested the notion that children often did not play an important role in providing support for their elderly parents in the eighteenth- and nineteenth-century United States.[4]

Steeped in this cultural heritage, it is not surprising that Lindert and others greet with skepticism the suggestion for contemporary developing countries that parental concern about old-age security motivates reproductive behavior. The impulse to generalize from the specific and familiar is powerful in the social sciences. In the case of social and economic development, this impulse is all the more powerful due to the still pervasive influence of the modernization paradigm—the conception of development as a uniform process that transforms societies from "traditional" to "modern" in a series of stages, each with a distinctive institutional configuration. Once a society has been located at a particular stage, institutional structure may be inferred according to what one understands it should be at that stage. This paradigm facilitates movement between "premodern" societies of the past and those of the present: Thus, evidence of

---

[3]I rely here on Smith (in press). See also Smith (1981: 601–611) and Lesthaeghe (1980: 531–534).

[4]Others who have reached similar conclusions include Vinovskis (in press) and Achenbaum (1978).

weak filial ties in eighteenth-century America provides a basis for questioning the strength of filial ties in present day developing countries.[5]

John Hajnal's elegant study of household formation systems illustrates how treacherous such movement between the past and the present can be when the powerful role of cultural differences is disregarded (Hajnal, 1982). Hajnal describes the distinctive system of household formation rules that characterized preindustrial Northwest Europe (late marriage for both sexes, the formation of independent households at the time of marriage, and the circulation of young unmarried people as servants) and contrasts it with the joint-household system that is found in much of the developing world today (earlier marriage for men and very early marriage for women, the newly married couple often remaining for a period as part of a household in which an older couple or person is in charge, and households with several married couples sometimes splitting to form two or more households, each containing one or more couples). In the joint-household system, property transfer may await the death of the elder generation, while a shift in farm management responsibility to the younger generation and the needs of weak and aging parents are seen to within an undivided family. By contrast, the economic and physical independence of children from parents that accompanied marriage in the Northwest European system required alternative mechanisms to effect property transfer between generations and to provide for the needs of aging parents. The solution for those with property was (primarily) the retirement contract and for the propertyless, publicly provided poor relief (Hajnal, 1982, p. 477). The retirement contract typically stipulated the transfer of property rights in return for maintenance for a specified period or until death. While the partners in a contract were frequently parents and their children, they were at least as often, it seems, unrelated. A study of such contracts in fourteenth-century East Anglia, for example, revealed that "before 1350 about one-half of the pensioners negotiated contracts with their own children; after 1350, less than one-quarter of the agreements involved parents and children" (Clark, 1982, p. 315). The kinship identity of partners in retirement contracts held no special significance with respect to enforcement because both the courts and the administrative hierarchy of the manor had the power to ensure that obligations were honored.

In contrast to joint-household systems, transfers among family members played a relatively minor role in smoothing consumption over the individual life

---

[5]It is just as common to find that evidence from currently developing societies is used as a basis for inferring conditions in the past. It is still not unusual, for example, to encounter depictions of premodern English households as extended in form or references to a secular trend from extended toward nuclear household structure in the course of Western development, whereas, in fact, neither of these assertions is correct, as was shown by the work of Laslett and others over a decade ago (Laslett & Wall, 1972). It is also not unusual to find demographic transition in the West partially explained by the erosion of the value of children as old-age security assets. For a recent example, see Birdsall (1983: 116).

cycle in Northwest European societies. Smoothing was achieved instead by transfers from communal funds and through the private pension plans noted above. Other contrasts between the Northwest European and joint-household formation systems suggest themselves. The former might be described as a system in which the elderly were tolerated while in the latter they are venerated. More generally, age and kinship appear to be much less significant principles of social organization in the former than in the latter. Some degree of gerontocracy is characteristic of all societies displaying the joint-household formation pattern. The process of aging thus entails, *ceteris paribus*, the accumulation of power and prestige. This cannot be said of the process of aging in Northwest Europe, where neolocal marriage and an ideology of generational self-sufficiency prevailed. Richard Smith (in press) has recently noted that among those without property in England "aging and increased poverty were to be seen as synonymous." He describes a pattern of individual "life-cycle poverty" that produced a *predictable* disparity between the economic status of an elderly parent and his or her children. While such disparities may be found in societies with joint-family systems, they are hardly predictable. Such instances instead represent deviant behavior on the part of the young—violations of a normative structure geared toward generating and maintaining a strong sense of filial obligation. Indeed, the very notion of *individual* fortunes as distinct from *family* fortunes is foreign to joint-family cultures.

One would probably be correct in saying that children did not have appreciable value as security assets to parents in those societies in which the Northwest European family formation system existed. It thus seems unlikely that the security asset value of children was an issue in the timing of fertility decline. It also appears that Lindert's concept of *relative child cost*, with its emphasis on the time and commodity costs and benefits of children through their teens, would find useful application to fertility transitions in these societies. The same thing cannot, however, be said of societies in which joint-household formation systems operate. Welfare and insurance functions that in Northwest European societies were performed by guild, manor, and parish are, in joint-household societies, fulfilled by the family. Support of the elderly, which in Northwest European societies was achieved either through impersonal retirement contracts, effectively enforced by law, or through public poor relief is, in joint-household societies, accomplished through implicit intergenerational contracts between parent and child. Accordingly, for the latter societies, one can reasonably presume (1) that the security asset value of children to parents is potentially high; (2) that this must be reckoned with in considering the circumstances and timing of fertility decline; and (3) that the relative child cost framework as applied by Lindert is inappropriate.

Children as Security Assets

In rural South Asia (and, indeed, many other parts of the developing world), where financial and insurance markets are poorly developed and where, consistent with the joint-household formation system, there is no tradition of extrafamilial welfare institutions, children have a number of desirable properties as security assets. Most importantly, with respect to security for elderly parents, they fulfill the need for an annuity. Uncertainty about length of life and the period and severity of debility that may preceed death requires an investment that yields an assured income for an indefinite period. A strategy of asset accumulation followed by dissaving is not responsive to this requirement. Although the accumulation of wealth will clearly contribute to security in old age, one can rarely be certain that contingencies, such as unusual longevity, will not arise for which the sale of a fixed quantity of assets proves to be inadequate.

It is sometimes suggested that investment in agricultural land is an attractive alternative to children for security purposes in settings like rural South Asia (Schutjer & Stokes, 1982; Vlassoff & Vlassoff, 1980). Land, because it yields income, also holds the potential of performing as a "second best" annuity. Nevertheless, there are, I believe, convincing reasons for rejecting the proposition that land should be regarded as either a superior investment or even a close substitute for children. These reasons pertain to the imperfections in and incompleteness of markets for labor and capital and the weakness of complementary social and legal institutions.

Land, for example, has to be closely managed in order to yield an income. This is true in most developing countries even if the land is leased out. Monitoring, supervising, and managing are labor-intensive, exacting, and costly activities. Neglect will threaten yields and income; and despite the existence of active labor markets in most settings, managerial services cannot easily be purchased. Because of monitoring and enforcement problems, such services must instead be provided by the owner or his immediate family.[6]

Agricultural yields vary from year to year under the best of circumstances; under the worst, these variations can be extreme and cause serious interruptions in income streams. Prolonged flooding or drought can cause virtual suspension of productive activity for considerable periods. Conditions such as these will, of course, affect the incomes of owner–operators, tenants, and landlords alike, and thus rental income is no more protected than labor or management income. Unlike the economically developed countries, developing countries generally lack institutional mechanisms (such as commodity futures markets, capital markets, and disaster insurance) to help the farmer adjust to production-related fluctuations in income.[7] Thus, the integrity of agricultural holdings is threatened because adjustment to such adverse conditions may often be achieved only through the distress sale of land.[8] With the exception of those segments of rural

----

[6]On the role of information and enforcement problems in the organization of exchange, see Ben-Porath (1980).

[7]For an explanation of why insurance markets and financial intermediation emerge in rural areas only at a late stage in economic development, see Binswanger and Rosenzweig (1982).

[8]For the case of Bangladesh, see Cain (1981) and van Schendel (1981).

society that have either great wealth or alternative, lucrative sources of income that are not subject to such risk, it is much easier to shed land assets than it is to accumulate them. Because catastrophe does not have an "up side" counterpart, there is typically little symmetry to the process of gain and loss. This asymmetry is accentuated because, for the vast majority, the same failure of capital and insurance markets that hastens the loss of land impedes recovery and accumulation.

Weather-induced risk is, moreover, only one of several threats to the security of land assets. More direct threats include physical expropriation and fraudulent manipulation of land records and titles. A not inconsequential threat, or, at least, one that may be strongly perceived by landowners, is posed by the state through land reform rhetoric or legislation.

Many amenities and necessary services illustrate the desirability of receiving "annuity payments" in the form of labor and argue for the superiority of children as a security investment. A partial list might include health care, food preparation, and companionship. (The labor in these instances is more likely to be provided by a son's wife than by a son.) Although one could conceivably obtain some of these services in the market, they would be highly imperfect substitutes for those provided by kin.

Children are neither costless nor risk-free investments. They may die or become disabled; and they may refuse to honor their obligations to parents. Despite the risks entailed in investing in children as security assets, however, they embody qualities that set them apart from land. First among these is the quality of support they provide to parents, which is another way of acknowledging the central position of the family in southern Asian societies, and that life without family is barely worth living. Although the maintenance of an adequate level of subsistence in old age represents an important goal, individuals aspire to a good deal more. They may aspire as much or more to their due as elders: Deference from others, comfort, peace, and companionship. For such "commodities," there are clearly no substitutes for their children and their children's families. Second is the versatility of children as security assets in settings where insecurity is rife and derives from many different sources, of which the process of aging is only one. Third, in many settings the security of land itself and of income derived from land is in doubt. In such circumstances, children may, in fact, serve as an important means of insuring against property loss. In general, therefore, it is probably more useful to think of land and children as security complements rather than substitutes.

Modeling Fertility Decisions

Accepting the proposition that parents in some developing countries place a high value on children as security assets, how does one best incorporate this into models of reproductive decision making? It is possible to accommodate a high security value of children within Lindert's cost-accounting framework: For example, one can impute a very high value to old-age support so that its estimated present value is nonnegligible, or one can tinker with the discount rate, perhaps even allow for a negative rate, to accomplish the same thing. Operationally, however, it is very difficult to estimate the value of old-age security relative to the time and commodity costs of young children, especially if there truly is no alternative to children providing such support. On balance, then, it may be preferable to consider alternative ways of conceptualizing both the method of valuation and the decision process.

There are other compelling reasons for pursuing alternatives to the global optimization decision model implicit in Lindert's framework when considering how concerns about future security figure in reproductive decisions. In the case of old-age support and security, and, equally important, an individual's expectations of what this should entail, the attempt to distinguish the economic from the noneconomic seems peculiarly artificial. Should, for example, a "feeling of security" be regarded as a psychic benefit (akin, say, to pleasure derived from playing with children), or is it a tangible economic benefit? Perhaps old-age security should be viewed as an integral package—a composite of the economic and the noneconomic. While children may indeed serve the purpose of a crude annuity for parents in many developing societies, they also provide a family setting in which to grow old.[9]

One class of decision models, which draws partially on bounded rationality theory, seems particularly promising in application to old-age security concerns and reproductive decisions: Lexicographic ordering of decision rules based on the criterion of "safety-first."[10] Unlike the neoclassical approach to household

---

[9]McNicoll (1980) provides a more general argument for pursuing alternatives to the global optimization approach to modeling fertility behavior. In this article, he elaborates the concept of *bounded rationality* as applied to reproductive decisions. One of his examples of how particular institutional settings may generate a segmented decision environment is particularly relevant to our discussion:

Notwithstanding the strong liking of economists for uniform rates of time preference across all decisions by an individual, empirically this may not be the case. The need for long-haul risk management, either by and for individual parents over their lifetime or by and for the family conceived as an ongoing corporate entity, may set up a domain of consistency separate from the domain of short-run economic decisions. For example, a near zero rate of time preference may apply to the former domain (such as with reference to old-age support perhaps decades in the future), while a high rate of time preference is implicit in the latter. Decisions on family size and timing of births may typically be counted in the former, as an aspect of family risk management. (1980: 452–453)

[10]Bounded rationality decision theory posits that choice is exercised over a subset of available options. Lexicographic ordering refers to a hierarchy of decision rules. The assumption of neoclassical microeconomics—implicit in Lindert's approach to child cost accounting—is that choice is exercised over the full range of options (*global optimization*). On bounded rationality, see Simon (1957). On Lexicographic Safety First (LSF) decision models and other approaches to modeling uncertain decisions, see Roumasset (1976) and Roumasset, Boussard, and Singh (1979). Lexicographic decision rules based on other criteria are discussed in Leibenstein (1981).

behavior, which focuses exclusively on so-called outcome rationality (individuals must behave only *as if* they were global optimizers), this approach is concerned with the decision process itself. Developed to study innovation–adoption behavior of farmers, Lexicographic Safety First (LSF) models assume that farmers, in making production decisions, are motivated not only by a desire to maximize net returns but also by the condition that net returns not fall beneath some specified "disaster level."

The results of field experiments by agricultural economists in a variety of developing country settings suggest that farmers are indeed risk averse (Binswanger, 1982). Other evidence relative to risk in agricultural production indicates that perceptions of risk tend to conform to objective probabilities (Walker, 1981). Moreover, in one study, which succeeded in overcoming the formidable measurement problems involved in testing the relative merits of different choice models, LSF rules were more successful than both expected utility and profit maximization criteria in predicting farmers' behavior (Walker, 1981).[11] Even without direct evidence, it is reasonable to suppose that if the likelihood of "disaster," however defined, is high and if the probability of its occurrence depends importantly on decisions over which an individual has some control, then the individual will act so as to minimize the probability of its occurrence. In the case of agricultural production, disaster is crop failure, and the choice variable is crop variety (or some other input decision). In our case, the disaster is income insufficiency in old age (and/or other contingencies), and the choice variable is fertility.

To elaborate, the analogy in the case of reproductive decisions is to assume that parents wish to maximize "utility" subject to the chance constraint that the probability of inadequate support and quality of life in old age is less than or equal to some target probability. Parents will seek to minimize the probability of disaster whenever the chance constraint is not met and to maximize utility when it is. Here, the first priority is to make adequate provision for the future with reasonable certainty. Only after this constraint is fulfilled do parents concern themselves with the fertility implications of the more familiar time and commodity costs and benefits of children.

The LSF model as applied to reproductive decisions suggests that parents define minimum requirements for old-age security in terms of a certain number of surviving children. Suppose, for example, that this minimum is one healthy and loyal surviving son. The fertility level that is consistent with this goal will depend primarily on the probability of child survival and the probability of child default. The higher the level of child mortality, the greater the fertility necessary to achieve the goal. Similarly, concern over child default should induce higher

---

[11]Both expected utility and profit maximization assume global optimization. The former allows for uncertainty, whereas the latter does not. In addition to Walker (1981), see Roumasset (1976) and Roumasset et al. (1979).

fertility than if there were no such concern.[12] Mortality and default risks may cause the operational "rule of thumb" to be revised upward, such that two sons surviving through infancy becomes the goal. In particular developing societies, the way in which targets are defined and, thus, their implications for fertility strategies will depend on several factors. For example, the kinship system will influence the extent to which sex of offspring is relevant to framing targets. For some societies, only sons will do, while in others it may only be necessary to have x surviving children, irrespective of sex. Kinship organization will also affect the range of alternative kin-based risk management arrangements that are available to individuals. The similarity in kinship organization among joint-household formation cultures that is so apparent when they are contrasted with the Northwest European household formation system of course masks important differences between societies in which the joint-family system operates. One dimension along which they vary is the degree of economic interdependence among laterally (as distinct from lineally) extended kin. The weaker the lateral bonds of obligation and cooperation, the more an individual will depend on lineal kin (Cain, 1982).

The target may be adjusted upward in response to the need for additional insurance against other contingencies (Cain, 1981). For example, if the security of property rights is dependent upon strength in numbers, the target may be raised from two sons to three. Culturally determined restrictions on the economic activities of women may create dependency that places them at extraordinary risk in the event of widowhood or divorce and thus have a similar effect. The presence of additional sources of risk would not necessarily require an adjustment in the target, however. It could well be that the target set for old-age security is sufficiently high to satisfy additional needs. Nevertheless, multiple sources of risk would serve to reinforce reproductive goals and increase the significance of attaining them. Moreover, the harsher the environment of risk, the more likely that parents will overshoot goals just to be on the safe side.

Economic Development and Fertility Decline

How would one's expectations about change in fertility in response to economic development differ with the LSF model as compared to Lindert's relative cost framework? For the LSF model, one should distinguish change that influences the number of children required to satisfy the security constraint (the target) from change affecting other aspects of the cost calculus relating to children (the residual).

Some variables may affect both "target" and "residual" but in opposite ways. For example, an improvement in infant and child mortality should have,

---

[12]If the frequency of default were high enough, parents might conceivably give up on children. However, if there were no alternative to children, the frequency would have to be very high before this would happen.

according to Lindert's framework, an unambiguous negative effect on the relative cost of children because time costs in particular are heaviest in the first few years of a child's life, while the returns from child labor do not begin to accrue until after the period of highest mortality risk. On the other hand, in the LSF model an improvement in infant and child mortality would, other things being equal, reduce the number of births needed to achieve the target. Unless this number still exceeded the level of natural fertility, one would expect an improvement in mortality to have a negative effect on fertility.

According to the LSF model, change in the time and commodity costs of childrearing or in the value of child labor can be expected to exert a negative influence on fertility only if fertility exceeds the level associated with the target. If fertility is less than or equal to the target level, such change should have no impact on demand for children or fertility. Suppose, for example, that the absolute value of children (considering only costs and returns up to age 15 or 20) is negative according to Lindert's formula. One can imagine several sources of change that would make children even more costly: For example, an increase in female wages or labor force participation that raises the time costs of children or technological change that erodes the market for child labor, thus reducing the potential contributions of children. These changes, however, could quite plausibly leave the target unaffected and thus have no effect on fertility: The cost of insurance will have risen, yet the need for insurance will remain. According to the unconstrained utility maximization model, on the other hand, an increase in the absolute or relative cost of children should, *ceteris paribus*, decrease the demand for children and result in an appropriate adjustment in fertility. The operation of a security constraint, such as described by the LSF model, may help to explain the disappointing results of empirical tests of microeconomic utility maximization models in developing countries and the failure to discover, for example, a consistent and significant relationship between women's work activity and fertility (Standing, 1983).

Other things equal, a sharp decline in mortality should produce a decline in fertility. The important exception to this, as noted above, is the situation in which the target exceeds the number of surviving children implied by natural fertility and initial mortality levels. An additional complication in predicting response to mortality change (and, indeed, determining a target with precision) is that one is dealing with behavior under uncertainty. If people are motivated by a principle of safety-first, they may be influenced less by *average* mortality experience than by variance in that experience and particularly the tail of the distribution that contains the worst records of child survivorship.

Reductions in the target itself could be produced by elimination or moderation of sources of risk, or the replacement of children by other sources of insurance, or some combination of these. Administrative and political development, for example, may eliminate the need for the political self-insurance that a large family provides. Growth in income and savings opportunities may reduce dependence on children for security. However, even with income growth, as long as insurance and financial markets remain badly incomplete, children will not be easily displaced as primary sources of security.

In settings characterized by multiple sources of serious risk for which children represent the best or only means of insurance, the target for surviving children may be particularly resistant to change. If little separates the targets implied by different sources of risk, then all sources must be moderated in order to induce a fertility response.[13]

The LSF model suggests a different pattern of fertility transition from that experienced in the West and depicted by conventional demographic transition theory. The latter describes a smooth and irreversible transition from high to low fertility. By contrast, the LSF model suggests a two-stage transition. In the first stage, fertility adjusts to a new mortality regime. The very sharp and nearly global improvements in mortality that followed World War II in many cases decreased the level of fertility necessary for achieving security goals. (The targets themselves need not have been altered.) The extent of fertility decline in the first stage will vary from society to society depending on the extent of mortality decline and the level of the security target. This security level, in turn, is dependent upon kinship structure and the environment of risk. Improvements in mortality need not produce any fertility response if the security target is sufficiently high (e.g., as in Bangladesh). The second stage of fertility transition is triggered by change that reduces the target itself, that is, improvement in the environment of risk and/or development of alternative sources of insurance. In exceptional cases, postwar economic development will have been so rapid that the two stages merge together and produce an unbroken transition from high to low fertility (e.g., as in Singapore). More typically, however, fertility will remain at an intermediate level between the first and second stages, possibly for a considerable period.

There is evidence, partial and incomplete because of data shortages and the recency of declines, that after an initial period of quite rapid decline, fertility has,

---

[13]There is an important set of circumstances that could lead to the suspension of LSF decision rules and quite different fertility behavior. The LSF model presumes a planning horizon extending (at least) to the end of a person's life. If a family is living in a state of economic desperation, their planning period may be drastically shortened—perhaps to just a few days or weeks. Concern over survival in the immediate future would overwhelm more distant security concerns. Under these circumstances, one can imagine that the modest incentive payments offered by many family planning programs for sterilization could prove irresistible. Even without incentives, the current costs of providing for young children would loom large and might precipitate a decision to terminate childbearing. Certainly in Bangladesh a disproportionate number of sterilization "clients" are drawn from the poorest segment of the society.

indeed, leveled off considerably above replacement rates in many developing countries.[14] Moreover, the fertility levels at which these plateaus occur vary from country to country. Although it would be premature to suggest that an explanation for these developments is at hand, one can nevertheless note the consistency of both the plateau phenomenon and variation in level of plateau with the safety-first model sketched above.

References

Achenbaum, W. A. *Old age in the new land*. Baltimore: The Johns Hopkins University Press, 1978.

Ben-Porath, Y. The F-connection: Families, friends, and firms and the organization of exchange. *Population and Development Review*, 1980, *6*, 1–30.

Binswanger, H. P. Risk aversion, collateral requirements and markets for credit and insurance in rural areas. *Studies in employment and rural development No. 79*, Development Economics Department, World Bank, Washington D.C., 1982.

Binswanger, H. P., & Rosenzweig, M. R. *Production relations in agriculture*. Discussion Paper No. 105, Research Program in Development Studies, Woodrow Wilson School, Princeton University, 1982.

Birdsall, N. Fertility and economic change in eighteenth and nineteenth century Europe: A comment. *Population and Development Review*, 1983, *9*, 111–123.

Bulatao, R. A., & Lee, R. D., with Hollerbach, P. E., & Bongaarts, J. (Eds.). *Determinants of fertility in developing countries* (2 Vols.). New York: Academic Press, 1983.

Cain, M. The household life cycle and economic mobility in rural Bangladesh. *Population and Development Review*, 1978, *4*, 421–438.

Cain, M. Risk and insurance: Perspectives on fertility and agrarian change in India and Bangladesh. *Population and Development Review*, 1981, *7*, 435–474.

Cain, M. Perspectives on family and fertility in developing countries. *Population Studies*, 1982, *36*, 159–175.

Clark, E. Some aspects of social security in medieval England. *Journal of Family History*, 1982, *7*, 307–320.

Hajnal, J. Two kinds of preindustrial household formation system. *Population and Development Review*, 1982, *8*, 449–494.

Knodel, J., Chamratrithirong, A., Chayovan, N., & Debavalya, N. *Fertility in Thailand: Trends, differentials, and proximate determinants*. Washington D.C.: National Academy Press, 1982.

Laslett, P., & Wall, R. (Eds.). *Household and family in past time*. Cambridge: Cambridge University Press, 1972.

Lee, R. D., & Bulatao, R. A. The demand for children: A critical essay. In R. A. Bulatao, R. D. Lee, with P. E. Hollerbach, & J. Bongaarts (Eds.), *Determinants of*

---

[14]Among those countries with relatively good data, Sri Lanka (total fertility rate of 3.8), Tunisia (5.3), Costa Rica (3.8), Fiji (3.4), and Malaysia (4.0) are examples (United Nations, forthcoming). It is tempting to extend this list to other countries where data are less complete. For example, the most recent contraceptive prevalence survey in Thailand (1981) gives the first indications that the rapid fertility decline experienced by that country may be "bottoming out" at a fertility rate of about 3.5 (Knodel, Chamratrithirong, Chayovan, & Debavalya, 1982). However, as the authors note, it is only one survey, and one that is methodologically suspect at that.

fertility in developing countries (Vol. 1). New York: Academic Press, 1983, pp. 191–233.

Leibenstein, H. Economic decision theory and human fertility behavior. *Population and Development Review*, 1981, *7*, 381–400.

Lesthaeghe, R. On the social control of human reproduction. *Population and Development Review*, 1980, *6*, 527–548.

Lindert, P. H. *Fertility and scarcity in America*. Princeton, N.J.: Princeton University Press, 1978.

Lindert, P. H. Child costs and economic development. In R. A. Easterlin (Ed.), *Population and economic change in developing countries*. Chicago, Ill.: University of Chicago Press, 1980, pp. 5–79.

Lindert, P. H. The changing economic costs and benefits of having children. In R. A. Bulatao, R. D. Lee, with P. E. Hollerbach, & J. Bongaarts (Eds.), *Determinants of fertility in developing countries* (Vol. 1). New York: Academic Press, 1983, pp. 398–415.

McNicoll, G. Institutional determinants of fertility change. *Population and Development Review*, 1980, *6*, 441–462.

Roumasset, J. A. *Rice and risk*. Amsterdam: North-Holland Publishing Company, 1976.

Roumasset, J. A., Boussard, J., & Singh, I. (Eds.). *Risk, uncertainty and agricultural development*. New York: Agricultural Development Council, 1979.

Schutjer, W. A., & Stokes, C. S. Agricultural policies and human fertility: Some emerging connections. *Population Research and Policy Review*, 1982, *1*, 225–244.

Simon, H. A. *Administrative behavior* (2nd ed.). New York: Macmillan, 1957.

Smith, R. M. Fertility, economy, and household formation in England over three centuries. *Population and Development Review*, 1981, *7*, 595–622.

Smith, R. M. Some issues concerning families and their property in rural England 1250–1800. In R. M. Smith (Ed.), *Land, kinship, and life-cycle*. Cambridge: Cambridge University Press, in press.

Standing, G. Women's work activity and fertility. In R. A. Bulatao, R. D. Lee, with P. E. Hollerbach, & J. Bongaarts (Eds.), *Determinants of fertility in developing countries* (Vol. 1). New York: Academic Press, 1983, pp. 416–438.

United Nations. *World population trends and policies 1982 monitoring report* (Vol. 1). New York: United Nations, 1983.

van Schendel, W. *Peasant mobility: The odds of life in rural Bangladesh*. Assen, The Netherlands: van Goreum, 1981.

Vinovskis, M. A. Historical perspectives on rural development and human fertility in nineteenth century America. In W. A. Schutjer & C. S. Stokes (Eds.), *Rural development and human fertility*. New York: Macmillan, in press.

Vlassoff, M., & Vlassoff, C. Old age security and the utility of children in rural India. *Population Studies*, 1980, *34*, 487–499.

Walker, T. S. Risk and adoption of hybrid maize in El Salvador. *Food Research Institute Studies*, 1981, *18*, 59–88.

9

Gender and Parenthood*

ALICE S. ROSSI
University of Massachusetts

Introduction

This analysis of gender and parenthood begins with the judgment that none of the theories prevalent in family sociology—exchange, symbolic interaction, general systems, conflict, phenomenology, feminist, or developmental—is adequate to an understanding and explanation of human parenting because they do not seek an integration of biological and social constructs. Research on age and aging has attempted such an integration, whereas research on gender has studiously avoided efforts in this direction. Gender differentiation is not simply a function of socialization, capitalist production, or patriarchy. It is grounded in a sex dimorphism that serves the fundamental purpose of reproducing the species. Hence, sociological units of analysis such as roles, groups, networks, and classes divert attention from the fact that the subjects of our work are male and female animals with genes, glands, bone, and flesh occupying an ecological niche of a particular kind in a tiny fragment of time. And human sexual dimorphism emerged from the long prehistory of mammalian and primate evolution. Theories that neglect these characteristics of sex and gender carry a high risk of eventual irrelevance against the mounting evidence of sexual dimorphism from the biological and neurosciences.

It had been my hope, over the course of the past decade, that the life-span perspective in developmental psychology and the life-course perspective in

*This is a slightly longer version of the Presidential Address presented at the American Sociological Association annual meeting in Detroit, September 1, 1983 than the version published in the February 1984 issue of the *American Sociological Review*. The author is grateful to the University of Massachusetts for the award of a faculty research fellowship for the 1983–1984 academic year; to colleagues who provided support and editorial feedback during the writing of several drafts of this chapter; and to Jeanne Reinle and Cindy Coffman for their patience and diligence in manuscript preparation.

sociology might develop in the direction of integrated biosocial theories, but this has not yet been the case. The "in" concept in adult development these days is "change," but the change both life-span and life-course social scientists are currently enamored of consists of cohort, historical period, and timing effects rather than maturation, and neither perspective has systematically dealt with sex and gender. Their assumptions vacillate between the view that men and women are free, purposive actors charting their own lives (or would be if the economy permitted them to do so) and the view that we are chameleons responsive to changing currents of opinion and historical events.[1]

By contrast, my assumption is that persistent differences between men and women and variations in the extent to which such differences are found along the life line are a function of underlying biological processes of sexual differentiation and maturation as well as social and historical processes.

The chapter proposes no formal theory integrating biological and social constructs. Its goal is necessarily more humble, to clear the ground for the emergence of biosocial theories in future. It begins with an examination of several demographic trends relevant to parenthood in individual lives and to the social ambiance surrounding childbearing and rearing in contemporary society. I begin with demographic trends because they suggest an unprecedented trend with important implications for a new pattern of gender differentiation. Second, the chapter reviews gender differences in parenting as reflected in recent research on traditional and nontraditional family arrangements and the effect of significant male investment in parenting for child outcome. With the evidence on these two topics before us, I will then assess the adequacy of current explanations of gender differences in parenting and demonstrate the relevance of an expanded explanatory model that draws upon bioevolutionary theory and the neurosciences.

Demographic Trends Affecting Gender Roles and Parenting

A good starting place for understanding change in gender and parenting roles is several demographic trends: Longevity and the sex ration, marriage and fertility, and household composition.

Longevity and the Sex Ratio

For most of human history, it was a rare child who reached adulthood without intimate acquaintance with the death of a sibling and of one, if not both, parents.

---

[1]This is not to downplay the great intellectual excitement of much recent research guided by a life-course perspective in sociology and demography (Easterlin, 1980; Elder, 1974, 1982; Elder & Liker, 1982; Elder & Rockwell, 1976, 1978; Riley, 1976; Riley & Waring, 1976; L. Russell, 1982). Such work provides major insights into the processes through which specific historical events and demographic trends impact on social systems and individual lives.

Many contemporary elderly people never knew their grandparents and have memories of their own parents only as middle-aged adults. Since mortality reduction is more palatable politically and psychologically than fertility reduction, longevity differences are narrowing between developed and developing societies. Davis and van de Oever (1982) calculate the life expectancy for men in 16 developing countries in the late 1970s at 60 years, while it was 68 in 20 developed nations. The counterpart averages for women were 64 and 75 in the two sets of countries.

A gender gap in length of life has accompanied the revolution in human longevity, greater in developed nations than in developing countries, with the result that women in countries like our own enjoy, on average, 15 more years of life than men in developing countries (Davis & van den Oever, 1982).

The reason the overall sex ratio in developed countries is not lower than it is, is interesting: Mortality reduction that produces a *female surplus* in old age is balanced by mortality reduction in infancy and childhood that produces a *male surplus* in the younger years. Countries that led the world in reducing infant deaths now show a male surplus well into the fourth decade of life. In the United States between 1910 and 1980, the sex ratio rose among those under 50 years of age, whereas it declined among those over 50 years of age (Davis & van den Oever, 1982).

The sex ratio will continue to rise among the young in the future because of improved diet and prenatal care for pregnant women and the widespread increase in heroic medical efforts to keep alive premature neonates.[2] The reason recent medical efforts affect the sex ratio is rooted in a genetic difference between male and female: There are more points at which aberrations may occur in the fetal development of the male than of the female. Indeed, the estimated sex ratio at conception is about 125, which compensates for the higher rates of spontaneous abortion of male fetuses and higher neonatal death rates of male babies that characterized most of human history.[3]

Increased longevity has particular relevance for the probability of parenthood for men compared to women. A longer life does not increase the reproductive

[2]One 1980 report showed that 40% of babies from 1–1.5 pounds of birth weight survived to the point of hospital discharge (Yu & Hollingsworth, 1980). A randomized prospective trial on the effect of intensive care versus standard care of low birth weight babies showed that the higher survival rate of newborns receiving intensive care was achieved at the expense of producing severely handicapped children (Kitchen, Richards, Ryan, McDougall, Billson, Hier, & Naylor, 1979). Handicapped babies cause stress in a family that in turn triggers an increase in the rate of separation and divorce of the parents. Since divorce is typically followed by becoming single for men but becoming single parents for women, these often difficult babies then become women's primary responsibility under circumstances of great financial and emotional stress.

[3]The male surplus among the young is not unprecedented in human history. In fact, a male surplus characterized all known traditional societies in virtually all of Eurasia until the nineteenth century as a consequence of female infanticide or neglect that led to higher mortality rates among female infants than male.

potential of women, despite a secular trend to a younger age at menarche and a slightly older age at menopause (Lancaster & King, 1982), whereas a longer life can considerably expand the reproductive potential of men. This basic gender difference in reproductive span produces age selectivity in marriage in nonindustrial as well as industrial societies. Davis and van den Oever (1982, p. 501) suggest "we are dealing with a phenomenon so fundamental that it is independent of economic development." Age hypergyny is also found among nonhuman primates, despite the fact that female primates remain fertile as long as they live (Altmann, 1983). Nor is it simply a matter of courtship initiative by old and young males competing for and winning young females, for many primate females actively select older, high status males with demonstrated abilities (Lancaster, 1976), much as many human females do. The shorter reproductive span of the female compared to the male, coupled with earlier ages of sexual and social maturation of women and a probable persistence of high divorce rates suggests that age hypergyny in marriage formation will remain highly resistant to change.

Marriage Rates

A male surplus in the younger years coupled with age hypergyny might be expected to produce higher marriage rates at younger ages for women, but this is clearly not the contemporary pattern. Increasing educational attainment contributes to marital postponement, but even among those in their late twenties, there has been a tripling of the proportion of women not married in 1980 compared to as short a time ago as 1967 (30% vs. 9%). Some portion of this increase is due to the marriage squeeze 20 years after a period of rising fertility rates, which produces a shortage of males a few years older than females, but the remainder represents voluntary postponement of marriage, an increase in preference for remaining unmarried, an increase in homosexuality, and the toll of divorce that leads to fewer remarriages among women than men. For men, social acceptance of sex outside marriage, economic uncertainty facing new entrants to the labor force, and the knowledge that their chances for marriage are not drastically reduced with age press for a postponement of marriage to older ages. Masnick and Bane (1980) predict that by 1990, 48% of men in their late twenties will still be unmarried.

Following a review of these trends and the observation that for many women from one-half to two-thirds of their adult lives will be without a husband, Davis and van den Oever (1982) suggest that marriage is "falling out of fashion."

Fertility

It is not clear whether becoming a parent is also "falling out of fashion." It is now generally accepted that the babyboom of the post-World War II period is the anomaly calling for explanation and not the drop in fertility rates since the late

1950s (Cherlin, 1981). Population growth continues with an "echo boom" as the tailend of the babyboom cohort moves through the childbearing years, but expectations are that the "primary forces of social change conducive to later marriage and low fertility will persist" (Westoff, 1983, p. 99). The lifetime birth expectations of young women are now below replacement level for their generation, and employment status has only a modest effect on these birth expectations (National Center for Health Statistics, 1982).[4]

But while families are becoming smaller and recent research shows a desire to postpone parenthood after marriage (Knaub, Eversoll, & Voss, 1983), almost all adults take on parenting responsibilities at some point in their lives. There has been only a slight increase in voluntary childlessness (Houseknecht, 1979; Veevers, 1979). Surveys among young women continue to show fewer than 10% enter adulthood with no expectation or desire for children (Blake, 1974, 1982). This figure may increase as public disapproval of childlessness softens (Blake, 1979). Huber and Spitze (1983) report a dramatic drop in the view that remaining childless is "selfish": only 21% of the women in their 1978 sample took this view, while more than 70% endorsed it in surveys 5 years earlier.[5]

The fertility trend worth watching concerns out-of-wedlock births. The overall rate of childbearing for unmarried women 15–44 years of age (29.4 per 1000 women) is now the highest rate ever recorded and represents 18% of all births. In the past, perhaps guided by an acceptance of Malinowski's principle of legitimacy (1930), sociologists tended to view out-of-wedlock births as an unfortunate consequence of economic hardship, sexual exploitation of women, family disorganization, and lack of access to contraception and abortion. It has clearly not been seen as a pattern freely chosen by women. Yet such a trend has been in place for some time in Scandinavian countries (Westoff, 1978), where such births are not stigmatized, and unmarried mothers are not subjected to the "putdown" of characterizing their children as fatherless rather than as having a status derived from their mothers. Blake (1982) suggests a comparable trend is occurring in the United States.

Little is known as yet about what proportion of these births are motivated by a desire for a child coupled with no wish for a spouse. One trend worth watching is the growth of sperm banks and artificial insemination. Most women who seek artificial insemination do so because of infertility on the part of their partners, but

---

[4]As of June 1980, the lifetime birth expectations of women aged 18–24 was 2023 births per 1000 women (National Center for Health Statistics, 1982).

[5]Huber and Spitze are careful to point out that their item asked whether a "couple" was selfish if they did not have at least one child, which might have lowered the disapproval rate compared to earlier studies that asked about a "woman" remaining childless. In the latter case, 86% of a 1973 survey considered childless women selfish (Mason, Czajka, & Arber, 1976) compared to the 21% reported by Huber and Spitze. On the other hand, Huber points out that rapid opinion shifts do occur, and concludes there has probably been a reduction in social pressure to have children (Huber & Spitze, 1983, pp. 135–137).

there are also women in their late twenties and early thirties with no Mr. Right on the horizon and strong desires for a child before they run out of reproductive prime time. The Feminist Women's Health Center in Oakland, California added insemination to its services in the fall of 1982 in response to local demand, and by the summer of 1983, close to 100 women were being inseminated a month, one-third of them single women who wished children but not marriage (Bagne, 1983). Some proportion of this group are lesbian women, many in stable sexual relationships. The purposive choice of parenthood through artificial insemination and adoption by single women with economic independence is a trend worth monitoring in the future.

There is little evidence, then, for the view that parenting is falling out of fashion, at least among women. What these trends do suggest is that we may be moving through a period during which parenting is being separated from marriage, as sex was separated from marriage in an earlier period. If this happens, there will be a widening gap in the proportion of each sex carrying family responsibilities.

Household Composition

The modal household in the United States has shifted from one headed by a marital pair rearing dependent-age children to a household headed by a single adult (Kobrin, 1976a, 1976b; Masnick & Bane, 1980). Postponement of marriage, rising rates of separation and divorce, and longer years of widowhood have combined to effect an increase in single adult-headed households, from 25% in 1960 to 35% by 1975 and a projected 45% in 1990. The trend to independent residence is particularly striking among young adults. Masnick (1983) has recently shown that as late as 1950, only 17% of unmarried women in their late twenties headed their own households; by 1980, this had jumped to 60%.[6]

---

[6]College attendance in the United States typically involves living apart from parents, which may represent the entering wedge toward independent residence and geographic migration once schooling is completed. The parental generation was the pioneer cohort that moved to the suburbs, also opening up housing in central cities and, hence, further facilitating the independent residence of young adults, whether or not they attend college. Indeed, Frey and Kobrin (1982) have recently examined the city-to-suburb and suburb-to-city migration in the United States from 1955 to 1975. The pattern in the 1950s of family migration to the suburbs and an increasing concentration of young and old individuals in central cities is now showing regional differences. In the South and West, the old pattern persists, but in the large northern Standard Metropolitan Statistical Areas (SMSAs), primary individuals are three times more likely to move to the suburbs than in the late 1950s, while husband–wife families show no further suburban movement. Unattached adults are buying suburban homes in the belt from Boston to Baltimore, while they are renting or buying central city apartments and condominiums in such cities as San Francisco and Denver.

For an increasing proportion of well-educated young adults, there is now almost a decade between departure from their parents' household and the formation of a marital household. This moratorium from family living in early adulthood may eventually have positive effects, in the sense of greater equity, upon gender roles in employment and household division of labor, but less positive, if not negative effects, upon adjustment to parenthood. Increasing proportions of women are acquiring economic and social self-sufficiency through career commitment and employment continuity, which in turn reinforces independent political and social values and an expectation of equitable sharing of family and household responsibilities after marriage. By the same token, more young men are living on their own, acquiring competence in the domestic skills they bring to marriage.[7]

What is not clear is the impact of early adult independence for a couple's ability to shift concerns from their own personal gratifications to a shared and greater concern for the welfare and care of children. Solo living may increase skills in household maintenance, cooking and clothes care, but it contributes nothing to skill in caring for a child or placing the needs and desires of others above one's own. Premarital independent living and postponement of childbearing after marriage may pave the way, for some couples, to an eventual decision to remain childless. That there may be greater difficulty when parenting is opted for was suggested in a pilot study of mine, in which late timing of parenthood was associated with greater reported difficulty in childrearing than early "on-time" parenting (Rossi, 1980a, 1980b).

Looking back over these various demographic trends suggests three general points relevant to the place of parenthood in individual lives and the ambiance surrounding childrearing in the larger society. For one, small families with closely spaced births, coupled with greatly extended life spans, means childbearing and rearing have become truncated, sharply contracted as a phase of life that previously occupied a significant proportion of adulthood. Only one in four American households now includes even one dependent age child. On a societal level, this may carry with it an erosion of a major source of social integration. Slater (1964/1974) pointed out 20 years ago that parenting serves social functions by linking dyads to the community. More recently, Fischer, Jackson, Stueve, Gerson, Jones and Baldassare (1977) and O'Donnell (1983) found that

---

[7]Research on the division of labor in household maintenance (Berk, 1980; Berk & Berk, 1979; Pleck, 1977, 1979; Robinson, 1977, 1980) reports very little change away from traditional gender roles. In the Michigan time budget studies comparing 1975 with 1965 data, Robinson (1980) reports an average increase in married men's contribution to house and child care of 6 minutes a day over the decade. Huber and Spitze (1983) report very little contribution by married men to home maintenance; their modest contribution is in response to the sheer fact of their wives' employment on a steady basis, with no effect on husbands' sharing domestic duties or the domestic competence and taste of either spouse.

parents in the active stages of childrearing are more involved in neighborhood and community affairs than childless or postparental adults. Looking ahead, children's needs may have a lower priority on public agendas, since only a minority of political constituents will be rearing children, thus undercutting the responsiveness of elected public officials to the needs of the very young.

Second, there is a growing difference in the proportion of each sex that is carrying family responsibilities. Despite a slight shift toward shared or primary father custody of children, women overwhelmingly carry the major childrearing responsibility following divorce. An increasing proportion of women are having children outside marriage, which implies a larger proportion of women than of men are tied into communal activities and institutions.

This gender gap in embeddedness in the caring institutions of society also carries broader political and social deviance implications. One may not go so far as French social scientist Gaston Bouthol (1969), who argues that the best predictor of war is a surplus in the number of young unattached males, but sociologists need no reminder that the same subpopulation group predominates in sexual violence, alcohol and drug abuse, crime, and social deviance. Unattached males roam the interstices between socially cohesive groups, kill, and are themselves killed and maimed, but the machine cultures of the West have shown no inventiveness in developing new social institutions capable of providing individual loyalty and social integration to replace the bonds of family. Our only answers have been armies and prisons.

Gender Differences in Parenting

There has been a significant shift in the language used in the social sciences to refer to human parenting. Twenty years ago, parenting meant mothering, and studies either frankly labelled their subjects ''mothers'' or one quickly learned that all the subjects were women, though the title referred to parents. A decade ago, one began to see the label ''caregiver,'' presumably to project the notion that parenting can be done not only by fathers as well as mothers but by non-parent surrogates, too (Lewis & Rosenblum, 1974). By the 1980s, the research literature has become richer, and we can begin to compare fathering and mothering.

Three types of research permit a close-up view of what it is that men do when they carry primary child-care responsibility and how they differ from the more traditional circumstance of women carrying this responsibility. The first type is solo fathers, men whose wives died or who hold custody of their children following divorce; these studies permit us to compare solo fathering with the more prevalent pattern of solo mothering. The second type are men in nontraditional family circumstances—communal groups or social contract couples. The third type are men in intact marriages who carry primary child-care responsibilities out of a commitment to marriage and parenthood as a full partnership.

Solo Fathers

The best research on solo fathering has been conducted in England where Hipgrave (1981) estimated fathers were 12% of all solo parents.[8] Three factors are found in common between solo fathers and solo mothers: A more restricted social life, a somewhat more democratic style in family management, and when a new partner enters the domestic setting, some difficulty in deciding what responsibilities to delegate to the partner. Although solo mothers are far more apt to slip below the poverty level than solo fathers, there is a considerable negative impact on income for solo fathers as well. Hipgrave found *one-half* the men experienced a decline in income after taking on childrearing responsibilities, only 12% attributable to the loss of a wife's earnings. In another study, some 35% of solo fathers left their jobs in order to meet their parental responsibilities for young children (George & Wilding, 1972). Most of the income drop was a direct result of increased parental responsibility: Shifting to less demanding but lower-paying jobs; loss of overtime pay in order to mesh with children's schedules; absenteeism to care for ill children; and a drop in social ties with business or professional associates that had increased income in the past.

The problems of solo parenting differ for men and women. Solo fathers receive more volunteer help from friends and kin, probably because men are assumed to be less capable of childrearing than women, but when men do not receive unsolicited help and they need it, they are less apt to seek it out than solo mothers do. Solo fathers make fewer new social contacts than solo mothers, because men make new contacts primarily through informal association with work colleagues, which they have little time for once they become solo parents.[9]

Solo fathers show anxiety about their role just as solo mothers do, but on different grounds: Many men report that although their children seemed to be faring well at the moment, they expect trouble in future, some anticipating a "volcanic eruption" when their children enter puberty. The men feel they fall down in providing intimate emotional support to their children, particularly their daughters, a finding also reported in American studies (Santrock & Warshak,

---

[8]Ferri (1973, 1976) estimated that solo fathers were twice as likely to be rearing sons as daughters, while solo mothers were only slightly more apt to be rearing girls than boys, and 90% of the fathers who took on primary care did so when the children were over 5 years of age (Ferri, 1976).

[9]Social expectations also play a role in the response of neighbors to solo fathers, particularly if the fathers had to leave their jobs, as 35% of solo fathers did in a study by George and Wilding (1972): Many of these fathers report suspicion and malicious gossip from neighbors concerning their being at home full time. Similar themes emerge in intact egalitarian couples when the fathers are at home a good deal in the daytime: G. Russell's (1982) study of Australian couples also reports social disapproval of paternal child care from friends who thought him a "bit of a woman" and from neighbors who would not let their children play in the home of a primary father caregiver, suggesting an element of sexual and aggression fears linked to intimacy between men and unrelated young children.

1979; Santrock, Warshak, & Elliott, 1982). Solo mothers' anxiety centers on inability to maintain past living standards and a breakdown of disciplinary control, particularly where sons are concerned. Discipline problems do not emerge in the experience of solo fathers, who follow stricter rules and are more consistent in disciplining their children.

That there is some reality to these parental concerns is suggested by the changes that attend remarriage by solo parents. Daughters in solo-father households benefit with the entry of a stepmother—as sons do in solo-mother households with the entry of a stepfather. Wallerstein and Kelly (1980) report increased self-control and a growth of emotional maturity in boys who acquire stepfathers and increased emotional maturity and subjective self-confidence for girls who acquire a stepmother. Hence, it seems to be the absence of a same-sex parent that has a negative impact on children, while the *kind* of impact varies by gender.

Alternate Family Forms

The best single study of the impact of alternate family forms upon child development is a longitudinal study in Los Angeles that has run for 6 years, beginning with a first interview with the mothers in their third trimester of pregnancy (Eiduson, Kornfein, Zimmerman, & Weisner, 1982). Four family forms are being studied for their impact on child development: Communal living groups, unmarried social contract couples, unmarried solo mothers, and traditional two-parent families.

Two findings hold for all four family types. One is a shift to greater social conventionality, predictable from the assumption that parenthood ties adults more closely into social institutions. The reversion to more traditional gender roles that has been noted in other studies of the transition to parenthood (Entwisle & Doering, 1981; Fischer, 1979; Shapiro, 1979) is also found in the nontraditional family types in Eiduson's study. The second pattern shown in all four family types is for the mother to provide the primary care for the children up to the age of 18 months. Men entered the child care scene only when the child was walking and talking.

The unmarried mothers in this study are of special interest because they consist of two distinct types: Predictably, most are young women who accepted unintended pregnancies and kept their babies; the second type were nestbuilding women who became pregnant intentionally, who are well educated, hold good jobs, and enjoy reasonable incomes—a first empirical example of the type discussed earlier. As a group, the solo mothers report a problem similar to that found in studies of divorced mothers, though their children are still too young to see its full ramifications: Their sons verge on problem behavior more often then daughters or sons in the other three family types. In none of the family arrangement types have men played any significant role in childrearing. Hence, marital styles seem more amenable to change than parenting styles.

Egalitarian fathers. The most interesting study, for our purposes, of intact couples in which the father carried primary child care responsibility was conducted by Radin (1982) with middle-class Michigan couples with a child between 3 and 6 years of age. She compared families in which men took on primary childcare while their wives worked or attended school, with traditional couples in which women were the primary caregivers. Her interest in doing the study was to test whether it was sex or social role that explains the unique effects of fathers on children and their different treatment of sons and daughters.

One important finding from the Radin study is the absence of any differences between parents in egalitarian and traditional families on sex-role orientation (Bem scale) or strictness on a child-discipline measure of family rules. That may seem surprising until one notes that the *children* in egalitarian families perceive their fathers to be more forceful, assertive, and strict than children did from traditional families. It was the daily exposure to the egalitarian fathers that mattered, since these men followed the rules they felt important and enforced discipline on their children.[10] Traditional fathers were simply not there to exercise the norms they espoused to the researcher.

A second finding relevant to Radin's major question concerning sex vs. social role is a difference between men and women in the problems they experienced in their childrearing pattern. The majority of the egalitarian fathers reported personal costs in terms of impeded careers as their major problem, while the counterpart problem for their wives was loss of close involvement with their children. This finding prompts Radin to conclude that "even when parents choose to violate sex role expectations, there are still internal pressures to fulfill the tasks for which they were socialized" (Radin, 1982, p. 198). It is dubious whether these results merely reflect residual effects of prior socialization.

Finally, there are decided contrasts in child outcome between the egalitarian and traditional patterns of childrearing: Egalitarian fathers engage in more cognitive stimulation of both sons and daughters than occurs in traditional families. They engage in more direct teaching efforts, and their children show the effect of such input from their fathers: Children of egalitarian fathers scored higher on internal locus of control and on verbal intelligence than did the children in traditional families. These children were too young to test for arithmetic ability, but the results are consistent with Biller's finding that children of solo mothers score less well on mathematical aptitude tests than children in intact families (Biller, 1974).

In none of the studies were primary caregiver fathers in charge of babies and toddlers. All the children were 3 years of age or older. Why 18 months of age is a significant watershed in paternal child care is not readily apparent, particularly

---

[10]G. Russell's study of Australian couples (1982), comparable in many ways to Radin's American study, also reports that both spouses in co-parenting couples consider the father to have higher standards for child behavior and to be stricter in rule enforcement than men in traditional families.

since breast-feeding is now a minor pattern in American infant feeding. Some clues are provided in qualitative material on a couple in LaRossa and LaRossa's study (1981) of the transition to parenthood, unusual in that the husband was caring for an infant son on a regular basis. I will describe this case in some detail since it illustrates points I shall elaborate on later.

Stuart is a history professor who gave four mornings a week to infant care while his wife taught and an older child attended nursery school. The father reported things went well for the first 3 months, because the baby slept most of the morning, and he could put in 3 hours on lecture preparations. As the baby began to sleep less, trouble began, and Stuart reported he was unable to comfort the child. Asked about his feelings under such circumstances, he reported he felt "anger," "frustration," "sometimes I go pound my fist on the wall or something like that."

By contrast, he took increasing pleasure in his 2-year-old daughter. Note what it is that delighted Stuart in this passage from an interview:

> My older child now is verbal . . . she dresses herself, takes care of herself, goes to the bathroom by herself, everything, a more or less autonomous being . . . and I just enjoy that tremendously. (LaRossa & LaRossa, 1981, pp. 193–194)

The daughter's skills in taking care of herself reduced the need for physical caregiving by the father; she was accessible to verbal communication and her autonomy permitted Stuart to get on with his own work.

To do fathering for Stuart involved being in charge and teaching the child. This made for a good part of his frustration in dealing with his infant son. As much as he was able to, he seemed to avoid direct interaction. Asked what he does when the baby is awake, Stuart said:

> I try to do something constructive still, maybe a little reading or some project around the house . . . sometimes I'll be in here in the same room with him, other times I'll just let him play by himself. (LaRossa & LaRossa, 1981, p. 194)

When the interviewer suggested Stuart seemed not to interact much with his son, he explained:

> Uh, not on a continuous basis . . . I mean, I give him a bottle; he's just learning to hold it up for himself now. I continually will teach him things or try to: how to hold his bottle, how to get it if it's fallen over to one side. . . . Right now I am trying to teach him how to roll over . . . he should know by now, but he's got this funny way. He tries to roll over with his arms stuck straight out . . . also, I will interact with him . . . by trying out new toys. (LaRossa & LaRossa, 1981, p. 195)

Later in the interview, Stuart confessed to finding a "certain degeneracy" in himself. He reported that when the baby is too fussy to permit him to concentrate on his work, he invents little things to do "to sort of occupy my time." Eating is one of these things, and he admitted he has put on "fifteen or twenty pounds" since his son's birth.[11]

Most of the fathers in the Georgia study did not even try to become significantly involved in the care of the newborn. The LaRossas use two concepts to capture the contrast between the mothers and fathers in their early induction to the parenting role: *Role distance* and *role embracement*. They suggest men distance themselves from the parental role in early infant care: The men act clumsy when handling the baby and show less skill than they actually possess when in company. The fathers also tended to "reify" the baby, that is, act toward the infants as if they were "things" rather than persons they can interact with.

Women, by contrast, tend to *embrace* the mother role; submerging themselves in the role and trying to act more skillfully than they in fact feel. Role-embracing mothers deny that one cannot interact with a baby, pointing out that one must simply interact on a largely nonverbal level. Hence, the new mothers quickly gain the sense that the infant has "interpersonal competence," whereas fathers by and large see no such competence and prefer to relate to an older child.

Were it the case that this gender difference in early parenting merely reflected the lesser opportunity men have earlier in life from sibcare or babysitting to learn the skills involved in handling an infant, one would predict that second-time fathers feel more comfortable and become more involved in the care of the second infant than the first. Shapiro's study (1979) does not confirm this expectation, however. Second-time fathers showed no effect of greater familiarity with babies: They were enamored with the growing abilities of their 2- and 3-year-olds and left the new infant to the mother while they took over more of the care of the older child. Their wives encouraged this because they themselves felt more experienced in infant care by the second birth and were pleased to have their husbands' help with the older child while they enjoyed the new infant.[12]

Several general results emerge from the three types of research. For one, solo fathers, like solo and traditional mothers, experience social isolation, income loss, and career restrictions as a consequence of primary responsibility for child care. Second, co-parenting of children in intact families, like solo fathering, tends to involve children beyond the toddler stage, rarely infants under 18

---

[11]At last follow-up, Stuart was back at the university full time, his wife teaching part time, and a babysitter was taking care of his son during the morning. A similar reversion to a more traditional pattern is also found in Russell's Australian co-parenting couples, only one-fifth of whom continued the primary father caregiver pattern in a 2-year follow-up (Russell, 1982).

[12]Entwisle and Doering (1981) found that working-class men were less likely to assist in child care when they had had prior experience in caring for young children than when they had no such experience, which may reflect the ambivalence of working-class women who experience parenting as their major source of self-worth. This may encourage their keeping their husbands as "mother's helpers" rather than as a sharing partner in parenting, something easier to do when the husband has had no prior experience.

months of age. Third, solo parenting involves anxiety for the parents primarily where the opposite-sex child is concerned, with problems of emotional deprivation of daughters for solo fathers and disciplinary control of sons for solo mothers. Fourth, exclusive or high levels of paternal investment in childrearing yields an internal locus of control and cognitive growth in the child, while exclusive rearing by women restricts young children's environmental exploration and encourages emotional dependence. We do not know if children of solo mothers show greater empathy and social skills than children of solo fathers, since this has not been investigated, though there was a hint of this in Eiduson's Los Angeles study.

The consistency with which one finds low paternal involvement with very young infants, who can neither walk nor talk, is of particular interest. Experimental work on response to infants supports the view that the underlying psychophysiological responses to infants are similar in men and women, but their behavioral responses differ in a way consistent with role distancing in the male and role embracing in the female: Women show approach behavior of a nurturant kind toward the infant, whereas men respond by ignoring or withdrawing from the infant (Frodi & Lamb, 1978). Lamb (1977) and Lamb and Goldberg (1982) have found that fathers differ in the *type* of interaction they engage in with children under 1 year of age: Fathers hold babies to play with them, mothers to take care of and sooth them. Altogether, one may suggest that men tend to avoid high involvement in infant care because infants do not respond to their repertoire of skills, and men have difficulty acquiring the skills needed to comfort the infant.

What shows in this new research on parenting are gender differences of the same kind that emerge in psychological research: Greater empathy, affiliation, sensitivity to nonverbal cues, and social skills in women; greater emphasis on skill mastery, autonomy, and cognitive achievement in men. The other side of these generally desirable attributes is a tendency for men to feel discomfort with intimacy and women with impersonal situations. Gilligan (1982), using Thematic Apperception Test (TAT) story-telling protocols varying in whether the central characters are in isolated, competitive situations or intimate relational situations, found that women perceive danger and project violence into impersonal achievement situations, whereas men perceive danger and project violence into close personal situations.[13] Intimacy is threatening to the male, impersonality to the female. These results are consistent with the role distance in men and role embracement in women in relating to the newborn child, since infant care involves a high degree of physical and emotional intimacy.

Prior socialization no doubt presents difficulties to contemporary young adults who attempt co-parenting and solo fathering. They are negotiating new turf with

---

[13]These gender differences are found not only in samples of average college students but among Harvard and Radcliffe men and women who went on to law and medical schools, where one might expect self-selection to produce a closer approximation to the male response among the women students (Gilligan, 1982).

few cultural guidelines and little social support. On the other hand, the fact that the same gender differences between solo mothers and solo fathers are found between men and women in intact families and in general psychological research of the kind Gilligan and others have conducted suggests there is more involved than a need to unlearn old habits and learn new ones specific to parenting. That the issue is not simply past socialization running against current ideological commitment is also suggested by developments on the Israeli kibbutzim in recent years. Spiro's (1980) 25-year follow-up on the kibbutz he first studied in the 1950s shows it is women in the *sabra* generation—born and reared totally under the collective childrearing of the kibbutz—who have pressed the hardest for greater contact with children, overnight visiting privileges for children, and more room for home-based family activities.[14]

Spiro concluded, against his earlier presuppositions as a cultural anthropologist, that "precultural sex differences" must be at work, but he gives no detail on what he thinks those "precultural" factors might be. Neither does Gilligan propose any theory to explain *why* intimacy is threatening to men and impersonality to women, or *why* she finds women's mode of thinking to be contextual and narrative, whereas men's is formal, linear, and abstract. She merely argues that theories of human development have used male lives as a norm and tried to fashion women out of a masculine cloth that does not fit.

Still another example of a lack of explanation of gender differences is found in studies demonstrating a sex-role inversion in the later years of the life span. It has been noted in a variety of studies that with age, men become less assertive, more tender and nurturant, whereas with age, women become more self-assured and assertive (Gutmann, 1964, 1969, 1975; Neugarten & Gutmann, 1958). The same massive involution of gender role with age was found in four very different societies, but the researchers have not proposed any biosocial or biopsychological mechanism through which this transformation takes place in the postparental years of life. The lack of explanatory specificity in all three examples—Spiro, Gilligan, and Gutmann—is based on the entrenched but erroneous view that biology is properly left outside the ken of the social sciences.

Evolutionary Perspective on Gender and Parenting

Parenting styles show the same gender differences found in other contexts than the family, which refutes the idea that there is something particular to pregnancy and birthing that "predisposes" or "triggers" maternal attachment to

---

[14]There is great controversy in the interpretations given for the departure from sex equality on the kibbutzim (Palgi, Blasi, Rosner, & Safir, 1983). Blumberg (1983) argues that women never had a real chance, since they were "integrated into 'male' economic and political roles, but there was no systematic attempt to integrate kibbutz men into 'female' roles" (p. 136). See also Blasi (1983) for another critical perspective on Spiro's (1980) argument that the shift back to traditionalism reflects the greater strength of "precultural sex differences."

the newborn. It is not to a "maternal instinct" or "hormonal priming" at birth that one should look but to gender differences that are in place long before a first pregnancy. This makes very dubious a view prevalent in the infant development literature in the last decade that close contact of the mother with her newborn during the first hours after birth, when hormonal levels are still very high, are important to subsequent mother–infant attachment. Lamb and Hwang's (1982) review of this literature concludes that the post birth period is neither a critical nor a sensitive period[15] for maternal attachment.[16]

Indeed, a rethinking of this issue from an evolutionary perspective suggests it is highly unlikely that small variations in early contact could be critical to human attachment to infants. For a complex organism like a human being, fixing of an essential bond is not likely to be dependent on a brief period or specific experience following childbirth. There will be considerable redundancy in the processes that assure activation of parental attachment to a child, and this will take place over a considerably longer period than a few hours or days after birth.

Animal research shows that it is possible to experimentally invoke nurturant behavior toward the young through the administration of female sex hormones to virgin, prepubescent males and females, so some hormonal factors implicit in sex dimorphism are implicated (Moltz, Lubin, Leon, & Numan, 1970; Rosenblatt, 1967, 1969; Terkel & Rosenblatt, 1968). It is also the case that normal males show nurturant behavior if exposed to pups for a period of time. Adler (1973) suggests that hormones may *prime* nurturant behavior, but continuous proximity is necessary to *maintain* that behavior and may even stimulate it in the absence of hormonal priming.

For most primate species and most of human history, lactation assured the maintenance of proximity between mother and newborn. Then, too, the mother–infant dyad is not isolated but enmeshed in a group, whether a baboon troop, hunter–gatherer band, or contemporary family. Support by the group is enhanced by the general affiliative, socially responsive qualities of the female, since these

---

[15]A "critical" period refers to a discrete phase of development during which specific events *must* occur if development is to proceed normally, while a "sensitive" period refers to a phase of development during which an aspect of development may be *more readily* influenced than at other stages. Contact with the newborn in the hours after birth is neither a "must" in the critical period sense nor even "facilitative" in the sensitive period sense.

[16]The best known work in this area is that by Klaus and Kennell (1976), whose findings have not replicated. Klaus and Kennell used poor young clinic patients, who might have been more affected by the projected model of good parenting behavior when they were marked off for special treatment by having more time with their newborn infants (Hawthorne effect). Studies with middle-class women at Stanford and in Sweden did not show any comparable effect of increased time with neonates for subsequent mother–infant attachment that Klaus and Kennell claim to have established. See Lamb and Hwang (1982) for a detailed critical review.

qualities elicit aid from the group and assure persistence in providing nurturant care to the young by all the females in the group.[17]

Thus, an evolutionary perspective not only suggests that no specific experience will be critical for parental attachment to and care of the young, it also argues against the possibility of leaving to a late stage of development, close to or following a pregnancy, the acquisition of qualities necessary for so important a function as reproduction. The attributes of mothering and fathering are inherent parts of sex differentiation that paves the way to reproduction. This is where the sociological analogy so often drawn between race and sex breaks down in the most fundamental sense. Genetic assimilation is possible through interracial mating, and we can envisage a society that is colorblind. But genetic assimilation of male and female is impossible, and no society will be sexblind. Except for a small minority, awareness of and attraction to differences between male and female are essential features of the species.

If the parenting styles of men and women build upon underlying features rooted in basic sexual dimorphism, then increased male involvement in primary care of the very young child will not have the effect that some theorists expect. For example, Chodorow (1974, 1978) argues that gender differences are themselves the consequence of the fact that it is women who do the parenting of both sons and daughters. By this thesis, if fathers had primary care responsibility for their same-sex child, boys, like girls today, would grow up with less individuation, greater relational affiliation, less clearly marked-off ego boundaries.

But there is no evidence from the studies of solo or co-parenting fathers to date to suggest this is a likely outcome. Men bring their maleness to parenting, as women bring their femaleness. Hence, the effect of increased male investment in primary care of sons is not to produce sons who would be more like daughters but to either enhance gender differences or, if there is significant co-parenting, to enlarge the range of characteristics shown by both sons and daughters.

Biological Components of Gender

It is one thing to criticize psychosocial theories for their inadequacy in explaining empirical findings on gender differences in parenting. It is quite another to supplement them with biological factors. Sociologists share enough ground in

---

[17]Gender-differentiated persistence in seeking contact with the newborn is found among siblings in both monkey and human groups. In monkey groups, mothers often try to keep both male and female siblings away from the newborn, but pubescent females *persist* in seeking proximity, whereas males do not (Suomi, 1982). Human toddlers show similar behavior, with girls seeking contact, while boys go off more readily when the mother is with a newborn (Dunn & Kendrick, 1982; Nadelman & Begun, 1982). Ember (1973) found that helping to care for younger children increased nurturing and socially responsible behavior in boys.

theory and method with psychologists to readily work across both disciplines. This is not the case where biological contributions to gender differences are concerned. My treatment must be very selective, but it is nonetheless necessary to make a few general points.

One, it makes no sense to view biology and social experience as separate domains contesting for election as "primary causes." Biological processes unfold in a cultural context and are themselves malleable, not stable and inevitable. So, too, cultural processes take place within and through the biological organism; they do not take place in a biological vacuum.

Second, there is a good deal of ferment in the biological sciences these days in opposition to the Cartesian reductionism that has characterized Western science for three centuries.[18] That model worked well in physics and chemistry and the technology they spawned. It has not worked well in embryology and the brain sciences. Reductionism in the biomedical fields works via the experimental mode in which one perturbs the normal working of the system under study, but as a consequence it runs the risk of confusing the nature of the perturbation with the cause of the system's normal functioning. An example from medical research illustrates this point: If you give patients the drug dopamine and it reduces Parkinsonian tremors, then Parkinson's disease is thought to be "caused" by a deficiency of dopamine (Lewontin, 1983). Sociobiologists rely on the same reductionist model: They consider properties of society to be determined by intrinsic properties of individual human beings; individuals in turn are expressions of their genes, and genes are self-replicating molecules. Following this logic leads to such claims as Dawkins (1976) for a "selfish gene," others for an "altruistic gene." Under fire from social scientists, Edward Wilson has revised his earlier gene-determinist theory to include the evolution of culture itself, using the concept of *gene-culture coevolution* to explain the emergence of "mind" (Lumsden & Wilson, 1981, 1982). But the revised theory remains a reductionist theory.[19]

The challenge to the reductionist model has come from biological scientists here and in western Europe, particularly among Marxist biologists, who argue in favor of a dialectical model. This is based on an interesting set of assumptions: One, organisms grow and change throughout their life spans through an interplay of biological, psychological, and sociocultural processes (Parsons, 1982; Petersen, 1980; Riegel, 1976; Rose, 1982a, 1982b). Second, biological processes are assumed to have greater influence at some points in the life span than at

---

[18]Two books of essays, from a 1980 conference in Bressanone, Italy, are a useful introduction to the dialectic perspective in biology (Rose, 1982a, 1982b). For a brief overview of the major ideas from this conference, see Lewontin's review of these books (Lewontin, 1983).

[19]See Gould (1983) for a review of Lumsden and Wilson's book, *Promethean Fire* (1982). A critical review of the companion volume, *Genes, Mind, Culture* (Lumsden & Wilson, 1981) can be found in Smith and Warre (1982).

others. For example, they are critical in fetal development, at puberty, during pregnancy, but less potent during latency or early middle age. Thus, for example, there are quite high correlations between testosterone level and aggression among young men, but no significant correlations among older men, since the latter's greater social maturation permits higher levels of impulse control (Persky, Smith, & Basu, 1971). So too, Gutmann's theory of the parental imperative is illuminated by an awareness of the ebb and flow along the life span in the significance of hormonal processes: Childbearing and rearing take place during that phase of the life span with the greatest sex dimorphism in hormonal secretion and body morphology and with very great pressure to perform in culturally specified ways in adult male and female roles. Along with the relaxation of social pressure from middle age on, there is also a change in body, a blurring of sexual and hormonal differences between men and women. It is the interaction of lowered inner hormonal pressures and lowered external social pressures, combined with psychologically coming to terms with a shortened life span, that I believe produces the sex-role involution noted in studies of personality in the later years.

In sum, organisms are not passive objects acted upon by internal genetic forces, as some sociobiologists claim, nor are they passive objects acted upon by external environmental forces, as some social scientists claim. Genes, organisms, and environment interpenetrate and mutually determine each other. To discuss biological predispositions is to attempt a specification of biological processes, in the same way sociologists try to specify social processes. Awareness of *both* social and biological processes adds a synergistic increment to knowledge, knowledge that can then be used to provide the means for modification and change; they do not imply that we are locked into an unchangeable body or social system. Ignorance of biological processes may doom efforts at social change to failure because we misidentify what the targets for change should be and, hence, what our means should be to attain the change we desire.

But for social scientists to specify what biological processes are relevant to the phenomenon they study can easily lead to flimsy argument by selective analogy of the aggressive–territorial, male-animal variety. One must adhere to some guidelines in exploring whether and in what specific way gender differences may be shaped by biological processes. The biological factors relevant to gender differences in social behavior will be located at some point on the chain of development that runs from genetic sex at conception (a female XX chromosome or a male XY chromosome), through gonadal differentiation during the first trimester of fetal development, to hormones produced by the gonads and related pituitary glands, to neural organization of the brain, and from there to social behavior.

We can study the effect of variation at any one of these points on the chain for subsequent social behavior of the organism. For example, a normal conceptus has two sex chromosomes (XX or XY) but occasionally may have three, either an extra X (XXY) or an extra Y (XYY). The Y chromosome is critical in gonadal differentiation of the male and the level of androgenic hormones the gonads produce. If androgens affect behavior, as they do, then we can see what social behavior and physical characteristics vary between say a normal XY male and an XYY male or an XXY male. Compared to a normal male, the XYY male with his extra dose of maleness, if you will, will be taller than average, more muscular, have more body hair, higher activity levels, more impulsivity, and more acute visual–spatial abilities. A male with an extra dose of femaleness, the XXY male with Klinefelter's Syndrome, is shorter and less muscular, has less body hair and smaller testicles, lower sexual arousability, and is more timid and passive in behavior than the average male. Family and social circumstances will obviously affect how and the extent to which the behavioral characteristics are shown, but we have identified a very specific and important biological component in the behavior of such males.

Sex hormones affect social behavior in one of two ways: They can have *direct* effects—what biologists call activational effects—or *indirect* effects—what biologists call inductive or organizational effects (Goy & McEwen, 1980; Hoyenga & Hoyenga, 1979). A direct effect means secretion level, hormone production rate or type of hormone is a *proximate* contributor to behavior. Think of the contrast in behavior of a 10-year-old and an 18-year-old male; one contributor to the different social behavior they show is androgens: The older boy will have on average an eight times higher level of androgen secretion than a 10-year-old boy (Ellis, 1982), and a good deal of the behavior of the two males is affected by that difference.

The indirect or organizational effect of sex hormones refers to the influence of hormones during the critical phase of neural development in the third trimester of pregnancy when the brain is undergoing rapid development and differentiation. Hormonal influence at this critical stage is important for gender differentiation, since brain cells acquire a "set" (like a thermostat setting), highly resistant to change after birth. It is this organizational effect of hormones on neural circuitry that led neuroscientists to speak of a "male" or a "female" brain at birth. Note too, that the amount of androgens circulating in a male fetus during the first trimester of pregnancy is the equivalent by body weight to four times the amount he will have from birth to approximately 10 years of age (Ellis, 1982). Hormones, then, have powerful effects during fetal development, go into a relatively quiescent period for the first decade of life, and then rapidly again during the second decade of life. To the extent that hormones affect behavior, it is simply not true that an absence of a gender difference in behavior at age 4 and the emergence of such a difference at 14 means the difference is culturally produced, because the adolescent's behavior is strongly influenced by the activational effects of sex hormones.

With these comments as background, we can specify the criteria for determining whether biology is involved in a gender difference in social behavior. Parsons (1982) suggests four such criteria and proposes that if two or more of them are met, there is strong evidence implicating biology in the observed gender difference. Slightly modified from those Parsons proposed,[20] the criteria are: (1) consistent correlations between social behavior and a physiological sex attribute (body morphology, sex chromosome type, hormonal type and secretion level, neural organization in the brain); (2) the pattern is found in infants and young children prior to major socialization influences, or the pattern emerges with the onset of puberty when body morphology and hormonal secretion change rapidly; (3) the pattern is stable across cultures; and (4) similar behavior is noted across species, particularly the higher primates most genetically similar to humans.

Using these four criteria, sex dimorphism with biological contributions can be claimed in four areas: (1) sensory sensitivity (sight, hearing, smell, touch) and body morphology; (2) aggression or, more aptly, general activity level; (3) cognitive skills in spatial visualization, mathematical reasoning, and, to a lesser extent, verbal fluency; and (4) parenting behavior (Petersen, 1980).

Parenting as a sex dimorphic pattern clearly meets two of the four criteria: In almost all cultures and most species, it is primarily a female responsibility to care for the young. In most cultures, siblings provide more caregiving to the very young than fathers do (Weisner, 1982; Whiting & Whiting, 1975). Paternal caregiving among nonhuman primates tends to be among New World monkeys who typically have multiple litters, unlike large apes and humans who typically have one infant at a time and a prolonged period of immature dependency (Redican, 1976).

Redican's assessment of the structural conditions that predict paternal involvement among nonhuman primates is remarkably similar to a comparable review by West and Konner (1976) of the conditions that predict human paternal involvement. For nonhuman primate males, paternal involvement is high when there is a monogamous social organization and paternity is readily identifiable; when males are not needed for the role of warrior–hunter; and when females are permissive and encourage paternal caregiving. For human males, West and Konner observe that men take care of their children if they are sure they are the fathers, if they are not needed as warriors and hunters, if mothers contribute to food resources, and if male parenting is encouraged by women.

The structural conditions specified by Redican (1976) and West and Konner (1976) apply for the most part to modern societies. There are limits, of course, on confidence in paternity, but sharing of the economic provider role is increasingly the pattern and spills over to rising pressure from women for greater participation by their husbands in child care. We can assume, then, that structural conditions are ripe for higher levels of paternal involvement in future. Two criteria remain at issue concerning biological implications: Do the differences between male and female on hormones, sensory sensitivity, activity level, or

---

[20]I have expanded Parsons' criterion "1" from just hormones to the factors cited in the text and modified criterion "2" by including pubertal change.

social and cognitive skills lead one to predict different styles of parenting on the part of men compared to women as they move toward greater co-parenting? It is my working hypothesis that all sexually dimorphic characteristics contribute to the species function of reproduction and, hence, have persisted as biological predispositions across cultures and through historical time.

A profile of gender differences in sensory modalities reads like this:[21] Females show greater sensitivity to touch, sound, and odor; have greater fine motor coordination and finger dexterity. Sounds are judged to be twice as loud by women as men; women pick up nuances of voice and music more readily and are six times more likely to sing in tune as men. The sense modality in which men show greater acuity than women is vision: Men show greater sensitivity to light, responding more quickly to changes in light intensity than women do. At birth, females are 4 to 6 weeks more mature neurologically than males, which persists in their earlier acquisition of language, verbal fluency, and memory retention. Language disabilities like stuttering and dyslexia are several times more prevalent among males than females.

Gender differences in social and cognitive skills are also found: Females are more sensitive to context, show greater skill in picking up peripheral information, and process information faster; they are more attracted to human faces and respond to nuances of facial expression as they do to nuances of sound. Males are better at object manipulation in space, can rotate objects in their mind, read maps, and perform in mazes better, and show a better sense of direction. Males are more rule-bound, less sensitive to situational nuance. Most of these differences meet the criterion of precultural influence in that they show up at very early ages. Male infants are more attracted to the movement of objects, females to the play of expression on human faces. Girl babies startle to sound more quickly than boy babies and respond to the soothing effect of a human voice, while boys respond to physical contact and movement.

Viewed as a composite profile, there is some predisposition in the female to be responsive to people and sounds, an edge in receiving, interpreting, and giving back communication. Males have an edge on finer differentiation of the physical world through better spatial visualization and physical object manipulation. The female combination of sensitivity to sound and face and rapid processing of peripheral information implies a quicker judgment of emotional nuance, a profile that carries a putdown tone when labelled "female intuition." It also suggests an easier connection between feelings and their expression in words among women. Spatial perception, good gross motor control, visual acuity, and

---

[21]Several sources contribute to this overview profile: Durden-Smith and DeSimone (1983), Gove and Carpenter (1982), Hoyenga and Hoyenga (1979), and Parsons (1980, 1982).

a more rigid division between emotional and cognitive responsivity combine in a counterpart profile of the male.

One ingenious study illustrates both the greater sound acuity of women and greater spatial perception ability of men. The test was simply mentally to search the alphabet for two types of capital letters: Those with a curve in their shape like an "S" and those with a long "ee" sound like a "Z". As predicted, men were faster and made fewer errors than women on the letter *shape* task, while women were faster and more accurate on the verbal *sound* task (Coltheart, Hull, & Slater, 1975).

When these gender differences are viewed in connection with caring for a nonverbal, fragile infant, then women have a headstart in easier reading of an infant's facial expressions, smoothness of body motions, greater ease in handling a tiny creature with tactile gentleness, and in soothing through a high, soft, rhythmic use of the voice. By contrast, men have tendencies more congenial to interaction with an older child, with whom rough-and-tumble physical play, physical coordination, teaching of object manipulation is easier and more congenial. Note however, that these are general tendencies, many of them exaggerated through sex-differentiated socialization practices; they should not be taken to mean they are either biologically immutable or invariant across individuals or cultures. Some cultures may reinforce these predispositions, as ours does, whereas others may socialize against or reverse them.

There is, however, a good deal of evidence in animal and human research to support the view that sex hormones and sex differentiation in neurological organization of the brain contribute to these differences. Androgens have been the most intensively studied for their effects on spatial visualization, maze running, aggression, and sexual behavior. Animals given androgen either neonatally or as adults show improvement in complex maze scores, whereas the administration of the female hormone, estrogen, depresses maze learning. Sons of diabetic mothers who were given estrogen during pregnancy show reduced spatial ability and more field dependence than control males. Turner's syndrome women, genetic females with only one sex chromosome (XO type), do not develop ovaries and, hence, are deprived of fetal androgens, and they show poor spatial and numerical ability.

As noted earlier, hormones can operate in either an activational or organization manner. There is evidence that certain of the gender differences cited above are not acquired after birth, when they could be the result of the interactive effect of both biological and social factors, but before birth, in the organization of the brain under the influence of gonadal hormones. Neuroscience research has established that the right hemisphere of the brain is dominant in emotions, facial recognition, music, visual tasks, and identification of spatial relationships, while language skills are dominant in the left hemisphere of the brain (Goy & McEwen, 1980; Kinsbourne, 1978). Human males show more rigid separation of function between the two brain hemispheres, while the female brain is less lateralized, less tightly organized than males. Thus, the brains of 4-year-old girls show more advanced cell growth in the left, language-dominant hemisphere, boys in the right, spatial-perception-dominant hemisphere.[22]

Anatomical research further established that a larger proportion of space in the right hemisphere is devoted to the visual–spatial function in males than females. McGuinness suggests that as a consequence males have more restricted verbal access to their emotions than females (Durden-Smith & DeSimone, 1983; McGuinness, 1976). Brain lateralization differences between men and women also suggest that one reason males show greater mathematical ability than females is that females approach mathematical problems through left hemisphere *verbal* means, whereas males rely more directly on right hemisphere *symbols*, which is a more efficient route to problem solving.

Until 1982, a prevalent interpretation for why and how gender differentiation in hemisphere organization occurs was linked to the earlier maturation of girls generally. Lateralization, beginning earlier in girls, might give them an advantage in verbal skills, while delayed lateralization gives males an advantage in spatial skills (Harris, 1978). This interpretation has been challenged by new research that found the divider between the brain hemispheres called the *corpus callosum* (a bundle of fibers that carries information between the two halves of the brain) was larger and more bulbous in females than in males, suggesting greater ease and frequency of communication between the two hemispheres in females (deLaCoste-Utamsing & Holloway, 1982; Durden-Smith & DeSimone, 1983).

If further research substantiates these findings, they do not mean we simply accept a gender difference in spatial visualization and mathematical ability as immutable. A postindustrial society in which an increasing proportion of occupations rely on mathematical and spatial skills, coupled with these findings, can as readily lead to a shift in mathematical training of girls away from dealing narrowly with their assumed ''math anxiety'' to biofeedback training to encourage greater direct reliance on symbols rather than words in problem solving.

Conclusion

Let us assume that the neurosciences continue to affirm what is a growing accumulation of evidence of biological processes that differentiate the sexes, and let us assume further that the social trend toward greater co-parenting continues in future. What are the likely outcomes in gender characteristics of a future generation of children?

---

[22]Male victims whose left-brain hemispheres were affected by stroke or epileptic seizure show more language impairment during recovery than female victims because of the much greater male reliance on the left hemisphere for language; female victims compensate by relying on their unimpaired right hemisphere.

I take the research findings to mean that at birth the child brings gender predispositions that interact with gender differences in the parents, whose own differences reflect biological predispositions either reinforced or downplayed by adult socialization and role pressure. Biological predispositions in the child do not preclude their supplementation by psychological qualities of the parents or encouraged in the child by parents who do not themselves possess a given characteristic. Quite traditional parents encourage their children to develop in ways they perceive to be useful when their children are adults, even when they themselves do not possess the qualities they encourage in their children. Differences between parents and children do not mean that parental influence is nil, nor that children have rebelled under peer pressure. The qualities in question might have been actively encouraged by the parent.

If you assume further, as I do, that there are many socially desirable attributes among traditional male and female traits, then an equal exposure of children to them from parents who both invest a great deal in caregiving could have the effect of encouraging more androgyny in the children. Several researchers have shown that cognitive ability and even scientific productivity is higher when subjects are neither strongly feminine nor strongly masculine but possess in equal measure the socially desirable traits of both sexes. Spence and Helmreich (1978) show that when socially desirable attributes of men and women are measured, they vary independently of each other within each sex. In other words, masculine qualities and feminine qualities do not preclude each other in the same person, although that combination is still not prevalent in American society. Furthermore, those with the highest levels of self-esteem and self-confidence were subjects *high* on *both sets* of attributes.

Spence and Helmreich used their masculinity–femininity scales in a study of established scientists that also included measures of work commitment, subject mastery, degree of overall competitiveness in work, and productivity. The measure of scientific productivity was an external criterion, the number of references to their subjects' publications in the Science Citation Index. They found that those scientists high on both the masculinity and the femininity scales were the most scientifically productive. Further analysis found the highest scientific attainment to be among those high in subject mastery and work commitment and lowest in competitiveness, a profile that again combines traditionally feminine with masculine characteristics.

Productive labor in all sectors of the occupational system and creativity in critical professions may benefit, therefore, by a blending of the attributes traditionally associated with male and female. That blending may be encouraged by movement away from sex-segregated occupations with token minority representation of one sex, toward compositional sex parity, on the assumption of an eventual reciprocal influence on each other of equal numbers of men and women incumbents.

But in the long run, on an individual as well as societal level, the socially desirable attributes of both sexes can be acquired by each sex only if we properly identify their sources in both biology and culture. Biological predispositions make certain things easier for one sex to learn than the other; knowing this in advance would permit a specification of how to provide compensatory training for each sex, in rearing children within families, in teaching children in schools, or in training adults on the job. No individual and no society can benefit from a circumstance in which men fear intimacy and women fear impersonality.

As adults, there are limits on the extent to which we can change our deeply engrained characteristics. But a first step is to understand and to respect the qualities of each sex and to actively encourage children to absorb the socially desirable attributes of both sexes. To the extent this is done, whether by solo fathers, solo mothers, or egalitarian co-parents, a future generation of boys and men may temper competitive self-interest with affiliative concern for the welfare of others and skills in intimate relations, and girls and women may temper their affiliative concern for others with a sense of effective, actualized selves.

No society on this tiny planet provides a model for us to emulate. It was my hope in recent years that feminism provided a guide to such a future, as it had been earlier that socialism did. But neither Marxism nor feminism, to say nothing of mainstream social science, has yet taken up the challenge of the biological component to human behavior, despite the fact that sex dimorphism is central to both production and reproduction. An ideology that does not confront this basic issue is an exercise in wishful thinking, and a social science that does not confront it is sterile. Whether one's motivation as a sociologist is rooted in a passionate commitment to social change or a passionate commitment to scientific advance, or both, it is my firm conviction, and conclusion, that the goals we seek are best approached through an integrated biosocial science.

References

Adler, N. The biopsychology of hormones and behavior. In D. A. Dewbery & D. A. Rethlingshafer (Eds.), *Comparative psychology: A modern survey.* New York: McGraw-Hill, 1973, pp. 301–343.

Altmann, J. *Lifespan and evolutionary aspects of parental care in nonhuman primates.* Paper prepared for the SSRC Conference on Biosocial Life-Span approaches to Parental and Offspring Development, Belmont Conference Center, Elkridge, Maryland, May 22–25, 1983.

Bagne, P. High-tech breeding. *Mother Jones,* 1983, *8*(7), 23–29, 35.

Berk, S. F. (Ed.). *Women and household labor.* Beverly Hills, Calif.: Sage, 1980.

Berk, R., & Berk, S. F. *Labor and leisure at home.* Beverly Hills, Calif.: Sage, 1979.

Biller, H. B. Parental and sex-role factors in cognitive and academic functioning. In J. K. Cole & R. Dienstbier (Eds.), *Nebraska Symposium on Motivation.* Lincoln, Nebraska: University of Nebraska Press, 1974, pp. 83–123.

Blake, J. Can we believe recent data on birth expectations in the United States? *Demography,* 1974, *11*, 25–43.

Blake, J. Is zero preferred? American attitudes toward childlessness in the 1970s. *Journal of Marriage and the Family,* 1979, *41*(2), 245–257.

Blake, J. Demographic revolution and family evolution: Some implications for American women. In P. W. Berman & E. R. Ramey (Eds.), *Women: A developmental perspec-*

tive. U.S. Department of Health and Human Services, NIH Publication No. 82-2298, 1982, pp. 299–312.

Blasi, J. R. A critique of gender and culture: Kibbutz women revisited. In M. Palgi, J. R. Blasi, M. Rosner, & M. Safir (Eds.), *Sexual equality: The Israeli Kibbutz tests the theories*. Norwood, Pa.: Norwood Editions, 1983, pp. 91–99.

Blumberg, R. L. Kibbutz women: From the fields of revolution to the laundries of discontent. In M. Palgi, J. R. Blasi, M. Rosner, & M. Safir (Eds.). *Sexual equality: The Israeli Kibbutz tests the theories*. Norwood, Pa.: Norwood Editions, 1983, pp. 130–150.

Bouthol, G. *La Guerre*. Paris: Presses Universitaires de France, 1969.

Cherlin, A. J. Explaining the postwar baby boom. New York: Social Science Research Council, *Items, 35*(4), 1981, 57–63.

Chodorow, N. Family structure and feminine personality. In M. Z. Rosaldo & L. Lamphere (Eds.), *Women, culture and society*. Palo Alto, Calif.: Stanford University Press, 1974, pp. 43–66.

Chodorow, N. *The reproduction of mothering: Psychoanalysis and the sociology of gender*. Los Angeles, Calif.: University of California Press, 1978.

Coltheart, M., Hull, E., & Slater, D. Sex differences in imagery and reading. *Nature, 1975, 253*, 438–440.

Davis, K., & van den Oever, P. Demographic foundations of new sex roles. *Population and Development Review*, 1982, *8*(3), 495–511.

Dawkins, R. *The selfish gene*. London: Oxford University Press, 1976.

de LaCoste-Utamsing, C., & Holloway, R. Sexual dimorphism in the human corpus callosum. *Science, 1982, 216*, 1431–1432.

Dunn, J., & Kendrick, C. Siblings and their mothers: Developing relationships within the family. In M. E. Lamb & B. Sutton-Smith (Eds.), *Sibling Relationships: Their Nature and Significance across the Lifespan*. Hillsdale, N.J.: Erlbaum, 1982, pp. 39–60.

Durden-Smith, J., & DeSimone, D. *Sex and the brain*. New York: Arbor House, 1983.

Easterlin, R. A. *Birth and fortune*. New York: Basic Books, 1980.

Eiduson, B. T., Kornfein, M., Zimmerman, I. L., & Weisner, T. S. Comparative socialization practices in traditional and alternative families. In M. E. Lamb (Ed.), *Nontraditional families: Parenting and child development*. Hillsdale, N.J.: Erlbaum, 1982, pp. 315–346.

Elder, G. H., Jr. *Children of the great depression*. Chicago, Ill.: University of Chicago Press, 1974.

Elder, G. H., Jr. Historical experience in the later years. In T. K. Hareven (Ed.), *Patterns of aging*. New York: Guilford, 1982, pp. 75–107.

Elder, G. H. Jr., & Liker, J. K. Hard times in women's lives: Historical influences across forty years. *American Journal of Sociology*, 1982, *88*(2), 241–269.

Elder, G. H. Jr., & Rockwell, R. C. Marital timing in women's life patterns. *Journal of Family History*, 1976, *1*, 34–53.

Elder, G. H. Jr., & Rockwell, R. C. Economic depression and postwar opportunity: A study of life patterns and health. In R. A. Simmons (Ed.), *Research on community and mental health*. Greenwich, Conn.: JAI, 1978, pp. 249–303.

Ellis, L. Developmental androgen fluctuations and the five dimensions of mammalian sex (with emphasis upon the behavioral dimension and the human species). *Ethology and Sociobiology, 1982, 3*, 171–197.

Ember, C. R. The effects of feminine task assignment on the social behavior of boys. *Ethos, 1973, 1*, 424–439.

Entwisle, D. R., & Doering, S. G. *The first birth: A family turning point*. Baltimore: Johns Hopkins University Press, 1981.

Ferri, E. Characteristics of motherless families. *British Journal of Social Work*, 1973, *3*, 91–100.

Ferri, E. *Growing up in a one parent family*. Slough, Great Britain: National Foundation for Educational Research, 1976.

Fischer, C., Jackson, R. M., Stueve, C. A., Gerson, K., Jones, L. M., & Baldassare, M. *Networks and places*. New York: The Free Press, 1977.

Fischer, L. R. *When daughters become mothers*. Unpublished doctoral dissertation, University of Massachusetts, Amherst, 1979.

Frey, W. H., & Kobrin, F. E. Changing families and changing mobility: Their impact on the central city. *Demography*, 1982, *19*(3), 261–277.

Frodi, A. M., & Lamb, M. E. Sex differences in responsiveness to infants: A developmental study of psychophysiological and behavioral responses. *Child Development*, 1978, *49*, 1182–1188.

George, V., & Wilding, P. *Motherless families*. London: Routledge and Kegan Paul, 1972.

Gilligan, C. *In a different voice: Psychological theory and women's development*. Cambridge, Mass.: Harvard University Press, 1982.

Gould, S. J. Genes on the brain. *New York Review of Books*, 1983, *30*(11), 5–6, 8, 10.

Gove, W. R., & Carpenter, G. R. *The fundamental connection between nature and nurture*. Lexington, Mass.: Lexington Books, 1982.

Goy, R. W., & McEwen, B. S. *Sexual differentiation of the brain*. Cambridge, Mass.: MIT Press, 1980.

Gutmann, D. An exploration of ego configurations in middle and later life. In B. L. Neugarten (Ed.), *Personality in middle and later life*. New York: Atherton, 1964, pp. 114–148.

Gutmann, D. *The country of old men: Cross cultural studies in the psychology of later life*. Ann Arbor, Mich.: Institute of Gerontology, 1969 (Occasional Papers in Gerontology, No. 5).

Gutmann, D. Parenthood: A key to the comparative study of the life cycle. In N. Datan & L. H. Ginsberg (Eds.), *Life span development and psychology: Normative life crises*. New York: Academic Press, 1975, pp. 167–184.

Harris, L. J. Sex differences in spatial ability: Possible environmental, genetic and neurological factors. In M. Kinsbourne (Ed.), *Asymmetrical functions of the brain*. Cambridge, Mass.: Cambridge University Press, 1978, pp. 405–522.

Hipgrave, T. Child rearing by lone fathers. In R. Chester, P. Diggory, & M. B. Sutherland (Eds.), *Changing patterns of child-bearing and child rearing*. London: Academic Press, 1981, pp. 149–166.

Houseknecht, S. K. Timing of the decision to remain voluntarily childless: Evidence for continuous socialization. *Psychology of Women Quarterly*, 1979, *41*, 81–96.

Hoyenga, K. B., & Hoyenga, K. T. *The question of sex differences: Psychological, cultural and biological issues*. Boston, Mass.: Little-Brown, 1979.

Huber, J., & Spitze, G. *Stratification: Children, housework, and jobs*. New York: Academic Press, 1983.

Kinsbourne, M. (Ed.). *Asymmetrical functions of the brain*. Cambridge, Mass.: Cambridge University Press, 1978.

Kitchen, W. H., Richards, A., Ryan, M. M., McDougall, A. B., Billson, F. A., Hier, E. H., & Naylor, F. D. A longitudinal study of very low birthweight infants. II. Results of a controlled trial of intensive care and incidence of handicap. *Developmental Medicine and Child Neurology*, 1979, *21*, 582–589.

Klaus, M. H., & Kennell, J. H. *Maternal–infant bonding: The impact of early separation or loss on family development*. St. Louis, Missouri: Mosby, 1976.

Knaub, P. K., Eversoll, D. B., & Voss, J. H. Is parenthood a desirable adult role? An assessment of attitudes held by contemporary women. *Sex Roles: A Journal of Research*, 1983, *9*(3), 355–362.

Kobrin, F. E. The fall in household size and the rise of the primary individual in the United States. *Demography,* 1976, *13,* 127–138. (a)

Kobrin, F. E. The primary individual and the family: Changes in living arrangements in the United States since 1940. *Journal of Marriage and the Family,* 1976, *38,* 233–239. (b)

Lamb, M. E. Father–infant and mother–infant interaction in the first year of life. *Child Development,* 1977, *48,* 167–181.

Lamb, M. E., & Goldberg, W. A. The father–child relationship: A synthesis of biological, evolutionary and social perspectives. In L. W. Hoffman, R. Gandelman & H. R. Schiffman (Eds.), *Parenting. Its causes and consequences.* Hillsdale, N.J.: Erlbaum, 1982, pp. 55–73.

Lamb, M. E., & Hwang, C. P. Maternal attachment and mother–neonate bonding: A critical review. In M. E. Lamb & A. L. Brown (Eds.), *Advances in developmental psychology* (Vol. 2). Hillsdale, N.J.: Erlbaum, 1982, pp. 1–38.

Lancaster, J. B. Sex roles in primate societies. In M. S. Teitelbaum (Ed.), *Sex differences: Social and biological perspectives.* Garden City, N.Y.: Doubleday-Anchor, 1976, pp. 22–62.

Lancaster, J. B., & King, B. J. *An Evolutionary Perspective on Menopause.* Paper presented at the American Anthropological Association, Washington, D.C., December 1982.

LaRossa, R., & LaRossa, M. M. *Transition to parenthood.* Beverly Hills, Calif: Sage, 1981.

Lewis, M., & Rosenblum, L. A. *The effect of the infant on its caregiver.* New York: Wiley, 1974.

Lewontin, R. The corpse in the elevator. *New York Review of Books,* 1983, *29*(21 and 22), 34–37.

Lumsden, C. J., & Wilson, E. O. *Genes, mind, culture,* Cambridge, Mass.: Harvard University Press, 1981.

Lumsden, C. J., & Wilson, E. O. *Promethean fire: Reflections on the origin of mind.* Cambridge, Mass.: Harvard University Press, 1982.

McGuinness, D. Away from a unisex psychology: Individual differences in visual, sensory and perceptual processes. *Perception,* 1976, *5,* 279–294.

Malinowski, B. Parenthood: The basis of social structure. In V. F. Calverton & S. D. Schmalhausen (Eds.), *The new generation.* New York: Macauley, 1930, pp. 113–168.

Masnick, G. *Some continuities and discontinuities in historical trends in household structure in the United States.* Unpublished discussion paper prepared for the Seminar on Family History and Historical Demography. Cambridge: Harvard Center for Population Studies, March 10, 1983.

Masnick, G., & Bane, M. J. *The nation's families: 1960 to 1990.* Cambridge: Joint Center for Urban Studies, 1980.

Mason, K. O., Czajka, J., & Arber, S. Change in U.S. women's sex-role attitudes, 1964–1974. *American Sociological Review,* 1976, *41,* 573–596.

Moltz, H., Lubin, M., Leon, M., & Numan, M. Hormonal induction of maternal behavior in the ovariectomized nulliparous rat. *Physiology and Behavior,* 1970, *5,* 1373–1377.

Nadelman, L., & Begun, A. The effect of the newborn on the older sibling: Mothers' questionnaires. In M. E. Lamb & B. Sutton-Smith (Eds.), *Sibling relationships: Their nature and significance across the lifespan.* Hillsdale, N.J.: Erlbaum, 1982, pp. 13–38.

National Center for Health Statistics. Advance report of final natality statistics, 1980. *Monthly Vital Statistics Report,* 1982, *31* (8 Supplement).

Neugarten, B. L., & Gutmann, D. Age–sex roles and personality in middle age: A thematic apperception study. *Psychological Monographs,* 1958, *72,* 33 pp.

O'Donnell, L. The social world of parents. *Marriage and Family Review,* 1983, *5*(4), 9–36.

Palgi, M., Blasi, J. R., Rosner, M., & Safir, M. (Eds.). *Sexual equality: The Israeli Kibbutz tests the theories.* Norwood, Pa.: Norwood Editions, 1983.

Parsons, J. E. Biology, experience and sex dimorphic behaviors. In W. R. Gove & G. R. Carpenter (Eds.), *The fundamental connection between nature and nurture.* Lexington, Mass.: Lexington Books, 1982, pp. 137–170.

Parsons, J. E. (Ed.). *The psychobiology of sex differences and sex roles.* Washington, D.C.: Hemisphere, 1980.

Persky, H., Smith, K. D., & Basu, G. K. Relation of psychologic measures of aggression and hostility to testosterone production in man. *Psychosomatic Medicine,* 1971, *33,* 265–277.

Petersen, A. C. Biopsychosocial processes in the development of sex-related differences. In J. E. Parsons (Ed.), *The psychology of sex differences and sex roles.* Washington, D.C.: Hemisphere, 1980, pp. 31–56.

Pleck, J. H. The work–family role system. *Social Problems,* 1977, *24,* 417–427.

Pleck, J. H. Men's family work: Three new perspectives and some new data. *The Family Coordinator,* 1979, *28,* 481–488.

Radin, N. Primary caregiving and role-sharing fathers. In M. E. Lamb (Ed.), *Nontraditional families: Parenting and child development.* Hillsdale, N. J.: Erlbaum, 1982, pp. 173–204.

Redican, W. K. Adult male–infant interactions in nonhuman primates. In M. E. Lamb (Ed.), *The role of the father in child development.* New York: Wiley, 1976, pp. 345–386.

Riegel, K. F. The dialectics of human development. *American Psychologist,* 1976, *31,* 689–700.

Riley, M. W. Age strata in social systems. In R. H. Binstock & E. Shanas (Eds.), *Handbook of aging and the social sciences.* New York: Van Nostrand Reinhold, 1976, pp. 189–217.

Riley, M. W., & Waring, J. M. Age and aging. In R. K. Merton & R. Nisbet (Eds.), *Contemporary social problems.* New York: Harcourt Brace Jovanovich, 1976, pp. 355–410.

Robinson, J. P. *How Americans use time.* New York: Praeger, 1977.

Robinson, J. P. Housework technology and household work. In S. F. Berk (Ed.), *Women and household labor.* Beverly Hills, Calif.: Sage, 1980, pp. 53–68.

Rose, S. (Ed.) *Against biological determinism.* New York: Schocken, 1982. (a)

Rose, S. (Ed.) *Towards a liberatory biology.* New York: Schocken, 1982. (b)

Rosenblatt, J. S. Nonhormonal basis of maternal behavior in the rat. *Science,* 1967, *156,* 1512–1514.

Rosenblatt, J. S. The development of maternal responsiveness in the rat. *American Journal of Orthopsychiatry,* 1969, *39,* 36–56.

Rossi, A. S. Aging and parenthood in the middle years. In P. Baltes & O. G. Brim, Jr. (Eds.), *Life span development and behavior* (Vol. 3). New York: Academic Press, 1980, pp. 137–205. (a)

Rossi, A. S. Life span theories and women's lives. *Signs: Journal of Women in Culture and Society,* 1980, *6*(1), 4–32. (b)

Russell, G. Shared-caregiving families: An Australian study. In M. E. Lamb (Ed.), *Nontraditional families: Parenting and child development.* Hillsdale, N.J.: Erlbaum, 1982, pp. 139–171.

Russell, L. B. *The baby boom generation and the economy.* Washington, D.C.: The Brookings Institution, 1982.

Santrock, J. W., & Warshak, R. A. Father custody and social development in boys and girls. *Journal of Social Issues,* 1979, *35,* 112–125.

Santrock, J. W., Warshak, R. A., & Elliott, G. L. Social development and parent–child interaction in father-custody and stepmother families. In M. E. Lamb (Ed.), *Nontraditional families: Parenting and child development*. Hillsdale, N.J.: Erlbaum, 1982, pp. 289–314.

Shapiro, E. R. *Transition to Parenthood in Adult and Family Development*. Unpublished doctoral dissertation, University of Massachusetts, Amherst, 1979.

Slater, P. Social limitations on libidinal withdrawal. In R. L. Coser (Ed.), *The family: Its structure and functions* (2nd ed.). New York: St. Martins Press, 1974, pp. 111–133. (Originally published, 1964.)

Smith, J. M., & Warre, N. Models of cultural and genetic change. *Evolution*, 1982, *36*, 620 621.

Spence, J. T., & Helmreich, R. L. *Masculinity and femininity: Their psychological dimensions, correlates and antecedents*. Austin, Tex.: University of Texas Press, 1978.

Spiro, M. E. *Gender and culture: Kibbutz women revisited*. New York: Schocken, 1980.

Suomi, S. J. Sibling relationships in nonhuman primates. In M. E. Lamb & B. Sutton-Smith (Eds.), *Sibling relationships: Their nature and significance across the lifespan*. Hillsdale, N.J.: Erlbaum, 1982, pp. 329–356.

Terkel, J., & Rosenblatt, J. S. Maternal behavior induced by maternal blood plasma injected into virgin rats. *Journal of Comparative and Physiological Psychology*, 1968, *65*, 479–482.

Veevers, J. Voluntary childlessness: A review of issues and evidence. *Marriage and Family Review*, 1979, *2*, 1–26.

Wallerstein, J. S., & Kelly, J. B. *Surviving the breakup: How children and parents cope with divorce*. New York: Basic Books, 1980.

Weisner, T. S. Sibling interdependence and child caretaking: A cross-cultural view. In M. E. Lamb & B. Sutton-Smith (Eds.), *Sibling relationships: Their nature and significance across the lifespan*. Hillsdale, N.J.: Erlbaum, 1982, pp. 305–328.

West, M. M., & Konner, M. L. The role of the father: An anthropological perspective. In M. E. Lamb (Ed.), *The role of the father in child development*. New York: Wiley, 1976, pp. 185–218.

Westoff, C. F. Marriage and fertility in the developed countries. *Scientific American*, 1978, *239*(6), 51–57.

Westoff, C. F. Fertility decline in the west: Causes and prospects. *Population and Development Review*, 1983, *9*(1), 99–105.

Whiting, B., & Whiting, J. W. *Children of six cultures: A psycho-cultural analysis*. Cambridge, Mass.: Harvard University Press, 1975.

Yu, V. Y. H., & Hollingsworth, E. Improved prognosis for infants weighing 1000 g. or less at birth. *Archives of Diseases in Childhood*, 1980, *55*, 422–426.

10

Family, Gender, and Occupation in Industrial France: Past and Present*

LOUISE A. TILLY
University of Michigan

Introduction

Occupational segregation by gender is a problem that has come of age. Everett Hughes' comments on ethnic relations in industry offer a perspective for examining gender stratification as well and, as he notes, for uncovering very general problems concerning industry and society (Hughes, 1949). He puts forward three "sweeping statements," as he calls them, about industry and social relations. The first is that "industry is always and everywhere a grand mixer of peoples" (p. 211). Nineteenth-century observers (Michelet, 1860) indeed protested what they perceived as the moral dangers of the mixing of the sexes in industrial work.

Hughes' second and third propositions modify his first in a paradoxical fashion. Second is that "modern industry, by virtue of being the great mixer, has inevitably been a colossal agent of racial, ethnic and religious segregation" (p. 212). (It was Hughes' purpose to confront research findings on colonial regions undergoing capitalist penetration and those on race relations in American industry. It is worth noting, however, that he made no mention of gender as a characteristic along which stratification of an industrial labor force occurs.) The third sweeping statement is that "industry is almost universally an agent of racial and ethnic discrimination" (p. 212).

Hughes' generalizations suggest both *why* occupational segregation by gender is now a critical problem and *how* better to understand it. He argues that as groups whose wages are kept low by segregation and discrimination become

*Thanks to Wendell Bell (commentator at the American Sociological Association panel at which this paper was first presented), Samuel Cohn, Karen Mason, and Charles Tilly for their comments and suggestions for revision.

increasingly dependent on industrial wages, they recognize their own inferior position and organize to improve their wages or to gain access to promotion and mobility in the system (or both). This fits the case of contemporary women, who have been the losers in a labor force segregated by gender. Increased interest in the problem (often posed and analyzed by women social scientists, as illustrated by the studies referred to in this chapter) has accompanied greatly increased female labor force participation in the past 20 years.

Hughes' analysis further suggests that when industries are new, or when they seek labor from new sources, they must make choices about the characteristics of their workers. Historical data can illuminate that process. A more recent study by Snyder and Hudis (1976) likewise concludes from a comparison of wage levels and occupation that occupational stratification contributes to income differentials. The origins of low female wages, they conclude, are to be found in the historical factors that determined patterns of occupational segregation. The purpose of this chapter is to bring historical evidence from France to bear on the following questions: (1) What have been the relationships among family, gender, and occupation, and how have they changed over time? (2) In the nineteenth and twentieth centuries, what determined the gender and age or marital status patterns of occupations? (3) Who or what institutions shaped the process?

The argument presented here (with reference to France in the nineteenth and twentieth centuries) is that with increasing capitalist industrial differentiation, employers in a given location graded jobs by gender, age, and marital status and recruited labor accordingly. Households had earlier had their own division of labor; tasks were assigned by age, sex, and family position even in household production. Industrial employers in search of the labor best fitting their perceived needs seem to have exaggerated these divisions. Marital status became a characteristic along which women could be excluded from jobs or from a career progression through jobs. All women were seen as eventually married women. Employers' task assignments were less flexible than those of households, because capital investment and work organization reinforced the gender designation of jobs. As higher levels of capital concentration, large-scale industrial production, and wage labor, with radical spatial separation of home and work, came to prevail, gender and marital status qualifications for employment affected more individuals and households. These employer decisions interacted with the strategies of households constrained by their need for wages and by their own internal division of labor. Wives' responsibilities for child care and housework did not disappear with the movement of production out of the household. To the contrary, that very removal made possible a development and elaboration of wives' tasks in the household. This process led to the generalization of the housewife occupation, the most segregated occupation of all.

This chapter is organized in the following fashion. It first establishes that France, like other contemporary Western industrial nations, has a labor force that is segregated by sex. The next section reviews how large-scale structural change shaped the overall gender configuration of occupations in industrializing and industrial France. The discussion then turns to occupational structure and family strategies in two French cities in the first decade of this century. It examines the behavior of employers and families both through their own statements of what they were about and in the ensuing patterns of labor-force distribution. The chapter concludes with a discussion of the implications of this historical evidence for understanding occupational segregation.

Occupational Segregation in Cross-National Perspective

Historical and cross-sectional studies have established that occupational segregation by sex has been the pattern in the United States since at least 1900 (Blau & Jusenius, 1976; Gross, 1968; Oppenheimer, 1970). For Europe, scholarly analysis of the causes, correlates, and consequences of occupational segregation and wage inequality is practically nonexistent.[1] Nevertheless, several comparative cross-national studies have shown that the patterns exist in most European nations. Katherine Gaskin's (1979) and Patricia Roos' (1981) recent dissertations show strong occupational segregation by sex in all the industrial economies they examined. The studies of Gaskin and Roos greatly improve on earlier cross-national comparisons by Galenson (1973) and Darling (1975) in their establishment of systematically comparable data sets and in their sophisticated analyses of these data, but neither study includes France in its comparison.[2]

To illustrate where France fits in the international picture, I calculated female to male ratios in seven large occupational groups (the only comparable occupational distribution by sex readily available) for France and six other nations, including the United States, as of 1970. These ratios are arrayed in Table 10.1, along with the Index of Dissimilarity for each labor force. (The Index of Dissimilarity is the proportion of workers of either sex who would have to change jobs to equalize job distributions across sex). The latter measure is sensitive to the number of categories across which it is calculated, so it is relatively low compared to the same measure calculated on the more detailed occupational categories used in the Gaskin and Roos studies. France is precisely in the middle of the range of national cases, and its segregation pattern is quite similar to that of the United States, except for a higher proportion female in services and agriculture. In this rough cross-national comparison calculated on large, crude categories, the lowest female/male ratio occurs in administrative, managerial, and production occupations in all cases; these occupations are highly male dominated. The female/male sex ratio in the agricultural category is the most

---

[1] See *Les femmes en France dans une société d'inégalités,* especially pp. 40–44 and 52–54, for a discussion of occupational segregation and wage inequality by the special commission on the status of women appointed by President Mitterrand in 1981.

[2] A special issue of *Signs* (1976), edited by Blaxall and Reagan, included interdisciplinary, cross-cultural, and historical studies, but none on France.

TABLE 10.1 Female to Male Ratio in Seven Occupational Groups in Seven Western Nations, ca. 1970

Occupation group	Canada 1971	United Kingdom 1971	Sweden 1970	France 1968	United States 1970	German Federal Republic 1970	Italy 1971
1. Professional, technical, and related	.92	.62	.72	.76	.67	.52	.86
2. Administrative and managerial	.19	.09	.18	.13	.20	.16	.07
3. Clerical and related	2.17	1.52	1.16	1.67	2.78	1.20	.53
4. Sales	.44	.90	.91	1.00	.65	1.12	.57
5. Service	.85	.23	2.59	2.35	1.25	1.20	.64
6. Agriculture, forestry, fishing	.22	.15	.25	.47	.11	.93	.41
7. Production	.13	.21	.17	.18	.22	.21	.21
Proportion female in total labor force	33.5	36.3	35.5	35.3	36.9	36.0	27.1
Index of Dissimilarity[a]	43.5	42.2	39.4	38.9	35.7	35.2	23.3

Source: International Labour Office, *Year Book of Labour Statistics,* 1977, Table 2B.

[a]Proportion of workers of either sex who would have to change jobs to equalize job distributions across sex.

variable among the cases, likely due both to real differences in the scale of agricultural units and linked patterns of labor supply (peasant vs. large-scale agriculture), but possibly also to varying practice in counting nonpaid, part-time or part-year workers.

Hence, although the historical path to industrialization differed among these nations, occupational segregation is a pattern all hold in common. There have been no occupation and wage analyses for France of the kind done for the United States; nevertheless, it is safe to assume that systematic wage inequality exists in France as does occupational segregation itself. I turn next to a sweeping overview of large-scale economic change in nineteenth- and twentieth-century France and its consequence for the age and sex patterns of occupations.

Gender and Occupation in France, 1700–1950

Peasant agricultural economies have universally been characterized by a division of labor by age and sex, affected by demographic and technological factors, including size of holding and type of crop. Household production prevailed in rural France well into the twentieth century: The penetration of capitalism into the countryside and the growth of large-scale agriculture was slow compared to England. Women's and men's work in peasant agriculture before the twentieth century had relatively fluid boundaries, for life was unpredictable; the number and the age and sex mix of a family work force did not always match the tasks to be done at a given moment. There were two solutions to this problem: (a) hiring live-in servants to do needed farm tasks or (b) having family members do the customary tasks of the other sex on a short-term basis. Despite this flexibility, a normative division of labor was in place. Women's tasks usually were concentrated in the house and nearby courtyard; they were charged with child care, domestic work, raising poultry, and managing the dairy. Men ranged further, to plow and cultivate the fields and to do most of the work of the harvest. Women also processed food and produced cloth and clothing, while men did whatever metal and wood working that was done domestically. (See Segalen, 1983, for a more nuanced picture of the French peasant household economy which emphasizes the range of variation in performance of tasks.)

Urban craft occupations were more clearly demarcated by sex in patterns whose origins are lost in time. Before 1789 and the French Revolution, the guilds, self-governing associations, controlled access to the craft and oversaw the quality of products. The small craft shop or household was the chief unit of production. In some cities, there were women's guilds, usually in cloth production or sewing; their number was never large and decreased as the textile industry concentrated and increased in scale. Women who were the widows of guild masters usually had the right to carry on their craft; since they were unlikely to be skilled craftworkers themselves, they most often managed the business with hired artisans to do the actual production. Girls could be apprenticed, as boys were, but to female craftworkers only; married women were likely to be helpers to their artisan husbands.

By no means all urban workers belonged to guilds, even in northern France, where guild organization was more pervasive. The cities were full of workers who earned a living outside guilds: Petty traders (among these, many women), laborers hired by the day, and numerous servants—male and female—on long-term (usually annual) contracts. Often these servants performed domestic service as we know it today along with productive work in their master's household. For most rural and urban people, then, work life was a movement through and among households, for that was where most production took place. Gender, age, and marital status were powerful predictors of where individuals would be located as workers and family members.

The coming of industrial capitalism was a slow and uneven process in France and late as compared to England. Wage earning outside households became the pattern. The concept of *labor force*, or active population, appeared at this time. French censuses before the mid-nineteenth century counted households, assuming a common economic activity, although it was not designated in these early censuses. It was only in the 1851 census and later that the notion of individually held jobs and, hence, individual occupations was introduced.

A French government questionnaire issued in 1872 to mayors of towns of 15,000 population or more illustrates both the categories of the older urban distribution of craft occupations by gender and the fluidity of early industrial designations. (The questionnaire was intended for the purpose of reporting local wages to the state.)[3] It demonstrates the endurance of craft household production in France. The questionnaire first lists categories of "industries" (these are actually occupations) under the heading "small scale industry"; there is a long alphabetical list of crafts, starting with *bijoutiers* (jewelers) and proceeding through *vitriers* (glaziers).[4] There is no classification by sex for these occupations because conceptually each one of them was *either* male or female, as reflected in the gender ending of the job title. Of the 62 occupations, 11 are female; 10 of these are connected with the sewing of clothing (including artificial flower making and shoemaking), one with the care of clothing (laundress–ironer). Occupations are simply classified as employer-housed, nonhoused, or apprentices. The rest of the questionnaire falls into three much briefer sections: One for large-scale industry, which consists exclusively of the textile industry; a second for retail trade; and a third for domestic service. Unlike the crafts, store

---

[3]Completed questionnaires for Amiens, 1874, 1876, 1877, 1884, 1887, 1888, were found in the Municipal Archives of Amiens (AMA [Archives municipales de la ville d'Amiens] 5F13).

[4]Three government investigations—on the textile, shoemaking, and garment industries—in the first decade of the twentieth century provide the employers' point of view in their extensive reports of employer and worker testimony at their hearings and site visits. Full citations for the latter two reports are found in the List of References under Ministère du Travail. There is no published report of the Parliamentary Enquête Textile, 1903–1904. Its papers and the reports submitted to it are found in the French national and departmental archives.

clerks are conceived as *necessarily* resident in the establishment; like the crafts, their sex and age is conveyed by occupation title only. Domestic servants are also conceived by definition to be resident with their masters, but they are classified by sex and the type of work they do. There is one common type of work—personal service—and three sex-differentiated ones: Male outdoor servants (coachmen, gardeners), female cooks, and females who combine personal service and cooking. The large-scale textile industry categories are the only ones arranged within rough categories of activity (spinning and weaving), along lines of age and sex: Men, women, and children.

Large-scale, concentrated industry with relatively unskilled worker needs required that employers choose among workers according to characteristics other than the customary craft–sex designation and take into account work-life trajectories that could be quite different from the craft model progression from apprentice to master, proceeding along a path of skill acquisition and increasing competence. These employers, with their specific technological needs, were operating within labor markets with different mixes of potential workers shaped by urban economic activity, household structure, migration, and, ultimately, law (cf. Saxonhouse & Wright, 1982).

Before examining urban labor force patterns further, the aggregate picture needs to be completed. The early growth of the large-scale textile industry offered jobs to boys and girls, young people of both sexes, and older workers, of whom the majority were men. There were married women workers, but they were a small proportion of married women, even of married women in textile towns, and a very small proportion of the labor force. As capital-concentrated manufacturing increased and pervaded the economy in the later nineteenth century, married women tended to drop out of industry, except for textiles, in which they continued to be welcomed as workers. Home work in garment and shoemaking emerged as an important source of wages for women and a way to accommodate the needs of both married and unmarried women. These isolated workers were part of capitalist–industrial reorganization of production, which combined shop and home work to tap women's labor at low cost and low risk.

A third female occupation that also increased in importance in nineteenth-century France was servanthood. This increase linked two changes: (*a*) increased numbers of prosperous servant-hiring households in the growing cities and (*b*) need for a livelihood for more and more rural women displaced from agriculture whose skills had been used in domestic industries. These domestic industries, such as hand weaving of textiles and small metal production, had provided wages for members of rural families who were either not needed on farms or were underemployed there. The growth of urban–industrial manufacturing undermined rural industry and with it women's jobs, but it did not provide new urban–industrial jobs for such women. The expansion of servanthood along with the growth of domesticity filled the gap.

Industrialized textile production, garment making, and domestic service, all industries transformed indirectly or directly by industrialization, were the largest employers of females in nineteenth-century France. Unlike the late twentieth century, in which there is a weak connection between marital status and labor force participation or occupational characteristics, these nineteenth-century women-employing industries had a work force that varied systematically by marital status. Servants were all single women, by definition; sewing for others was an occupation preferred by married women if done at home, but garment making in shops occupied mostly single women; and textile work was primarily done by single women. Of men's occupations, only craft apprenticeship (usually) and servanthood (sometimes) required single status. Like most women's occupations, these male occupations were linked to life cycle and age. The dilemma of urban French women was the acute problem of the married woman. To the extent that they did wage work outside their households, in textiles or other industries, married women assumed a double burden of wage labor and domestic responsibility. If they did home work, they accepted exploitative wage conditions in order to combine home responsibilities with wage earning.

Industrial–capitalist concentration reduced women's employment even more in other industries such as mining, metallurgy, and glassmaking. Earlier occupational patterns, which included jobs for young and married women as helpers, disappeared. Most occupations in these industries became almost exclusively male. Boys could find jobs when they were young and work their way through an age-graded career that in some respects resembled older craft patterns.

Cities and towns dominated by these heavy industries had few jobs for women. Servanthood, sewing, keeping small shops, cabarets, or boarding houses exhaust the possibilities. The household responsibilities of workers' wives in these towns were especially time-consuming. Fertility remained high in coal mining areas, as labor market conditions and company policy promoted reproduction of the work force *en place*, rather than through migration (Tilly, 1983). It was in the predominantly male-employing heavy industries and the communities that housed their workers that the housewife emerged: A wife with a set of tasks centered in the household and clearly differentiated from the tasks of those family members who did wage labor in the work place. Thus, although women as productive workers preceded the Industrial Revolution, the isolated and specialized *housewife* only emerged as a consequence of that revolution.

In most of urban France in the period, an adult male's earnings (given not only low wages but also an early peaking wage profile and high likelihood of cyclical unemployment or underemployment) were unlikely to be adequate to support a family on a regular basis. Children or wives were needed as wage earners to keep the working-class family afloat. In the course of the century, working-class families became more likely to depend on children (adolescents and young adults who lived in their parents' household until marriage) rather than wives as wage workers (Tilly, in press). The heavy-industry community pattern of the specialized housewife/mother generalized as wives more often came to manage the household and serve their wage-earning husbands and children.

These aggregate outcomes represent the balance of changes operating on the scale of regional and urban labor markets. Employers' designation of worker characteristics meshed with household's division of labor. By the first decade of this century, the labor force of many French cities was an industrial one. Most urban workers were employed for wages in relatively large-scale, capitalistically organized manufacturing. There exists unusually rich evidence about the employer policies for that period that provides the core of the data in the next section. The outcome of these employer strategies will be observed in the distribution by age, sex, and household position of the urban labor force.

Employers and Households in Amiens and Roubaix around 1900

Urban industrial economies differed in striking ways, as can be seen in the comparison of two cities, Roubaix and Amiens.[5] Roubaix, located in the Lille industrial triangle of the department of the Nord near the Belgian border, had an urban landscape dominated by red brick factories veiled in sooty smoke. It was the "Manchester of France"—a heavily concentrated, industrialized textile city specializing in both wool and cotton. In 1906, 44% of its work force was in textile production.[6] Although it had a substantial commercial sector (employing 20.8% of its labor force), it had few professional or domestic servants (2.5 and 5.9%, respectively). The city had a strong proletarian cast, with a full 76.4% of its household heads listing manual-worker occupations in the census.

The economy of Amiens (also a northern city, but in Picardy, closer to Paris) was both primarily small scale and more diversified than that of Roubaix. There was a textile sector, divided into large-scale spinning and a craft-organized sector specializing in velvet cutting, cloth dyeing, and fulling. Both types of textile manufacturing together employed only 11% of the labor force, while garment making employed 12.7%. Boot and shoemaking and railroad work (Amiens housed a large repair depot) were also important. The total employed in all types of manufacturing was 58.8% of the labor force; domestic servants made up 10.6%, professionals 7%, and the commercial sector 22.9%. A large part of the Amiens economy was based on the government offices located there and on the commerce this generated. A much smaller proportion (61% of employed heads of households) than in Roubaix (76.4%) reported manual occupations in 1906. Compared to the textile giant, Amiens was a bourgeois city.

_____

[5]The Roubaix and Amiens material cited here is part of an ongoing research project on family and class from 1850 to 1914 in the cities of Amiens, Anzin, Avesnes-les-Aubert, and Roubaix, each with a different economic base. The main sources are census nominal lists of individuals within households, government and company reports on industry, commerce and collective action, and newspapers.

[6]All census-based data are calculated from a 10% sample of individuals in households from the nominal lists of the 1906 census of Roubaix and Amiens.

Despite their differences, however, a similar process of employer decisions intersecting household strategies about their members' wage labor shaped the age, gender, and household position characteristics of each city's labor force. Simply put, neither employers nor households promoted married women's wage labor; both were willing to allow (and in fact needed) young, unmarried women to work but primarily in jobs that required little training and had no future as a "career." Let us look first at the effects of two types of employer decisions: Choice of location and designation of job by sex.

New industries, particularly boot and shoe, and garment making, moved to Amiens as the textile industry and crafts declined in importance in the nineteenth century. By the early twentieth century, however, the Amiens boot and shoe industry, which was organized both in factories and in putting out, was in trouble. The continued use of urban and rural home workers (including 25% women, survivors of an earlier domestic textile industry) was a business strategem, according to one boss' testimony, "to regularize factory production." By this he meant that it made it easier to hire home workers to meet exceptional demand with no additional capital investment; when demand was low, the workers could be easily laid off. The capitalist justification was that home work avoided "family disorganization" (Ministère du Travail, 1914, p. 374).

The boot and shoe industrialists of Amiens, with their mixed home and workshop organization of production, were trying to keep costs down as competition from mechanized producers elsewhere undercut their markets. Their workers complained that the quality of the shoes they were making was declining; they no longer sewed uppers to soles, but nailed them. Their bosses actually set up new job categories in order to reduce wages; for example, the category "*grande fillette*" (older girl) had been substituted, with lower pay, for "*femme*" (woman).[7] The shoemakers felt they were being exploited, but they had no easy solution to their situation. If home work were ended, would there be work for all in the factories? The employers were enjoying a buyers' market with an excess of labor that made it possible for them to pay low wages.

The garment industry had also been attracted to Amiens to take advantage of surplus labor, in this case, especially wives. In Amiens, the entrepreneurs in lingerie (underwear and shirts) were divided between those who ran factories and those who gave out home work. One home work advocate insisted that the wives he hired were working for extras ("*un appoint*"), hence, factory work was not suitable for them. He insisted that industrialists needed to be rid of social legislation that interfered with their freedom of action (Ministère du Travail, 1909, p. 156).

Albert Aftalion, an economist and indefatigable investigator of industrial conditions in the period, believed that the majority of seamstresses in Amiens

---

[7]Although industry is the unit of analysis for the labor force distributions discussed above, occupation and job are the categories used in contemporary statements of employer strategies.

sewed at home (Aftalion, 1906, pp. 74–75). An Amiens home-work manufacturer argued that home organization of production was moral, its workers less prone to organize and strike. He concurred that the women who sewed at home were relatively well off, "the wives of customs employees, police officers, tramway workers, commercial clerks" who could combine wage earning with housework (Ministère du Travail, 1909, p. 158).

In fact, a survey of garment workers and their households revealed that 11–30% of the wage resources of the household came from the seamstresses' wage, proportions suggesting that they were working for more than extras. In fact, further, garment workers complained that the prices paid for their work were continuing to decline. There was a superabundance of labor, they believed, and women were competing among themselves for the available jobs (Ministère du Travail, 1909, pp. 218 and 221). Again, here is evidence that manufacturers located in Amiens to tap abundant, and cheap, labor.

Employers also created job hierarchies and promotion ladders within gender categories. A contemporary ethnographic account of factory work in a huge Roubaix cotton spinning mill is explicit on this matter. Teams of five workers were assigned to each "self-acting" spinning machine: One spinner, two piecers, two bobbin girls or boys. At ages 13–16, children worked at replacing the filled bobbins; if boys were quick and attentive, they were promoted to piecing. At ages 25–30, men moved on to become spinners, "in command" of the team and responsible for its output. Technically, no apprenticeship was needed for spinning, but the "gift of organization and command" was necessary.

The sociologist who reported his observations of the mill believed that it was possible for women to have such a gift, but the selection and promotion process from bobbin worker to piecer to spinner left women at the lowest level. Employers believed that women did wage work for relatively short periods, except when they were young; hence, they kept women circulating in the lower ranks rather than moving up (Descamps, 1909, pp. 9–11). Some women were working in a discontinuous way over much of their lives, but employers acted as though they were temporary workers exclusively in their youth. They thus perpetuated girls' and women's access to jobs only at the base of the job hierarchy.

Similar detailed description of wool carding, combing, and weaving processes was also based on direct observation. Again, it appeared that women were not trained by employers; they were also limited to certain jobs only in these industries (Descamps, 1909, p. 13). The segregated nature of industrial textile jobs and the clustering of girls and women at the bottom of the job hierachy is illustrated also in the wage reports by job title in the papers of the Parliamentary Commission on the Textile Industry (Archives Nationales C 7318, 1922/805–818, 825–829 [Hereafter AN]). In the Roubaix mills they visited, women sometimes did preparation tasks, including loading thread for shuttles and warp making, in addition to bobbin work and, sometimes, piecing. They were almost never spinners. In the few cases where women had the same job title as men, their wages were listed at about 60% of the male wage (AN C 7318, 1922/593).

The Amiens textile industry employed proportionately more females than that of Roubaix. Employers there assigned workers by sex in different ways. The Parliamentary Commission reported that many more adult women than men worked in both the weaving and spinning mills, but especially in the latter (AN C 7318, 1922/805–818). The wage list of a small spinning mill shows only two male workers out of a total of 62. Women's job titles included spinner and other relatively high-ranked jobs from which they were usually excluded in Roubaix. Their wages were systematically lower, however, than those of the tiny minority of male workers, whose job title was comber (AN C 7318, 1922/707).

How did families respond to these employer actions? In the Amiens boot and shoe industry, according to a 1909 survey, families simply refused to send their sons into apprenticeship in the industry. The great majority of the workers who were interviewed were over 30; new blood was not being recruited (Ministère du Travail, 1914, pp. 385 and 377). Women were the home workers who supplied supplemental labor when their wages were needed. When they could, families were sending their sons to work elsewhere. The survey does not indicate which industries were considered more desirable, but in textiles and in commerce boys outnumbered girls, which may be a clue.

What about daughters? Most of them worked in the garment industry, an industry that had an excess of labor supply. The family strategy that sent girls to work as seamstresses seems to have been based on an unwillingness to pay for girls to develop skills and the expectation that with marriage, their wage labor would be limited. Furthermore, the sewing that girls did as seamstresses fitted them for housework.

Worker families in the Roubaix textile industry expected their sons to move ahead in the job hierarchy. The testimony of the textile union before the Parliamentary Commission illustrates family expectations. Wool weavers, the report states, were increasingly expected to tend two looms, an intensification of the rhythm of work and the effort needed to perform it. The union expressed its alarm that one of the consequences of this practice was the almost complete disappearance of apprenticeship and opportunities for child labor. The number of workers was also being reduced in the spinning process; again, the strength needed to operate the new machines meant that adult males were recruited directly, and the old system of working up to the spinner slot was no longer possible in the newer installations. The loss was to the sons of workers (Archives departementales du Nord M 625/1 [hereafter ADN]). Another document of the commission that lists jobs and wages for several mills suggests how the system worked. In Firm ''C'', eight sons of workers who had completed their schooling were working in the mill for very low wages while waiting for better posts (AN C 7318, 1922/610).

Roubaix families were investing in sons' futures while accepting limited prospects for their daughters. Because Roubaix textile mills hired several members of a family, some family members were likely to be in the low ranks. Household strategy as well as employer decisions dictated that it be women and girls, for the household division of labor reserved house work for them; it was based on the self-fulfilling assumption that men would be the major family wage earners.

In the Amiens textile industry, girls and women were to be found in a greater variety of jobs; adult males primarily worked elsewhere. Nevertheless, the relatively few males in the mills held the high ranking, better-paying occupations. Since women were so important as workers, the Chamber of Commerce officially favored a five-and-a-half-day week, so that wives could do their housework on Saturday afternoon. The division of labor in the household was unchallenged, but working wives' double burden could be eased in this way, or so the Chamber appeared to believe (AN C 7318, 1922/825–829). In Roubaix, where textile unionization was more advanced than in Amiens, male unionists complained that girls were taking jobs from men when employers tried to hire females for a formerly male-dominated job. There the male wage earner wife–housekeeper division of labor was reinforced by job assignments that male unionists, at least, supported (ADN M 625/106).[8]

What was the outcome of these employer and household labor allocation decisions? The structure of the labor force itself is the best answer our data can offer to this question. Tables 10.2 and 10.3 show the proportion of workers by household position—head, child, wife—in selected industries.[9]

Let us look at male *household heads* first. In Roubaix, 69% of them worked in manufacturing, with 42.3% in textiles. In Amiens, only 44% worked in manufacturing, and those were scattered among several industries, with fur/leather and textiles, 5.8 and 8.2%, respectively. Male *children* were even more likely than household heads to work in manufacturing and in textiles in both cities. In Roubaix, then, the dominant textile industry offered openings for fathers and sons. In Amiens, the textile industry provided proportionately more jobs for sons than for fathers, as did the manufacturing sector in general. Children were unlikely to be found in the higher status administrative professional jobs that employed household heads.

---

[8]Unions were sometimes active in opposing changes in gender designation of occupations in the late nineteenth and early twentieth centuries in textile and other industries. It is unlikely that they influenced gender and age designation of new jobs in early industrialization because they were seldom present. In speaking of households, I do not argue that there was a single objectively knowable interest for each household. If interests could be examined on an individual basis, they would certainly differ. Similarly, the costs to individuals of household strategies differ. Lack of information is a powerful hindrance to individual analysis, however, especially when it attempts to discern subjective interest. There were doubtless both bargaining and struggle within households, but the sources are poor for finding out about these matters. The few autobiographies of working-class individuals are not very helpful; court or police records might offer an entry to the problem, but full transcripts are not available. See Hartmann (1976, 1981), Hartmann and Markusen (1980), Humphries (1977, 1980), and Sen (1980) for debate on these issues.

[9]Household position here refers to relationship to household head; "children" are not an age group.

TABLE 10.2. Male Labor Force by Industry and Household Position, 1906

Industry	Household head (%)		Children (%)		All male workers (%)	
	Roubaix	Amiens	Roubaix	Amiens	Roubaix	Amiens
Fur/leather	1.7	5.8	2.5	6.8	1.9	5.7
Textiles	42.3	8.2	47.9	15.3	44.1	10.0
Garment making	1.2	1.6	1.7	2.6	1.4	1.9
Other manufacturing	23.3	28.5	23.5	31.9	23.3	28.5
Transportation	3.6	9.1	2.8	3.2	3.4	7.7
Commerce	19.4	27.2	18.6	30.4	18.6	27.5
Administrative/professional	3.5	10.6	1.1	3.7	2.8	9.1
Domestic	5.0	2.8	1.8	1.4	4.5	3.8
Agriculture	—	6.0	—	4.6	—	5.8
Total	100.0	99.8	99.9	99.9	100.0	100.0
Proportion of labor force in manufacturing	69	44	75	57	71	46
N	2254	1807	880	411	3379	2427

TABLE 10.3 Female Labor Force by Industry and Household Position, 1906

Industry	Household head (%)		Spouse (%)		Child (%)		All female workers (%)	
	Roubaix	Amiens	Roubaix	Amiens	Roubaix	Amiens	Roubaix	Amiens
Fur/leather	—	1.8	.3	4.7	.1	3.2	.2	3.0
Textiles	33.1	9.7	50.8	14.2	54.5	19.0	44.6	12.5
Garment making	9.5	28.6	4.9	35.7	13.0	40.0	9.2	30.4
Other manufacturing	11.1	5.9	10.1	3.6	18.2	12.7	17.0	7.6
Transportation	.4	.4	.9	.6	1.6	.3	1.1	.2
Commerce	35.0	19.7	25.0	20.5	7.9	12.6	17.6	15.4
Administrative/professional	1.9	7.4	2.0	3.9	2.3	1.3	1.9	3.5
Domestic	9.0	13.0	6.0	9.4	2.5	7.4	8.3	21.6[a]
Agriculture	—	13.0	—	6.2	—	3.4	—	5.7
Total	100.0	99.8	100.1	98.8	100.1	99.8	99.9	99.9
Proportion of labor force in manufacturing	54	46	66	58	86	75	71	54
N	257	269	599	487	694	378	1878	1491

[a]Includes all women working, including those in other household positions than head, spouse or child.

About equal proportions (roughly one-third) of employed female *household heads* worked in textiles and commerce in Roubaix; 21% was to be found also in garment making and other types of manufacturing. The overall proportion in manufacturing was much lower than that of females in other household positions. In Amiens, the largest proportion of women household heads was employed in the garment making industry, but their proportion among textile workers was also high; overall, their proportion in manufacturing was lower, as in Roubaix.

Wives were even more concentrated in manufacturing and in the textile industry in Roubaix; they were less often in commerce than were women household heads. Amiens wives were highly concentrated in garment-making, much less so in textiles, while commerce was in an intermediate position as an employer of wives.

Female *children* in Roubaix were more heavily concentrated in the textile industry than any other household group. Amiens daughters were also more often found employed in the textile industry, but they were also more heavily concentrated in garment-making than were other women. This was the reciprocal of their low proportion in commerce.

Because of the dominance of the large-scale textile industry as an employer in Roubaix, household position and gender affected the *industry* in which people worked less than in Amiens. The main exceptions to this generalization were that daughters were much less likely to be in commerce than were their mothers or female household heads, and that daughters *and* sons were even *more* concentrated in the textile industry than their parents. The relative lack of gender differentiation by industry in Roubaix is further illustrated by Table 10.4, which shows that the proportion female in most industries was quite close to the overall proportion female in the labor force. The exceptions were administrative/professional work and domestic service. Men and women did not have the same

TABLE 10.4. Proportion Female in Selected Industries, 1906

	Female (%)	
Industry	Roubaix	Amiens
Fur/leather	4.5	24.6
Textiles	36.0	43.6
Garment making	76.9	90.8
Other manufacturing	30.3	14.1
Transportation	13.9	2.1
Commerce	34.5	25.6
Administrative/professional	27.7	19.1
Domestic	50.5	77.5
Agriculture	—	37.4
Total labor force	35.7	38.0

occupations and jobs, however, as we have seen: In the city with a large-scale single industry, hierarchical gender segregation internal to the textile industry was the pattern.

In Amiens, matters were quite different. There, daughters were crowded into the textile and garment industries; the female child was most likely to have a job in manufacturing. Male children were also much more likely than their fathers to be in textiles and manufacturing. Three Amiens *industries* were female dominated, out of proportion to the female share of the labor force: Textiles, garment making, and domestic and household service. On the other hand, transport, other manufacturing, and administrative/professional occupations were dominated by males. These industrial patterns were the result of linked decisions and behavior by households and employers.

In both cities, as different as were their urban economies, age- and gender-differentiated occupational patterns prevailed. In Amiens, the patterns varied between industries; in Roubaix, between levels of jobs. In Amiens, girls were placed by families in few industries; married women were likely to be found in the same industries—but often doing home work—if they worked at all. Boys and men were both in different industries (better paying on the whole) and in more varied jobs with promotion prospects. In Roubaix, there was less segregation by sex in industry, more by status. Girls and women were kept circulating at the bottom of the job hierarchy, whereas boys had the chance to move up. In neither city, moreover, were women seen as potential supervisors of others and moved into positions of "command." In both cities, there was an apparent acceptance by households of the segregation of occupations because of its fit with the domestic division of labor both in current households and people's anticipated future households.

Conclusion

Everett Hughes' generalizations about industry and its labor force hold true with reference to the sex of workers in early industrial France. The French historical evidence shows that although industry brought together men and women, and boys and girls in one setting, it also segregated them into occupations and jobs along lines of gender, age, and marital status. In doing this, industry discriminated (in the sense Hughes used the word, that is, made distinctions) among them. Employers were the chief agents of this segregation and discrimination in their designation of the characteristics of workers in a given occupation.

What were the motives of employers? First, they wished to minimize their wage bill. They also wanted a stable and reliable force of skilled and supervisory workers. Such workers had to be trained and preferably retained within the organization long enough for that training to pay off. The contemporary ethnography of the two Roubaisien textile mills shows that employers excluded girls and women by design from the ladders that led to positions of "command."

Less skilled jobs could be done at low wages by women and young people, workers who were perceived as easily hired and dismissed. Such workers were also believed to be controlled, to some extent, by their families, hence more malleable and less independent as workers. The two groups—the trained, permanent workers, and the unskilled, replaceable one—offered flexibility to the employer faced with uncertain demand for his product.

Employers' motives are puzzling from our contemporary analytic perspective, which sees workers as individual wage earners with qualifications and needs individually attributed. The motives make sense only when individuals are put into relationship with households, which was the normative expectation (and common living arrangement) of the period. Households also made discriminatory decisions about male and female children's education and first jobs and how a wife and mother should spend her time. Neither employers nor households were interested in an infinite expansion of women's low-waged employment. Both preferred its containment: Employers because of added flexibility in any commitments to workers and the greater reliability of male workers, with their domestic needs serviced by wives and mothers; households because of the wages of unmarried daughters and the housework of wives. Both employers and households promoted the household location of reproduction, in both its biological and its social sense.

The world was not "turned upside down" by capitalist industrialization in France, as moralists and traditionalists feared. Production was reorganized and a new work force recruited by employers who followed earlier craft designations of men's and women's jobs or chose among workers of various gender, age, and marital statuses for new types of jobs for the reasons suggested above. The household division of labor was challenged, perhaps, but in the end it was reinforced by employer hiring decisions. These decisions permitted reproduction and family life to flourish in private ways that reflected social decisions. Different labor supply situations could shape the specifics of labor-force structure, as in Roubaix and Amiens. Employers and households in both cities shared one strategy, however—that of preventing women's full commitment to waged labor in the expectation that as childbearer, she would also do child care and housework. The gender of occupations, designated as they were by employers, as Hughes argued, both shaped and were shaped by the division of labor in workers' households.

References

Aftalion, A. *Le developpment de la fabrique et du travail à domicile dans les industries de l'habillement*. Paris: Larose et Tenin, 1906.
Archives departementales du Nord [ADN]. M 625/1. Rapport de la Chambre syndicale ouvrière de Roubaix et environs, à la Commission d'Enquête Parlementaire textile. No date.
Archives municipales de la Ville d'Amiens [AMA]. 5F13. Salaires industriels. Varied dates.

Archives nationales [AN]. C 7318/1922: Enquête parlementaire textile: 593, Roubaix wage list, 1903; 610, Roubaix wage and job list for several factories; 707, Amiens wage list, 1903; 782–797, Testimony of the Syndicat des ouvriers teinturiers et apprêteurs d'Amiens, 1903; 805–818, Rapport de la Chambre syndicale des ouvriers et ouvrières tisseurs et fileurs et partis similaires, Amiens, 1904; 825–829, Rapport de la Chambre de Commerce d'Amiens, 1904.

Blau, F. D., & Jusenius, C. L. Economists' approaches to sex segregation in the labor market: An appraisal. *Signs*, 1976, *1*, 181–200.

Blaxall, M., & Reagan, B. B. (Eds.). Women and the workplace: The implications of occupational segregation. *Signs*, 1976, *1*, (entire).

Cohn, S. *The feminization of the clerical labor force*. Unpublished doctoral dissertation, University of Michigan, 1981.

Darling, M. *The role of women in the economy*. Paris: Organization for Economic Cooperation and Development, 1975.

Descamps, P. La Flandre française: L'ouvrier de l'industrie textile. *La Science Sociale*, 1909, *59*, (entire).

Les femmes en France dans une société d'inégalités. Rapport au ministre des Droits de la Femme, January 1982. Paris: La Documentation française, 1982.

Galenson, M. *Women and work: An international comparison*. Ithaca, N.Y.: New York State School of Industrial and Labor Relations, 1973.

Gaskin, K. A. *Occupational differentiation by sex: An international comparison*. Unpublished doctoral dissertation, University of Michigan, 1979.

Gross, E. Plus ça change. . . ? The sexual structure of occupations over time. *Social Problems*, 1968, *16*, 198–208.

Hartmann, H. I. Capitalism, patriarchy, and job segregation by sex. *Signs*, 1976, *1*, 137–169.

Hartmann, H. I. The family as locus of gender, class and political struggle: The example of housework. *Signs*, 1981, *6*, 366–394.

Hartmann, H. I., & Markusen, A. R. Contemporary Marxist theory and practice: A feminist critique. *Review of Radical Political Economics*, 1980, *12*, 87–94.

Hughes, E. C. Queries concerning industry and society growing out of study of ethnic relations in industry. *American Sociological Review*, 1949, *14*, 211–220.

Humphries, J. The working class family, women's liberation, and class struggle: The case of nineteenth century British history. *Review of Radical Political Economics*, 1977, *9*, 25–41.

Humphries, J. An open letter (response to Hartmann and Markusen). *Review of Radical Political Economics*, 1980, *12*, 94.

Michelet, J. *La femme*. Paris: Hachette, 1860.

Ministère du Travail et de la Prevoyance sociale, Office du Travail. *Enquête sur le travail à domicile dans l'industrie de la lingerie* (Vol. 3). Paris, 1909.

Ministère du Travail et de la Prevoyance sociale, Office du Travail. *Enquête sur le travail à domicile dans l'industrie de la chaussure*. Paris, 1914.

Oppenheimer, V. K. *The female labor force in the United States: Demographic and economic factors concerning its growth and changing composition*. Berkeley, Calif.: Institute for International Studies, University of California, 1970.

Roos, P. A. *Occupational segregation in industrial society: A twelve-nation comparison of gender and marital differences in occupational attainment*. Unpublished doctoral dissertation, University of California, Los Angeles, 1981.

Saxonhouse, G., & Wright, G. *Two forms of cheap labor in textile history*. Unpublished manuscript, Economics Department, University of Michigan, 1982.

Segalen, M. *Love and power in the peasant family*. Chicago, Ill.: University of Chicago Press, 1983.

Sen, G. The sexual division of labor and the working-class family: Towards a conceptual synthesis of class relations and the subordination of women. *Review of Radical Political Economics*, 1980, *12*, 76–86.

Snyder, D., & Hudis, P. M. Occupational income and the effects of minority competition and segregation: A reanalysis and some new evidence. *American Sociological Review*, 1976, *41*, 209–234.

Tilly, L. A. *Reflections on families and coal mining in nineteenth century France*. Paper prepared for Convegno su strutture e rapporti familiari in epoca moderna, Trieste, September 1983.

Tilly, L. A. Worker families and occupation in industrial France. *Tocqueville Review*, in press.

Treiman, D. J., & Hartmann, H. I. *Women, work, and wages: Equal pay for jobs of equal value*. Washington, D.C.: National Academy Press, 1981.

11

The Work Histories of Women and Men: What We Know and What We Need to Find Out*

DONALD J. TREIMAN
University of California, Los Angeles

Introduction

This chapter is just what its title says it is—a review of what we know about the work histories of women and men in the United States and what we need to find out to gain an adequate understanding of this rich and complex topic.

A "work history" is a description of the socioeconomic activities of an individual over the course of his or her lifetime. In practice, most work histories are restricted to information about paid work; to be comprehensive, however, such histories should include information on such activities as school attendance, military service, and housework that represent alternatives to work for pay, since they influence and are influenced by participation in the paid labor force.

Data on work histories are basically of two types: Continuous event histories and information on events at selected points in the life course. Continuous event histories, which are by far the richest source of data, are usually obtained from sample surveys in which respondents are asked to describe the sequence of activities in which they were engaged over the course of their lives, from some beginning age to the time of the survey. For example, respondents might be asked to recall the first job they worked at for longer than 6 months, to describe the job, and to specify the starting month and year, the ending month and year, and the reason for leaving. The respondent would then be asked to recall and describe each subsequent activity. In this way, a complete description of the socioeconomic life course is built up.

*This chapter is a revision of a paper presented to the American Sociological Association, Detroit, 1983. I am indebted to the discussants, Francine Blau and Pamela Cain, and the session chair, Karen O. Mason, for stimulating and helpful comments.

Surveys of this type are very expensive, because they require lengthy interviews and a great deal of postsurvey coding and data reduction. For this reason, they are relatively rare. Only one major continuous work history survey based on a national sample has been conducted in the United States, the 1968 Johns Hopkins Life History Survey of a sample of males aged 30–39 (Blum, Karweit, & Sørensen, 1969); there are no continuous work-history data for a national sample of American women. (A number of continuous work-history surveys have been conducted in other countries; data on women are available for Austria, Hungary, and Japan, and data on men are available for these countries plus Germany, Ireland, Norway, and Poland.)

Much more common are surveys that inquire about events at selected points in the life course or selected points in time: First job, major job between school and marriage, major job between marriage and the birth of the first child, occupation 1 year ago, occupation 5 years ago, etc. The National Longitudinal Surveys of Labor Force Experience (the "Parnes' surveys"—see Parnes, Shea, & Spitz, 1970) are well-known examples. The Panel Study of Income Dynamics (Duncan & Morgan, 1974), which has been following 5000 American families annually since 1968, is another important data source of this type. Obviously, the kinds of inferences that can be drawn from these data are much more limited than the inferences possible from continuous-event-history data. However, most of what we now know about the work histories of women and men comes from such "snap shot" surveys, both because there is simply much more data of the "snap shot" variety and because analysts have had difficulty exploiting the full richness of continuous work-history data: There is so much of it that one hardly knows what to do with it.

What can we learn from work-history data of either sort—continuous—event-history data or data on activities at selected points in the life cycle? Or, to put it differently, why should we care about describing the socioeconomic life cycle?

The obvious reason is that, as has been increasingly recognized (e.g, Spilerman, 1977), the occupational attainments of individuals are historical events; that is, the occupational position of an individual at any point in time is the outcome of a sequence of previous activities, where such sequences are heavily dependent upon the structure of labor markets. Thus, information about the socioeconomic histories of individuals helps to inform analysis of their socioeconomic status at any one point in time. Work-history analysis can enrich the understanding of status attainment developed thus far largely on the basis of cross-sectional data, and this has begun to happen to a substantial degree. To date, however, most such analysis has been restricted to men, perhaps because their histories tend to be simpler than those of women. But it is precisely the complexity of women's socioeconomic experience, involving for many women time out of the labor force associated with childrearing and a subsequent return to work, that makes attention to their sequence of socioeconomic activities so crucial.

A central case in point is the role of labor-force experience in explaining earnings differences between men and women. Current theories about income differences between men and women turn heavily upon assumptions about gender differences in the extent and pattern of work experience. Specifically, the claim is made frequently that an important reason why women earn much less than men do—among full time workers, women earn about 60% of what men do, and this ratio has held constant for at least the past 25 years (Treiman & Hartmann, 1981, p. 16)—is that they tend to have much less work experience than men and moreover tend to have discontinuous work experience, with all the special difficulties that entails (about which more below). Data on work histories are required to test these claims, which have played a central role in theories of gender differences in earnings.

Labor-Force Participation over the Life Cycle

The pattern of labor-force participation over the life cycle has changed dramatically for women, and substantially for men, in the period since 1940, with very important implications for patterns of occupational mobility over the life course.

Let us consider women first. The major changes can be summarized briefly, although the details are relatively complex. First, the rate of female labor-force participation has increased steadily over the course of the twentieth century and dramatically since 1940, initially as the result of the wartime demand for labor and subsequently as the result of changes in the demand for female labor (Oppenheimer, 1972). Second, this shift was accompanied by a marked shift in age-specific participation patterns. (These are shown graphically in Figure 11.1, which gives female labor-force participation rates by age for selected birth cohorts from 1881–1885 to 1951–1955). Among cohorts entering the labor force prior to the beginning of the twentieth century, and hence reaching retirement age prior to World War II, women who worked at all tended to do so only before marriage or before the birth of their first child, leaving the labor force and not returning. But women who were still of working age during the war entered the labor force in substantial numbers during that time, and many of them remained in the labor force after the war. Hence, a "double-peak" pattern of labor-force participation was created, in which women worked before marriage or childbearing, left the labor force to raise children, and then returned after their children were partially grown, albeit at younger and younger ages. This pattern held for all cohorts entering the labor force from just after the turn of the century until the late 1960s, when a new pattern began to emerge in which women who entered the labor force after completing school *did not* leave for childrearing.[1]

---

[1]Readers familiar with data on trends in female labor-force participation rates by age may find these results somewhat surprising. But the fact is that the common interpretation of a shift from an early-peak pattern of labor-force participation in 1940 to a double-peak pattern in the 1950s to a single-peak pattern at present is somewhat misleading, since it confounds increases across cohorts in age-specific rates of labor-force participation with changes in the participation rates of specific cohorts as they age. The cohort approach makes clear the specific impact of the demand for labor in World War II on each cohort and its effect on the subsequent labor-force participation of each cohort as well as the steady increase over cohorts in the proportion of young women entering the labor force. See Robinson (1980) for a detailed discussion of this issue.

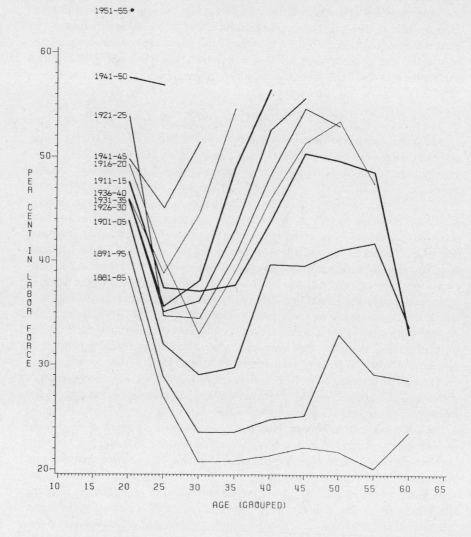

FIGURE 11.1. Percentage in labor force by age, 5-year birth cohorts 1911–1955
and alternate 5-year birth cohorts 1881–1910, U.S. women.
(Adapted from Robinson, 1980, Table 2.)

It is still too early to tell how stable this new pattern is and also too early to tell whether additional members of these cohorts will enter the labor force after childrearing or whether these cohorts are already permanently divided into a working and nonworking sector. In either event, the implications for women's occupational opportunities are large. In all but the youngest cohorts now of working age, a large fraction of women have returned to work after a period of time out of the labor force for childrearing. On average, these women have been at a considerable disadvantage in the competition for jobs. This circumstance no doubt accounts in large part for the downward mobility over the course of the work career experienced by the average woman, as we will see below.

Thus, if the pattern of female labor-force participation changes so that the typical woman worker remains in the labor force throughout her working life, we might well expect substantial improvement in the mobility chances of the average woman. Specifically, insofar as human capital arguments are correct, women who work continuously should have the same sorts of mobility patterns over the life course as men, and hence an increase in the proportion of women with continuous careers should result in a convergence of the occupational (and earnings) careers of women and men. The difficulty with this prediction is that, as we shall see below, currently women with continuous work experience have careers very different from those of men: They work at different sorts of jobs, they have less upward mobility over the course of their working lives, and they earn a great deal less. But at present, such women are in a small minority. It may be that as continuous labor-force participation comes to be the norm for women—which it certainly appears will happen considering that two-thirds of the youngest cohorts are currently in the labor force and show no signs of dropping out for childrearing—there will be a reduction in occupational segregation and a convergence in the earnings of men and women. On the other hand, the experience of Eastern European countries is not encouraging in this respect, since there is fully as much occupational segregation and nearly as large an earnings gap in most of those countries as in the United States, despite their long-standing patterns of full female labor-force participation.

The same sort of data on cohort trends in labor-force participation is not available for men. Nonetheless, it is evident from inspection of trends in cross-sectional age-participation profiles that most men work most of the time from the age they leave school until retirement, except for those who have military experience early in their careers. Male labor-force participation patterns have not changed much in recent years, except that participation rates of young men have declined because they are remaining in school longer than they used to. Participation rates, then, rise to near unity among those in their thirties and forties and subsequently decline as men begin to retire in their fifties, some because they can afford to and some because they are unable to continue working as the result of injury or illness. The interesting observation about gender differences in labor-force participation is that it is not so large as is commonly supposed. Among the adult population (i.e., age 18 and over) about 50% of the

women and 75% of the men are in the labor force, which is why women constitute 40% of the United States labor force at the present time.

The effect of these participation patterns on the extent of work experience can
be seen in data from the Panel Study of Income Dynamics, which has been
following a national sample with yearly interviews since 1968. Corcoran, Duncan, and Ponza (1982) present data on patterns of work experience from 1968 to
1980 for adult men and women aged 23–47 in 1968 (and, hence, 35–59 in 1980).
The gender differences are striking. Only 6% of the women worked full-time
(defined as at least 1500 hours for the year) all 13 years, compared to 64% of the
men, and 77% of the women, compared to 11% of the men, had at least 1 year in
which they hardly worked at all ("hardly at all" being defined as less than 250
hours of work for the year). These data, to be sure, overstate the gender difference in work experience among those with an appreciable amount of experience,
because they include the substantial fraction of women who have never worked
or who have worked for only a brief period. It is probable that if the comparison
were restricted to those persons with at least 1 year of full-time work experience,
the gender difference in experience would be much smaller. The difficulty in
choosing an appropriate comparison illustrates the complexity of patterns of
labor-force participation over the life cycle, especially for women.

Occupational Mobility over the Life Cycle

The Extent of Mobility

The first thing to note about occupational mobility over the course of the
career is that there is a lot of it. In the United States, people change jobs
frequently, apparently much more frequently than in other industrialized countries. In Detroit, for example, job-changing rates are about twice what they are in
Yokohama, a similar industrial city in Japan (Cole, 1979). But individuals not
only change jobs frequently, they change occupations as well. For example, 10%
of the labor force changed detailed (3-digit) occupations between 1980 and 1981
(Jacobs, 1983, p. 419). (Hereafter, "occupation" means categories of the census 3-digit classification and "occupational mobility" means a change between
these categories, unless otherwise specified.) Among those employed in both
1965 and 1970, 42% had a different occupation in the 2 years, as can be seen in
Table 11.1. And nearly 90% of the men in the National Longitudinal Survey of
Mature Men had changed occupations between their first job and the job they
held in 1975, when they were 54–68 years old (Jacobs, 1983, pp. 416–417).[2]

---

[2]To be sure, these estimates may overstate the true extent of occupational mobility,
because they include error in recall as well as true mobility. However, recall error could
also result in an underestimation of mobility to the extent that people erroneously report
their current occupation as their past one as well. Unfortunately, the data do not exist that
would permit us to decide between these possibilities.

Not surprisingly, the propensity to change occupations declines with age for both men and women until the very end of the career when it increases slightly. The beginning of the career until about age 30 is apparently a period of trial and error for a sizable fraction of the labor force, involving frequent job and occupational shifts as well as movements into and out of the labor force. Among those under age 20 in 1965 with a job, only 20% worked at the same occupation 5 years later, and among those aged 20–29, only about two-fifths of the men and one-third of the women did. But even after age 30, there is a great deal of occupational mobility. Among those employed in both years, about two-fifths of those aged 30–39 and about one-third of those over 40 had a different occupation in 1965 and 1970, as can be seen in column 8 of Table 11.1.

Interestingly, among those who were in the labor force in both years, men and women were about equally likely to change occupations: Approximately 40% of each sex had a different occupation in 1965 and 1970. However (except for those

TABLE 11.1. Distribution of 1970 Employment Status of Persons Employed in 1965, by Sex and Age, United States (in Percentage)

Age	Sex	(1) Not in labor force	(2) Dead	(3) Armed forces	(4) Unem-ployed	(5) Different occupa-tion	(6) Same occupa-tion	(7) Total	(8)[a] Percent Mobile
16–19	Male	7.7	0.8	10.0	3.9	57.6	20.0	100.0	74.2
	Female	38.9	0.3	0.0	3.2	37.6	19.9	100.0	65.6
20–29	Male	2.7	0.9	1.4	2.6	51.4	41.1	100.0	55.6
	Female	36.0	0.4	0.0	2.5	28.9	32.1	100.0	47.4
30–39	Male	2.3	1.5	0.8	2.1	37.5	55.9	100.0	40.1
	Female	17.6	0.9	0.0	2.5	31.5	47.5	100.0	39.9
40–49	Male	3.5	3.6	0.2	2.1	31.6	59.0	100.0	34.9
	Female	14.6	2.1	0.0	2.3	30.2	50.9	100.0	37.2
50–59	Male	10.9	8.7	0.0	2.2	25.5	52.6	100.0	32.7
	Female	21.3	4.4	0.0	1.9	24.8	47.5	100.0	34.3
60+	Male	35.2	30.3	0.0	1.4	11.9	21.2	100.0	36.0
	Female	39.7	25.6	0.0	1.2	12.0	21.4	100.0	35.9
Total									
	Male	7.9	6.1	1.1	2.3	34.6	47.2	100.0	42.3
	Female	26.0	4.0	0.0	2.3	27.2	40.3	100.0	40.3
All workers		14.8	5.3	0.7	2.3	32.2	44.8	100.0	41.8

Source: Adapted from Sommers and Eck (1977, Table 1). Data are from the 1970 Census of population, adjusted by taking account of deaths between 1965 and 1970 and differential rates of recall error by age and sex (see Sommers & Eck, 1977, p. 19, for details).

[a]This is the percentage who changed jobs between 1965 and 1970 among those who were in the labor force in both years. It is calculated by dividing column 5 by the sum of columns 5 and 6.

aged 60 or more), women were substantially more likely than men to leave the labor force and were also substantially more likely to enter the labor force. Except for retirement, labor-force leaving was greatest among women in their twenties and early thirties, which is consistent with the notion that women mainly leave the labor force to bear and rear children. But it is worth noting that substantial fractions of women left the labor force at every age, which means that it is incorrect to think of women as leaving the labor force for childrearing but then returning and remaining in the labor force until retirement, as some have supposed. Unfortunately, we do not have information on sequences of labor-force entries and exits over the life cycle and hence do not know—for either men or women—just how common patterns of multiple entry and reentry are. (The Panel Study of Income Dynamics data could, however, be used to partially overcome this gap.) But we do have data on the 1965 employment status of those employed in 1970, from which we can learn something about labor-force reentry patterns. As Table 11.2 shows, at every age substantial fractions of women

TABLE 11.2. Distribution of 1965 Employment Status of Persons Employed in 1970, by Sex and Age, United States (in Percentage)

Age	Sex	(1) Not in labor force or unemployed	(2) Armed forces	(3) Different occupa- tion	(4) Same occupa- tion	(5) Total	(6)[a] Percent Mobile
21–24	Male	50.5	9.9	29.4	10.2	100.0	74.2
	Female	71.4	0.0	18.7	9.9	100.0	65.4
25–34	Male	12.6	9.7	43.2	34.5	100.0	55.6
	Female	43.5	0.0	26.8	29.7	100.0	47.4
35–44	Male	5.3	2.0	37.2	55.5	100.0	40.1
	Female	36.9	0.0	25.2	38.0	100.1	39.9
45–54	Male	4.9	1.3	32.7	61.1	100.0	34.9
	Female	24.9	0.0	28.0	47.1	100.0	37.3
55–64	Male	5.9	0.5	30.6	63.0	100.0	32.7
	Female	18.0	0.0	28.1	53.9	100.0	34.3
65 +	Male	12.5	0.3	31.3	55.9	100.0	35.9
	Female	21.8	0.0	28.1	50.1	100.0	35.9
Total							
	Male	11.7	4.1	35.6	48.6	100.0	42.3
	Female	36.3	0.2	25.9	37.6	100.0	40.8
All workers		20.8	2.7	32.0	44.5	100.0	41.8

Source: Adapted from Sommers and Eck (1977, Table 2).

[a]This is the percentage who changed jobs between 1965 and 1970 among those who were in the labor force in both years. It is calculated by dividing column 3 by the sum of columns 3 and 4. The figures in this column are, by definition, identical to those in column 8 of Table 11.1, within the limits of rounding error.

employed in 1970 had not been employed in 1965. Especially striking is the observation that about one-fifth of women over 55 employed in 1970 had not been employed in 1965. These may be widows returning to work (or working for the first time) out of economic necessity.

The Pattern of Mobility

These results help to explain the striking gender difference in the pattern of occupational attainment over the life cycle that recently has been identified by Sewell and his colleagues (Sewell, Hauser, & Wolf, 1980). While previous studies, based on general samples of labor-force incumbents across broad age ranges (Featherman & Hauser, 1976; McClendon, 1976; Treiman & Terrell, 1975), had concluded that the process and average level of occupational attainment were essentially the same for men and women, Sewell's study, based on a sample of Wisconsin high school graduates from a single year, reached quite different conclusions. The essence of the pattern is this: Women begin their careers in higher status occupations than do men, because a large fraction of them begin as clerical workers while a large fraction of men begin as semiskilled or unskilled workers; the average Duncan Socioeconomic Index (SEI)[3] score of women's first jobs in the Sewell sample was 47 and that for men was 41, about one-third of a standard deviation lower (the average SEI scores are shown in Table 11.3 and the occupational distributions are shown in Table 11.4). Many men, then, experience substantial upward mobility over the course of their careers. By age 32, in the Sewell sample, substantial fractions of men had moved into managerial and skilled manual positions and out of semiskilled and unskilled jobs; the result was that by age 32, this cohort of men had experienced an average increase of 9 points on the Duncan SEI scale relative to their career beginnings.

By contrast, women on the average experienced slight *downward* mobility—a loss of 2 points on the Duncan scale.[4] The exact pattern of occupational mobility

---

[3]Duncan's Socioeconomic Index is conventionally used to measure occupational status in studies of status attainment. The index provides scores for each occupation in the U.S. Census detailed (3-digit) occupational classification and for the United States labor force, which has a mean of about 40 and a standard deviation of about 22. Originally developed by Duncan (1961a, 1961b) for the categories of the 1950 Census occupational classification, the index has been updated for use with the 1970 classification by Hauser and Featherman (1977) and by Stevens and Featherman (1981).

[4]Rosenfeld (1980), using data from the National Longitudinal Survey of Labor Market Experience of *Young* Women, does not find this pattern with respect to SEI, although she does with respect to income. In her data, the average SEI of women is higher than that of men at the beginning of their careers and remains higher 6 years later. This is probably explained by the fact that at the time of the initial interview, her sample was 14–24 years old, which means that 6 years later it was 20–30 years old. Not only is the sample too young for strong career trends to emerge, but the relatively broad age range distorts the results by including individuals of a variety of ages in each year for which data were collected. What is interesting is not the lack of growth of SEI for males in these data but

TABLE 11.3. Means and Standard Deviations of Status[a] of First and 1975 (or Last) Job, by Sex and Marital/Child Status, 1961 Wisconsin High School Graduates Employed Within Five Years prior to 1975[b]

	Mean		Standard deviation		
	First	1975	First	1975	N
Men	41.0	50.0	26.7	22.7	3411
Women					
All	47.1	44.7	18.3	20.0	2620
Never married	51.2	54.1	18.0	18.0	197
Ever married					
Childless	50.3	51.4	17.5	19.3	200
1–2 children	50.4	48.9	18.0	19.0	888
3+ children	43.8	39.6	18.1	19.6	1326

Source: Adapted from Sewell, Hauser, and Wolf (1980, p. 561, Table 5).
[a]Occupational status was measured by Duncan's Socioeconomic Index (Duncan, 1961a, 1961b).
[b]The modal age of this cohort in 1975 was 32.

that produced this outcome for women is, however, not nearly so clear as it is for men. Inspecting the distribution of women's first and current jobs over major occupation groups (Table 11.4) reveals mainly a decrease in the proportion in clerical jobs (15%) and an increase in the proportion in managerial jobs (7%), which would suggest that the status of the average woman's job should have increased. However, closer inspection reveals in addition a 2% increase in manual workers, a 4% increase in service workers, and a 2% increase in farmers and farm workers. Moreover, it is well known that women in managerial jobs tend to be concentrated at the low end—apartment managers, retail store managers, etc. Taken together, these shifts apparently result in the 2-point decline in average SEI.[5]

---

the much more rapid growth in hourly earnings for males than for females during this period. This result is particularly striking considering that Rosenfeld restricted her sample to those who were in the labor force in each of the 6 years for which data were collected, so that the gender difference in the growth of earnings cannot be attributed to differences in the length or continuity of labor-force experience.

[5]These conclusions are drawn from a comparison of occupational distributions at two points in time rather than from occupational turnover tables. While turnover tables would be preferable, because they would reveal the pattern of movement between occupations, comparable turnover tables for males and females that show occupational position at two points in the life cycle are not available. While a number of such tables have been published for each sex (e.g., for males, Blau & Duncan, 1967, p. 50; Featherman & Hauser, 1978, pp. 116, 538–539; and for females, Parnes et al., 1970, p. 154; Rosenfeld, 1979, pp. 292–293), noncomparabilities of sample definition and occupational classification preclude their direct comparison.

TABLE 11.4. Distribution of Major Occupation Group of First and 1975 (or Last) Job, by Sex and Marital/Child Status, 1961 Wisconsin High School Graduates Employed Within Five Years prior to 1975 (in Percentage)

		Professional, technical	Managers, proprietors[a]	Clerical, retail sales	Skilled workers	Semi, unskilled workers	Service workers	Farm, farm laborers	Total
Men	1st	26.9	9.8	9.5	11.2	32.2	2.5	7.9	100.0
	1975	24.8	27.2	6.7	17.6	15.9	3.2	4.7	100.0
Women									
All	1st	22.8	1.8	54.0	0.8	7.9	11.9	0.8	100.0
	1975	23.1	8.6	39.0	1.5	9.0	15.7	3.2	100.0
Never married	1st	39.6	3.0	41.1	2.0	7.6	6.1	0.5	100.0
	1975	39.1	12.7	34.0	2.0	5.1	6.6	0.5	100.0
Ever married									
Childless	1st	32.5	2.5	47.0	1.0	5.5	11.0	0.5	100.0
	1975	32.0	14.5	33.5	1.0	7.0	10.0	2.0	100.0
1–2 children	1st	29.2	2.1	52.4	0.4	5.6	9.5	0.8	100.0
	1975	27.6	9.5	42.0	1.0	5.7	12.3	1.9	100.0
3+ children	1st	14.8	1.1	58.0	0.8	9.9	14.5	1.0	100.0
	1975	16.4	6.5	38.6	1.8	12.0	20.1	4.6	100.0

Source: Adapted from Sewell, Hauser, and Wolf (1980, p. 559, Table 4).
[a]Includes those in nonretail sales.

How can the difference in the upward mobility propensities of men and women be explained? An obvious possibility is that women's mobility prospects are hindered by their labor-force discontinuity. There is some indirect support for this supposition in Sewell's finding that the mobility patterns of women are related to their marital and maternal status. (These results are also shown in Tables 11.3 and 11.4.) Women without children, and particularly those who have never married, experience slight upward mobility on the average whereas those with children, and especially the half of the sample with three or more children, experience slight downward mobility. Since women who have never married by the time they are past 30 tend to have continuous labor-force experience whereas those who have married tend to have some discontinuity in their labor-force participation (Treiman & Terrell, 1975, Table 4), the Sewell results are consistent with the notion that differences in labor-force participation affect mobility opportunities.

In considering these results, we need to keep two important points in mind. First, the upward mobility of never-married women is not very substantial, despite their essentially continuous labor-force participation. On average, they experience a 3-point increase in SEI between their first job and their job at age 32 compared with the 9-point increase for men noted above. There are at least two possible reasons why such women have less upward mobility than men. Women who have not married by their thirties tend to be disproportionately well educated and disproportionately likely to begin their careers in professional jobs. It may thus be simply that they cannot move up in occupational status because they have started at the top. If we were to compare these women to a sample of comparably educated men, we might find that the men, too, have very high status career beginnings and little upward mobility with respect to occupational status over the course of their careers. Alternatively, it may be that women in any circumstances—that is, regardless of level of education or status of first job—find upward mobility more difficult than do men. It is notable that never-married women are much less likely than men to move into managerial and nonretail sales jobs, despite presumably being better qualified than the average man. Moreover, these women, like women in general, get a much smaller income return on their labor-force experience than do men. Unfortunately, limitations of space preclude a review of gender differences in earnings over the life cycle (see Treiman & Hartmann, 1981, for such a review).

Second, even accepting the claim that labor-force discontinuity accounts, in part, for the inferior occupational mobility chances of women, the reasons for this association remain unclear. There are several alternative hypotheses: The orthodox human capital claim that time out of the labor force depreciates skills; various modifications of that basic hypothesis; and a hypothesis I wish to propose—that labor-force reentry creates an inferior bargaining position.

The argument has been made, quite forcibly, by economists of the "human capital school" (e.g., Mincer & Polachek, 1974; Polachek, 1975) that labor-force experience enhances human capital and hence productivity, while time out of the labor force depreciates human capital. Thus, those with more labor-force experience should, *ceteris paribus,* have more human capital and should thus be able to command higher incomes and—by extension—higher status jobs. Moreover, since—according to this theory—human capital depreciates if it is not increasing, those who spend time out of the labor force will typically earn less upon their return than at the time they left and, again by extension, should on average reenter the labor force in lower status jobs than those they left. Proponents of this view claim some support for it, mostly by demonstrating a nontrivial net effect of extent of labor-force experience on earnings (for a review of this evidence see Treiman & Hartmann, 1981, chap. 2), and by showing that earnings of labor-force reentrants are typically lower than when they left (for a review of the evidence see Corcoran, Duncan, & Ponza, 1982, and the papers cited there). But it turns out that very quickly (within the first year or so of labor-force reentry) wages rebound to their prelabor-force withdrawal level, a phenomenon that Mincer and Ofek (1982) attribute to the "repair" of human capital and Corcoran and her colleagues (1982) attribute to temporary mismatches between worker skills and jobs together with employer insistence on a low-wage probationary period during which a worker's productivity can be assessed.

An alternative reason why labor-force discontinuity may impair opportunities for upward mobility is that it creates a disadvantageous bargaining position. Those returning to work after a period out of the labor force are essentially like new job applicants, even though they have previous experience. Whereas someone who already has a job will not voluntarily change jobs except to move to a better one, the unemployed job seeker does not have this luxury but must take what she or he can get. Employers know this and need not make many concessions to secure the services of those returning to work. Moreover, many large firms tend to fill all but entry-level jobs by promotion from within through an internal labor market (Doeringer & Piore, 1971). Hence, those returning to work may find their opportunities largely restricted to entry-level jobs regardless of their experience.

Despite the plausibility of the "bargaining position" hypothesis, however, there has been no research directed to testing it. The only pertinent evidence comes from studies of gender differences in the consequences of geographical mobility. Typically, families move for the benefit of the husband's job opportunities. The consequence is that whereas men who are geographically mobile tend to earn more in their new job than they did in their old job, women who are geographically mobile tend to earn less in their new job than in their old one (Gallaway, 1969a, 1969b)—if they even get a new job. Data from the 1970 Census of population show that women employed in 1965 who were geographically mobile (defined as changing county of residence) were less likely to be employed in 1970 than were women who were not geographically mobile (Long, 1974, Table 2), which may be an indication of the difficulty of securing a suitable job from a position of unemployment.

A test of the "reduced bargaining power" vs. the "human capital deprecia-tion" hypothesis could be made by comparing geographically mobile women who move for their husbands' benefit with women returning to work after a time out of the labor force. Insofar as time out of the labor force results in human capital depreciation, women returning to work should fare less well than compar-able women moving directly from one job to another in a move forced by geographical mobility. But the bargaining power hypothesis would predict no difference between the two groups. The advantage of geographically mobile women as a test population is that there is no implication of lack of competence of the job changers, as there is when considering other involuntary job changers, such as those who are fired or laid off. However, a comprehensive study would consider the prospects—in terms of occupational status and income—of several groups of workers, divided by gender: New labor force entrants, those returning to work, those seeking a new job as the consequence of geographic mobility, those seeking a new job as the result of a layoff or firing, and those changing jobs as the result of "pull" rather than "push" factors.

In addition, for a definitive test we need a much more precise specification of what is meant by "human capital depreciation." While it is evident that in some highly technical areas skill obsolescence is a major problem so that those return-ing to work after more than a few months' absence find themselves unfamiliar with new techniques or procedures, it is not at all evident how pervasive the problem is. It may be the case that for the great majority of jobs, new techniques and procedures can be learned in a matter of hours or days. Careful studies of job requirements and of the match between requirements and qualifications need to be undertaken before attributing income losses and downward mobility associ-ated with time out of the labor force to productivity declines due to depreciation of human capital, especially given the quick rebound of incomes within the first year after labor-force reentry noted above.

Sequences of Jobs

Spilerman (1977), in an influential paper, has called for the identification of "career lines" or "job trajectories," which he defines as work histories common to some portion of the labor force. He suggests that much can be learned from the study of the properties of such job trajectories, a judgment that I share. Much of our impressionistic understanding of the life chances of individuals derives from knowledge of their work histories: How they started, what sorts of promotions they were offered, what choices they had, what decisions they made when they had choices, and so on. The trick is to find a way to aggregate these individual histories into coherent sequences—if indeed, there are coherent sequences rather than a melange of highly idiosyncratic experiences—to try to determine whether there are systematic differences in career trajectories between men and women, between those in different types of occupations, and so on. The assumption is that there are—that career trajectories differ on the average between men and women and between women with and without family and childrearing responsibilities, and also that they differ among occupational groups. As we know from the work of Hodge (1966) the notion of a career in the sense of a coherent set of occupational changes leading inexorably upward is inconsistent with the reality of occupational histories. People not only change jobs and occupations often, as we have seen above, but many of them—men and women both—also change jobs in a more or less random way, moving from one job to another in no discernible upward progression. The reason for this is obvious enough—a great fraction of job changing in contemporary American society is not voluntary but is rather the consequence of layoffs, plant closings, involuntary transfers, etc. And among women, job changing results in addition from "forced" geographic mobility and labor-force reentry after a period of absence, neither of which is conducive to career continuity, as we have seen.

Career continuity, in the sense of a sequence of jobs that follows a clear and systematic upward trajectory with respect to rank, status, or income is probably characteristic of only a small fraction of the labor force: Those who begin in or move into a profession, skilled craft, or administrative position. And even with respect to such occupations, there is a very large amount of mobility over the career, as Evans and Laumann (1983) have shown. Among 23 detailed (3-digit) occupations with large numbers of incumbents in the 1970 Census major-group "professional, technical, and kindred workers," in only 5 were more than one-half of those who had begun their careers in the profession still practicing it by age 55 (as estimated via a synthetic cohort analysis). If there is that much career discontinuity in the professions, there is little reason to expect much stability in other occupations.

Of course, Evans and Laumann's results do not tell us that careers are disorderly, only that they often involve occupational mobility. An obvious next step would be to use the same data, the 1970 Census public-use sample that includes a question on 1965 occupation, to develop career trajectories for the professions they studied and for other occupational groups as well. It is commonly held, for example, that engineering is a young man's field, and that a successful career as an engineer involves moving out of the profession and upward into management. It would be easy enough to test this claim by studying the mobility patterns of those who begin their careers as engineers. A variety of similar hypotheses could be tested, including those regarding the relative prospects of men and women who were in a given occupation in 1965 and who remained in the labor force in 1970. This, indeed, is similar to the strategy proposed by Spilerman (1977), but it has not actually been implemented with the 1970 Census data, perhaps because it is extremely expensive in computer time.

A different and somewhat more efficient—albeit ultimately less informative—approach to the analysis of careers has been proposed by Sørensen (1975; see also Sørensen & Tuma, 1981). In this approach, the main interest is in the "growth," that is, increase, in occupational status and earnings over the life course. Changes in occupational status and earnings are presumed to depend upon the personal characteritics of workers, features of labor markets, and time. Applying models of this sort to the Johns Hopkins Life History data and to various data sets from the National Longitudinal Surveys of Labor Market Experience, Sørensen and his associates have shown results consistent with but going beyond what we have already noted in the Sewell data: On average, the occupational status and income of men, especially white men, increases substantially over the course of the career (Sørensen, 1975); and attainment patterns of men depend upon the position of jobs within labor-market structures (Kalleberg & Hudis, 1979; Sørensen & Tuma, 1981). Women, by contrast, show little gain in occupational status over the course of the career, although there is a small return to work experience for women—much less than for men (Rosenfeld, 1978, 1980). But the careers of women, like those of men, are substantially affected by their labor-market position, with interfirm moves heavily dependent upon women's personal characteristics and job moves within internal labor markets heavily dependent on age and job duration (Felmlee, 1982).

These results suggest the importance of, but do not directly address, gender differences in the functioning of internal labor markets. It has been claimed (e.g., Kanter, 1977) that a major reason for the lack of career advancement of women is that women's jobs, in contrast to men's jobs, are often dead-end positions with no promotion opportunities within the internal labor market. This is clearly a crucial issue but one that has not been much studied in a systematic way (see, however, the interesting discussion of gender differences in promotion opportunities in Chapter 12, this volume, by Baron and Bielby). Once again the difficulty is the lack of suitable data. It is difficult to study internal labor markets without data for particular firms, and there have been few such data sets available to researchers. The study of particular firms has both advantages and disadvantages. The major advantage is that a great deal of career mobility occurs within internal labor markets and involves job changes within census occupation and industry categories. Such changes are difficult to capture in work histories not only because they are often not so well remembered as are interfirm changes but also because we have no conventional way of coding job changes other than with the census occupation and industry categories. Reliance on personnel records solves both problems. The major disadvantage of utilizing the records of a single firm to study career mobility patterns is that the average worker changes firms quite frequently so that personnel records will on average cover only a small part of each worker's career. The obvious solution is to do studies of several kinds to build up a comprehensive picture of career mobility processes.

Unfinished Business

As is evident from the topics thus far reviewed, there is a great deal of work left to be done. The study of careers is barely beginning, and each new piece of research typically raises more questions than it answers. Thus far, the outlines of gender differences in patterns of labor-force participation have been reasonably well established, although a great deal more needs to be learned about this topic, particularly with respect to sequences of movement into and out of the labor force. Studies of labor-force reentry and of job mobility will be helpful in testing theories of income differences between men and women, as suggested above; but virtually no work has yet been done in this area. By far the greatest need, however, is to begin to identify job trajectories—that is, systematic sequences of successive jobs—of the kind proposed by Spilerman. This is a difficult task, made even more difficult by the paucity of appropriate data. But it is the area of greatest potential payoff. With the exception of a few professions, we cannot even be sure at this point that there is such a thing as a career trajectory. It may be that for the great majority of workers, job sequences are quite idiosyncratic— even though for men there appears to be an average upward movement in status and income. But this could be caused by the fact that managers almost never begin as managers but are promoted from within the ranks. The promotion of about one-fifth of all men who begin their careers in jobs other than the professions or managerial positions to managerial responsibilities would be sufficient to account for the observed pattern of average upward mobility over the course of the career. But this leaves the 80% who do not become managers. For them, career trajectories may consist either of more or less random movement among jobs and occupations or of no movement at all. The difficulty is that at this point we simply do not know and have little basis for making inferences other than to observe that the rates of both job and occupational changes decline with age but, nonetheless, remain high In absolute terms throughout the life course.

If we know so little about the situation of men, we know even less about women, since the data are even skimpier for women. In gross terms, it is evident that most women experience little upward mobility over the course of their careers, and that upward mobility prospects are particularly poor for married women with children. But we have virtually no direct information on the effect of patterns of work experience on mobility prospects or on the consequences of starting in one occupation rather than in another. Finally, although the structure of labor markets and the position of a job in a labor market are obviously crucial determinants of career opportunities, the effect of labor-market position has been studied in only the most limited way. The application of a typology of mobility types of the kind proposed by Kalleberg and Hudis (1979) to a general sample including both men and women at various career stages would be extremely useful.

One way of summarizing our unfinished business is to point out that we need to move beyond the analysis of labor-force subgroups specified only by sex, race, and age to identify specific career trajectories and to relate these trajectories to variations in labor-force position, entry occupation, family and life-cycle circumstances, and all of the other factors that we know are implicated in careers. To do this will require not only more imaginative exploitation of existing data but also the generation of new and more suitable data—in particular, con-

230 Work Histories of Women and Men

tinuous work-history data for a large representative sample of both women and men. Such data are currently available for a number of other countries. It is time we had such data for the United States as well and time we addressed these questions both here and abroad. Indeed, a comparison of United States patterns with those of other countries would take us a long way toward a better understanding of the socioeconomic life course in industrial societies.

References

Blau, P. M., & Duncan, O. D. *The American occupational structure.* New York: Wiley, 1967.

Blum, Z. D., Karweit, N. L., & Sørensen, A. B. *A method for the collection and analysis of retrospective life histories* (Report No. 48). Baltimore: The Johns Hopkins University, Center for the Study of the Social Organization of Schools, 1969.

Cole, R. E. *Work, mobility, and participation: A comparative study of American and Japanese industry.* Berkeley, Calif.: University of California Press, 1979.

Corcoran, M., Duncan, G. J., & Ponza, M. *Work experience, job segregation, and wages.* Paper presented to the Conference on Job Segregation by Sex, National Academy of Sciences, Washington, D.C., May 1982.

Doeringer, P., & Piore, M. *Internal labor markets and manpower analysis.* Lexington, Mass.: D. C. Heath, 1971.

Duncan, O. D. Properties and characteristics of the socioeconomic index. In A. J. Reise, Jr. (Ed.), *Occupations and social status.* New York: Free Press of Glencoe, Inc., 1961, pp. 139–161. (a)

Duncan, O. D. A socioeconomic index for all occupations. In A. J. Reise, Jr. (Ed.), *Occupations and social status.* New York: The Free Press of Glencoe, Inc., 1961, pp. 109–138. (b)

Duncan, G. J., & Morgan, J. N. *Five thousand American families: Patterns of progress* (Vol. 1). Ann Arbor, Michigan: University of Michigan, Institute for Social Research, 1974.

Evans, M. D., & Laumann, E. O. Professional commitment: Myth or reality? In D. J. Treiman & R. V. Robinson (Eds.), *Research in social stratification and mobility: A research annual* (Vol. 2). Greenwich, Conn.: JAI Press, 1983, pp. 3–40.

Featherman, D. L., & Hauser, R. M. Sexual inequalities and socioeconomic achievement in the U.S., 1962–1973. *American Sociological Review,* 1976, *41,* 462–483.

Featherman, D. L., & Hauser, R. M. *Opportunity and change.* New York: Academic Press, 1978.

Felmlee, D. H. Women's job mobility processes within and between employers. *American Sociological Review,* 1982, *47,* 142–150.

Gallaway, L. E. The effect of geographic labor mobility on income: A brief comment. *Journal of Human Resources,* 1969, *4,* 103–109. (a)

Gallaway, L. E. *Geographic labor mobility in the United States: 1957 to 1960.* Washington, D.C.: U.S. Government Printing Office, 1969. (b)

Hauser, R. M., & Featherman, D. L. *The process of stratification.* New York: Academic Press, 1977.

Hodge, R. W. Occupational mobility as a probability process. *Demography,* 1966, *3,* 19–34.

Jacobs, J. Industrial sector and career mobility reconsidered. *American Sociological Review,* 1983, *48,* 415–420.

Kalleberg, A. L., & Hudis, P. M. Wage change in the late career: A model for the outcomes of job sequences. *Social Science Research,* 1979, *7,* 61–80.

Kanter, R. M. *Men and women of the corporation*. New York: Basic Books, 1977.
Long, L. H. Women's labor force participation and the residential mobility of families. *Social Forces*, 1974, *52*, 342–348.
McClendon, M. J. The occupational status attainment processes of males and females. *American Sociological Review*, 1976, *41*, 52–64.
Mincer, J., & Ofek, H. Interrupted work careers. *Journal of Human Resources*, 1982, *17*, 3–24.
Mincer, J., & Polachek, S. W. Family investment in human capital: Earnings of women. *Journal of Political Economy*, 1974, *82*, S76–S108.
Oppenheimer, V. K. *The female labor force in the United States: Demographic and economic factors governing its growth and changing composition* (Population Monograph Series No. 5). Berkeley: University of California, Institute of International Studies, 1972.
Parnes, H. S., Shea, J. R., & Spitz, R. S. *Dual careers: A longitudinal study of labor market experience of women* (Manpower Research Monograph No. 21). Washington, D. C.: U.S. Government Printing Office, 1970.
Polachek, S. W. Discontinuous labor force participation and its effect on women's market earnings. In C. B. Lloyd (Ed.), *Sex, discrimination, and the division of labor*. New York: Columbia University Press, 1975, pp. 90–122.
Robinson, J. G. *Labor force participation rates of cohorts of women in the United States: 1890 to 1979*. Paper presented to the Population Association of America, Denver, 1980.
Rosenfeld, R. A. Women's employment patterns and occupational achievements. *Social Science Research*, 1978, *7*, 61–80.
Rosenfeld, R. A. Women's occupational careers: Individual and structural explanations. *Sociology of Work and Occupations*, 1979, *6*, 283–311.
Rosenfeld, R. A. Race and sex differences in career dynamics. *American Sociological Review*, 1980, *45*, 583–609.
Sewell, W. H., Hauser, R. M., & Wolf, W. C. Sex, schooling, and occupational success. *American Journal of Sociology*, 1980, *86*, 551–583.
Sommers, D., & Eck, A. Occupational mobility in the American labor force. *Monthly Labor Review*, 1977, *100* (January), 3–19.
Sørensen, A. B. The structure of intragenerational mobility. *American Sociological Review*, 1975, *40*, 456–471.
Sørensen, A. B., & Tuma, N. B. Labor market structures and job mobility. In D. J. Treiman & R. V. Robinson (Eds.), *Research in social stratification and mobility: A research annual* (Vol. 1). Greenwich, Conn.: JAI Press, 1981, pp. 67–94.
Spilerman, S. Careers, labor markets, and socioeconomic achievement. *American Journal of Sociology*, 1977, *83*, 551–593.
Stevens, G., & Featherman, D. L. A revised socioeconomic index of occupational status. *Social Science Research*, 1981, *10*, 364–395.
Treiman, D. J., & Hartmann, H. I. (Eds.). *Women, work, and wages: Equal pay for jobs of equal value*. Washington, D.C.: National Academy Press, 1981.
Treiman, D. J., & Terrell, K. Sex and the process of status attainment: A comparison of working women and men. *American Sociological Review*, 1975, *40*, 174–200.

12

Organizational Barriers to Gender Equality: Sex Segregation of Jobs and Opportunities*

JAMES N. BARON
Stanford University

WILLIAM T. BIELBY
University of California, Santa Barbara

Introduction

Something interesting has happened to the study of gender stratification. Nine years ago in the *American Sociological Review (ASR)*, Treiman and Terrell wrote:

> It is clear that labor market discrimination against women does not extend to the status of the work open to them nor to the qualifications demanded. Women work at jobs which are about as prestigious as those held by men and, like men, secure good jobs mainly on the basis of superior education. (1975, p. 182)

It is hard to imagine an *ASR* reviewer allowing that paragraph to pass today. It is not that Treiman and Terrell's conclusions were wrong nor that the world has changed so much since 1975, but rather that our way of conceptualizing and analyzing gender inequality has changed considerably.

Some researchers would take issue with comparing men's and women's careers in terms of occupational status. Treiman and Terrell (1975) found that income attainment (rather than status attainment) *does* differ dramatically by sex (also see Suter & Miller, 1973). Consequently, some investigators have argued against analyses based on conventional occupational status scales, since status rankings for men and women are incommensurable (e.g., Bose & Rossi, 1983). However, there is a more basic reason why Treiman and Terrell's conclusion

*The research reported here was supported in part by a grant from the National Science Foundation (SES 79-24905). Patricia Y. Martin provided helpful comments on an earlier version of this chapter, and David Callaway provided superb technical assistance.

would not pass muster today: Researchers have begun analyzing organizational barriers faced by women in the labor market.

In fact, from the standpoint of the sociology of knowledge, it is interesting how concepts and methods originally developed in studying men's careers were superimposed piecemeal on women's attainment (Acker, 1973, 1980). For instance, gender differences in labor-market outcomes are often summarized by analyses of covariance expressing differential rates of return to human capital, social background, and the like, which seems at odds with how we think about men's and women's careers. While modeling and analyzing career achievements by sex is an important enterprise, we need to know much more about the organizational structures and processes that generate gender inequalities.

We have labeled this shift in focus the "new structuralism" in stratification research (Baron & Bielby, 1980), which is being extended to the study of gender inequality. Women's inferior attainments are being traced to: (a) their supposed concentration in so-called secondary labor markets, devoid of opportunities for advancement; (b) their segregation into certain jobs, occupations, firms, and industries; (c) organizational arrangements restricting women's access to authority and responsibility in the work place; (d) familial norms and the household division of labor, which materially limit women's career involvement and symbolically limit the kinds of work available; (e) and class conflicts, in which male–female divisions are used by capitalists to divide and conquer the work force (see, for instance, Acker, 1980; Roos & Reskin, 1984; Treiman & Hartmann, 1981, chap. 3).

Much of this research has attempted to infer organizational arrangements from observed career patterns of individual women. For instance, the frequent finding that men's careers benefit more than women's from marriage and having children is usually taken as evidence of a parallelism between the division of labor in households and in organizations: Being married and having children serve as different "signals" to employers for a male vs. a female, and they also imply quite different things about household responsibilities (Bielby & Baron, 1983; Kanter, 1977; Pfeffer & Ross, 1982; Talbert & Bose, 1977). However, such an inference says very little about how employers use marriage as a signal. As Pfeffer and Ross (1982) note, marriage might signify conformity to organizational expectations, it might indicate worker attributes positively associated with performance, or it might cause employers to perceive the employee as needier than comparable unmarried workers.

Of course, women whose careers are impeded by specific employer practices may not care *why* employers behave this way. But those of us interested in sociological theory and, more importantly, those of us interested in changing the world of work, cannot content ourselves simply by demonstrating that specific variables do not affect men and women equally. Rather, we must subject competing perspectives on gender stratification to explicit empirical tests; otherwise, we preclude falsification, just as human capital theorists after the fact can explain away any aberration that makes labor markets appear inefficient.

How can the validity of various perspectives on gender inequality be assessed? On the one hand, there is a wealth of research on individuals' careers documenting differences in what happens to men vs. women; this research specifies the differential outcomes we are interested in explaining. On the other hand, we have some brilliant ethnographies of how organizations foster gender inequality (particularly, Kanter, 1977). This work specifies the *processes* fostering gender inequality, but, being restricted to specific organizations or occupations, it often lacks the comparative focus necessary to determine why organizations behave differently.

As an adjunct to ethnographic work and attainment studies, we believe large-scale comparative organizational research is required that documents how specific attributes of the work place affect gender inequalities. Accordingly, we have spent the last several years acquiring and analyzing data describing work arrangements in organizations across a variety of industrial settings in California. Our original intent was not to focus primarily on gender inequality in the work place. Rather, we were interested in examining various theories about economic segmentation and its relationship to the organization of work. However, the data we obtained also enumerated the gender composition of every job. In cleaning the data, men and women shared job assignments in organizations so rarely that we could usually be certain that an apparent exception reflected coding or keypunch error. This fact, coupled with subtle and not so subtle references in the data to gender-based employment practices, increasingly drew our attention to the primacy of the sexual division of labor within organizations. We were amazed at the pervasiveness of women's concentration in organizational ghettos.

Of course, it is no surprise that work is highly segregated by sex. Research on gender segregation has documented persistent differences in the work assignments of men and women since the turn of the century. In fact, roughly 60–70% of men (or women) would have had to change detailed occupations to equalize the occupational distribution by sex, and this has remained roughly constant since 1900 (Blau & Hendricks, 1978; England, 1981; Gross, 1968; Williams, 1979).[1] Occupations, however, are amorphous entities within which there is frequently stratification by sex (see Grimm & Stern, 1974). Consequently, organizational practices that segregate women within the lowest levels of occupational career ladders are obscured by studies examining occupational change. Furthermore, firms vary considerably in their sex-typing of occupations. For instance, male waiters are disproportionately employed in high-ticket restaurants, whereas women labor in low-priced restaurants; boys' schools hire male teachers, whereas girls' schools hire women. This organizational variation is also overlooked by studies at the individual and occupational levels.

In short, from a theoretical and policy point of view, we need to know: (1) How much organizational sex segregation exists; (2) what kinds of organizations

---

[1]Children's play and contributions to the household are also highly segregated by sex, even at an early age (White & Brinkerhoff, 1981).

segregate most; and (3) most importantly, what are the implications of sex segregation for women's career advancement? This chapter summarizes what we have been learning about gender inequality in organizations from our ongoing studies and outlines some implications of our work for future research and for policies aimed at achieving work-place equity. After briefly describing our sample, we review our findings with respect to these concerns.

Data

We have studied over 400 work organizations in California between 1959 and 1979. These data were collected by the California Occupational Analysis Field Center of the U.S. Employment Service, primarily for use in preparing the *Dictionary of Occupational Titles (DOT)* (for a description of data collection procedures, see Baron, 1982, chaps. 2–3; Cain & Treiman, 1981; Miller, Treiman, Cain, & Roos, 1980; U.S. Department of Labor, 1972). We measured segregation by the "index of dissimilarity" (or Δ), the percentage of women or men in a firm that would have to switch job titles to equalize job distributions across sex (Duncan & Duncan, 1955). Our sample of organizations is roughly representative of California during the two-decade period studied. These data include organizations ranging from 2 to almost 8000 employees, from a tortilleria to a women's bank, from heavy manufacturing to small-scale services. In fact, the industries excluded or underrepresented in our sample (particularly, insurance, trucking, construction, and retail trade) are probably more segregated by sex than average, so our results may actually understate work-place segregation.[2]

Findings

How Much Segregation Exists?

Among those organizations studied, over 59% were perfectly segregated by sex—that is, workers of one sex were either excluded entirely or were concentrated in job titles filled exclusively by the same sex. Even among the minority of firms that were not perfectly segregated (i.e., had indices of dissimilarity less than 100), the median was 84.1. Fewer than 10% of the work force was in jobs that included both sexes. Thus, most organizations are either perfectly segregated or closely approximate that state of affairs (Bielby & Baron, in press-b).

Occupational-level research overlooks much of this segregation, which occurs within detailed (3-digit) occupational classifications (Bielby & Baron, in press-

---

[2]Various reweightings of the data to improve their representativeness within and across industries did not affect the outcome of our statistical analyses.

a). For example, across seven major occupational categories, similar to those used by the Equal Employment Opportunity Commission (EEOC) in its publications, the index of dissimilarity was only 36.5 for nearly 51,000 workers employed in 290 organizations in our sample. At the level of 645 *DOT* occupations, somewhat more detailed than the Census 3-digit classification, the index was 75.1, ranging from 69.3 for nonmanual occupations to 81.2 for manual work. However, organizational job titles displayed an index of 96.3 (94.1 for nonmanual and 98.0 for manual jobs), and the index was virtually unchanged $(\Delta - 95.9)$ if jobs having only one incumbent (which are perfectly segregated by definition) were excluded from consideration.

Given these results, using major occupational categories to monitor trends in gender equity, as the EEOC often does, for instance, seems virtually worthless. In our view, studies of *occupational* segregation are misleading not only because they suffer from such aggregation biases, but also because they do not illuminate the organizational arrangements that foster and sustain segregated work. The next section briefly summarizes what our empirical analyses contribute on that score.

What Kinds of Organizations Segregate Most?

Armed with the conventional arsenal of multivariate statistical techniques, we had originally planned to run regressions explaining variance in organizational segregation patterns. However, given the descriptive results summarized above, such analyses would not tell us very much about sex segregation: It is hard to explain variance in a constant. To the extent that our results are generalizable, they suggest that firms differ less in the *extent* of sex segregation than in the processes generating and sustaining it. Accordingly, we looked at factors differentiating the minority of organizations that were not pervasively segregated from the majority that were. These analyses revealed that firms can become segregated in quite different ways.

Many of the perfectly segregated enterprises were very small entrepreneurial firms, in which male employers can indulge what Becker (1971) terms their "tastes" for an all-male work place. Furthermore, the absence of a detailed division of labor permits women either to be excluded or to be concentrated in a few job categories (e.g., receptionist). At the same time, large bureaucratic firms were also very segregated by sex. The hallmark of bureaucracy is that each individual is an expert: Accordingly, bureaucratic organizations approach a division of labor in which each individual monopolizes a job title, demarcating specific domains of expertise (Weber, 1922/1947). Clearly, an organization having only one worker per job has to be perfectly segregated by sex, and bureaucratization represents a move in that direction.

Large bureaucracies also have a detailed occupational division of labor that divides men's from women's work. In particular, large manufacturing organizations relying primarily on manual tasks were more highly segregated than others, since women have historically been excluded from many jobs involving physical labor. Even after laws in California limiting women's lifting were ruled unconstitutional in 1970, we observed no change in the segregation of women from positions previously closed to them by virtue of this legislation. Because these same work settings are the most unionized in our sample, we observed a negative effect of unionization on gender equity in job assignment. While collective bargaining and union governance may promote desegregation, they did not do so in our sample during the period under study (cf. Bridges, 1982; O'Farrell & Harlan, in press).

Another characteristic of bureaucratic control is the fragmentation of work into job titles considerably more detailed than warranted simply on technical grounds. This "hierarchy fetishism," according to Marxists, increases organizational loyalty, caters to workers' status needs, and imposes opportunities for advancement precluded by a more massified division of labor (Dreyfuss, 1938/1968; Edwards, 1979; Gordon, 1972; Wachtel, 1974). By comparing the establishment's distribution of job titles to the distribution of 6-digit *DOT* occupations catalogued by an independent government analyst, we assessed the extent to which such fragmentation characterized each organization (see Baron, 1982, chaps. 6–7). Not surprisingly, fragmentation was another basis of gender segregation, since women are grouped into the lower echelon of each set of occupation-specific job titles.

Segregation was also higher in enterprises where internal labor markets appear to operate. Formal bidding procedures for job advancement, combined with a work force occupying specialized nonentry jobs, inhibit the assignment of men and women to the same jobs, and in some cases women employees were excluded altogether from such settings (Bielby & Baron, in press-b). These findings are consistent with other research showing the adverse impact of promotion ladders on gender equity when men and women are assigned to separate entry classifications and department-specific seniority rules keep women from transferring into male career lines (Shaeffer & Lynton, 1979).

Not surprisingly, our analyses indicate that women are less likely to be segregated when they comprise a larger share of the firm's work force. Kanter (1977) has linked skewed sex ratios favoring men to the powerlessness of women in organizations. Access to resources (in this case, job opportunities monopolized by men) is severely restricted when women are grouped into occupational ghettos. Spangler, Gordon, and Pipkin (1978) have demonstrated the barriers that female law students confront when they comprise a minority of the student body, and our results seem consistent with theirs: Just as a token woman law student can expect to be segregated *socially* and excluded from the law review, so can a minority of women workers expect to be segregated *positionally* and barred from career opportunities in the firm.

Part of the relationship between sex ratios and segregation reflects characteristics of organizations associated with having a small percentage of female workers: Women are typically a smaller fraction of the work force in large, unionized, "core" manufacturing enterprises, which are among the most segregated in our sample. However, this by no means accounts for the entire relationship for which there may be a fairly simple explanation. Men seek to exclude women from their job classifications if only to preserve the status and opportunities they monopolize (Martin, 1983). Controlling for size and occupational composition—which our models do—a firm having a high percentage of female workers could only be *more* segregated than one tilted toward men if it: (1) added additional (segregated) job titles into which the women were allocated; or (2) grouped all of them within preexisting titles that remained perfectly segregated However, firms apparently do neither. In our sample, the (log) number of job titles is correlated almost perfectly with (log) firm size, so the creation of new female ghettos is constrained by organizational size. Therefore, *ceteris paribus,* an increase in the relative size of the female labor force implies that some women are likely to end up in jobs also staffed by men, even if only by accident, thereby reducing segregation.

Our results thus cast doubt on the generality of some recent studies that suggest increases in relative minority size enhance discrimination by making minorities appear more threatening (e.g., Frisbie & Neidert, 1977; South, Bonjean, Markham, & Corder, 1982). Of course, the relationship between sex ratios and segregation may not be linear—that is, there may be "tipping points" at which an increase in the proportion of women in a firm has a particularly strong effect (Kanter, 1977; but cf. South et al., 1982). Moreover, sex ratios may not have the same effect on segregation patterns across firms of all sizes; for instance, larger shifts in gender composition may be required to achieve a given amount of desegregation in big firms than in small ones (Martin, 1983). Hopefully, future research will explore these concerns. Disentangling the relationship between sex ratios, segregation, and opportunity will require a combination of ethnographic, comparative, experimental, and other methods.

To better understand factors affecting segregation, we looked in detail at the few aberrant instances in which firms were relatively less segregated. (Bear in mind that here, "relatively less segregated" establishments are those in which "only" 75% of women would have to switch jobs to equalize occupational distributions by sex.) These detailed analyses suggested that instances of apparent desegregation are often illusory. Desegregated establishments seem to be of four types.

One form of apparent integration occurs when men and women share job assignments in a firm, but their duties are segregated by sex. In a summer camp in our sample, for instance, counselors supervised same-sex children, while a language school hired both men and women as language instructors because the firm thought it important for students to gain experience conversing with members of both sexes. Thus, despite parity in job assignments, workers' duties reflect cultural sex-role expectations. We refer to this as *gender-based* desegregation.

Second, in a very small enterprise, if any job title is composed of men and women, this sharply reduces the index of dissimilarity, making the establishment appear integrated. Yet if small organizations are in fact bastions of traditionalism, as many suggest, then the lone female sharing a job assignment with men may in fact be segregated *within* that role, a victim of the gender-based desegregation described above. For instance, a store having two male and one female sales clerks may segregate them by product, shift, and the like (Talbert & Bose, 1977). We refer to this as *nominal* desegregation, since it reflects a nominal integration of men and women in a small establishment.

A third form of apparent desegregation occurs in multilocational establishments, in which men and women occupy the same job assignment but in different locations. Some real estate brokerages in our sample employed male and female managers and salespersons, but women managers supervised female clerks exclusively in some offices, while male managers supervised salespeople elsewhere. We term this *spatial* desegregation; again, it is an apparent exception that actually reflects another source of segregated work.

A similar sort of segregation occurs across organizations rather than across different sites in a single enterprise. Research on clerical and sales occupations (Blau, 1977; Talbert & Bose, 1977), travel agents (Mennerick, 1975), banking (Szafran, 1984), and other work settings demonstrates that men and women with the same nominal job assignment are often segregated organizationally. Joan Wallach Scott has described the same phenomenon in nineteenth-century textile manufacture:

> The specific jobs done by men and women varied from mill to mill, but the separation of male and female work was almost universal; in most mills many rooms were staffed entirely by women. Thus the separate realms of work for men and women remained undisturbed. (1982, pp. 171–172)

Ongoing research demonstrates this within our own data: Where an *occupation* appears to be integrated (for instance, it has 50% men and 50% women), men typically perform the job in some locations and women perform it elsewhere (Bielby & Baron, in press-a). Because mobility patterns and job content are often defined interorganizationally in professions, crafts, and technical roles, sex composition in those lines of work varies a bit less from firm to firm. In contrast, manufacturing organizations differ significantly in the gender definitions of specific jobs. While part of this reflects differences across firms in the skills required of particular jobs, the remainder may bespeak men's long-standing monopoly of employment in the most desirable manufacturing settings. Interestingly, "not elsewhere classified" ("n.e.c.") occupations were among the most segregated across enterprises. While occupational schemes do not distinguish between men and women in the same "n.e.c." classification, firms apparently have little difficulty in doing so, placing women and men in very different organizational contexts.

Finally, we did encounter a few instances of integrated job assignments that seemed consistent with mechanisms posited by human capital theorists, who argue that women invest in skills that are general and will not atrophy from disuse (Mincer & Polachek, 1974; Polachek, 1979). For example, integrated divisions of labor were observed in some agricultural and real estate establishments. In both lines of work, skills are highly transferable across firms, and rewards are distributed in ways that may attract qualified males as well as females with intermittent labor-force participation. We refer to this as *market desegregation*, since the labor market appears to function in these instances as posited by neoclassical theory.

Economists, of course, might criticize us for not taking into account the labor supply affecting each firm: Women may be segregated simply because they are not qualified for many jobs held exclusively by men, given their familial commitments and responsibilities. While this may explain a few instances of segregation or desegregation, it is difficult to explain the pervasive segregation of women across such diverse organizational and industrial contexts based solely on labor supply. (Nor does it explain segregation *within* detailed occupations.) One must assume that labor-supply constraints differ significantly among the establishments in our sample, covering the gamut of sizes, locations, technologies, industries, and the period between 1959 and 1979. In short, the independent variable (labor supply) varies dramatically, whereas the dependent variable (segregation) hardly varies at all. Thus, labor supply can hardly account for segregation patterns.

Rather, our research suggests that there is in some sense equifinality in work arrangements; that is, segregation occurs through a variety of organizational structures and processes. In small "periphery" firms, segregation may arise through traditional practices and face-to-face patriarchal work relations that concentrate women in stereotyped roles, even in the absence of a detailed division of labor. Manufacturing technologies relying intensively on manual labor also display high segregation, barring women from performing many duties on the outdated grounds that they cannot handle the physical demands. As noted above, bureaucratization, fragmented job titles, specialization, reliance on nonentry personnel, and sex ratios skewed toward men are other concomitants of segregation documented by our research. In short, each of the organizational control strategies outlined by Edwards (1979)—simple, technical, and bureaucratic—entails its own mechanisms of sex segregation. Organizations differ less in the amount of segregation than in the ways they produce it.

Sex Segregation and Careers

This segregation obviously has profound implications for the careers of men and women, which are the focus of studies in progress. Not surprisingly, the few jobs containing men and women were mostly in entry-level slots at the bottom of organizations; in fact, about 85% of workers in jobs containing men and women were at the entry level. However, entry-level jobs in our sample were almost as segregated as other jobs, demonstrating that distinctions between men's and women's work exist from the time most employees enter organizations. Career ladders embody and exacerbate this segregation, with women's promotion opportunities typically limited to moves one or two steps higher up the organizational ladder, in positions responsible for supervising women exclusively (see Baron, 1982, chapts. 7–8). In contrast, promotion ladders for men are longer.

An ordnance establishment in our sample illustates this pattern. In this plant, 555 women were employed as "Assemblers," while 243 men were employed as "Production Workers," both entry jobs involving the same duties and sharing the same detailed *DOT* code. Job analyses indicated few differences between the two slots, except that men occasionally lifted more than 25 pounds (11.34 kg), the limit that women could then legally lift without a special permit. Of course, a separate job title is not required to capture that distinction, and in most other respects, the jobs were identical. In fact, in certain respects, the women's job appeared more demanding, according to the job analyst.[3]

However, these jobs were conspicuously different in relation to organizational promotion hierarchies. Female Assemblers could be promoted into the Leadlady classification, while male Production Workers were promoted into the Leadman classification. In other words, workers were segregated by sex upon entry and then channeled into sex-specific career trajectories. There were 31 Leadmen supervising the 243 Production Workers, implying a span of control of about 8 workers per supervisor. Among women, however, there were only 10 Leadladies, indicating that the average female line supervisor oversaw 55 women. This not only suggests a more massified control structure confronting women on this assembly line than men but also implies quite different probabilities for promotion among men and women. If the span of control is 1:8 among men, but 1:55 among women, the average female Assembler seems much less likely to advance than the average male Production Worker, even though the employer states it is company policy to upgrade workers from within.

This asymmetry was perpetuated farther up this organization's ladder. The Leadlady and Leadman classifications promote to Foreman, a title composed of 32 male and 3 female incumbents in this establishment. Foremen could advance to become Supervisors, staffed by 14 men and no women. In other words, once men and women advanced far enough to vie for the same positions, women's chances diminished almost entirely. Toward the bottom of the ladder, separate job classifications were utilized to segregate women from men, lest the large number (and percentage) of women in this firm pose problems of social control. Farther up the hierarchy, sex ratios tipped in men's favor, and it apparently seemed "natural" that only 9% of the Foremen and none of the Supervisors in this plant should be women.[4] To assess whether this enterprise was typical, we

---

[3]The analyst believed its incumbents required 4 more years of education than the men, and the job involved slightly greater finger dexterity and training time, while the men's position required a bit more eye–hand–foot coordination.

[4]It is worth noting that this establishment did 100% of its business with Federal defense agencies and was studied in 1970, several years after Executive Order 11375 empowered the Office of Federal Contract Compliance Programs to punish government contractors who utilize ascriptive traits in employment.

examined each occurrence of a sex-integrated job in our sample that appeared to have opportunities for upward mobility, and in the vast majority of other establishments analyzed, women in those jobs seemed to have reached organizational dead ends as well.

Our data also provide numerous examples of men's apparent ability to circumvent formal promotion rules. In these cases, a position was monopolized by women at the bottom of an organization, and that position was listed as requisite experience for promotion to the next level. However, all occupants of the next highest position were men. Employment Service analysts were occasionally quite explicit in conveying such inequalities:

> [MOLDING MECHANIC] workers [three males] are usually obtained from outside the plant. . . . Promotion from [the position of] OPERATOR, MOLDING MACHINE [to MOLDING MECHANIC] within the company is not normal since these workers are all female (Job analysis schedule 2909975, pen and pencil company, 1965).

This recurrent pattern underscores the political aspect of credentials, skills, and experience (Collins, 1979). Apparently, men can substitute alternative qualifications for those required and obtained in the internal labor market, while women rarely experience this option.

To be sure, extremely skewed sex ratios favoring women had a similar effect to those favoring men: When virtually all incumbents of a slot were female, males were unlikely to occupy the next highest position. For instance, a wholesale firm (45 employees) that processes frozen fish employed 29 women and 1 man as entry-level "Peelers and Packers" within its production department. (There was also 1 male entry "Laborer" in that department.) Supervision within the production unit was performed by 5 female "Leadladies." Thus, the presence of a few male "tokens" in this department did not alter the gender-based nature of the hierarchy within this establishment.[5]

Yet unless sex ratios in entry jobs were so conspicuously skewed, the balance of females to males almost always worked to women's disadvantage. A phonograph record manufacturer, for instance, employed 16 men and 44 women in an entry slot called "Press Operator." Women thus comprised 73.3% of this organizational role, a value intermediate between what Kanter (1977) calls a "skewed" and "tilted" sex ratio. Although this establishment was subject to union bidding arrangements, the classification of "Set-up Man," to which "Press Operators" were promoted, consisted of 12 men and no women, and the next job up the organizational ladder, "Pressing Foreman," was also all male (3 men).[6] Similar patterns were observed in other establishments where females outnumbered males in entry jobs by ratios as high as 3:1.

---

[5]However, all administrative and sales personnel were male, implying the existence of two ladders within this enterprise: A one-step ladder for female production labor and a more finely graded one for men in the office.

[6]Indeed, as was often the case until recently, gender distinctions (the suffix "man") were incorporated in the job titles themselves.

Thus, while Kanter (1977, p. 209) posits that men are tokens when they comprise roughly 20% or less of a group, as are women within that range of percentages, our results suggest that "tipping points" are not symmetric. Rather, a category (in this case, a job) having 75% women and 25% men may be less "skewed" than one equally tilted in the other direction. Only when women virtually monopolize a subordinate job is one likely to find a female who managed a promotion to the next highest position. In terms of access to power and opportunities for building careers, women continue to be the subdominant category until they constitute a much larger percentage of the group. Men, on the other hand, can avoid some pitfalls of tokenism, even when their relative numbers are fairly small.

Our data inspire another interesting conjecture for the sociology of numbers: The effects of sex ratios may depend on absolute group size (see Martin, 1983). Anecdotal evidence from our data suggests that having a large percentage of women in a given slot is less likely to guarantee that the superordinate position contains female incumbents if the absolute numbers involved are large. For instance, if a job employs 2 men and 6 women, it is quite possible that the next highest job within the organization (if one exists) would be staffed predominantly or entirely by females. The same prediction about a job involving 200 men and 600 women, however, is likely to be incorrect, since there is a sufficiently large pool of men to dominate opportunities for subsequent advancement, despite their proportionate underrepresentation. Of course, given our findings on job segregation, such integrated jobs are definite rarities, and the ordnance firm discussed above illustrates that large organizations tend to handle this matter in a different way: Gender-specific supervisorial titles and promotion lines are utilized when large numbers of women and men are segregated into sex-typed entry jobs.

Consistent with theories of labor-market dualism, our findings suggest that women face better career prospects in monopolistic industries and so-called core firms—large, bureaucratized organizations that are dominant actors in their economic environment (Baron, 1982; Baron & Bielby, in press).[7] Within the core, approximately 19% of women in the "line" jobs analyzed by the Employment Service were employed above the entry level, compared to about 6% outside that sector of the economy. Among men, around 35% of those in the core were in nonentry jobs, compared to about 22% in the periphery sector. Women in the core were concentrated disproportionately in entry slots requiring no prior human capital (almost 80% are in such positions). In the periphery, the percentage in entry slots was even higher, roughly 90%, but a much greater proportion of these entry-level women (roughly 40%, compared to about 2% in the core) had some form of general human capital (college education, vocational training, or experience) they brought to the firm. However, entry-level men in both sectors—but especially in the core—were much better able than women to capitalize on their

---

[7]Findings reported here concerning differences in labor-market structure are preliminary; for more details, see Baron and Bielby (in press).

prior qualifications in landing a position with mobility prospects in an internal labor market.

Our analyses indicate that a high percentage of women in core firms (around 45%) are in entry slots that are not dead ends, suggesting avenues of upward mobility. However, this is largely illusory. Almost one-half of these women are concentrated in one job in one organization: The "Assembler" position in the ordnance plant discussed above. As we noted, the larger span of control of female supervisors over female subordinates there (relative to men) severely constrains promotion possibilities. Therefore, even when women occupy slots that are situated in a career ladder, their actual chances of advancing within it seem inferior to men's.

Not surprisingly, women also exhaust the promotional benefits of internal labor markets within core firms faster than men. A higher percentage of women employed above the entry level appears to have reached dead-end jobs, compared to men employed in the same firms.[8] In short, for women as for men, internal labor markets facilitate career attainment, but fewer women reap the rewards, and the benefits are more limited (see Felmlee, 1981).

Discussion

Our analyses portray segregation as pervasive, almost omnipresent, sustained by diverse organizational structures and processes. Moreover, this segregation drastically restricts women's career opportunities by blocking access to internal labor markets and their benefits. Is there no hope?

We combed our data for deviant cases in which firms successfully integrated jobs, hoping to identify factors that might counteract the inertia associated with past practices. One bank, studied in 1968, initiated a program to hire and promote women into officer classifications. Staffing patterns of the bank supported this claim: 7 of 81 vice-presidents were women, 18 of 108 assistant vice-presidents, 16 of 49 management trainees, and 29 of 118 operations officers. While females exclusively were used in such routine data-processing jobs as keypunch operator, 10 of 23 systems analysts were women. This represents substantial gender equity for women, but in a sense this bank's efforts are significant only when compared to the uniformly high levels of segregation in other large bureaucracies. Indeed, fully equalizing the job distribution by sex would have still required reassigning roughly 80% of the bank's female employees. Most managers and professionals were men, while few men were employed in routine clerical positions.

---

[8]The Employment Service rarely performs detailed analyses of administrative and clerical jobs, which are assumed to be comparable across organizational settings. Consequently, these estimates of gender differences in access to internal labor markets probably *understate* reality considerably, since they do not adequately reflect the concentration of women (relative to men) in dead-end office jobs.

Thus, organizational demography, history, technology, and available labor supply severely constrain the degree to which change can occur in short periods of time. This is particularly true for large bureaucracies employing many workers in nonentry jobs. Nonetheless, under GM's recent agreement with EEOC, the corporation will spend at least $42.5 million on antidiscriminatory measures. Northrup and Larsen (1979) concluded that women were the primary beneficiaries of the consent decree between AT&T and EEOC: White women garnered 40% of new managerial jobs in the company between 1973 and 1979. This AT&T decree is the most costly, complex, and comprehensive settlement to date aimed at achieving work-place gender equity. Yet despite mandated EEOC quotas, affirmative action overrides in promotion, and other measures to reduce segregation, the index of dissimilarity computed over only eight broad occupational categories (*not* detailed job titles), declined from 79.4 to 68.2 between 1973 and 1979. This is no small accomplishment, but the AT&T experience illustrates (as do our results) how far we still have to go.

The egalitarian policies of the above-mentioned bank seem to have overcome bureaucreatic inertia because they were implemented during a time of extraordinary organizational growth and change. When analyzed in 1968, the bank was described as one of the largest and fastest growing businesses in the nation; employment increased nearly 50% between 1961 and 1968. During this same period, the bank was also undergoing technological change, automating its data-processing operations, and establishing regional offices and branch banks throughout Southern California. Growth and technological change appear directly responsible for the desegregation of several management, administrative, and data-processing job classifications in this unusual firm.

The salutary effects of growth and technological change on gender equity appear to transcend this case. Various investigators have noted that growth has a "trickle down" effect, improving opportunities for women and other minorities (e.g., O'Farrell & Harlan, in press; Rosenbaum, 1979; Shaeffer & Lynton, 1979; Stewman & Konda, 1983). This is, of course, a double-edged sword, since if women benefit most from growth, they suffer most from decline.

The bank's experience demonstrates that the segregation observed in other bureaucracies is by no means inevitable. However, short of such fortuitous and idiosyncratic circumstances, large and systematic reductions in sex segregation seem unlikely to occur in the absence of fundamental shocks to society. For instance, during World War II, employers faced extreme labor shortages. California's Industrial Welfare Commission granted 60 permits exempting 4500 women from its restrictions on heavy lifting, allowing them to enter production jobs previously closed to females (Margaret Miller, Executive Director, Industrial Welfare Commission, State of California, personal communication). Thus, unusual circumstances outside organizations forced employers to abandon long-standing practices ostensibly based on physiological differences between men and women. Nevertheless, after the war, the same women were demobilized as quickly as they had been integrated into the work force. The same procedure for obtaining exemptions from the labor code remained in effect but was not utilized, and, until 1971, the code rationalized sex segregation of production jobs in manufacturing. Significantly, longitudinal analyses of segregation patterns in a subset of our firms revealed virtually no change in segregation patterns, even among enterprises analyzed after court decisions struck down California's restrictions on women's lifting (Bielby & Baron, in press-b). As Stinchcombe (1965) has noted, organizational practices often survive long after the conditions that gave rise to them have changed.

While we have related segregation patterns to technical and administrative exigencies within organizations, we tried to avoid casting specific actors as villains in this drama. As suggested earlier, it is difficult to imagine that such pervasive sex segregation arose solely from workers' vocational preferences—that is, that women chose this result. Male co-workers presumably are also implicated, as are unions, according to our results. Theories that reduce gender segregation to vocational choices or employer malevolence are equally simplistic.

However, whether or not employers are primarily responsible for producing segregation, historical and legal precedents exist for making them remedy it. Since intervention into the family—the other major locus of segregation—is impractical, society is left with little choice but to intervene within the work place. Toward that end, several policy implications of our study are clear. First, high levels of segregation seem likely to persist if policymakers adopt a laissez-faire approach. Neither demography, technological change, nor bureaucratization is a "natural" force leading to balanced sex ratios within organizations. Second, policy intervention appears unlikely to make things worse, since many establishments are as segregated as they could be. While there may be political or economic incentives for focusing on certain work settings, policy efforts could justifiably be directed at almost any area of the economy, since all sectors are extremely segregated.

Our research also suggests some strategies for attacking sex segregation. Policies that segregate men from women are most visible in large organizations, documented in written contracts, rules, job definitions, and procedures. They do not exist solely in subjective tastes of employers, workers, and clients. Large firms are often subject to public scrutiny, and greater dependence on government resources makes them susceptible to policy interventions (Salancik, 1979). They are also more likely to have slack resources with which to absorb the costs of social change, and the visibility of such firms makes them natural models to others.

Interventions also appear more likely to succeed when organizations already have a sizable female work force. Organizations having few or no women members are probably the most intransigent, and policy efforts there would benefit fewer women overall. Sex ratios affect the balance of power among organizational members, and our results show that when women comprise a larger percentage of the labor force, employers seem less likely to segregate them. The presence of a visible contingent of minority employees within an organization, even at the lowest ranks, may be a precondition for success in desegregating work. Consequently, it may be better to desegregate a particular key organizational subunit where women already command a presence than to try imposing work-place equity throughout the firm in the absence of such a constituency. In other words, there may be threshold effects in achieving work-place equity.

In fact, seeking integration by creating "tokens" or "solos" throughout the organization may solidify resistance by male workers and demoralize those who should champion and benefit from equal opportunity programs (Kanter, 1977; Northcraft & Martin, 1982). Tokenism underscores differences vis-à-vis members of the majority, exaggerating evaluations (positive and negative) of the token. Governmental timetables or organizational quotas mandating gender parity across all job titles may have the unintended consequence of making virtually every woman in the firm into a token, putting her in a "do or die" situation.

Given the connection between sex segregation and mobility barriers, job integration will require modifying organizational rules for advancement through career ladders. These changes are easier to accomplish when female workers command firm-specific experience and, more importantly, when that experience is *acknowledged* by relevant organizational gatekeepers. Definitions of relevant experience seem much more elastic for men than for women, as evidenced by the prevalence of men supervising women subordinates in our sample without the formal job experience supposedly required. Women are often told that they lack power in organizations because they lack experience, but it is equally true that they lack experience because they are denied the power to define their particular experiences as relevant. Functionalist theory in sociology is often criticized for failing to acknowledge alternative ways of satisfying the same functional requirement in society. The same criticism can be made of formalized job descriptions and promotion policies in many organizations: Even if men monopolize some trait that relates to effective job performance, women may possess alternative experience that is equally relevant. This highlights another reason why job integration efforts may be more successful when women comprise a nontrivial percentage of the work force, when they presumably can have more say in defining what characteristics are appropriate for hiring and promotion decisions.

To summarize, organizational structures and processes are among the principal sources of gender inequity in job assignments and opportunities. Understanding the causes of segregated work and remedying its effects requires that social scientists focus on the relationship between organizational arrangements and career outcomes, a topic also of keen interest to practitioners and officials charged with implementing egalitarian policies. This research, like our predecessors', has its limitations. Because our unit of analysis is the establishment rather than the corporation, our portrait of segregation focuses disproportionately on the "line" of organizations, rather than corporate hierarchies, where progress toward integration has been greater (Shaeffer & Lynton, 1979). Furthermore, gender equity has certainly increased in the last several yerars, which are not represented adequately in our analyses. Hopefully, these limitations will be remedied by future research, showing our disheartening findings to be obsolete.

References

Acker, J. R. Women and social stratification: A case of intellectual sexism. *American Journal of Sociology,* 1973, *78,* 936–945.

Acker, J. R. Women and stratification: A review of recent literature. *Contemporary Sociology,* 1980, *9,* 25–39.

Baron, J. N. *Economic segmentation and the organization of work.* Unpublished doctoral dissertation, University of California, Santa Barbara, 1982.

Baron, J. N., & Bielby, W. T. Bringing the firms back in: Stratification, segmentation, and the organization of work. *American Sociological Review,* 1980, *45,* 737–765.

Baron, J. N., & Bielby, W. T. *The organization of work in a segmented economy. American Sociological Review,* in press.

Becker, G. S. *The economics of discrimination* (2nd ed.). Chicago: University of Chicago Press, 1971.

Bielby, W. T., & Baron, J. N. Organizations, technology, and worker attachment to the firm. In D. J. Treiman & R. J. Robinson (Eds.), *Research in social stratification and mobility* (Vol. 2). Greenwich, Conn.: JAI Press, 1983, pp. 79–113.

Bielby, W. T., & Baron, J. N. *Men and women at work: gender segregation in organizations and occupations.* Submitted for publication, 1984. (a)

Bielby, W. T., & Baron, J. N. A woman's place is with other women: Sex segregation in organizations. In B. Reskin (Ed.), *Sex segregation in the workplace: Trends, explanations, remedies.* Washington, D.C.: National Academy Press, in press. (b)

Blau, F. D. *Equal pay in the office.* Lexington, Mass.: D. C. Heath, 1977.

Blau, F. D., & Hendricks, W. Occupational segregation by sex: Trends and prospects. *Journal of Human Resources,* 1978, *14,* 197–210.

Bose, C. E., & Rossi, P. H. Gender and jobs: Prestige standings of occupations as affected by gender. *American Sociological Review,* 1983, *48,* 316–330.

Bridges, W. P. The sexual segregation of occupations: Theories of labor stratification in industry. *American Journal of Sociology,* 1982, *88,* 270–295.

Cain, P. S., & Treiman, D. J. The dictionary of occupational titles as a source of occupational data. *American Sociological Review,* 1981, *46,* 253–278.

Collins, R. *The credential society.* New York: Academic Press, 1979.

Dreyfuss, C. Prestige grading: A mechanism of control. In B. G. Glaser (Ed.), *Organizational careers: A sourcebook for theory.* Chicago, Ill.: Aldine, 1968, pp. 145–149. (Originally published, 1938.)

Duncan, O. D., & Duncan, B. A methodological analysis of segregation indexes. *American Sociological Review,* 1955, *20,* 210–217.

Edwards, R. C. *Contested terrain.* New York: Basic Books, 1979.

England, P. Assessing trends in occupational sex segregation, 1900–1976. In I. Berg (Ed.), *Sociological perspectives on labor markets.* New York: Academic Press, 1981, pp. 273–295.

Felmlee, D. H. Women's job mobility processes within and between employers. *American Sociological Review,* 1981, *47,* 147–151.

Frisbie, W. P., & Neidert, L. Inequality and the relative size of minority populations: A comparative analysis. *American Journal of Sociology,* 1977, *82,* 1007–1030.

Gordon, D. M. *Theories of poverty and underemployment.* Lexington, Mass.: D. C. Heath, 1972.

Grimm, J. W., & Stern, R. N. Sex roles and internal labor market structures: The "female" semi-professions. *Social Problems,* 1974, *21,* 690–705.

Gross, E. Plus.ca change. . . ? The sexual structure of occupations over time. *Social Problems,* 1968, *16,* 198–204.

Kanter, R. M. *Men and women of the corporation.* New York: Basic Books, 1977.

Martin, P. Y. *Towards a structural theory of group sex composition in work organizations.* Unpublished manuscript, School of Social Work, Florida State University, 1983.

Mennerick, L. A. Organizational structuring of sex roles in a nonstereotyped industry. *Administrative Science Quarterly,* 1975, *20,* 570–586.

Miller, A. R., Treiman, D. J., Cain, P. S., & Roos, P. A. (Eds.), *Work, jobs, and occupations: A critical review of the dictionary of occupational titles.* Washington, D. C.: National Academy Press, 1980.

Mincer, J., & Polachek, S. W. Family investments in human capital: Earnings of women. *Journal of Political Economy,* 1974, *82,* S76–S106.

Northcraft, G. B., & Martin, J. Double jeopardy: Resistance to affirmative action from potential beneficiaries. In B. A. Gutek (Ed.), *Sex role stereotyping and affirmative action policy.* Los Angeles: Institute of Industrial Relations, UCLA, 1982, pp. 81–130.

Northrup, H. R., & Larsen, J. A. *The Impact of the AT&T–EEO Consent Decree.* Philadelphia: Wharton School, University of Pennsylvania, 1979.

O'Farrell, B., & Harlan, S. Job integration strategies: Today's programs and tomorrow's needs. In B. Reskin (Ed.), *Sex segregation in the workplace: Trends, explanations, remedies.* Washington, D.C.: National Academy Press, in press.

Pfeffer, J. & Ross, J. The effects of marriage and a working wife on occupational and wage attainment. *Administrative Science Quarterly,* 1982, *27,* 66–80.

Polachek, S. W. Occupational segregation among women: Theory, evidence, and a prognosis. In C. B. Lloyd, E. S. Andrews, & C. L. Gilroy (Eds.), *Women in the labor market.* New York: Columbia University Press, 1979, pp. 137–157.

Roos, P.A., & Reskin, B. Institutional Factors contributing to sex segregation in the workplace. In B. Reskin (Ed.), *Sex segregation in the workplace: Trends, explanations, remedies.* Washington, D.C.: National Academy Press, in press.

Rosenbaum, J. A. Organizational career mobility: Promotion chances in a corporation during periods of growth and contraction. *American Journal of Sociology,* 1979, *85,* 21–48.

Salancik, G. R. Interorganizational dependence and responsiveness to affirmative action: The case of women and defense contractors. *Academy of Management Journal,* 1979, *22,* 375–394.

Scott, J. W. The mechanization of women's work. *Scientific American,* 1982, *247,* 166–187.

Shaeffer, R. G., & Lynton, E. F. *Corporate experiences in improving women's job opportunities* (Report No. 755). New York: The Conference Board, 1979.

South, S. J., Bonjean, C. M., Markham, W. T., & Corder, J. Social structure and intergroup interaction: Men and women of the federal bureaucracy. *American Sociological Review,* 1982, *47,* 587–599.

Spangler, E., Gordon, M. A., & Pipkin, R. M. Token women: An empirical test of Kanter's hypothesis. *American Journal of Sociology,* 1978, *84,* 160–170.

Stewman, S., & Konda, S. L. Careers and organizational labor markets: Demographic models of organizational behavior. *American Journal of Sociology,* 1983, *88,* 637–685.

Stinchcombe, A. L. Social structure and organizations. In J. G. March (Ed.), *Handbook of organizations*. Chicago, Ill.: Rand McNally, 1965, pp. 142–193.

Szafran, R. F. Female and minority employment patterns in banks. *Work and Occupations*, 1984, *11*, 55–76.

Suter, L., & Miller, H. Income differences between men and career women. *American Journal of Sociology*, 1973, *78*, 962–974.

Talbert, J., & Bose, C. E. Wage-attainment processes: The retail clerk case. *American Journal of Sociology*, 1977, *83*, 403–424.

Treiman, D. J., & Hartmann, H. I. (Eds.). *Women, work, and wages: Equal pay for jobs of equal value*. Washington, D.C.: National Academy Press, 1981.

Treiman, D. J., & Terrell, K. Sex and the process of status attainment: A comparison of working women and men. *American Sociological Review*, 1975, *40*, 174–200.

U.S. Department of Labor. *Handbook for analyzing jobs*. Washington, D.C.: U.S. Government Printing Office, 1972.

Wachtel, H. M. Class consciousness and stratification in the labor process. *Review of Radical Political Economics*, 1974, *6*, 1–31.

Weber, M. [Bureaucracy.] In H. H. Gerth, & C. W. Mills (Eds. and trans.), *Max Weber, essays in sociology*. New York: Oxford University Press, 1947. (Originally published, 1922.)

White, L. K., & Brinkerhoff, D. B. The sexual division of labor: Evidence from childhood. *Social Forces*, 1981, *60*, 170–181.

Williams, G. The changing U.S. labor force and occupational differentiation by sex. *Demography*, 1979, *16*, 73–88.

13

Gender Politics: Love and Power in the Private and Public Spheres*

FRANCESCA M. CANCIAN
University of California, at Irvine

Introduction

Love has been a feminine specialty and preoccupation since the nineteenth century, a central part of women's sphere. Women's dependency on men's love has been attacked by feminists as a mystification that gives men power over women (Flax, 1982). And their argument makes sense in terms of an exchange theory of power—if women need men more than men need women, then men will have the power advantage in marriage and couple relationships.

This chapter presents a perspective on the social organization of love that clarifies the links between love, dependency, and power. My perspective is based, first of all, on the empirical generalization that women and men prefer different styles of love that are consistent with their gender role. Women prefer emotional closeness and verbal expression; men prefer giving instrumental help and sex, forms of love that permit men to deny their dependency on women. Second, I argue that love is feminized in our society; that is, only women's style of love is recognized, and women are assumed to be more skilled at love and more in need of it.

My perspective clarifies how the social organization of love bolsters the power of men over women in close relationships, but it also suggests that men's power advantage in the private sphere is quite limited. It is primarily in the public sphere that feminized love promotes inequality in power. The feminization of love implies that men are independent individuals and by so doing obscures relations of dependency and exploitation in the work place and the community.

*I am indebted to Frank Cancian, Henry Fagin, Steven Gordon and Ann Swidler for helpful comments and discussions.

Definitions

Let me begin by defining love and power. I will then describe the feminization of love, summarize the evidence on men's and women's styles of love, and consider the effects of love on power.

My definition of love includes instrumental assistance and emotional expression and deemphasizes verbal self-disclosure. I define love between adults as a relatively enduring bond where a small number of people are affectionate and emotionally committed to each other, define their collective well-being as a major goal, and feel obliged to provide care and practical assistance for each other. People who love each other also usually share physical contact; they talk to each other frequently and cooperate in some routine tasks of daily life. This definition is similar to definitions of companionate love as opposed to passionate love (Walster & Walster, 1978). It resembles Tönnies' concept of *Gemeinschaft* and is very different from the Parsonian conception of love as expressive but not instrumental.[1]

I define power as the ability to impose one's will on others despite resistance or the ability to prevail when decisions are made (Blau, 1964).

The Feminization of Love

In contrast to the broad definition of love that I have just given, our culture has been dominated by a much narrower conception of love for over a century, which I label "feminized love" (see Douglas, 1977).

The feminization of love in contemporary culture is evident in the way love is defined. Researchers who study love, intimacy, and close friendship often use operational definitions of love that consider only emotional expression, verbal self-disclosure, and affection. They typically ignore providing instrumental help or sharing physical activities.

For example, the study of marriage by Stinnett, Carter, and Montgomery (1972) among older people emphasized emotional expression and cognitive understanding in defining the basic needs in marriage. Six basic marital needs were identified: Love, personality fulfillment, respect, communication, finding meaning, and integrating past experiences. Love was measured by four questions about feelings, for example, whether one's spouse expressed "a feeling of being emotionally close to me." Providing money, practical help, or sex were not considered to be among the basic needs satisfied by marriage (Stinnett et al., 1972).

---

[1]Alternative definitions of love are reviewed in Walster and Walster (1978), Hendrick and Hendrick (1983), and Reedy (1977). Frederich Tönnies' concept of *Gemeinschaft* includes economic exchange, physical proximity, routine cooperation, and affection; later generations of sociologists, like myself, incorrectly believed that Talcott Parsons' pattern variables restated Tönnies' *Gemeinschaft-Gessellschaft* distinction. In fact, Tönnies' *Gemeinschaft* tends to integrate the instrumental and expressive aspects of action.

Research on friendship usually distinguishes close friends from acquaintances on the basis of how much personal information is disclosed (Booth & Hess, 1974; Lowenthal & Haven, 1968), and many recent studies of married couples and lovers emphasize communication and self-disclosure. Thus, a recent book on marital love by Lillian Rubin (1983) focuses on intimacy, which she defines as "reciprocal expression of feeling and thought, not out of fear or dependent need, but out of a wish to know another's inner life and be able to share one's own" (p. 90). She argues that intimacy is distinct from nurturance or caretaking, and that men are usually unable to be intimate.

The general public also defines love primarily as expressing feelings and verbal disclosure, not as instrumental help; this is especially true for middle-class as opposed to working-class people.[2] In a study I conducted in 1980, 130 adults from a wide range of social backgrounds were interviewed about the qualities that make a good love relationship. The most frequent response referred to honest and open communication. Similar findings have been reported by others (Quinn, 1982; Swidler, 1982). Finally, *Webster's New Collegiate Dictionary* (1977) defines love as "strong affection for another arising out of kinship or personal ties" and as attraction based on sexual desire, affection, and tenderness.

These contemporary definitions of love obviously focus on qualities that are seen as feminine in our culture. A study of gender roles by Rosenkrantz, Vogel, Bee, Broverman and Broverman (1968) found that warmth, expressiveness, and talkativeness were usually seen as appropriate for females but not males. When this study was repeated in 1978, the core features of gender stereotypes were unchanged although fewer qualities were seen as appropriate for only one sex. Expressing tender feelings, being gentle, and being aware of the feelings of others were still ideal qualities for women and not men. The desirable qualities for men but not women included being independent, competent, unemotional, and interested in sex (Rosenkrantz, 1982). Thus, sexuality is the only masculine component in our culture's conception of love.

Evidence on Women's and Men's Style of Love

There is a fairly extensive body of research on women's and men's styles of love—on the kind of behavior that each sex prefers in close relationships with their lovers, spouse, or close friends. The results show that women prefer to talk about their personal experiences, especially their fears and troubles, and want to

---

[2]The greater emphasis on mutual aid and instrumental love among poor people is described in Miller and Riessman (1964), Rapp (1982), and Rubin (1976). The masculine role also seems less focused on independence and individualism in the working class. In the middle class, love is more feminized and women are more dependent on love with a man, probably because middle-class men can provide a high income and enviable lifestyle. Working-class women are more likely to look to their kin and children for intimacy, not their husbands (see Schneider & Smith, 1973).

feel emotionally close and secure. Men prefer to show their love by instrumental help, doing activities together, and sex (see reviews of this research in Cancian, n.d.[b]; Peplau & Gordon, in press).

For example, the two styles of love emerged clearly in a study of seven couples by Wills, Weiss and Patterson (1974). The couples recorded their own interactions for several days. They noted how pleasant their relations were and also counted how often their spouse did a helpful chore, like cooking a good meal or repairing a faucet, and how often the spouse expressed acceptance or affection. The social scientists followed traditional usage and labeled practical help as "instrumental behavior" and expressing acceptance as "affectionate behavior," thereby denying the affectionate aspect of practical help. The wives seemed to be using the same scheme; they thought their marital relations were pleasant that day if their husband had directed a lot of affectionate behavior to them, regardless of his positive instrumental behavior. But the husbands' enjoyment of their marital relations depended on their wife's instrumental actions, not her affection (Wills et al., 1974). One husband, when told by the researchers to increase his affectionate behavior toward his wife, decided to wash her car, and was surprised when neither his wife nor the researchers accepted that as an "affectionate" act.

Other studies of married couples and friends report similar findings. Margaret Reedy (1977) surveyed 102 married couples and asked them how well a series of statements described their marriage. The men emphasized practical help and spending time together and gave higher ratings to statements like: "When she needs help I help her," and "She would rather spend her time with me than with anyone else." Men also described themselves as more sexually attracted. The women emphasized emotional security and were more likely to describe the relationship as secure, safe, and comforting. Another study of the ideal and actual relationship of several hundred young couples found that the husbands gave greater emphasis to feeling responsible for the partner's well-being and putting the spouse's needs first, as well as to spending time together. The wives gave greater importance to emotional involvement and verbal self-disclosure (Parelman, 1980). In friendships also, men value sharing activities, while women emphasize confiding their troubles and establishing a supportive emotional attachment (Dickens & Perlman, 1981).

There is also a large body of research showing that women are more skilled and more interested in love than men. Women are closer to their relatives and are more likely to have intimate friends (Adams, 1968; Dickens & Perlman, 1981). Women are more skilled in verbal self-disclosure and emotional expression (Henley, 1977; Komarovsky, 1962). When asked about what is most important in their lives, women usually put family relations first, while men are more likely to put work first.

However, this evidence of women's superiority in love is not so strong as it first seems. Many of the studies show very small differences between the sexes, and the measures of love are usually biased against men and focus on verbal self-disclosure or willingness to say one "feels close" to someone. For example, in a careful study of kinship relations among young adults in a Southern city, Bert Adams found that women were much more likely than men to say that their parents and relatives were very important to their lives (58% of women and 37% of men). However, when he looked at actual contact with relatives, he found much smaller differences (88% of women and 81% of men whose parents lived in the city saw their parents weekly). He concludes that "differences between males and females in relations with parents are discernible primarily in the subjective sphere; contact frequencies are quite similar" (Adams, 1968, p. 169).

In sum, women and men have different styles of love, but love is feminized. It is identified with qualities that are stereotypically feminine and with styles of love that women prefer.

Social historians help us identify the causes of this social organization of love. They describe how love became feminized in the nineteenth century as economic production became separated from the home and from personal relationships (see Degler, 1980; Ryan, 1979, 1981; Welter, 1966). They have shown how the increasing divergence of men's and women's daily activities produced a polarization of gender roles. Wives became economically dependent on their husbands, and an ideology of separate spheres developed that exaggerated the differences between women and men and between the loving home and the ruthless work place.

Building on this historical research, I interpret the feminization of love and gender differences in styles of love as caused primarily by: (1) the sexual division of labor that makes wives economically dependent on their husbands and makes women responsible for childrearing; (2) the separation of the public and private spheres; and (3) beliefs about gender roles. Thus, there are both socioeconomic and cultural causes of our social organization of love.

Love and the Power of Men over Women

In the private sphere of marriage and close relationships, the social organization of love bolsters men's power over women in two ways. First it exaggerates women's dependency on men. If most people believe that women need heterosexual love more than men, then women will be at a power disadvantage, as many feminists have pointed out (Flax, 1982).

In fact, there is strong medical and sociological evidence that men depend on marriage as much as, or more than, women. For example, the mortality rate of unmarried men is much higher than married men, while marriage has a weaker effect on the mortality of women (Gove, 1973). The fact that men's health benefits from marriage more than women's health suggests that men depend more on marriage, whether or not they acknowledge this need. Men's dependency on marriage is also suggested by the tendency for women to have closer ties with friends and relatives than men; thus, men are more dependent on their spouses for social support (Cancian, n.d.[a], chap. 3). Men also remarry at higher rates than women (Stein, 1981, p. 358) and when they are asked about their major goals in life, a happy marriage is usually first or second on their list (Campbell, Converse, & Rodgers, 1976). But the centrality of independence to the masculine role seems to make us forget these facts. A dominant picture of gender politics in our culture is still a woman trying to entrap a man into an enduring love relationship, while all he wants is temporary sex.

Because of the social organization of love, men's dependency on close relationships remains covert and repressed, whereas women's dependency is overt and exaggerated. And it is overt dependency that affects power, according to social exchange theory. Thus, a woman gains power over her husband if he clearly places a high value on her company or if he expresses a high demand or need for what she supplies (Blau, 1964; Homans, 1967). If his need for her and high evaluation of her remain covert and unexpressed, her power will be low.

The denial of dependency is also evident in the styles of love that men prefer. Insofar as men admit that they are loving, their styles of love involve fulfilling women's needs and not on being dependent and needy themselves. Providing practical help, protection, and money implies superiority over the one who receives these things. Sex also expresses male dominance insofar as the man takes the initiative and intercourse is defined either as him "taking" his pleasure or being skilled at "giving" her pleasure, in either case defining her as passive. The man's power advantage will also be strengthened if the couple assumes that his need for sex can be filled by any attractive woman, while her sexual needs can only be filled by the man she loves.

In contrast, women's preferred ways of loving involve admitting dependency and sharing or losing power. The intimate talk about personal troubles that appeals to women requires a mutual vulnerability, an ability to see oneself as weak and in need of support. Women's love is also associated with being responsive to the needs of others; this leads to giving up control, in the sense of being "on call" to provide care whenever it is requested.[3]

In addition to affecting the balance of dependency between women and men, the feminization of love bolsters men's power by devaluing women's sphere of activities. Defining love as expressive devalues love, since our society tends to glorify instrumental achievement and to disparage emotional expression as sentimental and foolish (Fiedler, 1966; Inkeles, 1979). In fact, much of women's love consists of instrumental acts like preparing meals, washing clothes, or providing care during illness, but this is obscured by focusing on the expressive side of love. In our culture, a woman washing her husband's shirt tends to be seen as expressing loving feelings, while a man washing his wife's car tends to be seen as doing a job.

The well-known study of gender stereotypes among mental health workers by Broverman, Broverman, Clarkson, Rosenkrantz and Vogel (1970) vividly dem-

---

[3]A nurturant woman can be a formidable power, and taking care of someone easily slides over into controlling them; but the tendency to deny the active and powerful aspect of women's nurturance often obscures this aspect of women's power.

onstrates how defining love as expressive is connected to decreasing women's status and power. In the study, therapists were asked to describe mentally healthy adults, femininity, and masculinity. They associated both mental health and masculinity with being independent, unemotional, dominant, and businesslike, qualities that the researchers labeled as "competence." In contrast, "expressive" qualities like being tactful, gentle, or aware of the feelings of others were associated with femininity and not with mental health. These results document a devaluation of femininity and show how the dominant concept of mental health is biased against women and against love and attachment (see Gilligan, 1982).

In sum, the power of men over women in close relationships is strengthened by the feminization of love and by men's and women's different styles of love.

But Men Are Not That Powerful

Men clearly dominate women in close relationships. Husbands tend to have more power in making decisions, a situation that has not changed in recent decades (Blood & Wolfe, 1960; Duncan, Schuman, & Duncan, 1973). The evidence on the superior mental and physical health of married men vs. women has led some researchers, like Jessie Bernard (1972), to conclude that the institution of marriage is controlled by men for men's benefit.

However, given that power means the ability to get what one wants from another, men's power over women in intimate relationships is severely limited by the social organization of love. First, the legitimacy of men's style of love is denied. He will probably fail to persuade her that his practical help is a sign of love and that his sexual advances are a request for intimacy. As one of the working-class husbands interviewed by Lillian Rubin said, "She complains that all I want from her is sex, and I try to make her understand that it's an expression of love"; and a wife commented, "he keeps saying he wants to make love, but it just doesn't feel like love to me" (1976, p. 146). In contrast, the legitimacy of her desire for intimate communication is supported by the mass media and by therapists. Thus, there is probably more social pressure for him to express his feelings than for her to enjoy sex.

Moreover, because of the avoidance of dependency associated with the male role, he may not even know what he wants or needs from her and, therefore, may be unable to try to get it. Thus, the covert nature of a man's dependency may increase his power by hiding his neediness from women. But it may also decrease his power by hiding his needs from himself.

Women's responsibility for love and their overt dependence can also leave both partners feeling controlled by the other.[4] Insofar as love is defined as the

---

[4]Other negative consequences of women's dependency on love are described in Cancian (1984); for example, her dependency may lead her to seek frequent reassurance from him that he loves her, and she may be so needy that he will inevitably fail to meet her needs.

woman's "turf," an area where she sets the rules and expectations, a man is likely to feel threatened and controlled when she seeks more intimacy. Talking about the relationship, like she wants, feels like taking a test that she made up and he will fail. The husband is likely to react with withdrawal and passive aggression. He is blocked from straightforward counterattack insofar as he believes that intimacy is good.

From a woman's perspective, since love is in her sphere and she is responsible for success, she is very highly motivated to have a successful relationship. When there are problems in the relationship, she typically wants to take steps to make things better. She is likely to propose solutions such as discussing their problem or taking a vacation; and he is likely to respond with passive resistance and act as if she were pushy, demanding, and unfeminine. His withdrawal and veiled accusations will probably make her feel helpless and controlled.

Thus, a woman's control of the sphere of love ends up making her feel less powerful, not more, because she can succeed in her sphere only by getting the right response from him. Women's separate sphere of love and the family probably produced much more power for women in Victorian times, when a woman could succeed in love through her relations with her children and women friends and through sacrificing herself for her husband; in those times, being a loving woman was less dependent on the behavior of men (Ryan, 1979).

In these times, one of the most frequent marital conflicts reported by therapists is the conflict between a woman who wants more intimacy, more love, something more from her husband, and the man who withdraws and feels pressured (Raush, Barry, Hertel, & Swain, 1974; Rubin, 1983). The same pattern showed up in a survey of middle-class couples that asked how people wanted their spouse to change. The major sex difference was that husbands wanted their spouse to be less emotional and create less stress, while wives wanted their spouse to be more responsive and receptive (Burke, Weir, & Harrison, 1976).

Similar conflicts emerge from interview studies, although men's sexual frustrations come out more clearly in interviews (Cancian, 1984; Rubin, 1976). One young wife who had been married 3 years exploded: "Words! If only my husband could talk to me more. Sometimes he listens, but he hardly ever talks back. It's hard to talk to a drunk, and yet it's the only time he shows me any real feelings." Her husband acknowledges: "She always says that I don't talk to her. I don't understand. I'm sure she knows what I'm thinking, but that isn't good enough for her." For him, "I feel we have really communicated after we have made love."[5]

In sum, feminized love seems to give men some power advantage, but neither sex wins in the conflicts it creates.

---

[5]This quote is from an interview by Cynthia Garlich, a student in an undergraduate seminar I taught, in which students did intensive, open-ended interviews about close relationships.

Power in the Public Sphere

Love may have a more important effect on power relations in the public sphere than in the private sphere. Feminized love covers up the material dependency of women on men and the interdependence of all people. It is part of a world view that explains people's life situation by their inherent nature and not by the relations of exchange, sharing, or exploitation between them.

The way feminized love mystifies social relations of dependency and exploitation was especially clear in the nineteenth century, when wives were totally dependent economically on their husbands and the ideology of woman's special sphere of love was emerging. A central argument in this ideology was that women were powerless and dependent because they were naturally submissive and affectionate. An article by an antislavery writer in the mid-nineteenth century illustrates this perspective:

> The comparison between women and the colored race is striking. Both are characterized by affection more than by intellect; both have a strong development of the religious sentiment; both are exceedingly adhesive in their attachments; both, comparatively speaking, have a tendency to submission, and hence, both have been kept in subjection by physical force, and considered rather in the light of property, than as individuals. (Rose, 1982, p. 45)

This perspective denies the material basis of women's dependency. It also defines religious morality and the need for affection as qualities peculiar to women.

The other side of defining women as naturally dependent, moral, and affectionate is defining men as naturally independent, amoral, and isolated. As Marxist scholars have pointed out, the ideology of the isolated individual accompanied and justified the rise of capitalism (Zaretsky, 1976). Men were encouraged to see themselves as independent, competitive, and self-made. If they were rich or poor, it was the result of their own individual merit, not relations of dependency with other people. And if they were real men, they would thrive on the impersonal, competitive relationships that prevailed at work.

Contemporary views of human nature often perpetuate the ideology of separate spheres and the self-made man. They assume that independence is the central human virtue, and dependency and attachments are feminine qualities associated with weakness. As Carol Gilligan has documented (1982), current psychological theories of human development assert that a healthy person develops from a dependent child into an independent, autonomous adult. For example, Daniel Levinson's conception of development for men centers on the "Dream" of glorious achievement in his occupation. Attachments are subservient to the goals of becoming an autonomous person and attaining the "Dream"; a man who has not progressed toward his "Dream" by mid-life should break out of his established way of life by "leaving his wife, quitting his job, or moving to another region" (1978, p. 206). This concept of a healthy man condemns men without challenging careers, which includes most middle- and working-class men. It also ignores the fact that "successful" men depend on others: On wives and mothers who raised them and their children, on men and women who worked with them and for them. In many ways, Levinson's position is a restatement of the ideology of the self-made man, an excellent justification of meritocracy and inequality.

Thus, defining affection and dependency as feminine supports inequality in the public sphere in addition to maintaining men's power over women at home. It also motivates men to work hard at impersonal jobs and to blame themselves for their poverty or failure.

More generally, the ideology of separate spheres leads people to tolerate immoral, exploitative relationships in the work place or the community.[6] For example, this ideology suggests that it is acceptable for a manager to underpay his workers or for the faculty at a university to ignore an assistant professor who has been fired. Their behavior is not unloving or immoral; they are being businesslike or are respecting individual privacy. From this perspective, it is natural to treat people like objects at work; personal relationships, morality, and love are reserved for the private sphere and the feminine role.

There are other ways that the social organization of love contributes to economic and political inequality (see Sokoloff, 1980). In particular, it strengthens the power of men over women at the work place not only by encouraging women to devote themselves to love and the family but also by supporting the belief that money and dreams of achievement are not very important to women.

The consequences of love would be more positive if love were the responsibility of men as well as women and if love were defined more broadly to include instrumental help as well as emotional expression. Our current social organization of love maintains a situation where at home, women and men are in conflict, and where at work, men oppress women and managers oppress workers.

Conclusion

I have focused on how love effects power relations. In conclusion, I want to return to the causes of our current social organization of love. The foregoing analysis suggests that one reason for the persistence of the feminization of love and the accompanying emphasis on the independence of men is that these patterns serve the interests of the ruling classes. This functional explanation is weak until we can specify the mechanisms by which ruling groups manage to establish beliefs and social practices that benefit them. The historical research on the origins of the feminization of love in the nineteenth century suggest that the major causes were the differentiation of the harsh public sphere and the loving private sphere and also the sexual division of labor, especially the economic dependency of women on men.

---

[6]The concept of *love* has been closely tied to moral values in American culture, as Ann Swidler (1980) has pointed out.

This explanation suggests that our conceptions of love will change now that women are less economically dependent. It also suggests that in societies where the public sphere is seen as cooperative and helpful, love will be identified with men as well as women and with instrumental as well as expressive activity; a small socialist society might be an example. These issues should be explored in future research. We also need to focus on the masculine gender role and clarify how men's identification with the marketplace effects gender roles and love relationships. By clarifying the causes of our patterns of love, hopefully we can also clarify the social conditions that would encourage a more androgynous kind of love that combined emotional expression and practical help and acknowledged the interdependence of men and women.

References

Adams, B. *Kinship in an urban setting*. Chicago, Ill.: Markham, 1968.

Bernard, J. *The future of marriage*. New York: Bantam Books, 1972.

Blau, P. M. *Exchange and power in social life*. New York: John Wiley, 1964.

Blood, R. O., & Wolfe, D. *Husbands and wives*. New York: The Free Press, 1960.

Booth, A., & Hess, E. Cross-sex friendship. *Journal of Marriage and the Family*, 1974, *36*, 38–47.

Broverman, I. K., Broverman, D. M., Clarkson, F., Rosenkrantz, P., & Vogel, S. Sex-role stereotypes and clinical judgments of mental health. *Journal of Consulting Psychology*, 1970, *34*, 1–7.

Burke, R., Weir, T., & Harrison, D. Disclosure of problems and tensions experienced by marital partners. *Psychological Reports*, 1976, *38*, 531–542.

Campbell, A., Converse, P. E., & Rodgers, W. *The quality of American life*. New York: Russell Sage Foundation, 1976.

Cancian, F. M. Marital conflict over intimacy. In G. Handel (Ed.), *The psychosocial interior of the family* (3rd ed.). New York: Aldine, 1984.

Cancian, F. M. *Attachment and freedom*. Unpublished manuscript, University of California, Irvine, n.d.(a)

Cancian, F. M. *The feminization of love*. Unpublished manuscript, University of California, Irvine, n.d.(b)

Degler, C. N. *At odds: Women and the family in America from the Revolution to the present*. New York: Oxford University Press, 1980.

Dickens, W., & Perlman, C. Friendship over the life cycle. In S. Duck & R. Gilmour (Eds.), *Personal relationships* (Vol. 2). London: Academic Press, 1981.

Douglas, A. *The feminization of American culture*. New York: Knopf, 1977.

Duncan, O. D., Schuman, H., & Duncan, B. *Social change in a metropolitan community*. New York: Rusell Sage Foundation, 1973.

Fiedler, L. *Love and death in the American novel*. New York: Stein and Day, 1966.

Flax, J. The family in contemporary feminist thought: A critical review. In J. Elshtain (Ed.), *The family in political thought*. Amherst, Mass.: University of Massachusetts Press, 1982.

Gilligan, C. *In a different voice*. Cambridge, Mass.: Harvard University Press, 1982.

Gove, W. Sex, marital status and mortality. *American Journal of Sociology*, 1973, *79*, 45–67.

Hendrick, C., & Hendrick, S. *Liking, loving and relating*. Belmont, Calif.: Wadsworth, 1983.

Henley, N. *Body politics*. Englewood Cliffs, N.J.: Prentice-Hall, 1977.

Homans, G. Fundamental social processes. In N. Smelser (Ed.), *Sociology*. New York: John Wiley, 1967.

Inkeles, A. Continuity and change in the American national character. In S. Lipset (Ed.), *The third century*. Stanford, Calif.: Hoover Institution Press, 1979.

Komarovsky, M. *Blue-collar marriage*. New York: Random House, 1962.

Levinson, D. J. *The seasons of a man's life*. New York: Knopf, 1978.

Lowenthal, M. F., & Haven, C. Interaction and adaptation: Intimacy as a critical variable. *American Sociological Review*, 1968, *33*, 20–40.

Miller, S. M., & Riessman, F. The working-class subculture. In A. Shostak, & W. Greenberg (Eds.), *Blue-collar world*. Englewood Cliffs, N.J.: Prentice-Hall, 1964.

Parelman, S. A. *Dimensions of emotional intimacy in marriage*. Unpublished doctoral dissertation, University of California, Los Angeles, 1980.

Peplau, L., & Gordon, S. Women and men in love: Sex differences in close relationships. In V. O'Leary, R. Unger, & B. Wallston (Eds.), *Women, gender and social psychology*. Hillsdale, N.J.: Erlbaum, in press.

Quinn, N. Commitment in American marriage. *American Ethnologist*, 1982, *9*, 775–798.

Rapp, R. Family and class in contemporary America. In B. Thorne (Ed.), *Rethinking the family*. New York: Longman, 1982.

Raush, H. L., Barry, W. A., Hertel, R. K., & Swain, M. A. *Communication, conflict and marriage*. San Francisco: Jossey-Bass, 1974.

Reedy, M. *Age and sex differences in personal needs and the nature of love*. Unpublished doctoral dissertation, University of Southern California, 1977.

Rose, W. L. Reforming women. *New York Review of Books, 29*, October 7, 1982.

Rosenkrantz, P. Changes in stereotypes about men and women. *Second Century Radcliffe News*, June 1982.

Rosenkrantz, P., Vogel, S. R., Bee, H., Broverman, I. K., & Broverman, D. M. Sex role stereotypes and self-concepts in college students. *Journal of Consulting and Clinical Psychology*, 1968, *32*, 287–295.

Rubin, L. B. *Worlds of pain*. New York: Basic Books, 1976.

Rubin, L. B. *Intimate strangers*. New York: Harper and Row, 1983.

Ryan, M. *Womanhood in America* (2nd ed.). New York: New Viewpoints, 1979.

Ryan, M. *The cradle of the middle class: The family in Oneida County, New York, 1790–1865*. New York: Cambridge University Press, 1981.

Schneider, D. M., & Smith, R. *Class difference and sex roles in American kinship and family structure*. Englewood Cliffs, N.J.: Prentice-Hall, 1973.

Sokoloff, N. *Between money and love: The dialectics of women's home and market work*. New York: Praeger, 1980.

Stein, P. *Single life*. New York: St. Martin's Press, 1981.

Stinnett, N., Carter, L., & Montgomery, J. Older persons' perception of their marriages. *Journal of Marriage and the Family*, 1972, *34*, 665–670.

Swidler, A. Love and adulthood in American culture. In N. Smelser & E. Erikson (Eds.), *Themes of work and love in adulthood*. Cambridge, Mass.: Harvard University Press, 1980, pp. 120–147.

Swidler, A. *Ideologies of love in middle class America*. Paper presented to the Annual Meeting of Pacific Sociological Association, San Diego, 1982.

Walster, E., & Walster, W. G. *A new look at love*. Reading, Mass.: Addison-Wesley, 1978.

Welter, B. The cult of true womanhood: 1820–1860. *American Quarterly*, 1966, *18*, 151–174.

Wills, T., Weiss, R., & Patterson, G. A behavioral analysis of the determinants of marital satisfaction. *Journal of Consulting and Clinical Psychology*, 1974, *42*, 802–811.

Zaretsky, E. *Capitalism, the family and personal life*. New York: Harper & Row, 1976.

14

Women and the State: Ideology, Power, and the Welfare State*

FRANCES FOX PIVEN
City University of New York

Introduction

Much of the feminist literature of the last few years evinces an almost categorical antipathy to the state. Among socialist feminists, the antipathy is signaled by the use of such terms as *social patriarchy* or *public patriarchy* to describe state policies that bear on the lives of women.[1] And among cultural feminists, it takes form in the nostalgic evocation of the private world of women in an era before state programs intruded on the family (Elshtain, 1982, 1983).

There is some irony in this. While women intellectuals characterize relationships with the state as "dependence," women activists turn increasingly to the state as the arena for political organization and influence. At least as important, the intellectual animus toward the state flies in the face of the attitudes of the mass of American women evident in survey data. While the data show most women are opposed to a defense buildup and presumably, therefore, hostile to the military aspects of state power, in domestic policy areas they evidently believe in a large measure of state responsibility for economic and social well-

*An earlier version of this chapter was prepared for the Research Planning Group on Women and the Welfare State, sponsored by the Council for European Studies. I would like to thank members of that group as well as Richard A. Cloward, Barbara Ehrenreich, Temma Kaplan, Evelyn Fox Keller, Joel Rogers, and Alice Rossi for their comments.

[1]See, for example, Barrett (1983), Boris and Bardaglio (1983), Brown (1980), Eisenstein (1981, 1983), Kickbusch (1983), McIntosh (1978), Polan (1982), Schirmer (1982), and Wilson (1977). Happily, however, some of the most recent work, a good deal of it still unpublished, has begun to explore the political and ideological resources yielded by women in and through the welfare state. See, for example, Balbo (1981, 1983), Borchorst and Siim (1983), Dahlerup (1983), Ergas (1983), Hernes (1983), Rossi (1983), and Schirmer (1983).

being, suggesting a belief in the strong and interventionist state that some feminist intellectuals abjure.[2]

Of course, activist women may be erring "liberals," and popular attitudes, including the attitudes of women, can be wrong. But in this instance, I think it is an undiscriminating antipathy to the state that is wrong, for it is based on a series of misleading and simplistic alternatives. On the one hand, there is somehow the possibility of power and autonomy; on the other, dependence on a controlling state. But these polarities are unreal: All social relationships involve elements of social control, and yet there is no possibility for power except in social relationships. In fact, I think the main opportunities for women to exercise power today inhere precisely in their "dependent" relationships with the state, and in this chapter I explain why.

Before I turn directly to this issue, I want to consider the shift in the political beliefs signaled by the gender gap, for I think it important as well as evidence of my main contentions about power. Of course, everyone agrees the gender gap is important as well as evidence of something. The media has bombarded us with information on the gap and also has given us our main explanation, attributing the new cleavage of opinion and voting behavior between men and women to the policies of the Reagan administration.[3] This is not wrong, for the Reagan policies may well have had a catalytic effect on the expression of women's political attitudes. The organized women's movement has also been given credit for generating the gap, and despite the poor match between the largely middle-class constituency of the movement and the cross-class constituency of the gap, and between the issues emphasized by the movement and the issues that highlight the gap, this is probably not entirely wrong either.[4] Nevertheless, I think a development of this scale is likely to have deeper sources than have heretofore been

---

[2]Attitudes toward defense spending accounted for a good part of the difference between male and female preferences in the 1980 election. This pattern persisted into 1982, when 40% of men favored increased defense spending but only 25% of women did. However, by 1982 women had come to place concerns about defense second to their concerns about the economy (Miller & Malanchuk, 1983). Gurin (cited in Rossi, 1983) also shows an increase of gender identification among women through the 1970s. See also Schlichting and Tuckel (1983) for an examination of differences in the attitudes of married and unmarried and employed and unemployed women, which concludes that the gender gap holds regardless of marital or labor-force status.

[3]Rossi (1983) reviews studies that show the beginning of a gender gap as early as the 1950s. However, exit poll data after the 1980 election revealed an unprecedented 9% spread in the voting choices of men and women. In subsequent polls, the spread substantially widened to a 15% difference between men and women in response to whether Reagan deserved reelection in a *New York Times* poll reported in December 1983. Moreover, while male ratings of the President rose with the upturn in economic indicators and the invasion of Grenada, the unfavorable ratings by women remained virtually unchanged.

[4]Attitudes about the reproductive and legal rights of women, which have been the central issues of the movement, do not differentiate male and female respondents in the surveys. Single women, however, are much more likely than men to support the "women's rights" issues.

proposed. I will conclude that those roots are in the expanding relationships women have developed with the state and in the new possibilities for power yielded by those relationships. But because the connection between beliefs and this new institutional relationship is not simple and direct, I want first to evaluate and give due weight to other influences on the shift in political opinion that has occurred among women.

Rather than showing the imprint of the women's movement, with its clearly modernizing tendencies, the emphasis on peace, economic equality, and social needs associated with the gender gap suggests the imprint of what are usually taken as traditional female values. This oft-made observation suggests the gender gap is not a fleeting response to particular current events but has deep and authentic roots. At the same time, traditional values of themselves cannot account for this development. The caretaking values of women are old, but the sharp divergence between women and men is entirely new. However, much tradition may color the politics of women: The fact that traditional values associated with the family are now being asserted as public values is a large transformation. Or, as Kathy Wilson told a reporter on the occasion of the convening of the National Women's Political Caucus in 1983, "women are recognizing that their private values are good enough to be their public values." More than that, the beliefs associated with the gender gap are specifically about the obligations of government to protect these values. Women are asserting that the state should represent women, in their terms.

All of this suggests the possibility that a major transformation of consciousness is occurring on a scale that argues powerful historical forces must be at work, whatever the precipitating role of current Administration policies. While the comparisons may seem at first glance too grand, I think the public articulation and *politicization* of formerly insular female values may even be comparable to such historic developments as the emergence of the idea of personal freedom among a bonded European peasantry, or the spread of the idea of democratic rights among the small farmers of the American colonies and the preindustrial workers of England and France, or the emergence of the conviction among industrial workers at different times and places of their right to organize and strike. Each of these ideological developments reflected the interplay of traditional and transforming influences. And each brought enormous political consequences in its wake.

Ideological Transformation and the Gender Gap

If the gender gap is evidence of an ideological transformation, how do we begin to explain it? It is worth observing the primitive state of our theorizing about ideology.[5] This is probably due in no small part to the treatment of ideas by

---

[5]Geertz (1973) made this point 11 years ago, but it remains largely true today. The main exceptions are in those branches of social theory descended from the European-language philosophers, particularly phenomenology and hermeneutics, which are con-

the dominant sociological tradition as not requiring much explanation. It is not that ideas were unimportant in this tradition. To the contrary, consensual ideas were taken as axiomatic, as the very essence of society. In this view, ideas were not attributed to human actors but to the social structure. It seemed to follow that the emergence of deviant or oppositional ideas could be explained as the result of strains or ruptures in the social structure. This sort of reasoning tended to deflect attention away from ideology, for it was not a dynamic factor in social life. Ideology was either consensual and axiomatic, in which case it changed little or only gradually; or if the ideas of particular groups changed sharply, then it was the stresses in the social structure that had generated the deviation that deserved scrutiny. Emile Durkheim pointed the direction as he set out to develop his analysis of the causes of suicide: "Disregarding the individual as such, his motives and his ideas, we shall see, directly, the states of the various social environments . . . in terms of which the variations in suicide occur" (1951, p. 151).[6]

For a long time, studies of oppositional movements followed Durkheim's lead in dismissing the significance of the ideas of social actors as causes of their behavior, and in searching instead for explanations in the "social environment." Movements were not reflections of ideas, albeit deviant ideas, but rather the result of stresses or breakdowns in the social structure. The result, as Tilly, Tilly and Tilly (1975) have pointed out (although surely not to argue the significance of ideology), was that movements came to be characterized by a mindless eruptive imagery, as in Crane Brinton's metaphor of fevers (1952). Or, when attention was paid to the ideas associated with movements, as in the work of Neil Smelser (1962), these ideas were treated not as possible causes of movements but as additional symptoms of the derangement in the social environment that alone explained the movement.

The variety of Marxist structural interpretations that gained prominence in the last decade overtook and to some extent displaced the sociological perspective generated mainly by Durkheim and Parsons. The classical Marxists, including Marx himself, at least sometimes had appreciated the importance of oppositional ideology and even had given it explanatory weight, although the issue remained ambiguous and contradictory. However, this theme remained subordinate, at least in the American Marxist revival. Instead, the Marxist structuralists sought to challenge and supplant the ideational characterization of social structure that

cerned precisely with intersubjective meaning systems. But these developments have remained isolated from the mainstream of social analysis because the significance of objective social reality in patterning human action, including symbolic action, is ignored or denied. See Giddens (1976).

[6]If the ideas of men were inconsequential in explaining their action, the ideas of women were apparently even less consequential in Durkheim's view. Indeed, women were not even much influenced by social environment, for "being a more instinctive creature than man, woman has only to follow her instincts to find calmness and peace" (1951, p. 272).

had come to dominate sociology with a characterization of social structure as rooted in the mode of production. In doing so, they continued to focus on social structure as the overriding determinant of political action and for the most part did not accord ideology a significant role in its own right.

Only very recently, with the waning of conviction in the various structural-isms and the renewed attention to Gramsci (1971) has ideology, particularly the ideology of ordinary people, come into focus. There is at least a developing agreement that ideas pattern action, and that oppositional ideas underlie op-positional action. The signal importance of even this beginning is suggested by Lukes (1975) when he argues that if politics is reduced to structural determi-nants, whatever those structural determinants, the realm of the political is effec-tively eliminated.

Even so, a good deal of the recent interest in ideology owes more to empirical than to theoretical work, and particularly to studies of peasant movements that proliferated in the wake of the war in Southeast Asia. These studies derived much of their inspiration from the earlier historical work on peasant and pre-industrial popular movements of Eric Hobsbawm (1965), E. P. Thompson (1966), and Barrington Moore (1966). I will draw on this literature, partly for its insights on ideology, and partly because I think there are certain parallels be-tween the situation of women and peasants. As with women, the focus on the politics of the peasantry was long overdue, if only because, like women, they are so numerous and have so long been ignored. Most peasants lived at the periphery of the modern world of the market and the state. So did many women, especially those whose lives were delimited by the insular and patriarchal family system that spread in the West with industrialization. And women were like peasants in that many lived within a kind of subsistence economy, the family economy where women provided unpaid services to men in exchange for a share of the income men earned in the wider world.

The significant thrust of the literature on peasant movements is its insistence that peasants have ideas that inform their action, including revolts. This theme recurs in the work of such otherwise rather different analysts as Moore, Rudé, Womack, Wolf, and Thompson, to name only a few. Peasant ideas are tradi-tional ideas, rooted in what Hobsbawm calls the "double chains of lordship and labour" (1981, p. 2). Peasant ideas are formed, in other words, in reflection of the centuries-old relations of deference to overlords and the centuries-old travails of wrenching a subsistence from the land. These are the ideas that Thompson (1971) calls the "moral economy of the English crowd."

Much of this may be said of women. Like peasants, women developed ideas that reflected their lived experience within the subsistence economy of the pat-riarchal family and that described and justified that experience. They valued the family, they celebrated maternity and the nurturing services they provided their children and their men, and they honored the family bonds that seemed to guarantee them and their children a measure of security in exchange for their services.

In other words, women also developed a traditional moral economy, a moral economy of domesticity, reflecting both their universal life tasks of motherhood, which Sarah Ruddick (1982) has, I think, rightly argued are formative in the development of a cognitive and moral orientation she calls "maternal thinking," and their more particular experience within a Western patriarchal family that made them dependent on male wages. Surely it is these large and compelling features of their circumstances—no less compelling than the double shackles of lordship and labor—that account for the startling differences in the moral development of women, with its greater emphasis on relationship, care, and obligation (Gilligan, 1982) compared to the moral development of men.

What I call the moral economy of domesticity makes many of us uncomfortable. After all, these ideas justified and helped ensure the confinement and subservience of most women within the family. If they were political actors at all, it was only within sexual and family relations where, as social inferiors and economic dependents, their leverage was limited. Accordingly, even when women in traditional situations are viewed as social actors, their action is often characterized as devious, manipulative, evasive. (Here, again, the parallel with characterizations of peasants, with slaves, and other subject groups is striking and almost surely partly true.) Dignity seems to require that we see the ideas that thus limited women and ensured their subservience as the impositions of others.

The literature on the peasantry is instructive, however, for it demands we feel more empathy for subject peoples and give them more credit as well. Peasants are the "collosal majority" of all the people who have lived on this earth, John Berger (1979) says, and yet they have rarely been treated as historically significant actors. To be an historical actor means not only to change the world by one's action—the winds and the tides do that—but to act with purpose. Purpose implies ideas. It also implies some measure of agency, however constricted, for if ideas are simply imposed, then people are victims, not actors. To see purpose, the ideas implied by purpose, and some assertion of agency in the action of ordinary people was a major step forward. We had learned that peasants were not inanimate.

Peasant ideas were formed out of the centuries-old experience of domination by rural overlords and centuries-old bondage to the soil. But even thus "shackled," peasants were not entirely powerless, and their ideas were not the ideas of utterly powerless people. In fact, many of these ideas reflect a series of political accommodations won by peasants from other more powerful groups in the peasant communities. Thus, the traditions of peasants included firm standards defining the obligations of lords, landlords, and central rulers to the peasant community.

It was, we are told, when these standards and the political accommodations they implied were violated that the peasantry became political actors. Thus, in Scott's (1976) work on Southeast Asia, in Thompson's (1971) analysis of the English food riots, in Womack's (1968) account of the Zapata wars, rebellion is provoked when others violate traditional standards: When the landlord fails to fulfill his customary obligations to reduce his rent if the crop fails; or when he demands an increased share of the peasants' crops, or seizes the peasants' historic holdings; or when magistrates fail to conform with ancient customs requiring the "fair" distribution of local food supplies during periods of shortage. In these and many other instances, transgressions against traditional standards provoked the peasantry to defiant political action. In this sense, tradition itself armed people to enter history.[7]

We can also see the strong imprint of the traditional ideas of women on their actions when they moved beyond the realm of the family, and beyond the politics of personal relations, to do battle with the large forces they perceived as threatening to destroy and transform their lives. Women, like peasants, sometimes entered history. And they did so when the traditional moral economy of domesticity, with its emphasis on the primacy of caretaking values, was violated. Women joined and even lead the food riots that swept across Europe in the eighteenth and nineteenth centuries in resistance to the "new-fangled" doctrine of the market. Women reformers in the United States and Europe at the end of the nineteenth century pioneered in the struggle for social welfare protections. In the United States in the 1960s, black women who could not feed and clothe their children asserted their *right* to welfare as mothers. The women who joined in the general looting during the New York blackout in 1977 might have been saying something of the same thing when they ignored the television sets and stereos in favor of baby food and canned spinach. And Polish women who joined in the Solidarity strikes explained it was because their families, and especially their children, needed food. In each instance, we can see the traditional caretaking values of the moral economy of the family that provoked the political action of women and also guided its forms, much as "the moral economy of subsistence" or the "moral economy of the English crowd" provoked and guided the political action of peasants. More than that, caretaking values sometimes armed women to challenge or defy the dominant values of the public world, and particularly the values of the market, for when women entered the public world, the moral economy of domesticity inevitably clashed with the doctrines of *laissez faire*.[8]

All of this is surely very appealing for the dignity it gives to simple people. And it also bears on an explanation of the gender gap, since the issues on which the polarization of the political opinions of men and women has occurred seem to

[7]This argument is actually not new. Like much else, it should probably be credited to Tocqueville who, in setting out to explain the upheavals associated with the French Revolution, also emphasized the importance of traditional ideas. He thought the peasantry were goaded to rebel because the nobility had defaulted on their obligations to the community spelled out by those traditional ideas.

[8]Kaplan (1982) provides an eloquent exposition of the force and potential radicalism of traditional women's values in a series of episodes of collective protests in Barcelona early in this century. Margaret Somers' current work on "collective memory and the claim to regulative liberty and narrative justice" among women in early nineteenth-century England makes a broadly similar argument (1983).

be patterned broadly by the traditional values of the moral economy of domesticity. But there is a large difficulty if the matter is left there. That caretaking values
are being asserted as public values, that domestic rights are being asserted as
public rights, is of itself a very large change that cannot be explained by tradition
alone.

Nor is an emphasis on traditional ideas by itself usually an adequate explanation of the political action of peasants and other peoples. If traditional ideas
sometimes provoke people to deviant political action, these ideas can, by definition, only generate traditional modes of political action, calling for the restoration of traditional social arrangements. Much of the literature on peasant politics
seems to me so enraptured by the recognition of the force of traditional ideas as
to overlook or understate the elements of innovation and transformation implied
by the events recounted. True, there may be instances when popular custom itself
prescribes the occasions and forms of protest, as in Hobsbawm's characterization
of the riots of the *menu peuple* (1965) as a virtually ritualized communication
between the preindustrial urban crowd and the Prince. But tradition mainly
prescribes the forms of acquiescence to prince or lord, and not the forms of
rebellion. If peasant political action is guided by ideas as this literature rightly
insists, then rebellion implies the existence of new ideas that cannot be ascribed
to tradition alone.

Even those movements that seem to be entirely restorative often contain
strong elements of innovation that are generally ignored in the literature. Thus,
the extensive literature on the food riots (Rudé, 1964; Thompson, 1971; Tilly,
1975) portrays these as if literally scripted by traditions governing the distribution of food. The *actions* of the market crowds who commandeered grain or
bread to sell it for a ''just'' price in fact challenged the growing central gov-
ernments of Europe and the spread of the market. The *intentions* ascribed to the
crowds, however, were to merely enforce the edicts of medieval law and custom.
But they enforced tradition by breaking with it, by usurping the authority that had
heretofore belonged only to local rulers. Surely this was no small thing and
implied something more than traditional ideas.

The same observation can be made of the contemporary antifeminist movements. Much about the movements seems to fit the mold suggested by the study
of restorative peasant movements. The women participants in these movements
may well have been activated by transgressions of the traditional moral economy
of domesticity. The insular and patriarchal family is eroding, jeopardizing the
old rights that had guaranteed women and their children a life and a livelihood
within the family. The metaphor of family breakdown usually applied to these
developments is somewhat misleading, for it suggests an evolutionary development beyond the control of human actors, and people usually do not oppose
developments that they do not ascribe to human agents. Peasants do not protest
drought, for example, for they see it as the result of forces beyond anyone's
control. They are more likely to protest new extractions by tax collectors, for
they can see the human actors whose transgressions of traditional arrangements

arc causing them hardship. As Pearce (1982) points out, the rate of marital dissolution has in fact not increased over the past century. But where once it was mainly through death that women or men were left alone to raise their children, now it is mainly through desertion and divorce or the failure to marry in the first place, and it is mainly women who are left.[9]

If ideas guide action, then we would expect transgressions of the moral economy of domesticity to generate a restorative or reactionary politics. There is ample evidence just this happened, with the rise of movements expressing in-dignation at the violations of the old family norms and calling for the restoration of the old family order. But even in these most restorative of movements, there were new modes of action and therefore new ideas. Women in the pro-life and anti-ERA movements mobilized in activist and public ways to demand that the state intervene to accomplish the restoration of tradition, none of which, as a number of commentators have pointed out, was traditional at all.

The question is, then, even recognizing the great weight of past beliefs, how do ideas change? And what are the conditions in our own time that account for the changing political ideas of women? There are two main explanations in my opinion. I will call the first *idealist*, for it posits that ideologies change as a consequence of exposure to other ideologies, and the second *objectivist*, to capture the focus on change in objective socioeconomic conditions. In the ideal-ist view, traditional ideologies are transformed by exposure to new ideas that come from some outside source. It is a popular argument, as when the stimulus for the suffragist movement is found in the abolitionists, the stimulus of the modern women's movement in the New Left. It is also an old argument. Tocqueville, for example, excoriated the men of letters of the eighteenth century for their responsibility in generating revolutionary sentiments. While the in-tellectuals of course disagreed among themselves, the argumentation itself had "fired the imagination even of women and peasants" (p. 139), leading them to think "what was wanted was to replace the complex of traditional customs" with rules derived from general and abstract theories.

This line of explanation has been elaborated by Rudé as the process by which the traditional or "inherent" popular culture absorbs different and (perhaps)

---

[9]While it is difficult to get firm empirical evidence on this question, I am inclined to agree with Ehrenreich (1983) when she argues the breakdown of the two-parent family is the result of a kind of male emancipation from the burdens of family support. The extreme disparity in the economic circumstances of men and women in the aftermath of separation provides some support for this view, for it argues a very substantial material advantage for men in marital breakup and disadvantage for women. Weitzman (1981) shows that the available income of men rose sharply 1 year after divorce by 42%, while the standard of living of women dropped sharply, by 73%. A recent Census Bureau report helps make sense of this finding. More than one-half of divorced men default entirely or partially on court-ordered child-support payments, which averaged only $2110 in 1981. Meanwhile, the practice of alimony payments has almost disappeared. Only 15% of the 17 million divorced or separated women were awarded alimony, and less than one-half of those were actually receiving the full payments due them.

forward-looking ideas (1980). In developing this distinction between inherent
and derived ideologies, he is self-consciously drawing on Gramsci's (1971)
distinction between ''organic'' and ''nonorganic'' ideologies. Rudé does not
think, however, that the external influences that transform popular ideologies are
necessarily the ideas of the class struggle. What he does think is that popular
political struggles could not advance ''without the native 'plebian culture' or
'inherent' ideology becoming supplemented by . . . the political, philosophical
or religious ideas, that at varying stages of sophistication, became absorbed in
the more specifically popular culture'' (1980, p. 33). This theme is also evident
in other analyses of peasant or preindustrial uprisings. Thus, Hobsbawm and
Rudé (1968) attribute great importance to the presence of educated shoemakers
in helping to stimulate the ''Captain Swing'' uprisings among English agricultural laborers; Thompson (1966) makes much of the dissemination of the idea of
the ''rights of men'' through the writings of Cobbett and others in accounting for
insurgency among the English working class in the early nineteenth century; and
Wolf (1969) attributes a large role to the Viet Minh who were able to draw upon
traditional village patterns to ''build a bridge between past and present''
(p. 189).

I call this the *idealist* explanation because it seems to posit a force to ideas that
is independent of the social circumstances of the people who adopt the ideas. Of
course, people sometimes absorb ideas from without, and this is what peasants
have done. The large and interesting question is why they are sometimes receptive and to which ideas they are receptive. Tocqueville (1955), in fact, asked this
question. He wondered why, ''instead of remaining as in the past the purely
intellectual concept of a few advanced thinkers,'' the new ideas found a welcome
among the masses (p. 139) and thought the answer was the dissolution of old
institutions as well as a ruling class so stupid as to articulate and justify the
grievances of the lower orders. Rudé (1980) also asks the question and answers
that derived ideas are more likely to be absorbed when they articulate popular
experience and belief (p. 29) and when, somehow, circumstances are right. This
is almost surely correct and points away from a pure idealism, but it is entirely
too vague.

The second, and I think more powerful explanation is an *objectivist* explanation. It is, quite simply, that new political ideas are developed in reflection of
changes in objective social circumstances, although not in a simple and direct
way and surely not apart from the continuing influence of preexisting ideas
formed in the context of other circumstances as well as the influence of derived
ideas. This way of accounting for ideological change is of course most familiar in
the broad Marxist view that class situation generates class ideologies (although in
the hands of some Marxists, the idealist error is reversed, and the imprint of
tradition on the ideas formed in response to new circumstances, and even on the
ability of people to respond to new circumstances with new ideas, is ignored).
But an objectivist explanation is also implicit in the literature on the peasantry. If
the traditional ideas of peasants reflect their particular social experience, then

changes in those experiences should generate new ideas, albeit new ideas shaped and limited by preexisting ideological traditions. And perhaps it is in the search for ways of accounting for new conditions that peasants are likely to be receptive to ideas that come from elsewhere. To argue otherwise, to regard ideas once formed into an ideological heritage as impervious to change except as a consequence of the influence of external ideas is either to argue that peasant circumstances never change or to withdraw from them the status of historical actors, capable of reflecting and acting on new objective possibilities and constraints.

Change in the Objective Circumstances of Women

I have come this far, by such a tortured path, to posit that the gender gap simultaneously reflects the influence of women's traditional beliefs and the transformation of those beliefs in response to radical changes in the objective circumstances of American women. I turn now to a consideration of those objective circumstances, of the way changes in the family, the labor market, and the state have altered the opportunities and constraints that confront women as political actors. If ideologies are, as I contend, forged in the crucible of memory and experience, then the scale of these institutional shifts lends weight to my opening contention that a major ideological transformation is at work.

One large change is in the family. Rising rates of divorce and separation, combined with growing numbers of women who bear children but do not marry, mean that fewer and fewer women are in situations that even outwardly resemble the traditional family. Moreover, even those women who remain within traditional families now confront the possibility, if not the probability, of desertion or divorce and the near-certainty of a long widowhood. Even within those shrinking numbers of apparently traditional families, relations have been altered by the fact that many no longer rely exclusively on the wages earned by men.

Even taken by itself, we should expect this large change in circumstance to have consequences for the politics of women. The firm contours of the insular and patriarchal family narrowly limited the options for action available to women, but it also created options for action, for exercising power in family relations, no matter how convulated the ways. Now these options are contracting. They do not exist in families where men are not present. And even when they are, the old forms of female power have almost surely been weakened if, as Ehrenreich (1983) argues, men in general are increasingly "liberated" from their obligations under the moral economy of domesticity and, thus, wield the threat of desertion or divorce.

But if the traditional family relations gave women some limited options for action, in the larger sense these relations made women dependent on men and, therefore, subject to them, even for access to the public world. It should not be surprising, therefore, that the political opinions of women followed those of men so closely in the past. The family was indeed an institution of social control, as of course all institutions are.

The shredding of marital bonds, together with the inability of families to maintain themselves on the wages earned by men, meant that more and more women, like peasants before them, were forced to enter the labor market. Women became wage workers on a mass scale. Whatever this actually meant in the lives of women, it clearly meant that women had entered the mainstream of ideas about power simply because most of those ideas are about marketplace power. There are few analysts indeed who do not think the economic resources and opportunities for organization generated by market relations are critical resources for power. In this very broad sense, the Left tradition is not different. For nearly a century, Left intellectuals have looked almost exclusively to production relations as the arena in which popular power could be organized and exercised. Production, by bringing people together as workers in mass-production industries, generated the solidarities that made collective action possible. And, once organized, workers in the mass-production industries also gained leverage over capital.

But the prospects for women generated by their mass entry into the labor market are neither so simple nor so happy. The situation is, of course, different for different women. For those who are better educated and perhaps younger, liberation from the constraints of the family has meant an opportunity to move into and upward in the realms of the market and politics. These women, among whom I count myself, have tried to shake themselves free of the old moral economy of domesticity and in their place developed new ideas to name their new opportunities and aspirations. These are the ideas of the women's movement, ideas about liberation, modernization, and market success. That movement not only took advantage of burgeoning opportunities for women in government, business, law, and medicine.[10] It helped create those opportunities. In this sense, changes in objective circumstances and ideology were interactive, as I think they always are. If new ideas reflect new conditions, new ideas in turn may well lead people to act in ways that help shape those conditions.

But most women did not become lawyers, nor will they. Most women, forced to sell their labor, sold it in the expanding low-wage service sector as fast-food workers, or hospital workers, or office-cleaning women where, perhaps as a result of the influx of vulnerable women workers, wages and working conditions actually deteriorated over the last decade (Rothschild, 1981). The stability of the ratio of female earnings to male earnings, *despite the large gains made by some women,* is striking evidence of the weak position of these workers.[11] They are located in industries where unionization has always been difficult and where

---

[10]Where only 4% of the nation's lawyers and judges were women in 1971, women accounted for 14% in 1981. In the same period, the percentage of physicians who are women rose from 9 to 22%, and the percentage of female engineers increased from 1 to 4%.

[11]See Peattie and Rein (1981) for a review of data on women's participation in the labor force that shows the persistence of part-time and irregular employment as well as the concentration of women in low paid jobs. See also Chapters 11 and 12, this volume.

those unions that did form realized few gains because widely scattered work sites made organization difficult, and a ready supply of unemployed workers weakened the strike power. The prospect of long-term, high levels of unemployment in the American economy makes it less likely than ever that these structural barriers, which prevented unionization and the use of the strike power in the past, can now be overcome.

Nor is it likely that women will gradually enter the manufacturing industries where workers did succeed in unionizing, if only because these industries are shrinking. New jobs are being created not in steel, autos, or rubber, but in fast foods, data processing, and health care. Of course, even if this were not so, even if women were likely to enter the smokestack industries in large numbers, it would be too late, for international competition and robotization have combined to crush the fabled power of mass-production workers. In fact, the broad shifts in the American economy from manufacturing to services and from skilled work to unskilled work, combined with the likelihood of continuing high levels of unemployment, mean that the possibilities for the exercise of popular power in the work place are eroding for both men and women.

Women are thus losing their old rights and their limited forms of power within the family. In the marketplace, their position is weak, and prospects for improvement through individual mobility or the development of collective power are grim. These circumstances have combined to lead women to turn to the state, and especially to the expanding programs of the welfare state. Income supports, social services, and government employment partly offset the deteriorating position of women in family and economy and have even given women a measure of protection and therefore power in the family and economy. In these ways, the state is turning out to be the main recourse of women.

The relationship of women to the welfare state hardly needs documenting. Women with children are the overwhelming majority among the beneficiaries of the main "means-tested" income maintenance programs, such as AFDC, foodstamps, and Medicaid.[12] Moreover, the numbers of women affected by these programs are far greater than the numbers of beneficiaries at any one time, for women in the low-wage service and clerical sectors of the labor force turn to welfare-state programs to tide them over during family emergencies or their frequent bouts of unemployment. Older women, for their part, depend on social security and medicare benefits, without which most would be very poor. However inadequately, all of these programs moderate the extremes of poverty and insecurity among women.

More than that, the programs that make women a little less insecure also make them a little less powerless. The availability of benefits and services reduces the dependence of younger women with children on male breadwinners, as it reduces

---

[12]Over one-third of female-headed families, or 3.3 million, received AFDC in 1979 (Census Bureau). An almost equal number received Medicaid, and 2.6 million were enrolled in the food stamp program (Erie, Rein, & Wiget, 1983).

the dependence of older women on adult children. The same holds in the relations of working women with employers. Most women work in situations without unions or effective work rules to shield them from the raw power of their bosses. Social-welfare programs provide some shield, for the availability of benefits reduces the fear that they and their children will go hungry and homeless if they are fired.

Women have also developed a large and important relationship to the welfare state as the employees of these programs. The proportion of such jobs held by women has actually increased, even as the total number of social-welfare jobs greatly expanded. By 1980, fully 70% of the 17.3 million social-service jobs on all levels of government, including education, were held by women (Erie, Rein, & Wiget, 1983), accounting for about one-third of all female nonagricultural employment and for the larger part of female job gains since 1960 (Erie, 1983). In these several ways, the welfare state has become critical in determining the lives and livelihood of women. The belief in a responsible state reflected in the gender gap is partly a reflection of this institutional reality. But will this new institutional context yield women the resources to particpate in the creation of their own lives as historical actors? Can it, in a word, yield them power?

Women and Political Power

Very little that has been written about the relationship of women to the state suggests we look to it for sources of power. To the contrary, the main characterization is of a state that exercises social control over women, supplanting the eroding patriarchal relations of the family with a patriarchal relationship with the state. In my opinion, the determination to affirm this conclusion is generally much stronger than the evidence for it. Even in the nineteenth century, state policies had a more complicated bearing on the situation of women. Thus, while it is clearly true that changes in family law that granted women some rights as individuals, including the right to own property, did not overcome their subordination, that is hardly evidence that the state by these actions was somehow moving "toward a new construction of male domination" (Boris & Bardaglio, 1983, p. 75).

This kind of argument is even more strongly made with regard to welfare state programs. From widows' pensions and laws regulating female labor in the nineteenth century, to AFDC today, state programs that provide income to women and children, or that regulate their treatment in the marketplace, are condemned as new forms of patriarchal social control. Now there is surely reason for not celebrating widows' pensions as emancipation or AFDC either. These programs never reached all of the women who needed support (widows' pensions reached hardly any), the benefits they provided were meager, and those who received them were made to pay a heavy price in pride. Similarly, government regulation of family and market relations never overcame economic and social discrimination and in some instances reinforced it. But perhaps because some income would seem to be better than none, and even weak regulations can be a beginning, the definitive argument of the social-control perspective is not that the welfare state is weak and insufficient, but that involvement with government exacts the price of dependence, somehow robbing women of their capacities for political action. It seems to follow that the massive expansion of these programs in the past two decades and the massive involvement of women and their children in them is cause for great pessimism about the prospects for women exerting power and surely for pessimism about the prospects for women exerting power on the state.

In general, I think this mode of argument is a reflection of the eagerness with which we have embraced a simplistic "social control" perspective on institutional life, straining to discover how every institutional change is functional for the maintenance of a system of hierarchical relations and, therefore, evidence of the power of ruling groups. Of course, ruling groups do have power, they do try to exercise social control, and they usually succeed, at least for a time. But they are not all powerful. They do not rule entirely on their terms, they do not exercise social control without accommodations. Even then, the institutional arrangements that achieve social control are never entirely secure, for people discover new resources and evolve new ideas, and sometimes these resources and ideas are generated by the very arrangements that, for a time, seemed to ensure their acquiescence.

The critique of the welfare state developed by radical feminists was surely strongly influenced by the major Left analyses of these programs. Overall, and despite the complexities in some of their arguments, the Left disparaged social-welfare programs as functional not for the maintenance of patriarchy but for the maintenance of capitalism. Where in other arenas there was sometimes readiness to see that institutional arrangements had been shaped by class conflict, and even to see a continuing capacity for class struggle, in the arena of social welfare there was mainly social control. In part, this reflected the view, almost axiomatic among many on the Left, that the only authentic popular power is working-class power arising out of production relations. It was at least consistent with this axiom to conclude that welfare-state programs weakened popular political capacities and in several ways. The complicated array of program and beneficiary categories, combined with regressive taxation, fragmented working-class solidarity; the programs provided puny benefits but considerable opportunities for coopting popular leaders and absorbing popular energies; and the very existence of social-welfare programs distracted working people from the main political issue which, of course, was the control of capital. In this view, the welfare state was mainly understood as an imposition from above.

But I do not think the evolution of the American welfare state can be understood as the result only or mainly of a politics of domination. Rather it was the result of complex institutional and ideological changes that occurred in American society and of the complex and conflictual politics associated with these changes. Over the course of the last century, the role of government (particularly the federal government) in American economic life progressively enlarged. This development was largely a reflection of the demands of businessmen in an increasingly concentrated economy. But it had other consequences beyond creating the framework for industrial growth. As government penetration of the economy became more pervasive and more obvious, *laissez-faire* doctrine lost much of its vigor, although it still echoed strongly in the rhetoric of politicians. Few analysts dispute the significance of the doctrine in the American past. It was not that the actual role of government in the economy was so restricted, for the record in that respect is complicated. Rather, the doctrine of limited government was important because it restricted the spheres in which democratic political rights had bearing. Eventually, however, the doctrine became untenable. The political ideas of Americans, like the ideas of peasants, gradually changed in reflection of a changing reality. An economy increasingly penetrated by government gave rise to the wide recognition of the role of the state in the economy and a gradual fusion of ideas about economic rights and political rights (Piven & Cloward, 1982).

This shift in belief is evident in a wealth of survey data that show that Americans think government is responsible for reducing economic inequality, for coping with unemployment, for supporting the needy, for, in short, the economic well-being of its citizens. It is also evident in electoral politics, as Tufte's (1978) analyses of the efforts of political leaders to coordinate the business cycle with the election cycle make evident, as do exit poll data on the popular concerns that generated electoral shifts in the 1980 election.[13]

And as with peasants, ideas undergird political action. The emerging recognition that government played a major role in the economy, and that the democratic right to participate in government extended to economic demands, increasingly shaped the character of political movements. Beginning with the protests of the unemployed, the aged, and industrial workers in the Great Depression, to the movements of blacks, women, and environmentalists in the 1960s and 1970s, government became the target of protest, and government action to redress grievances arising in economic spheres became the program. The gradually expanding American welfare state was mainly a response to these movements. It is not by any means that the movements were the only force in shaping the welfare state. On the one hand, the success of the protestors was owed to the growing legitimacy of their demands among a broader public and the threat they therefore wielded of precipitating electoral defections if government failed to respond. On the other hand, the programs that responded to protest demands were limited and modified by other powerful interests, mainly by business groups who resisted the programs or worked to shape them to their own interests.

------

[13]See Burnham (1981) for an excellent discussion of the issues that determined the outcome of the 1980 election. He concludes that worry over unemployment was the critical issue leading voters who had supported Carter in 1978 to defect to Reagan in 1980.

Nevertheless, popular movements were a critical force in creating and expanding the welfare state (Piven & Cloward, 1971, 1977).

If the welfare state was not an imposition, if it was forged at least in part by a politics from below, what then will be its consequences over the longer run for the continued exercise of political force from below? This of course is the main question raised by the social control thesis, and it is of enormous significance for women given their extensive involvement with the welfare state. Thus far, that involvement is not generating acquiescence, To the contrary, the expectations of government revealed by the gender gap, as well as the indignation and activism of women's organizations in reaction to the policies of the Reagan administration, are not the attitudes of people who feel themselves helpless. Rather, they suggest that women think they have rights vis-à-vis the state and some power to realize those rights. If, however, the wide involvement of women in the welfare state as beneficiaries and workers erodes their capacities for political action, then what we are witnessing is a deluded flurry of activity that will soon pass.

But perhaps not. Perhaps this is the beginning of women's politics that draws both ideological strength and political resources from the existence of the welfare state. One sense in which this may be so is that the welfare state provides some objective institutional affirmation of women's political convictions. I said earlier that the welfare state was in large part a response to the demands of popular political movements of both men and women. These movements, in turn, had been made possible by changes in the relationship of government to the economy which had encouraged the idea that democratic rights included at least some economic rights. Once in existence, the social programs strengthen the conviction that economic issues belong in political spheres, and that democratic rights include economic rights. In particular, the existence of the social programs are, for all their flaws, an objective and public affirmation of the values of economic security and nurturance that connect the moral economy of domesticity to the gender gap.

This kind of affirmation may well strengthen women for political action. To use a phrase suggested by Jane Jenson (1983) in connection with the rise of the French women's movement, the "universe of political discourse" helps determine the likelihood and success of political mobilizations. One can see the criticality of the universe of political discourse or ideological context in determining not only the success but the scale of past expressions of oppositional politics among women. I have already suggested that the participation of women in the food riots of the eighteenth and nineteenth centuries reflected the centrality of nurturance to women (as well as their institutional access to the markets where collective action could take place). But perhaps women were able to act as they did on so large a scale because their distinctive values as women were reinforced by the traditional belief, held by men and women alike, that the local poor had a prior claim on the local food supply. By contrast, when middle-class women reformers in the nineteenth-century United States tried to "bring homelike nurturing into public life" (Hayden, 1981, pp. 4–5), they were pitted against the still very vigorous doctrines of American *laissez faire*. Not only were their causes largely lost, but their movement remained small, failing to secure much popular support even from women. The situation is vastly different today. The women reformers who are mobilizing now in defense of social-welfare programs are not isolated voices challenging a dominant doctrine. The existence of the welfare state has contributed to the creation of an ideological context that has given them substantial influence in the Congress as well as mass support from women.

Women have also gained political resources from their relationship with the state. One critical resource would appear to be of very long standing. It is, quite simply, the vote and the potential electoral influence of women, given their large numbers. Of course, that resource is not new, and it is not owed to the welfare state. Women have been enfranchised for over six decades, but the promise of the franchise was never realized for the reason that women followed men in the voting booth as in much of their public life. Only now, with the emergence of the gender gap, does the promise of electoral power seem real.

Part of the reason for the new significance of women's electoral power is in the institutional changes I have described. The "breakdown" of the family, while it stripped women of old resources for the exercise of power within the family, nevertheless freed women to use other resources. In fact, I think the breakdown of any institutional pattern of social control can generate resources for power, Tilly and other resource mobilization theorists notwithstanding. Tilly may be right to scorn the long-held view that breakdown generates Durkheimian stress or disorganization. He is wrong, however, to go on to insist that what is usually viewed as social disorganization cannot yield people resources. The disintegration of particular social relationships may well mean that people are released from subjugation to others and thus freed to use resources that were previously effectively suppressed. The breakdown of the plantation system in the United States, for example, meant that rural blacks were removed from the virtually total power of the planter class, and only then was it possible for them to begin to use the infrastructure of the black Southern church as a focus for mobilization.

Similarly, only as women were at least partly liberated from the overweaning power of men by the "breakdown" of the family has the possibility of electoral power become real. The scale of the gender gap and the fact that it has persisted and widened in the face of the Reagan administration's ideological campaign suggests the enormous electoral potential of women. This, of course, is the media's preoccupation and the preoccupation of contenders in the 1984 election as well. But its importance extends beyond 1984. Women have moved into the forefront of electoral calculations because they are an enormous constituency that is showing an unprecedented coherence and conviction about the key issues of our time, a coherence and conviction that, I have argued, is intertwined with the development of the welfare state. This electorate could change American politics. In particular, it could change the politics of the welfare state, although not by itself.

The welfare state has generated other political resources that, it seems fair to say, are mainly women's resources. The expansion of social-welfare programs has created a far-flung and complex infrastructure of agencies and organizations that are so far proving to be a resource in the defense of the welfare state and may have even larger potential. The historic involvement of women in social welfare and their concentration in social welfare employment now have combined to make women preponderant in this infrastructure and to give them a large share of leadership positions as well.[14] The political potential of these organizations cannot be dismissed because they are part of the state apparatus. Such organizations, whether public or private, are part of the state, in the elementary sense that they owe their funding to government. Nevertheless, the byzantine complexity of welfare state organization, reflecting the fragmented and decentralized character of American government generally, as well as the historic bias in favor of private implementation of public programs, may afford the organizations a considerable degree of autonomy from the state. That so many of these organizations have lobbied as hard as they have against the several rounds of Reagan budget cuts is testimony to this measure of autonomy. They did not win, of course. But mounting federal deficits are evidence they did not lose either, and that is something to wonder about.

There is another aspect of the politics generated by this organizational infrastructure that deserves note. The welfare state brings together millions of poor women who depend on welfare-state programs. These constituencies are not, as is often thought, simply atomized and, therefore, helpless people. Rather, the structure of the welfare state itself has helped to create new solidarities and has also generated the political issues that cement and galvanize these solidarities. We can see evidence of this in the welfare-rights movement of the 1960s, where people were brought together in welfare waiting rooms, and where they acted together in terms of common grievances generated by welfare practices. We can see it again today, most dramatically in the mobilization of the aged to defend social security. The solidarities and issues generated by the welfare state are, of course, different from the solidarities and issues generated in the work place. But that difference does not argue their insignificance as sources of power, as the Left often argues, and especially for women who have small hope of following the path of industrial workers.

The infrastructure of the welfare state also creates the basis for cross-class alliances among women. The infrastructure is dominated, of course, by better-educated and middle-class women. But these women are firmly linked by organizational self-interest to the poor women who depend on welfare-state programs. It is poor women who give the welfare state its *raison d'etre* and who are

---

[14]Rossi (1982), in an analysis of the first National Women's Conference at Houston in 1977, reports that 72% of the delegates were employed either by government or by nonprofit social welfare organizations. See also Rossi (1983) for a discussion of "insider–outsider" coalitions made possible by government employment. This pattern exists in European welfare states as well (see Balbo, 1983; Ergas, 1983; Hernes, 1982).

ultimately its most reliable source of political support. Of course, the alliance between the organizational infrastructure and the beneficiaries of the welfare state is uneasy and difficult and sometimes over-shadowed by antagonisms that are also natural. Nevertheless, the welfare state has generated powerful cross-class ties between the different groups of women who have stakes in protecting it.

Conclusion

The erosion of the traditional family and their deteriorating position on the labor market has concentrated women in the welfare state. The future of these women, workers and beneficiaries alike, hangs on the future of these programs. They need to defend the programs, expand them, and reform them. They need, in short, to exert political power. The determined and concerted opposition to welfare-state programs that has emerged among corporate leaders and their Republican allies and the weak defense offered by the Democratic Party suggests that the situation will require a formidable political mobilization by women. The programs of the welfare state were won when movements of mass protest, by raising issues that galvanized an electoral following, forced the hand of political leaders. The defense and reform of the welfare state is not likely to be accomplished by less. There is this difference, however. The electoral and organizational support needed to nourish and sustain the movements through which women can become a major force in American political life is potentially enormous.

References

Balbo, L. Crazy quilts: Rethinking the welfare state debate from a woman's perspective. 1981, unpublished paper.

Balbo, L. Untitled paper presented to Conference on the Transformation of the Welfare State: Dangers and Potentialities for Women, Bellagio, Italy, August 1983.

Barrett, N. B. *The welfare system as state paternalism.* Paper presented to Conference on Women and Structural Transformation, Institute for Research on Women, Rutgers University, November 1983.

Berger, J. The peasant experience and the modern world. *New Society,* 1979, *17,* 376–378.

Borchorst, A., & Siim, B. *The Danish welfare state: A case for a strong social patriarchy.* Paper presented to the conference on the Transformation of the Welfare State: Dangers and Potentialities for Women, Bellagio, Italy, August 1983.

Boris, E., & Bardaglio, P. The transformation of patriarchy: The historic role of the state. In I. Diamond (Ed.), *Families, politics, and public policy.* New York: Longman, Green, 1983, pp. 70–93.

Brinton, C. *The anatomy of revolution.* Englewood Cliffs, N.J.: Prentice-Hall, 1952.

Brown, C. Mothers, fathers and children: From private to public patriarchy. In L. Sargent (Ed.), *Women and revolution.* Boston, Mass.: Southwood Press, 1980, pp. 239–267.

Burnham, W. D. The 1980 earthquake: Realignment, reaction, or what? In T. Ferguson & J. Rogers (Eds.), *The hidden election: Politics and economics in the 1980 presidential campaign.* New York: Pantheon Books, 1981, pp. 98–140.

Dahlerup, D. *Feminism and the state: An essay with a Scandinavian perspective*. Paper presented to the conference on the Transformation of the Welfare State: Dangers and Potentialities for Women, Bellagio, Italy, August 1983.

Durkheim, E. *Suicide*. Glencoe, Ill.: The Free Press, 1951.

Ehrenreich, B. *The hearts of men*. New York: Anchor Books, 1983.

Eisenstein, Z. *The radical future of liberal feminism*. New York: Longman, Green, 1981.

Eisenstein, Z. The state, the patriarchal family, and working mothers. In I. Diamond (Ed.), *Families, politics, and public policy*. New York: Longman, Green, 1983, pp. 41–58.

Elshtain, J. B. Feminism, family and community. *Dissent*, 1982 (Fall), 442–450.

Elshtain, J. D. Antigone's daughters: Reflections on female identity and the state. In I. Diamond (Ed.), *Families, politics, and public policy*. New York: Longman, Green, 1983, pp. 298–309.

Ergas, Y. *The disintegrative revolution: Welfare politics and emergent collective identities*. Paper presented to the conference on the Transformation of the Welfare State: Dangers and Potentialities for Women, Bellagio, Italy, August 1983.

Erie, S. P. *Women, Reagan and the welfare state: The hidden agenda of a new class war*. Paper presented to the Women's Caucus for Political Science, Chicago, Illinois, September 1–4, 1983.

Erie, S. P., Rein, M., & Wiget, B. Women and the Reagan revolution: Thermidor for the social welfare economy. In I. Diamond (Ed.), *Families, politics, and public policy*. New York: Longman, Green, 1983, pp. 94–123.

Geertz, C. *The interpretation of cultures*. New York: Basic Books, 1973.

Giddens, A. *New rules of sociological method: A positive critique of interpretive theories*. New York: Basic Books, 1976.

Gilligan, C. *In a different voice*. Cambridge, Mass.: Harvard University Press, 1982.

Gramsci, A, *Prison notebooks*. New York: International Publishers, 1971.

Hayden, D. *The grand domestic revolution*. Cambridge, Mass.: The MIT Press, 1981.

Hernes, H. M. *The role of women in voluntary associations*. Preliminary study submitted to the Council of Europe, Steering Committee of Human Rights (CDDH), December 1982.

Hernes, H. M. *Women and the welfare state: The transition from private to public dependence*. Paper presented to the conference on the Transformation of the Welfare State: Dangers and Potentialities for Women, Bellagio, Italy, August 1983.

Hobsbawm, E. J. *Primitive rebels: Studies in archaic forms of social movements in the 19th and 20th centuries*. New York: W. W. Norton, 1965.

Hobsbawm, E. J. *Bandits*. New York: Pantheon, 1981.

Hobsbawm, E. J., & Rudé, B. *Captain Swing*. New York: Pantheon, 1968.

Jenson, J. *"Success" without struggle? The modern women's movement in France*. Paper presented to a workshop at Cornell University on the Women's Movement in Comparative Perspective: Resource Mobilization, Cycles of Protest, and Movement Success, May 6–8, 1983.

Kaplan, T. Female consciousness and collective action: The case of Barcelona, 1910–1918. *Signs: Journal of Women in Society and Culture*, 1982, 7, 545–566.

Kickbusch, I. Family as profession—profession as family: The segregated labor market and the familialization of female labor. Unpublished paper. Copenhagen, 1983.

Lukes, S. *Power: A radical view*. London: Macmillan, 1975.

McIntosh, M. The state and the oppression of women. In A. Kuhn & A. Wolpe (Eds.), *Feminism and materialism*. London: Routledge and Kegan Paul, 1978, pp. 254–289.

Miller, A. H., & Malanchuk, O. *The gender gap in the 1982 elections*. Paper presented to the 38th Annual Conference of the American Association for Public Opinion Research, Buck Hill Falls, Pennsylvania, May 19–22, 1983.

Moore, B. *Social origins of dictatorship and democracy*. Boston, Mass.: Beacon, 1966.

Pearce, D. M. Farewell to alms: Women and welfare policy in the eighties. Paper presented to the American Sociological Association Annual Meeting, San Francisco, September 1982.

Peattie, L., & Rein, M. *Women's claims: A study in political economy*. Unpublished manuscript, 1981.

Piven, F. F. Deviant behavior and the remaking of the world. *Social Problems*, 1981, *28*, 489–509.

Piven, F. F., & Cloward, R. A. *Regulating the poor: The functions of public welfare*. New York: Pantheon, 1971.

Piven, F. F., & Cloward, R. A. *Poor people's movements: Why they succeed, how they fail*. New York: Pantheon, 1977.

Piven, F. F., & Cloward, R. A. *The new class war: Reagan's attack on the welfare state and its consequences*. New York: Pantheon, 1982.

Polan, D. Toward a theory of law and patriarchy. In D. Kairys (Ed.), *The politics of law: A progressive critique*. New York: Pantheon, 1982, pp. 294–303.

Rose, H. In practice supported, in theory denied: An account of an invisible urban movement. *International Journal of Urban and Regional Research*, 1978, *2*, 521–537.

Rossi, A. S. *Feminists in politics: A panel analysis of the first national women's conference*. New York: Academic Press, 1982.

Rossi, A. S. Beyond the gender gap: Women's bid for political power. *Social Science Quarterly*, 1983, *64*, 718–733.

Rothschild, E. Reagan and the real America. *New York Review of Books*, February 5, 1981, *28*.

Ruddick, S. *Preservative love and military destruction: Some reflections on mothers and peace*. Paper presented to the Annual Meeting of the American Political Science Association, Denver, Colorado, September 1982.

Rudé, G. *The crowd in history*. New York: Wiley, 1964.

Rudé, G. *Ideology and popular protest*. London: Lawrence and Wishart, 1980.

Schirmer, J. G. *The limits of reform: Women, capital and welfare*. New York: Shenkman, 1982.

Schirmer, J. G. *Cut off at the impasse: Women and the welfare state in Denmark*. Paper presented to the conference on the Transformation of the Welfare State: Dangers and Potentialities for Women, Bellagio, Italy, August 1983.

Schlichting, M., & Tuckel, P. *Beyond the gender gap: Working women and the 1982 election*. Paper presented to the 38th Annual Conference of the American Association for Public Opinion Research, Buck Hill Falls, Pennsylvania, May 19–22, 1983.

Scott, J. C. The moral economy of the peasant: *Rebellion and subsistence in Southeast Asia*. New Haven, Conn.: Yale University Press, 1976.

Smelser, N. J. *Theory of collective behavior*. London: Routledge and Kegan Paul, 1962.

Somers, M. R. Personal communication, 1983.

Thompson, E. P. *The making of the English working class*. New York: Vintage Books, 1966.

Thompson, E. P. Moral economy of the English crowd in the eighteenth century. *Past and Present*, 1971, *50*, 76–136.

Tilly, C. Food supply and public order in modern Europe. In C. Tilly (Ed.), *The formation of nation states in Western Europe*. Princeton, N.J.: Princeton University Press, 1975, pp. 380–455.

Tilly, C., Tilly, L. A., & Tilly, R. *The rebellious century*. Cambridge, Mass.: Harvard University Press, 1975.

Tocqueville, A. de. *The old regime and the French revolution*. Garden City, N.Y.: Doubleday, 1856/1955.

Tufte, E. R. *Political control of the economy*. Princeton, N.J.: Princeton University Press, 1978.

Weitzman, L. J. The economics of divorce: Social and economic consequences of property, alimony, and state support awards. *UCLA Law Review*, 1981, *28*, 1183–1268.

Wilson, E. *Women and the welfare state*. London: Tavistock, 1977.

Wolf, E. R. *Peasant wars of the twentieth century*. New York: Harper & Row, 1969.

Womack, J. *Zapata and the Mexican revolution*. New York: Vintage Books, 1968.

III

GENDER AND THE
LIFE COURSE IN
AGING SOCIETIES

15

Interpretive Social Science and Research on Aging

BERNICE L. NEUGARTEN
Northwestern University

Introduction

Some 40 years ago, most social scientists were preoccupied with how to make the social sciences scientific, which usually meant how to make them like the natural sciences. The major concerns were then, as now, how to perceive order in the chaotic social world; how to ask questions in ways that are researchable; how to build theories that can be supported by observations. Most investigators called themselves logical positivists or rational empiricists, for the concern was also how to create "objective" measures; how to explain and eventually predict—even more, eventually to control—human behavior; how to discover the "laws" of social behavior, of social structures, and of societies.

Most social scientists nodded to the notion that interdisciplinary approaches were important, but only a few did more than nod, for most researchers were then, as now, unprepared to undertake multidisciplinary, let alone interdisciplinary, approaches. The primary consideration was to build our disciplines in ways that would make them more distinctive and more rigorous.

The prevailing view was that there is a real world of social institutions and patterns of social interaction that can be objectively known, and that the various social-science disciplines were capturing various parts of that reality. To use an awkward metaphor: There was one true elephant, even though some investigators studied the trunk, others the leg, and still others, like the macro-sociologists, the overall configuration of the animal. The task was to focus one's lenses "correctly" in order to perceive one's own part of the "truth" and to leave it to someone else who someday would come along and put it all together in a grand scheme that would capture the essential nature of the beast.

Interpretive Social Science

Today, a different philosophy of science has emerged; and most students of social behavior—though surely not all—are moving toward the stance of what haṣ been called the interpretive social sciences (Rabinow & Sullivan, 1979). To attempt an oversimplified statement of this position and at the risk of repeating that which may have become common knowledge, interpretive social science begins with the acknowledgement that the social sciences have never developed agreement with regard to methods nor explanations in the way that has been characteristic of the natural sciences where, at successive points in time, one paradigm has prevailed and has then been replaced by another (Kuhn, 1962 1970).

More important, from this perspective, is that the models of the natural sciences are not the appropriate ones for social scientists to emulate. This is not because social sciences are new and have not yet had time to develop powerful paradigms: nor because the social sciences, like the natural sciences, undergo major changes in paradigms. The difference is more fundamental. The study of the human world can never be context-free: the observer can never stand outside his subject matter but must always share the context of cultures, languages, and symbols that constitute that world. In this view, the observer stands within the same circles of human meaning as do the objects of his study, and there is no outside, detached standpoint from which to gather observations. Even the anthropologists and historians who study different or earlier societies can be only partially detached. They remain not only part of the human world but culture-bound in their interpretations. Social scientists are all caught in a hermeneutic circle: Ultimately, a good explanation is one that makes sense of the behavior we see, but what makes sense is itself based on the kinds of sense we can make. In different words, there is no "objective" nor absolute verification procedure to fall back on. We can only continue to offer interpretations.

In this framework, there are no immutable laws; no reductionist models that are securely based in logical self-evidence; no "received" truths; and surely no value-free social science. Change is fundamental; change is dialectical; meanings are multiple and inexhaustible. The aim is understanding, within the limits of our cultural and historical present. The goal is not to discover universals, not to make predictions that will hold good over time, and certainly not to control; but, instead, to explicate contexts and thereby to achieve new insights and new understandings.

This view creates a more open world for social scientists. Although ambiguity and indeterminacy are inherent aspects of interpretations, the number and diversity of our means of comprehension become thereby increased. Techniques from a variety of disciplines become available. Investigators can become more comfortable with the fact that there is no commonality in the social sciences, for when our definitions and our methods are themselves products of consciousness, it can follow that we have very different views of what constitutes our subject matter and how it is to be examined. We become less defensive over the accusation that social scientists cannot find commonality either in the idea of social nor in the idea of science. We can acknowledge that the social sciences are anarchistic, and that attempts to discover laws or universals tell us perhaps more about their authors than about the world.

This does not mean, however, that anything goes. We do develop criteria of evidence, we do use criteria of logical inference and deduction, and we do strive for consensus and for communicability. We attempt to build theories of the middle range, even if theories are themselves interpretations; theories in which our constructs gain meaning by being systematically related to other constructs and are connected with our observations. We can attempt to represent the world that can be known to us, if not the "true" world. And if, because the known world is constantly changing and being reconfigured, we cannot make predictions except in very limited ways, we can attempt to explain what we observe.

Research Questions and Methodology

The tenets of interpretive social science lead directly to the relationship between research questions and methodological questions. Although this relationship is fundamental to all disciplines, it is in the limelight among sociologists these days, to judge from the heated interchanges now appearing in the sociological journals. This is because sociologists have been giving a certain priority to precise measurements and to quantitative methods, to the seeming neglect of more substantive issues. There is little disagreement that it is the formulation of the research question that must come first and the selection of method that must come second. But in adopting the stance of interpretive social sciences, we are more forcefully reminded that however refined our quantitative methods, they can only add precision to those selected phenomena (or variables) that lend themselves to those methods. Not, by any means, that refinement and clarity of relationships are unimportant; but they leave us as limited as before with regard to the "thick" descriptions (Geertz, 1972) that would add breadth and depth to our interpretations. This is only to say that newly elaborated techniques of regression and multivariate analyses and path analysis or cross-sequential designs or Jöreskogian designs are important steps in defining the relations between the particular variables in question, but they give the investigator no purchase on the innumerable other factors and other contexts that would add to understanding.

We are forcefully reminded also that our quantitative methods cannot help us escape the hermeneutic circle in which we are entrapped. They do not provide "objectivity" in the sense that they reflect the "real" world. Indeed, there is an opposite danger—that the focus on methods may lead us ever more to a reductionist approach, for there is the beguiling notion that the more clarity we can obtain about the relations between some three or five or six factors, the more we should limit our attention to those and leave the rest of the confusion to someone else.

These reminders are related to the concerns that many sociologists are now voicing. To quote Coser, who warned in his presidential address to the American Sociological Association:

> Concern with precision in measurement before theoretical clarification of what is worth measuring and what is not . . . is a roadblock to progress in sociological analysis. . . . What I am concerned with is not the uses but rather the abuses of these instruments of research. (1975, p.692)

And in arguing for the value of qualitative as well as quantitative methods, Coser went on to say:

> Sociology is not advanced enough solely to rely on precisely measured variables. (p. 693) . . . our discipline will be judged in the last analysis on the basis of the substantive enlightenment which it is able to supply about the social structures in which we are enmeshed. . . . If we neglect that major task . . . we shall degenerate into . . . specialized researchers who will learn more and more about less and less. (1975, p. 698)

Research on Aging

How does all this apply to research on aging? It might be said first that if ever there was an area of inquiry that should be approached from the perspective of interpretive social sciences, this is one. It is apparent even to the most casual observer that aging has multiple biological, psychological, and sociological components; that neither the behavior of older people nor the status of older people can be understood otherwise; and that the primary need is for explication of contexts and for multiplicity of methods. It should also be apparent that attention to change over time is fundamental in all disciplinary approaches to the study of aging, whether it be change in the individual or historical change in social, economic, and political institutions.

For the sociologist, in particular, the societal context is of paramount significance (a point that will be elaborated below), for it is not only that older people are different from each other, but that the very processes of aging are different in different societies, in different subgroups, at different points in history; so that aging is social destiny as well as biological destiny. In the field of gerontology, this point has been made clearly enough. It has been demonstrated over and over again that there is no single pattern of aging (we have only to consider the different trajectories of change in women and men); and there are no immutable laws, except at the most general level—namely, that in the normal course of events, men and women are born, grow up, and die; and that now, in industrialized societies, most people grow old before they die.

Sociological Foci in Aging Research

Bearing in mind that sociologists have come relatively late to the field of aging, trailing far behind anthropologists and psychologists, what, then, are the substantive questions that sociologists are addressing? In a recent review article, sociological research on aging was described as having been addressed primarily to four general issues (Maddox, 1979):

1. Chronological age as an explanatory variable (where the repeated finding is that age is a very weak variable).
2. The modernization of society as it affects the status and welfare of older people (and where, because the factors are complex, the relationship is not simply that modernization leads to lower status of the aged).
3. Adaptation in later life (and where, to oversimplify it, successful adaptation in late life has been found to be the rule rather than the exception).
4. The changing age structure of the population (where, so far as social implications are concerned, attention has been given primarily to the heterogeneity of successive cohorts).

It can be said, then (although the following distinction should not be over-drawn), that the first three of the four major issues relate to older people as an age group and accordingly that sociologists have been concentrating at the level of inquiry where subgroups of persons are the units of observation. At another level, where the society is the unit of observation (the fourth issue listed above), very little research has been carried out. Furthermore, when relating these two levels of inquiry, attention has gone almost entirely in one direction and to the question: How do social and societal changes influence the lives of older men and older women? Seldom have there been studies in the other direction, where the question is: How does the presence of increasing numbers of older people affect the society?

Gaps in Sociological Research

Social aging. It is worth speculating further about the major questions that sociologists have been ignoring. For instance, in focusing on persons, the question might well be: How is social or sociological aging to be defined? Is it to utilize the model of an age-stratified society and to define aging as the passage from one to another set of social roles and, thus, from one to another age stratum (Riley, Johnson, & Foner, 1972)? What additional analytical frameworks need to be formulated?

How does this question of the nature of social aging relate to one occasionally encountered in the writings of demographers: Presuming that the human species has a given biological potential with regard to maximum life span (a presumption that emerges from comparative studies of animal species), what is the nature and extent of the social constraints and social enhancements that influence that biological potential? How do they interact with gender, as, for instance, in accounting for the added longevity of women in some but not all societies?

The nature of social aging, whether for one or both sexes, has seldom been discussed by sociologists, in contrast to the wide-ranging debates among biologists over the definitions and the competing theories of biological aging.

If the nature of social aging is an appropriate question, then it would dictate that sociologists pay attention not only to the behavior or status or integration of men and women who are old but to the social processes of aging and, in turn, to appropriate methods for studying change. Next questions would then become more meaningful: What forms of social interaction, at micro- or macrosocial levels, and what social–institutional arrangements hasten or delay social aging? How do these vary, say, for men and for women?

Conflicts in studies of change. We might pursue one step further the question of how to study change and, in this instance, to consider the explication of contexts as one of the goals of interpretive social science. There has been considerable attention given to age, cohort, and time of measurement as indices for measuring change and how these interact statistically in accounting for observed differences between age groups, or age–sex groups, with regard to one or another type of behavior. Here, the method of cross-sequential analysis has often outweighed the significance of the substantive problem; and too often the inquiry has stopped where it might well have begun. In demonstrating, for example, that a cohort difference outweighs an age difference in adult performance on a particular psychometric test of intelligence—or that it is the calendar year in which a particular political or social attitude has been measured that outweighs age or cohort—the indices of age, cohort, and period remain "empty" as explanatory variables. That is, we do not know what it is that has occurred with the passage of lifetime that is being reflected in our index, age; nor what historical or economic or social events have actually affected the persons we study and that are represented by our index, cohort, or in our index, calendar year. This is not to deny that the age–cohort–period approach is itself a step in the explication of contexts; nor that rich or "thick" data sets are hard to come by. It is, rather, to say that we might sometimes do well to study a small rather than a large sample of persons, to make use of a broader range of variables in creating qualitative as well as quantitative data, and thereby to seek enlightenment not only about the meaning of those three indices but about other factors that are operating.

It is the rare instance when, in explicating what is meant by cohort and intracohort patterns, an investigator like Elder (1974) can select a major event like the Great Depression of the 1930s, identify families who did or did not suffer a significant loss of income, and then study the psychological and social changes that occurred over time in girls and boys in both types of families. This is a design that forwards interpretation and understanding and one that would be of particular value in studying change in older women and men.

Studies of the life course. To take a different example: This time, of how multiple contexts and multiple methods would forward interpretation, and this time, a substantive question that sociologists are already examining; namely, differences in the life course across historical time.

A distinction should first be made: Psychologists usually speak of life-span development, while sociologists usually speak of the life-course. The life-span orientation and the life-course perspective differ in their key intellectual concerns. While the former gives a good deal of attention to the "inner" life, the latter emphasizes turning points when the "social persona" undergoes change. A life-course approach concentrates on age-sex-related role transitions that are socially created, socially recognized, and socially shared. The age system of a society creates predictable role transitions, turning points that provide roadmaps for individuals and that outline life pathways.

A review of the sociological research on the life course (Hagestad & Neugarten, in press) indicates that patterns of role transitions across historical time have been explored mainly through intercohort comparisons. Individual life sequences have seldom been the object of study, but instead the focus has been on birth cohorts and on central tendencies. That is, we do not know how many of the individuals who were, say, at the median age on one transition are among those at the median age on the next. Because life pathways cannot be charted from most such studies, much of the research that sociologists have defined as life-course analysis does not analyze lives but presents the statistical histories of cohorts. (There are notable exceptions, such as the studies by Hogan [1981] and by Abeles, Steel, & Wise [1980]). Furthermore, most studies have been focused on the timing, sequencing, or spacing of transitions in young adult women or men, with little attention given to late-life transitions and, as the result, with little attention given to the long-term consequences of early transitions.

It is recognized that the kinds of data sets suitable for such analyses are seldom to be found, so that sociologists are often unable to do what they would like. Still, some students of the life course might set about creating small, if not large, data sets that would be more suitable in this respect.

Most important, for our present purposes, is the fact that in most of the studies of intercohort differences, the investigator has not attempted to explain the patterns observed. It is acknowledged that the collective biography of a birth cohort is shaped by societal change—by historic, economic, and political events as well as by the size and other characteristics of cohorts themselves—yet these factors have seldom been analyzed, for to do so requires not only an explication of the historical context but an understanding of how historical events are translated into changes in life patterns. Similarly, if we are to explicate contexts, we might look to anthropological studies of cultural values and cultural meanings of age and to social–psychological studies of age norms as all these change over time for women and for men.

Multiple methods. We might also make use of a broader array of methods: For one, autobiographical accounts that would help us understand the personal meanings attached to life transitions. To elaborate this point: Those of us who have gathered life histories and who have talked at length with the persons we are observing are usually impressed with the ways in which the individual seeks to make a life story out of a life history; to give new meanings to past events; to weave together the many threads of a life into a single tapestry. They describe past intentions and plans and why, when those plans succeeded or failed, they did or did not make some next transition. One important source of enrichment in studying the life course, then, is to examine the individual's own goal-setting.

It is true that individuals see their lives through their own lenses. But so, also, do observers wear their own lenses as they select their research questions and their methods. This point is one of the tenets of interpretive social science.

The use of the personal narrative need not remain off-limits to sociologists who study the life course. Neither is it true that to use personal narratives is to be unsystematic (Bertaux, 1981). There are standards for judgment. A life story must be "followable" and self-explanatory (Ricoeur, 1977); it must be judged in terms of its internal consistency and how well it accounts for the various events of the life course; it must make sense in ways that others can accept, which is to say it must be understandable in terms of socially shared meanings.

These are the same standards by which we judge the observations obtained by other methods. An interpretation that emerges from any set of observations must make sense to other observers. And only when an explanation makes sense to enough persons who share a common set of meanings does it become a good explanation.

But it is not easy for many sociologists to use personal narratives. We have been shaped not only by the culture of our society but also by the culture of our discipline, which has socialized us to be wary of what we call the "subjective." We often forget that "the subjective" lies in the observer as well as in the observed.

To use life histories would be at least one step in making use of multiple methods and multiple interpretations in understanding the life course. We might even venture further in broadening our methods of inquiry: In addition to the life history, to use the projective technique, the depth interview, and the analysis of symbols. All these can be utilized by sociologists to produce group data that can add new dimensions to our understanding.

Neglect of the Societal Level in Sociological Research on Aging

These examples of how an interpretive approach might alter both the questions and the methods pursued by sociologists have been drawn from that first level of inquiry mentioned earlier—from the study of persons. I turn now to the second level of analysis and to the collectivity we call "society."

In all parts of the world, societies are undergoing change that is perhaps as fundamental as any in human history, change that comes with the increase in longevity and the increasing proportions of older persons in the population. These demographic trends have proceeded rapidly since the turn of the century in the industrialized nations; and it is projected—barring catastrophic famines or wars—that the numbers of older people will increase as rapidly in the developing countries over the next 20 years as they increased in developed countries over the past 80 years. The lives of all persons at all ages will be altered as will patterns of social interaction and the structure of all our social institutions.

By and large, sociologists have as yet ignored the implications of the aging society. Only a few have begun to think about the research that needs to be carried out, the ways in which our views of society and our social theories need to be reassessed. Like everyone else, we are talking about the demographic imperative, but we are seldom studying it.

There are some exceptions, of course. There are those sociologists engaged in planning health and social services and in consulting with those government policymakers who are preoccupied with questions of labor-force participation and public and private pension systems. But, besides the demographers, why are there not more sociologists giving attention to the effects on the society and on the ways our social institutions are changing because of the changing age structure of the population?

A few examples will perhaps make the point more clearly: We have studies ad infinitum of the two-generation family of parents and children and now a few studies of grandparents and children; but where are the studies of social interaction in the four- and five-generation family that is becoming the modal family structure? We have looked at older persons in educational institutions: Who they are and what courses of study they elect, but we have seldom considered the influence of older students on our educational institutions themselves (e.g., on educational curricula, the distribution of resources, the growth of informal educational agencies, the attitudes of teachers). We have studies of the political activity of older people but few studies of how our political structures are themselves being altered. What is the effect of the aging society on corporate structures? On city and regional planning? On our laws and our legal institutions?

It is puzzling, given the subject matter of sociology, that we have given so little attention to questions like these. We have been thinking a great deal about the effects of technology on the society but not about the effects of longevity.

There are also questions of another type, for sociologists might soon be called upon by policymakers to help deal with the social changes that are already occurring because of the new age–sex distribution. How shall we help define equity among age–sex groups? How define an age-integrated society? How utilize the experience and abilities of older women and older men? How understand the values of long life?

Conclusion

If ever the sociologists were needed, it is now. If ever the time to reexamine our models of social change and to abandon the search for immutable laws of social behavior, it is now. And finally, to adopt the stance of interpretive social sciences, if ever we are to pursue the goal of understanding how people grow old and how societies grow old, then it is now.

References

Abeles, R. P., Steel, L., & Wise, L. L. Patterns and implications of life-course organization: Studies from Project TALENT. In P. Baltes & O. G. Brim, Jr.(Eds.), *Life-span development and behavior* (Vol. 3). New York: Academic Press, 1980, pp. 307–337.

Bertaux, D. (Ed.). *Biography and society: The life history approach in the social sciences.* Beverly Hills, Calif.: Sage, 1981.

Coser, L. A. Presidential address: Two methods in search of a substance. *American Sociological Review,* 1975, *40*, 691–700.

Elder, G. H., Jr. *Children of the great depression.* Chicago, Ill.: University of Chicago Press, 1974.

Geertz, C. Deep play: Notes on the Balinese cockfight. *Daedalus,* 1972, *101*, 1–37.

Hagestad, G. O., & Neugarten, B. L. Age and the life course. In R. Binstock & E. Shanas (Eds.), *Handbook of aging and the social sciences* (2nd ed.). New York: Van Nostrand Reinhold, in press.

Hogan, D. P. *Transitions and social change: The early lives of American men.* New York: Academic Press, 1981.

Kuhn, T. S. *The structure of scientific revolutions.* Chicago, Ill.: University of Chicago Press, 1970. (Originally published, 1962.)

Maddox, G. L. Sociology of later life. *Annual Review of Sociology,* 1979, *5*, 113–135.

Rabinow, P., & Sullivan, W. M. (Eds.). *Interpretive social science: A reader.* Berkeley, Calif.: University of California Press, 1979.

Ricoeur, P. The question of proof in Freud's psychoanalytic writings. *Journal of the American Psychoanalytic Association,* 1977, *25*, 835–872.

Riley, M. W., Johnson, M. E., & Foner, A. *Aging and society: A sociology of age.* New York: Russell Sage Foundation, 1972.

16

Life-Course Analysis in Social Gerontology: Using Replicated Social Surveys to Study Cohort Differences*

RICHARD T. CAMPBELL
JEFFERY ABOLAFIA
GEORGE L. MADDOX
Duke University

Introduction

This chapter examines the current state of methodology in research on aging. Like any topic, aging must be studied from many points of view. Here, we concentrate on the use of survey data within a cohort-comparative perspective in order to better understand social aspects of aging within the context of the life course as a whole. We are particularly concerned about the potential gulf that exists between those who study aging from a somewhat abstract theoretical level and those who are concerned with more applied aspects of the problem.[1] The latter group, often referred to as "social gerontologists," must deal with the day to day problems of an elderly population. There is, of course, a strong research tradition within social gerontology per se, but it rarely articulates with the more recent theoretical literature on aging and the life course.

---

*An earlier version of this chapter was presented as part of a symposium sponsored by the Section on the Sociology of Aging at the annual meeting of the American Sociological Association, Detroit, 1983. We are indebted to Gerda Fillenbaum, Linda George, and Kenneth Manton for help in locating data sources and to David Featherman, Victor Marshall, and Bernice Neugarten for helpful comments on the first version. Deborah C. Campbell and Betty Ray assisted with production of the manuscript. Partial support of the Sandoz Foundation (U.S.) is acknowledged.
[1]This is, of course, a false dichotomy; many researchers work at both levels. Yet the distinction is useful for analytical purposes and does no serious violence to the field as a whole.

An emerging generation of sociologists, economists, psychologists, and others have come to accept a point of view about the life course and the proper means of studying it that is somewhat at variance with traditions in social gerontology. This approach, generally referred to as the "life-course perspective," has had enormous impact in a number of disciplines; but it has had less of an impact on *the actual practice of research* in social gerontology than might be expected, given the wide circulation the basic ideas have received. To a degree, it is not hard to understand why this should be so. Researchers faced with understanding issues regarding, say, the social organization of nursing homes or meeting the transportation needs of the elderly are likely to be somewhat unimpressed by theorizing, however sophisticated, which does not hold at least some promise of delivering propositions that can be tested in the field and findings that will be of use to practitioners. The notion of disengagement with its concomitant psychological, social, and behavioral implications is a good example of a concept that is useful at both the theoretical and applied levels. Later, we will show how our understanding of disengagement is enhanced by a life-course approach.

To date, the actual contribution of the life-course approach to understanding the processes of aging in more applied terms has been modest. This chapter demonstrates that a life-course approach *is* relevant, indeed required, for an understanding of a variety of policy-related issues. We go on to argue that one way (although by no means the only way) to go about applying the perspective is through the careful analysis of replicated social surveys. Finally, we suggest that the process of data collection on the aging process needs to be rationalized on a level that has not been attempted heretofore.

The Life-Course Perspective

There is remarkable agreement among social scientists of many persuasions on some rather fundamental propositions with respect to the study of the life course. It will be useful to lay these out briefly here. More complete expositions can be found in Riley (in press), Featherman (1981), Easterlin (1980), and Baltes and Nesselroade (1979), all of whom provide the more fundamental sources.

1. Aging as either a biological or social process can not be understood adequately without reference to the whole of the life course.
2. Aging is multifaceted, composed of interdependent biological, psychological, and social processes. It is not a unitary or exclusively biological process.
3. Lives are played out in particular social and historical circumstances that must be understood if the life course of the individual is to be understood.
4. As individuals develop and change, social institutions both limit alternatives and are changed by new demands placed on them. The relationship between individual and society is interactive and dialectic.

5. Development and change occur throughout the life course. While change may be patterned and normative in early life, it becomes increasingly less so in middle and late adulthood such that older people show more, rather than less, variation than young adults.

In general, these assumptions require that any cross-sectional or cohort-specific longitudinal findings be treated as tentative until researchers determine how stable it is in the face of replication across time and space. Thus, the aging process—whether biological, psychological, or social—must be understood in terms of a flow of cohorts through social structures.

This point of view, while receiving wide acceptance within at least some precincts of social gerontology, has not had a strong impact on the way in which research is carried out, as even a cursory examination of recent journals in the field will make clear. Understanding the implications of these points for working researchers in gerontology requires a look at the roots of the discipline in somewhat closer detail.

Biological Stability vs. Cohort Differentiation

Gerontology is one of the few disciplines in the academic community that has managed to stay truly multidisciplinary over an extended period of time. The union of investigators with biological, psychological, and sociological perspectives with those of more applied interests (as symbolized in the structure of the *Journal of Gerontology*) has had both positive and negative implications for the field. While in some ways it has made acceptance of the principles outlined above easier, it has also retarded their implementation in actual research practice.

It seems fair to say that gerontology as a field, at least in the beginning, was dominated by a biological orientation to the study of aging.[2] At the heart of that orientation is an assumption that the fundamental processes of aging are inherently biological and constant. As one reads Shock's 1977 review of biological theories of aging, it is impossible to imagine the various approaches he discusses being based on an assumption of anything other than biological stability. That is, if aging is to be explained at the cellular level, or below, one has to assume that the processes are invariant with time (i.e., over cohorts). If one has a theory that emphasizes the declining ability of the body to ward off immunological threats, for example, it does not seem reasonable to argue that there is substantial variation between persons in the nature of the underlying phenomena, nor that one

[2]Several readers have pointed out that our characterization of the biological point of view is over simplified and does not reflect current controversies in the field. This is certainly true. For responses to biological reductionism see, for example, Reynolds (1980) and Rose (1982). Still, we think our characterization is historically accurate and reflects the predominant orientation that has affected the view of biology that social scientists bring to the field of aging.

needs to check each cohort for the stability of the process.[3] It is certainly true that the *environment* is not time invariant and may well present the body with new sources of insult, but the process by which the body "wears out" is not assumed to be cohort-specific by any means.

Thus, in the study of biological aging, human beings are seen as more or less interchangeable specimens. But there is an important proviso; an individual's particular history must be taken into account in order to understand the particular set of stimuli and influences to which he or she has been exposed. At the level of individual medical histories, that point has been understood for a long time, although rarely translated into effective survey data collection.

The implications of these assumptions are clear but bear restating. If a particular disease shows increased rates among cohorts entering old age, we have to assume that some (probably lagged) environmental influence is responsible; we do not assume that suddenly the aging process has changed in such a way that one disease has given way to another as a manifestation of physical decline. A rather widely known example these days is the effect of asbestos exposure on shipyard workers during and after World War II. It is now clear that many subsequent cohorts were exposed to this powerful carcinogen in school rooms and other institutional settings. Perhaps the most dramatic example of a lagged effect is the change in the sex-specific risk of lung cancer as a result of the more recent adoption of cigarette smoking by large proportions of women. A more controversial example is the effect of the high sodium content of canned foods on rates of hypertension. Assuming that the effect of sodium intake on blood pressure is a relatively stable biological constant that may show some variation from person to person, increased levels of hypertension across cohorts are assumed to come from changes in inputs rather than changes in process.[4]

It is difficult to trace exactly how the influence of biologically based thinking has affected social gerontology, and, in any case, that is not the purpose of this chapter. But it seems clear that a dominant assumption in the field has been that one should search for fundamental processes and parameters; that the psychology and sociology of aging should be understood in terms of basic, relatively immutable phenomena. The term, *normal aging*, which appears repeatedly in standard texts, implies a stable psychobiological process, one in tune with traditions in the disciplines that gave rise to gerontology, particularly its medical and psychological components.

It is not hard to see the linkage between the notion of biological stability in the process of aging and similar ideas among psychologists. Psychology as a discipline has assumed that it was dealing with a biologically homogenous human

---

[3]Modern cellular level theories of aging do, of course, emphasize the essentially stochastic aspects of aging and allow for substantial interindividual level variation but assume homogeneity of process.

[4]Expressed more mathematically, assume that the means of independent variables in an equation are changing over time (and therefore across cohorts) rather than the coefficients in the equation.

population about which certain basic truths were knowable. The study of child development, at least until the very recent past, can be seen as an attempt to understand the underlying parameters of a broadly defined growth process. Variations from developmental norms are understood in terms of environmental influence or defined as pathology.[5] With respect to the study of aging, until very recently, psychologists assumed that a (reverse) developmental process could be described that would delineate norms with respect to the aging process. Thus, biology was very close to the surface, and intersubject variation was taken to be environmentally determined and an annoyance to be "controlled." Of course, the most well-known example of an attempt to break out of an approach to psychology that assumes that one's findings generalize to all cohorts is the work of Schaie (1965, 1979) and his colleagues on age changes in measured intelligence. They have shown consistent cohort differences in cognitive measures, which, if ignored in data analysis, lead to an overstatement of the effect of age on intellectual performance.

The impact of a life-course perspective on the field of psychology can also be seen clearly in a recent book by Gergen (1982), who departed from the traditional approach to social psychology some years back after writing a devastating critique of classical experimentation in the field (Gergen, 1973). Gergen argued that much of what social psychologists take to be "facts" with respect to conformity, interpersonal attraction, influence processes, and similar concepts are in fact bound up in the particular culture and environment in which they are studied. No experimental finding can be taken as a reflection of underlying "truth" with respect to the nature of human things, and no experimental (or for that matter, nonexperimental) study can be evaluated or understood without knowledge of the shared culture and assumptions of subject and experiment.[6] Gergen sees the life-course approach in psychology as both reflecting the decreasing vitality of traditional science and as providing a reasonable alternative. In particular, he is responsive to the view advanced by Baltes and Schaie (1973), among others, which sees life-course development as historically dependent and increasingly subject to chance factors as the individual grows older. Thus, at least in classical experimental social psychology, the "life-span point of view" is having an impact.

A More Sociological Approach

Turning to sociological approaches to social gerontology, we find it more difficult to argue that researchers have been responsive to the biologist's assump-

---

[5]Many readers will object to being tarred with this brush. The point is not that *all* psychologists make such assumptions or that all of their work does, but rather that this perspective underlies training and research in psychology to a great degree.

[6]Gergen's arguments go far beyond the assertion that experimental findings might be cohort specific; indeed, he is challenging the whole of conventional science, at least as practiced by social scientists.

tion about aging processes. Notions of cohort flow, changes in macro-social structure, and the interplay of individual and environment have been at the heart of the discipline for a very long time. Ryder's seminal paper (1965) on the relationship of cohort replacement to social change (published, interestingly, in the same year as Schaie's equally seminal paper on the age–period–cohort issue), provided a generation of sociologists with a template for research. Still, sociologists studying aging have found it difficult to avoid the search for universality. Certainly, the best known example of a theoretical approach that assumed (not tested) universality is disengagement theory. Hochschild (1975) has provided a devastating analysis of the logical and theoretical shortcomings of that approach. She shows that the theory, at least as originally stated (Cumming & Henry, 1961), is untestable because it does not permit falsification. While her specific criticism is often cited, her recommendations for a more effective approach are rarely discussed. In fact, Hochschild, while not writing from a life-course perspective, suggests that replicated studies over time and space, which permit variation in social structure, are the only way to test the extent to which *rates or levels* of disengagement change, a point anticipated in a broader context by Neugarten (1969).[7]

It is conceivable that the proportion of a population that displays disengaged behavior and the timing of this display in the life course could change over time as a function of both the particular historical sequences to which different cohorts were exposed and also in response to contemporary social and economic factors. Thus, the emerging approach to the study of the life course would not have us ask whether disengagement theory was "correct" or not but rather to specify the circumstances under which greater or lesser numbers of people would disengage. For example, several analysts, particularly Uhlenberg (1979), have noted the striking differences (on a wide variety of variables) between United States cohorts born prior to about 1920 and those born after. Those cohorts now entering early old age are substantially better off in terms of economic and physical well-being than their predecessors. Is it not reasonable to assume that the rate of disengagement, holding age constant, should decline or appear later in the life course as a result? This is not to say that disengagement is an uninteresting concept. On the contrary, if it could be shown that cohort-specific rates of disengagement and activity reflect social and historical factors, one would have a useful way of anticipating variations in demands placed on a wide variety of social institutions as well as learning something of theoretical importance about situational determinants of aging process.

Applying the Cohort Perspective

Even if it is clear that social gerontology as a discipline has been slow to acknowledge the importance of cohort flow and cohort differences, it remains to

---

[7]We ignore for the moment the difficult issue of how one operationalizes disengagement including the problem of whether we are talking about a state (engaged or not) vs. a scaled variable such that one can talk about level of engagement.

be demonstrated why these ideas are important to those who actually deal with the problems of the aged and who make decisions about the delivery of services, the allocation of resources, the training of practitioners, and similar matters. Is the life-course perspective the academic white elephant that many fear it to be (Baltes, 1973)? And if it is not, then what must be done to make the power of its ideas available in the field?

To the first question we can only respond that the social institutions and the structure of social services faced by the elderly change slowly. If policymakers and practitioners can anticipate the changing needs, attitudes, and values of their clientele with greater lead time, then fewer individuals might face outdated and inappropriate facilities and services. If, for example, the "newer' cohorts of elderly persons born in the 1920s who are now in their sixties are less likely to show high levels of ill health at a given age, more likely to be financially self-sufficient, more likely to have several children available for social support, and more likely to remain independent into their eighties than previous cohorts, then perhaps we need to think hard about dealing with a population that begins to disengage around age 85–90. Anticipating the arrival of large numbers of intact "old-old" individuals in their late eighties by just a few years would be of great value to social planners and others. On the other hand, if for some reason still younger cohorts do not show such high levels of social resources as they enter old age (perhaps as a result of being members of the high fertility cohorts themselves) (Easterlin, 1980), then the demand for a particular mix of services and supports would change yet again.

Gender, a theme to which many of the other chapters in this volume are devoted, offers another example of the value of a life-course perspective. Differential mortality, combined with extended longevity, means that increasingly the oldest of the old will be predominantly female and will be well into their eighties. Dealing with this increasingly large, very old population will require an understanding of their modal life history and variations about it. But we dare not assume that women turning 80 at the turn of the next century will be the same as those women who turned 80 in 1970 (and who provided most of the data on which current research findings about human aging are based). Women born in 1890 led dramatically different lives from women born in 1920, and the birth cohorts of the years after World War II can be expected to be even more different. Taking these known differences in terms of marital histories, employment experience, income and wealth, family structure, and other variables into account will permit studies designed to help the gerontological community to anticipate the needs of an ever-changing clientele.

Answering the second question—how to use life-course concepts more effectively—requires exploration of the disengagement process a bit more carefully. There are at least two ways of looking at the issue, and they imply rather different ways of collecting and analyzing data. First, we might pick some specific age, say 70, and ask when and how levels of disengagement (depending on whether we think of disengagement as a state or continuous variable) might differ between cohorts.

Second, we might ask how the rate of transition from an engaged state to a disengaged state changes as a function of time (age) at the individual level. That is, using techniques developed for the study of event histories (see Featherman, in preparation; Tuma & Hannan, 1984), we can (*a*) model the likelihood of changing states as a function of characteristics of individuals and their particular histories and *(b)* add cohort-specific variables to the model (e.g., cohort size or exposure to different historical environments) in order to account for further variation in rates of transition. Framing the question in terms of levels or probabilities at a given age leads us to think of regression analysis or similar procedures. The event history approach is less familiar to many readers than regression analysis, perhaps, but it is quite similar to regression in the sense that we have an equation consisting of variables and coefficients, but the coefficients tell us how *rates* of change differ for individuals with differing characteristics including, of course, the aggregate characteristics of their cohort and the environment to which they were jointly exposed at a particular age. In each case, then, the aggregate outcome measure can change across cohorts for at least three reasons:

1. Cohort differences in the mean or distribution of one or more predictors (e.g., income levels, educational levels). As a special case, cohorts differ in aggregate characteristics such as size or in composition due to exogenous social factors such as birth rates, war, or disease.

2. Historical factors that vary by cohort (e.g., economic conditions affecting the cohort), at a particular transition point (e.g., moving from school to work), particular technological developments (e.g., vitamin additives in milk), or the provision of support services not previously available (e.g., day care).

3. Changes in the coefficients themselves as a result of social policy changes or other factors including the emergence of other variables not previously operative. A shift in social policy to make adult children responsible for nursing-home costs of parents if parents were unable to pay is an example. A policy like this would almost certainly affect other decisions made by both parents and their adult children.

Thus, the replication of studies across cohorts requires us to determine if the levels or distributions of the variables in the equation have changed, if the parameters of the equation have changed, or if both variables and coefficients have changed. Moreover, if we are to do the kind of social monitoring implied here, we need systematically replicated surveys, a corresponding data set of macro-social structural information, and a study design that permits answers to the exact questions posed.

Obviously, what is being proposed here is strongly reminiscent of the enthusiasm for social indicators that was expressed in the late 1960s and the early 1970s. While the excitement surrounding that notion has subsided somewhat, the idea is still viable, as a recent report by Reiss (1981) makes clear. Duncan (1968, 1975) has provided several convincing examples of how replicated survey data may be used to detect changes over time in various social values and behavioral choices. The analysis of replicated surveys also brings to mind the age–period–cohort issue and its associated statistical and conceptual problems. (For a full discussion, see Maddox & Campbell, in press.) However, before dealing with any of these issues in any detail, we must first consider the available data base, and, more importantly, envision what the data base might look like in the short and long term. Do currently available data resources permit the kind of cohort monitoring implied by the discussion thus far? If not, do we have the capacity to do so in the future?

The Survey Data Base

A recent publication by Taeuber and Rockwell (1982) provides a valuable compendium of machine-readable data sources classified by type, topic, and other criteria. Their work succinctly demonstrates that, although one can find some reasonably high quality data on the elderly population from as far back as the 1940s, for all practical purposes 1960 marks the beginning of the collection of a useable data archive. Prior to that date, it is difficult to find data resources that combine adequate sampling, machine readability, and reasonable item coverage. In some areas, particularly health, the systematic gathering of detailed information on national samples really began in the early 1970s.

Taking 1960 as a somewhat arbitrary baseline and using age 60 as a somewhat arbitrary entry point to old age, we have information collected on elderly individuals from the birth cohort of 1900 forward. That is, in 1983, we have information on a rather narrow 25-year window (at best) of birth cohorts, beginning in 1900 and ending in 1925, assuming that in 1985 researchers will have data of one kind or another on the cohort of 1925. On the other hand, by the end of this century, researchers will have extended that window to 40 years to include birth cohorts born under dramatically different circumstances. This information can be summarized easily in Table 16.1.

Arranging the information in this fashion illuminates several obvious aspects of the intersection of year of birth and the various social, political, and economic events faced by these various cohorts. For example:

1. The cohort of 1920 is remarkably advantaged relative to the cohort of 1900. Those born in 1920 (a) benefitted from the boom of the post-World War II period to a greater degree than the cohort of 1900; (b) had access to far more effective health care; (c) had relatively large families; (d) benefitted from a wealth of social legislation passed in the 1960s; and (e) spent most of their working careers in a relatively strong economy.

2. In many ways, the cohort of 1940 is even more advantaged, although it is not clear whether that advantage will continue given the current economic and political climate. It is conceivable that this cohort will enter old age with less accumulated wealth, a smaller immediate and extended family, and fewer social resources to draw on than its predecessors.

TABLE 16.1. Ages of Three Birth Cohorts,
1920–2000

Year	Cohort		
	1900	1920	1940
1920	20	—	—
1930	30	10	—
1940	40	20	—
1950	50	30	10
1960	60	40	20
1970	70	50	30
1980	80	60	40
1990	90	70	50
2000	100	80	60

As a mental exercise, it is interesting to imagine what could be done if the information in Table 16.1 were extended backward in time to include cohorts born between, say, 1840 and 1900. To what extent would our understanding of both aging and social change be extended or changed? Would we have greater ability to understand the difficulties faced by old people in the year 2000 if we had better data on old people in the year 1900 (i.e., the cohort of 1840)? The answer would seem to be self-evident; at the very least, one could compare the cohorts affected by the Civil War and its aftermath to those born in the period 1880–1900.

We are now in the process of accumulating data so that researchers in the year 2060 will, in fact, have a 100-year time series of survey data with which to work—a data base providing information on people in their sixtieth year beginning in the cohort of 1900 through the cohort of 2000. Even if we think in less grandiose terms, just 40 years from now, within the professional lifetime of persons now being trained as gerontologists, researchers will have a data base unavailable—and hardly imaginable—today.

What will that data base look like? Some of its characteristics are clear. We will have a long time series of macro-social data, not only from the United States, but from most other industrialized societies and, increasingly, from less developed societies as well. We will have scores, if not hundreds, of machine-readable surveys and in all likelihood the ability to analyze them at great speed with an inexpensive desk top computer. But will we have the best information possible? To this question, the answer is no.

The simple truth is that we are in the midst of collecting an accidental data base. In terms of the timing of surveys, their design, the topics they cover, sample composition, and many other more technical details, we are, in effect, collecting data at random. There are important exceptions to this conclusion, the most important being the data collection activities of the U.S. Bureau of the Census (although even these are in danger of being seriously compromised) including the Current Population Survey and the reconstruction of Public Use Samples of earlier censuses.[8] There are also several examples of carefully replicated social surveys in the academic sector, two of the best known being the Election Surveys being done at the Institute for Social Research at the University of Michigan and the NORC General Social Surveys. But generally, data collection is chaotic, accidental, and essentially unplanned.

The word *chaos* is perhaps a harsh word to use, but it is the only one appropriate to the current situation. At present, the process by which data are collected on the elderly population is an almost random result of decisions by private and federal funding agencies, investigator initiatives, review panel decisions, and current congressional interest. A few examples will suffice. (Details on the various surveys mentioned below can be found in the appendix):

1. During the 1970s, two major panel studies of the elderly population were in progress—the Parnes survey of older men (officially, the National Longitudinal Survey of Labor Market Experience) (Parnes, 1975) and the Social Security Administration's Longitudinal Retirement History Survey (LRHS) (Irelan, 1972). Together, they covered the birth cohorts of 1905–1921. LRHS, which was intended to cover the cohorts of 1905–1911 for 10 years, is now complete. The Parnes survey continues, studying men who were 45–59 in 1966. The cohorts becoming 65 + in 1985 and beyond were born in 1920 forward and are included in neither survey; hence researchers will have no longitudinal data on the "new elderly" unless one of the panels is replicated on a new population.

2. Between 1975 and 1981, there were at least four major national cross-sectional surveys of the elderly population. There is substantial overlap among them in item coverage, sample selection, and other aspects of the studies. On the other hand, the surveys are sufficiently disimilar in design, item construction, and objectives that one could not easily pool the data.

3. The Survey of Institutionalized Persons, a major study of patients in all kinds of facilities, not just nursing homes, which was carried out in the early 1970s, has never been replicated, nor has the National Survey of Nursing Homes been replicated since 1977.

4. Many major cross-sectional surveys carried out for a specific purpose (e.g., the Quality of American Life Studies done in 1971 and 1978) failed to oversample the elderly. As a result, coverage of the elderly population, particularly those over 75, is so thin as to be almost useless.

---

[8]With the cooperation of the U.S. Bureau of the Census, the Center for Demographic Studies at the University of Wisconsin is preparing public-use samples of the 1940 and 1950 censuses.

5. Federal data collection activities, both those conducted by the government itself and those contracted out, are not coordinated with activities of the academic community. Much of the latter, of course, is funded from federal sources. A good example of the problem is the area of health. The appendix contains a listing of many different studies that measure health-related variables conducted by the government or academic researchers. The list illustrates both substantial overlap and serious gaps.

It is a truism that the study of aging would benefit greatly from a more comprehensive approach to data collection. On the other hand, it is simply not within the American tradition to centralize these kinds of activities. Neither the academic community nor the public would benefit from a watch-dog agency with authority to veto specific projects or order others, as anyone who has had to deal with the Office of Management and Budget on survey approval can testify. On the other hand, there are a number of things that can be done that should make it possible to make the analysis and dissemination of cohort-based information more effective, and we turn to these now.

Some Recommendations

Our recommendations fall into three categories having to do with *(a)* rationalizing the data base, *(b)* survey methodology, and *(c)* training.

Rationalizing the Data Base

First, in recent years, several valuable compendia of data sets have appeared (e.g., Mednick & Baert, 1981; Migdal, Abeles, & Sherrod, 1981; Taeuber & Rockwell, 1982), but we lack a coherent picture of what we know about what populations. The appendix contains a very preliminary example of what might be done.

Second, a machine-readable time series of data on the *aggregate* characteristics of birth cohorts would also be desirable. Such information could be easily merged with micro-individual data for multilevel analysis.

Third, whether we prepare for it or not, data collection will continue. A conference on "The Data Base in the Year 2030" might be a useful way to come to grips with and reduce the chaotic state of our current efforts.

Survey Methodology

First, there is still a good deal of uncertainty about the reliability and validity of survey information obtained from elderly respondents. For relatively little cost, one could conduct experiments evaluating the effectiveness of various survey methods. For example, recontacting subjects surveyed at an earlier time would permit retrospective checks on prior contemporaneous reports as a reliability check.

Second, emerging data analytic tools require precise dating of events and life-course transitions. Survey researchers have little experience collecting such data. We need to experiment with various approaches to obtaining reliable life histories.

Third, surveys all too frequently isolate individuals from their environment. Yet to understand the behavior of the elderly, we often need to know what alternative resources and opportunities are or were available. Thus, surveys might be supplemented with a local area information file providing data on available facilities, programs, and the like. The recent "Mental Health Catchment Area" studies being conducted under the auspices of NIMH (Eaton, Regier, Locke, & Taube, 1981) are an excellent example of coordinated data collection involving sample surveys, institutional records, and inventories of local services.

Fourth, most sample surveys of the elderly continue to focus on the noninstitutional population. For many purposes, this is clearly a mistake. It *is* possible to survey the institutionalized elderly, and it is possible to develop weights to correct for the bias resulting from failure to do so. Both alternatives should be pursued.

Training

First, analyzing survey data is a demanding task. In addition to statistical issues, there are many technical details involving missing data, weights, index construction, item comparability, etc. to be mastered. At present, most gerontologists have not learned these techniques. As a result, we rely on a very small group of methodology specialists for information. The survey data base is very rich; to mine it properly we must provide training for practicing researchers in survey analysis techniques and insist that graduate students acquire the necessary skills and that newly trained professionals get them as soon as possible.

Second, most analysis of data relevant to aging involves nonexperimental methods, yet most gerontologists learn statistical techniques focused on the analysis of data from experiments. There is a great disjuncture between what gerontologists learn and what they are asked to do in the area of data analysis. Again, a continuing education program is required.

Summary and Conclusions

During the past two decades, we have made enormous strides in our ability to collect, manage, and effectively analyze data. At the same time, spurred in part by data availability, researchers have come to see that understanding the life course depends on information on successive cohorts. If one thinks of science as sitting on a three-legged stool of theory, data, and methods, it is rare that the legs are even; at any given moment, one area is ahead of the other two. For years, it was the case that our analytical methods were behind our creative imagination.

With the development of advanced statistical techniques and a theoretical perspective in which to apply them, we are now in a situation where we are often forced to deal with deficient data. Our point in this essay has been that gerontology as a discipline must attempt to get the process of data collection under control and to take advantage of the insights stemming from the life-course perspective.

Appendix

Table A.1 (pp. 315–316) lists 21 social surveys relevant in whole or in part to the study of health, broadly defined. The table does not purport to be exhaustive; there are probably other surveys that could have been listed, but those that appear are either *(a)* nationally based with a large sample size or *(b)* particularly informative, despite being based on a local sample. The studies vary widely in design, content, timing of measurement, and other details. Taken together, they provide a mass of information on cohort differences in health, illness, health care utilization, insurance coverage, and similar variables.

While the studies are immensely useful now, they will be far more useful over the next 20–40 years as cohort coverage extends to those born at mid-century and measured in late middle age. The table shows that survey coverage tends to be inconsistent, with some periods showing great duplication and overlap, whereas coverage of others is relatively sparse. During the next decade, it will be important to try and maintain reasonable coverage of the ''new'' elderly for use in conjunction with the extensive information already available on the cohorts of 1900–1920.

The huge volume of information already available has not been used with anything near the efficiency that would be desirable. In part, this reflects the difficulty of interagency collaboration within the federal government and the even greater difficulty of serious collaboration between the government and the academic sector. Recently, data tapes have been increasingly available to the academic research community, and they have been formatted in a way that makes it easier for researchers to use them. A great deal remains to be done.

References

Baltes, P. B. (Ed.). Life-span models of psychological aging: A white elephant? *Gerontologist*, 1973, *13*, 457–512.

Baltes, P. B., & Nesselroade, J. R. History and rationale of longitudinal research. In J. R. Nesselroade, & P. B. Baltes (Eds.), *Longitudinal research in the study of behavior and development*. New York: Academic Press, 1979, pp. 1–39.

Baltes, P. B., & Schaie, K. W. On life-span development research: Paridigms, retrospects, and prospects. In P. B. Baltes & K. W. Schaie (Eds.), *Lifespan developmental psychology: Personality and socialization*. New York: Academic Press, 1973, pp. 365–395.

California State Department of Public Health, Human Population Laboratory. The California human population laboratory for epidemiology, Series A, No. 6, 1964.

TABLE A.1. A Summary of Studies Assessing the Health of Cohorts Born between 1900–1960

Study	Cohort[a] coverage	Design	Measurement dates	Variables[b]	Reference
Alameda County	1900–1940	Longitudinal	1965, 1971	A C D O P	California State Department of Public Health, 1964
Evans County	1900–1930	Longitudinal	1958, 1967	C E K M O	McDonough et al., 1963
Framingham	1900–1930	Longitudinal	1948–present	C E K M	Dawber and Kannel, 1958
Health Examination Survey	1900–1960	Repeated cross section	1952–1962; 1963–1965; 1966–1970	A C F K O	NCHS, 1974
Health Interview Survey	1900–1960	Repeated cross section	Annually, 1957–present	A B C E F H I J K L N P	NCHS, 1975a
Health and Nutrition Examination Survey	1900–1960	Repeated cross section	1971–1974; 1976–1980	A B C F G K L N O P	NCHS, 1977a
Longitudinal Retirement History Survey	1905–1911	Longitudinal	Biennially, 1969–1979	A C D F H I J L N	Irelan, 1972
Longitudinal Sample of Disability Insurance Applicants	1900–1960	Case-specific	1968–present	A B C D K O	Social Security Administration, 1982
National Ambulatory Medical Care Survey	1900–1960	Repeated cross section	Annually, 1973–present	A B C J L N P	NCHS, 1975b
National Council on Aging—Lou Harris Surveys	1900–1960	Repeated cross section	1974, 1981	B C D E O	Henretta et al., 1977
National Hospital Discharge Survey	1900–1960	Repeated cross section	Annually, 1965–present	A C K L O	NCHS, 1977b
National Longitudinal Surveys of Labor Market Experience	1905–1921 (Males)	Longitudinal	1966–1980	D	Parnes, 1975
National Medical Care Expenditure Survey	1900–1960	Longitudinal	6 interviews: January 1977–June 1978	A B C D E H I J K L N	Taeuber and Rockwell, 1982

TABLE A.1. *(Continued)*

Study	Cohort[a] coverage	Design	Measurement dates	Variables[b]	Reference
National Medical Care Utilization and Expenditure Survey	1900–1960	Longitudinal	5 interviews: February 1980–March 1981	A B C D E F I J K L N	NCHS, 1983
National Nursing Home Survey	1900–1920	Repeated cross section	1969, 1973–1974, 1977	B C D L M O P	NCHS, 1979b
National Survey of Personal Health Practices and Consequences	1915–1960	Longitudinal	1979, 1980	A D E F G K L N O	NCHS, 1979a
National Survey of Trends in Health Services Utilization	1900–1960	Repeated cross section	1963, 1970	F I J L N	Taeuber and Rockwell, 1982
Survey of Disabled and Nondisabled	1900–1954	Longitudinal	1972, 1974	A B C D H I J K L N	Social Security Administration, 1982
Survey of Disability and Work	1900–1960	Cross section	1978	A B C D H I J K L N	Social Security Administration, 1982
Survey of the Elderly	1900–1910	Repeated cross section	1957, 1962, 1975	A B C D E F I J L N P	Shanas, 1962; Taeuber and Rockwell, 1982
Survey of Low Income and Disabled	1900–1955	Longitudinal	1973, 1974	A C D F I J L N	Tissue, 1977

[a]Cohort coverage may extend beyond dates shown.
[b]Letters correspond to the following topics: (A) acute conditions; (B) Arthritis; (C) chronic conditions; (D) limitations on daily activity; (E) cigarette smoking; (F) dental findings and visits; (G) dietary intake; (H) disability days; (I) health expenses; (J) health insurance; (K) heart disease; (L) hospitalization; (M) mortality and its causes; (N) physician visits and services; (O) mental health; (P) vision and hearing.

Cumming, E., & Henry, W. *Growing old*. New York: Basic Books, 1961.

Dawber, T. R., & Kannel, W. B. An epidemiologic study of heart disease: The Framingham study. *Nutrition Review*, 1958, *16*, 1–4.

Duncan, O. D. Social stratification and mobility: Problems in the measurement of trend. In E. B. Sheldon & W. E. Moore (Eds.), *Indicators of social change: Concepts and measurements*. New York: Russell Sage Foundation, 1968, pp. 675–719.

Duncan, O. D. Measuring social change via replication of surveys. In K. C. Land & S. Spilerman (Eds.), *Social indicator models*. New York: Russell Sage Foundation, 1975, pp. 105–127.

Easterlin, R. A. *Birth and fortune*. New York: Basic Books, 1980.

Eaton, W. M., Regier, D. A., Locke, B. Z., & Taube, C. A. The epidemiologic catchment area program of the National Institute of Mental Health. *Public Health Report*, 1981, *96*, 319–325.

Featherman, D. L. Retrospective longitudinal research: Methodological considerations. *Journal of Economics and Business*, 1977, *32*, 152–169.

Featherman, D. L. The life-span perspective in social science research. *The five year outlook on science and technology* (Vol. 2). Washington, D.C.: National Science Foundation, 1981, pp. 621–648.

Featherman, D. L. Biography, society and history: Individual development as a population process. In A. B. Sørensen, F. Weinert, & L. Sherrod (Eds.), *Human development: International perspectives*. (in preparation)

Gergen, K. J. Social psychology as history. *Journal of Personality and Social Psychology*, 1973, *26*, 309–320.

Gergen, K. J. *Toward transformation in social knowledge*. New York: Springer-Verlag, 1982.

Henretta, J. C., Campbell, R. T., & Gardocki, G. Survey research in aging: An evaluation of the Harris survey. *Gerontologist*, 1977, *17*, 160–167.

Hochschild, A. R. Disengagement theory: A critique and proposal. *American Sociological Review*, 1975, *40*, 553–569.

Irelan, L. M. Retirement history study: Introduction. *Social Security Bulletin*, 1972, *35*, 3–8.

Maddox, G. L., & Campbell, R. T. Scope, concepts and methods in the study of aging. In R. H. Binstock & E. Shanas (Eds.), *Handbook of aging and the social sciences* (2nd ed.). New York: Van Nostrand Reinhold, in press.

Mednick, S. A., & Baert, A. E. (Eds.). *Prospective longitudinal analysis: An empirical basis for the primary prevention of psychological disorder*. New York: Oxford University Press, 1981.

Migdal, S., Abeles, R. P., & Sherrod, L. *An inventory of longitudinal studies of middle and old age*. New York: Social Science Research Council, 1981.

McDonough, J. R., Hames, C. G., Stulb, M. S., & Garrison, G. E. Cardiovascular disease field study in Evans County, Georgia. *Public Health Reports*, 1963, *78*, 1051–1059.

National Center for Health Statistics. Plan and initial program of the health examination survey. *Vital and health statistics programs and collection procedures*, 1974, *Series 1, No. 4*.

National Center for Health Statistics. Health interview survey procedures: 1957–1974. *Vital and health statistics programs and collection procedures*, 1975, *Series 1, No. 11*. (a)

National Center for Health Statistics. The national ambulatory medical care survey. *Vital and health statistics programs and collection procedures*, 1975, *Series 13, No. 33*. (b)

National Center for Health Statistics. Plan and operation of the Health and Nutrition Examination Survey, United States, 1971–1973. *Vital and health statistics programs and collection procedures*, 1977, *Series 1, No. 10*. (a)

National Center for Health Statistics. Utilization of short stay hospitals by persons with heart disease and malignant neoplasms: National Hospital Discharge Survey. *Vital and health statistics programs and collection procedures, 1977, Series 13, No. 52.* (b)

National Center for Health Statistics. Basic data from wave I of the National Survey of Personal Health Practices and Consequences. *Vital and health statistics programs and collection procedures, 1979, Series 15, No. 2.* (a)

National Center for Health Statistics. The National Nursing Home Survey: 1977 summary for the United States. *Vital and health statistics: Data from the National Health Survey, 1979, Series 13, No. 43.* (b)

National Center for Health Statistics. Procedures and questionnaires of the National Medical Care Utilization and Expenditures Survey, 1983, *Series A, Methodological Report, No. 1.*

Neugarten, B. L., & Havighurst, R. J. Disengagement reconsidered in a cross-national context. In R. J. Havighurst, J. M. A. Munnichs, B. L. Neugarten, & H. Thomae (Eds.), *Adjustment to retirement.* Assen, The Netherlands: van Gorcum and Company, 1969, pp. 138–146.

Parnes, H. S. The National Longitudinal Surveys: New vistas for labor market research. *American Economic Review,* 1975, *65,* 224–249.

Reiss, A. J. Statistical measurement of social change. In *The five year outlook on science and technology* (Vol. 2). Washington, D.C.: The National Science Foundation, 1981, pp. 649–667.

Reynolds, V. *The biology of human action* (2nd ed.). San Francisco, Calif.: Freeman, 1980.

Riley, M. W. Age strata in social systems. In R. H. Binstock & E. Shanas (Eds.), *Handbook of aging and the social sciences* (2nd ed.). New York: Van Nostrand Reinhold, in press.

Rose, S. (Ed.). *Towards a liberatory biology.* New York: Schocken, 1982.

Ryder, N. B. The cohort as a concept in the study of social change. *American Sociological Review,* 1965, *30,* 843–861.

Schaie, K. W. A general model for the study of developmental problems. *Psychological Bulletin,* 1965, *64,* 92–107.

Schaie, K. W. The primary mental abilities in adulthood: An exploration in the development of psychometric intelligence. In P. B. Baltes & O. G. Brim Jr. (Eds.), *Life-span development and behavior* (Vol. 2). New York: Academic Press, 1979, pp. 68–117.

Shanas, E. *The health of older people: A social survey.* Cambridge, Mass.: Harvard University Press, 1962.

Shock, N. Biological theories of aging. In J. E. Birren & K. W. Schaie (Eds.), *Handbook of the psychology of aging.* New York: Van Nostrand Reinhold, 1977, pp. 103–115.

Social Security Administration. Users manual for the longitudinal sample of disability insurance applicants. SSA, ORS Pub. No. 019 (11–77), 1977.

Social Security Administration. 1978 Survey of Disability and Work: Data book, 1982.

Taeuber, R. C., & Rockwell, R. C. National data series: A compendium of brief descriptions. *Review of Public Data Use,* 1982, *10,* 23–111.

Tissue, T. The survey of low income aged and disabled: An introduction. *Social Security Bulletin,* 1977, *40,* 3–11.

Tuma, N. B., & Hannan, M. T. *Dynamic analysis.* New York: Academic Press, 1984.

Uhlenberg, P. Demographic change and problems of the aged. In M. W. Riley (Ed.). *Aging from birth to death: Interdisciplinary perspectives.* Boulder, Col.: Westview Press, 1979, pp. 153–166.

17

Aging Policies and Old Women: The Hidden Agenda

BETH B. HESS

County College of Morris, New Jersey

Introduction

The basic theme of this chapter is that public policy with respect to the elderly has not been gender-neutral—either in the past or, more crucially, the present. First, such policies have been consistently framed in terms of the male life course and concerns, despite the rather obvious facts that the majority of elderly are women, and that whatever problems are associated with advanced age in our society are overwhelmingly experienced by women. Second, the policy initiatives of the Reagan administration are shaped by a hidden agenda based on the ideology of private rather than public provision of services and on a commitment to traditional gender roles.

We begin with a few demographic observations; then describe what may be called the "gerontological gender gap"; discuss the differential impact by gender of public policy—past and present—in the areas of income maintenance, health care, and housing; and close with an analysis of the ideological foundations of recent federal policy formulations and their consequences for the elderly.

America's Elderly in the 1980s

Any discussion of America's elderly must begin with the secular trends in fertility and life expectancy that have combined to "age" our population and to bring the problems of old age into the public forum. For example, the proportion of our population aged 65 or older was 9.8% in 1970, stands at 11.5% today, is expected to reach 12.2% at the turn of century, and to rise to 17.6% in the year 2050 as the baby boom cohorts reach old age (Bureau of the Census, 1982b). Within that subpopulation, the older the age stratum, the faster its current rate of growth. People aged 85 or older increased by over 140% between 1960 and 1980

(American Council of Life Insurance, 1982), and the 1980 census counted 32,000 persons claiming to be 100 years of age or older. This rate of growth at the very oldest ages will, however, taper off in the next century when the age-group 65–74 will increase most rapidly (Siegel, 1979, p. 9; Soldo, 1980).

At the same time, female life expectancy has continued to increase relative to that for males (see Verbrugge [1983] for an extensive analysis of age–gender mortality rates). Whereas in 1900 there were more older men than older women, the sex ratio among the elderly has dramatically reversed throughout this century. Today, there are roughly 67 men aged 65 or over for every 100 women of that age and about 43 men per 100 women at 85 or older. These trends are expected to continue through the first half of the next century (Bureau of the Census, 1982b). In other words, as the population of old people increases numerically and proportionately, even more so does that of older women.

It has become conventional in gerontology to distinguish between the "young-old" and "old-old" (Neugarten, 1974), with the cutting point today at age 70 or 74. In this two-tiered scheme, members of the younger segment typically enjoy higher incomes, better health, are more likely to be living with a spouse, and to be active in the community, while members of the older segment manifest the conditions we have come to call the "problems" of aging—inadequate incomes, ill health, deteriorating housing, death of a spouse, increasing social isolation, and the like. Thus, when data on all people 65 or over are presented, the situation of the younger aged appears less favorable than it actually is, whereas the difficulties of the oldest are minimized.

The Gerontological Gender Gap

Most gerontologists were slow to realize that this young-old distinction was in most respects a gender difference, and that gender differences often cut across age lines. Paradoxically, the awareness of the "woman question" in gerontology might have been delayed in part by the relative prominence of a number of women in that field in the 1950s and early 1960s—a situation not unrelated to the low status and lack of major funding for aging studies during that period. The "discovery" of the aged in the mid-1960s, along with the funding available under the Older Americans Act for gerontological institutes and research projects, brought large numbers of men into the field and did little to change its major focus on issues related to the male experience, particularly studies of retirement in all its aspects—antecedents, correlates, and consequences.

Despite two published critiques of the research agenda and underlying assumptions of social gerontology in 1975 (Beeson, 1975; Hochschild, 1975), the leadership of the Gerontological Society scheduled their 1978 annual meeting in New Orleans, Louisiana—a state that had not ratified the Equal Rights Amendment. Only after a threatened boycott by several hundred feminist members of the Society were the meetings moved to Dallas, amid much acrimony and lingering ill-will.

Neither such activism on the part of feminist gerontologists nor the surge in research on aging women has been completely successful in changing the level or direction of the public and professional discourse on aging. For example, in his otherwise excellent recent analysis of public policy and aging, Stephen Crystal (1982) devotes a single page to "women" while talking of a gender-undifferentiated aged population on the other 190 pages, although every single problem of the elderly and every policy failure that he so carefully details has a differential impact by gender and race.

Not only have policy failures differentially affected old women—so have the successes. In their recent extensive analyses, both Crystal (1982) and Kutza (1981) demonstrate the ways in which government initiatives have succeeded in helping the least needy elderly. As Hudson (1978) has pointed out, one un-intended effect of the relative security of most old people has been to diminish concern for their less fortunate age-peers. Rather than push for further initiatives, the leaders of the "aging establishment" in the 1980s will probably settle for maintaining the current level of benefits and do so in an increasingly inhospitable public arena. The possibility of an aging "backlash," foreseen by Ragan (1976) and Hudson (1978), is a current reality. Age-based entitlements in what is commonly portrayed as a zero-sum policy game are being questioned as never before. What has not been fully addressed, however, are the gender biases already built into these programs.

A brief look at three major public policy areas will clarify this point:

Income. While the overall poverty rate for the elderly is about the same as that for the population as a whole—14.6 vs. 15% in 1982—only 8% of male heads of household aged 65 or older had incomes below the poverty level compared with 15% of their female counterparts. For unrelated individuals, these proportions rise to one-fourth for men and one-third for women. In addition, older women are far more likely than older men to be "unrelated individuals": Even at age 70 or over, 72% of men are living with a spouse, compared with only 23% of comparably aged women (Bureau of the Census, 1983a). Clearly, poverty in old age is overwhelmingly a problem of older widows and single women.

Is it only because they live so much longer that women exhaust savings and other resources? Actually, their income disadvantage in old age is built into the entire system of retirement income benefits. Retired men are more likely than women to receive maximum social security benefits and to have worked in companies that also provide private pensions. Private pensions are almost ex-clusively characteristic of the core rather than the peripheral economic sector (already stratified by race and gender), and most of these pension plans do not contain automatic provisions for widow benefits (Moss, 1983). Thus, for as long as the husband lives, the couple can maintain a comfortable standard of living, although not the luxurious "free ride" often depicted in conservative economic journals. Upon his death, however, income from private pensions and other sources is typically terminated. For most widowed old women, their dead hus-bands' Social Security check is their primary, if not the only, source of old-age income. Since this benefit is pegged to preretirement earning levels, income differences among classes of workers are perpetuated among their survivors, even though the "replacement ratio"—the proportion of preretirement income received as a Social Security benefit—is higher for lower earners. It is precisely this income-redistributing aspect of the Social Security system that has made it a prime target of conservative economists and politicians.

In addition, the 1972 amendments to the Social Security Act that protect against increases in the cost of living have been criticized as overly generous to the elderly, relative to younger wage-earners. But the argument that lowering the inflation rate will redound to the benefit of the most impoverished old people conveniently overlooks the fact that the two items that have accounted for the extreme fluctuations of the past decade—the prices of gasoline and of new homes—are of minimal importance to old widows, in comparison to health costs and rents, both of which are rising well in advance of the overall Consumer Price Index.

Health. Their longer life expectancy also means that most old women will experience the debilitation of chronic illness. In contrast, men are likely to die of accidents, cardiovascular diseases, and other "killer" conditions (Verbrugge, 1983). Thus, frail elderly women aged 75 or older—because of their health care needs and the absence of a caregiving spouse—are twice as likely as old and ill men to be in long-term care institutions. Yet we have devised a health-care delivery and financing system for the elderly based on the acute-care model. One can only speculate what our nursing-home system would be like if life expectancies were reversed and a large proportion of older men could expect to end their lives in an institution.

For the great majority of old women who remain in the community, the type of health-care services they utilize are only partially covered by Medicare. In fact, Medicare today covers only about two-fifths of the health-care costs of the elderly, with most of the rest coming out of the older person's pocket. Dental care, drugs, eyeglasses, hearing aids, and other prosthetics for the chronically ill are not covered. Both Medicare and private health insurance premiums are going up, while the range of services covered is narrowing, to the disadvantage of those who are least able to pay, who also happen to be the most ill (Pear, 1983). In other words, it costs the elderly person less to be cared for in a hospital rather than at home.

It is elderly widows who are primarily affected by these policies. Without a spouse to attend to their ordinary needs, those who require aid in daily living will find that most home-based services are not reimbursable. Since Medicare covers only a few months of skilled nursing services in nursing homes—and most beds are not skilled nursing, but simply custodial—disposing of all one's income and assets ("spending down") in the community or an institution in order to qualify for Medicaid is not uncommon. The "money-saving" changes in Medicare payment formulas currently proposed by the Reagan administration will make it even more difficult for older nonmarried women to remain in their own residences.

Housing. Because of their low incomes, increasing frailty, and singlehood, old women are the prime market for subsidized rental housing. The major federal programs for construction of such facilities—Sections 8 and 202—lost much of their funding in 1981 and 1982, while money for congregate-housing social services has been completely eliminated. Other changes in the programs have limited eligibility and increased the share paid by renters (U.S. Senate, Special Committee on Aging, 1982). The proposed solution for "asset rich/income poor" homeowners is a program whereby equity in their home is converted into an annuity, paying monthly benefits in exchange for ultimate title to the property. Such an arrangement would be of help to many elderly couples but has little impact on the well-being of the several million old widows who live in nonsubsidized rental housing (Bureau of the Census, 1981).

A great deal more could be said, but the main point should be clear: Public programs have been shaped by assumptions based on the life experience of men. In fact, the whole debate on aging is still often framed in what can only be considered masculinist terms: The need to work, the trauma of retirement, finding something like "work" to keep the old folk happy, or activity of any kind—as befits a society founded on the Protestant Ethic.

Yet not only are the real problems of old age disproportionately experienced by women, but it is women who are increasingly expected to bear the brunt of dealing with these problems.

Aging Policies in an Era of Retrenchment

Current public policy is essentially one of disinvestment, that is, there is a double-pronged effort to reduce the role of the federal government in providing income, health, housing, transportation, and social services to the elderly. One thrust has been to create a public climate in which it is believed that the private sector would be a more efficient and less costly provider. The other development is a renewed emphasis on the family as the "natural" locus of care and support.

"Poor-Mouthing" the Federal System

An example of the first policy thrust can be seen in the recent flap over the solvency of the Social Security system. Here, I borrow from the excellent treatment of the subject by John Myles (1981) who notes that attacks on the Social Security system from the political Right predate the Reagan administration, while the defenders of the Social Security system have failed to refute effectively the charge that the system is on the verge of bankruptcy. Without a murmur of dissent, the media invariably frame the issue in terms of impending doom— "almost bankrupt," "actuarially unsound," "a crisis of coming insolvency"—and similar phrases. And so it has come to be perceived by large numbers of citizens. A national survey by Louis Harris for the National Council on Aging in 1981, for example, found that a majority of respondents had "hardly any" confidence in the Social Security system, particularly the younger respondents and those in high-income brackets.

Another element in undermining confidence in the federal system is the suggestion that people, especially younger workers, could maximize their return by investing in a private pension plan rather than pay into Social Security. This position has been forcefully argued by members of conservative think-tanks such as the Heritage Foundation. In the business sector, millions of dollars were spent in 1982 on advertising for Individual Retirement Accounts, with tables showing how you could retire with over a million dollars, while a spate of newsmagazine articles quoted government and private sector economists on the superiority of private retirement savings plans.

Public support for the Social Security system can also be eroded by denying what the system's critics call "scare stories" about old age as a period of terminal misery. Not so, they claim, citing statistics to demonstrate that most elderly today are not living in poverty. This claim is essentially correct: The poverty rate of the population aged 65 or older was reduced by one-half between 1960 and 1980—but precisely *because* of the Social Security Act Amendments, including Medicare, that were passed as part of the Great Society program in 1965 and 1972. And if one only counted men, there is indeed very little old-age poverty, except among blacks, but that presumably will be reduced when the new prosperity trickles down far enough.

The dust jacket for a book published in 1980, for example, trumpeted that "most of America's senior citizens are not ill-housed, frail, or poor, though these notions are leading us to tragically wasteful public programs." The book's title was *Old Folks at Home* (Rabushka & Jacobs, 1980), and the research upon which the authors base their conclusions was a survey of elderly homeowners—a sample biased heavily in favor of the still-married, relatively affluent, healthy, and well-housed "young-old."

In addition, successive secretaries of Health and Human Services have frequently noted that programs for the elderly account for one-quarter to one-third of federal expenditures—without adding that this figure includes Social Security benefits and Medicare costs. Once Social Security and other fully or partially self-funded programs are excluded, the proportion of the federal budget spent on old-age programs is roughly 4% (U.S. Senate, Special Committee on Aging, 1983)—about the same as for veterans programs and only one-third of the interest on the national debt in fiscal year 1982.

This barrage of poor-mouthing not only undermines confidence in the Social Security system but also engenders intergenerational tension, particularly if young workers perceive themselves as overtaxed in order to let the aged live in luxury without assurances that they, too, will be taken care of adequately in their old age.

But in actuality, the Social Security system need not be in a financial bind. There are a number of relatively simple and effective remedies at hand—most of which were overlooked or underplayed in the 1983 report of a special Presidential Commission. Indeed, the Commission's analysis and the amendments that passed Congress in 1983, with White House blessing, continue most of the gender inequities already built into the system in addition to exacerbating intergenerational hostility. It is doubtful that such sweeping changes could have been made without the carefully nurtured public perception of crisis.

One major stumbling block to necessary reform of Social Security is the insistence on retaining the ideological fig leaf of retirement benefits as an insurance program linked to work history. To mention just one possible reform: A trust fund financed from general revenues and based on a percentage of the Gross National Product would avoid the effect of variation in labor-force participation rates or in the proportion of workers to nonworkers (the "dependency ratio"). In a largely automated postindustrial economy, the work lives of individuals may be both shorter and less continuous than in the past, making a retirement income system based on prior earnings less feasible than one computed on the basis of the total value of the goods and services being produced.

As for the relative virtue of a publicly guaranteed and administered system, economic gerontologists such as James Schulz (1980) and Juanita Kreps (1976) have amply demonstrated that Social Security remains the best bargain and the most certain source of income maintenance in old age for the vast majority of Americans.

Why, then, the attack on Social Security? In my judgement, efforts to discredit the system are rooted in the fact that Social Security, despite the intentions even of those who authored the legislation (Cates, 1983), has been a successful mechanism for redistributing income from the relatively affluent to the less well-off. It is this aspect of the system that exemplifies the evils of the welfare state to economic and political conservatives. If a program as deeply entrenched as Social Security can be discredited and dismantled, so presumably can any other attempt to disturb the "free play" of the market in allocating resources and income. Thus, the recent volley of criticism—not only of particular features but of the very rationale of the Social Security system—in such media as *The Wall Street Journal, Commentary, Fortune, Forbes,* and *The Public Interest.*

By mid-1983, these same media were running similarly worded articles about the Medicaid fund. Indeed, 2 days after the paper upon which this chapter is based was read at the annual meeting of the American Sociological Association, the *New York Times* featured an article entitled, "Medicare: The Next Crisis Over 'Entitlements'" (September 4, 1983:6E).

The role of private enterprise in delivery of health care to the aged began with the legislation that encouraged the building—and selling and reselling—of proprietary nursing homes and can be seen today in the home health care "boom" (Kleinfield, 1983), from a business that lost money in 1980 to one reporting earnings of 3 billion dollars in the first half of 1983. Unquestionably, many people have been able to leave the hospital and return to their homes because private home health services are now available and are covered by third-party insurers at considerably lower cost than hospital-based care. There is also no question that home health-care companies can deliver a necessary product at reasonable cost—but only to those who can afford it or who have health insurance coverage. Medicare does not currently reimburse services of this type, although several experimental waiver programs are in progress.

Forbes recently painted a glowing picture of the profits to be realized from the aging of America: "Gray gold" they call it. But there has been no discussion of the philosophical question raised by private ownership of health-care facilities and services for the elderly: Is a sense of public responsibility lost when we turn the tasks over to profit-making firms? One of the virtues of state-supported services is that, despite manifest inefficiencies and high costs, the message is nonetheless conveyed that care of the needy is an obligation of citizenship.

And Who Shall Care for the "Truly Needy"?

But what, then, is to be done for the "truly needy"? Undoubtedly, some frail elderly can be adequately cared for within the tax-subsidized profit-making nursing home industry, a system that uniquely combines the worst of private greed and public incompetence (Hess, 1978). There are, to be sure, many fine and well-run homes, mostly in the nonprofit sector, but the overall system created in deference to the private market, as well as the manifest shortcomings of underfinanced public institutions, have reinforced the negative image of institutional care. Perhaps our long-term care policy could be considered one of those "fatal remedies" (Sieber, 1981) or unintended consequences of doing good that penalize those one seeks to help and that generate resistance to further attempts to rectify the situation.

The solution? The emerging consensus is that frail elderly people should, of course, be cared for at home. Not their home—for that would entail further expenditures in community-based services, possibly exceeding the costs for congregate care. Where else but in the home of an adult child? And not just any adult child, but the one who can most easily put aside other interests and who is, anyway, equipped by nature to assume the task: The adult daughter.

For example, a distinguished physician who directs a major rehabilitation clinic, arguing for a change in Medicare regulations to permit payment to a family member for elder care, states that:

> [The current system] obliges many couples to institutionalize, at great public cost, a person who could be cared for better and far more economically at home if a reasonable salary were paid, enabling a daughter or granddaughter to give up outside employment for this purpose. (*New York Times*, April 25, 1983, p.24)

Notice how unquestioned these assumptions are: That the women should do it, that the only reason such women are employed is to earn pocket money, and that they would prefer to earn it by caring for an infirm older person. At least this letter used sex neutral terms for the patient. More typical are references to the nursing home patient as "he."

Actually, proposals of this nature solve a number of problems: Saving tax dollars, providing care to the frail elderly, and keeping women in the home, where they really wish to belong. Such are the assumptions underlying several features of the Family Protection legislation introduced into Congress in its last two sessions (Hess, 1983). As Senator Paul Laxalt put it in introducing the 1979 version, government policy has "actively encouraged placement of the elderly in outside institutions away from their families . . . [and] contributed to lessening concern by the younger generation for their parents" (Brown, 1981). Or, in the words of Senator Jepsen, the 1981 sponsor: "All too frequently, low and moderate-income families are forced to put their elderly parents into subsidized nursing homes because they cannot afford to keep them at home" (U.S. Senate, *Congressional Record,* June 17, 1981).

This legislation proposes a tax credit or deduction for families that provide a home to an elderly dependent. This will, of course, be welcomed by the many households that already provide such care. In fact, over 80% of home care for the frail elderly is given by relatives (Shanas, 1979), most of whom are wives caring for ill husbands. Adult children who care for elderly kin would much prefer services—respite care, home health aid, homemaking assistance, and the like— to tax credits (Horowitz & Shindelman, 1980; Sussman, 1979). In both the Sussman (1979) study and its replication by Horowitz and Shindelman (1980), caregivers to the elderly were asked to rank their preferences among a list of five economic-assistance programs and five social-support programs. For these re- spondents, tax credits ranked low, while monthly checks were somewhat more attractive, but the strongest preferences were for direct assistance in homemaking and health-care tasks. When asked to choose the single most beneficial of the 10 possible supports, over 80% of the Horowitz and Shindelman sample chose a service rather than financial support (with only 2% favoring a tax deduction). Not only were financial incentives relatively unpopular, but they often evoked negative reactions (Horowitz & Shindelman, 1980).

In any event, tax credits or deductions to their children are not likely to affect the outcome for most nursing home residents. The typical resident is female, extremely ill, never-married or with only one or two offspring, and over 80 years old, so that any "children" are likely also to be elderly if not deceased. For the elderly in the community, the research evidence (reviewed in Hess & Waring, 1978) is quite clear: Both old and young prefer to maintain independent resi- dences. It is the triumph of Social Security and Medicare that such independence has been realized by so many. Indeed, large numbers of elderly would prefer to go into a nursing home rather than live with their adult offspring if no other choice were available (Crystal, 1982).

Further, it is simply not true that old people are dumped into homes by uncaring kin. Institutionalization typically occurs after all other arrangements have been tried and found wanting or after some severe setback in the lives of the older person or her caregivers. Nor are old people sent to nursing homes to save their children money: Medicare does not pay one cent for most patients, and Medicaid takes over only at the point of utter impoverishment.

Nonetheless, in April 1983, the Reagan administration reinterpreted the Medicaid legislation as allowing states to require offspring to help pay for their parents' nursing home care. Such "filial support" rules have been extremely difficult to enforce in the past and contain several counterproductive features. From her extensive review of the laws and research evidence, Sandra Newman has concluded that "a weighing of the available evidence provides a convincing case that these laws are, at best, an irritant and, at worst, damaging to whatever family ties do exist, however weak" (Newman, 1980, p. 4). Nor is there much hope that the states will realize large sums of money from the exercise, since the families of most Medicaid patients who do have surviving offspring are themselves in financially straitened circumstances.

The Family-Support System

In light of these considerations, I am more guarded than other gerontologists in response to the recent outpouring of work on the family as a "natural support system" for the elderly. My fear is that this new-found enthusiasm could become the rationale for reducing commitment to public and community programs and in some quarters will be incorporated into a larger ideologically based attempt to reverse the gains of the women's movement.

Home care for the elderly is a feminist issue, then, on several grounds, the first being that in most cases, old women are the care-receivers and younger ones the caregivers. The other ground is that this issue has also become a litmus test of public vs. private assumption of social-welfare responsibilities. To the degree that public programs come to be perceived as inefficient, inhumane, and extravagant to boot, the private alternative will appear that much more attractive, but it must be cloaked in appeals to "filial responsibility" and virtues on a higher moral plane than mere money-saving or the integrity of the free-enterprise system.

Yet there is little reason to believe that the lot of the frail elderly will be vastly improved as a consequence. The daughters and sons who are both able and willing to assume the task of caregiving have always done so with little inducement. Second, it was precisely the uncertain nature of kinship resources and family supports that led to defining care of the frail elderly as a public responsibility. It can even be argued that removing claims for care from the interpersonal to the civic arena will actually enhance the quality of intergenerational relationships, because they will be based on voluntary rather than obligatory ties (Hess & Waring, 1978).

Our fear is that under the guise of protecting and revitalizing the American family, essential needs of the elderly will once more be left to the chance of the market place, available in quality and quantity to those who can afford it, but replete with ceremonies of degradation for those who cannot. When the cost of elder care must be factored into each family's personal budget, the unpaid service of adult women becomes an important resource. Disputes over the allocation of responsibility within families and among siblings will be aggravated. In no way will these developments contribute to family protection or cohesion.

If the goal is to enhance family-based supports for their elderly, this can be best achieved by reducing conflicting demands on the middle generation(s), allowing the voluntary exchange system to operate with a minimum of anguish or guilt. An enlightened public policy would first of all focus on maintaining old people in their own residences for as long as possible while also providing a spectrum of community-based services to relieve the burdens on caregiving kin: Visiting nurses and homemakers, meal delivery, an adult day-care center, transportation assistance, and respite services—in fact, all the programs that are currently losing their funding or being folded into block grants to be fought over at the state level.

Perhaps most distressing of all, the very successes of the aging establishment in having lifted so many elderly out of poverty and into self-sufficiency might have blunted further efforts to improve the conditions of the several million old people—primarily women—who remain ill-fed, ill-housed, ill-clothed, and just plain ill.

References

American Council of Life Insurance. *Data track 9: Older Americans*. Washington, D.C.: ACLI, 1982.

Beeson, D. Women in studies of aging: A critique and a suggestion. *Social Problems*, 1975, *23*, 52–59.

Brown, R. Blueprint for a moral America. *The Nation*, May 23, 1981, p. 622 ff.

Cates, J. R. *The political construction and maintenance of Social Security's anti-poor bias*. Paper presented to the Society for the Study of Social Problems, Detroit, 1983.

Crystal, S. *America's old age crisis: Public policy and the two worlds of aging*. New York: Basic Books, 1982.

Hess, B. B. The politics of aging. *Society*, 1978, *15*, 22–23.

Hess, B. B. Old women: Problems, potentials, and public policy implications. In E. W. Markson, & G. Batra, (Eds.), *Public policies for an aging population*. Lexington, Mass.: Lexington, 1980, pp. 39–60.

Hess, B. B. Protecting the American famliy: Public policy, family, and the New Right. In R. Genovese, (Ed.), *Families and change: Social needs and public policy*. South Hadley, Mass.: J. F. Bergin, 1983, pp. 11–21.

Hess, B. B., & Waring, J. M. Parent and child in later life: Rethinking the relationship. In R. M. Lerner, & G. Spanier, (Eds.), *Child influence on marital and family interaction*. New York: Academic Press, 1978, pp. 241–274.

Hess, B. B., & Waring, J. M. Family relationships of older women. In E. W. Markson, (Ed.), *Older women: Issues and prospects*. Lexington, Mass.: Lexington, 1983, pp. 227–251.

Hochschild, A. R. Disengagement theory: A critique and proposal. *American Sociological Review*, 1975, *40*, 553–569.

Horowitz, A., & Shindelman, L. W. *Social and economic incentives for family caregivers*. Paper presented to the Gerontological Society of America, San Diego, 1980.

Hudson, R. B. Emerging pressures on public policies for the aged. *Society*, 1978, *15*, 30–33.

Kleinfield, N. R. The home health care boom. *The New York Times*, June 30, 1983, p. D1 ff.

Kreps, J. M. Social security in the coming decade: Questions for a mature system. *Social Security Bulletin*, March 1976, pp. 21–29.

Kutza, E. A. *The benefits of old age: Social welfare policy for the elderly*. Chicago, Ill.: University of Chicago Press, 1981.

Moss, A. Social insecurity: Pension plans shortchange women. *Women's Political Times*, February 1983, p. 2.

Myles, J. *The trillion dollar misunderstanding*. Working Papers, July/August 1981, 23–31.

National Council on Aging. *Aging in the eighties: America in transition*. Washington, D.C.: NCOA, 1981.

Neugarten, B. L. Age groups in American society and the rise of the young-old. *Annals of the American Academy of Political and Social Science*, 1974, *415*, 189–198.

Newman, S. J. *Government policy and the relationship between adult children and their aging parents: Filial support, Medicare, and Medicaid*. Unpublished manuscript, Institute for Social Research, University of Michigan, Ann Arbor, 1980.

Pear, R. Medicare proposals said to burden those most ill. *The New York Times*, April 10, 1983, p. 28.

Rabushka, A., & Jacobs, B. *Old folks at home*. New York: The Free Press, 1980.

Ragan, P. K. *Another look at the politicizing of old age: Can we expect a backlash effect?* Paper presented to the Society for the Study of Social Problems, New York, 1976.

Schulz, J. *The economics of aging*. Belmont, Calif.: Wadsworth, 1980.

Shanas, E. The family as a social support system in old age. *The Gerontologist*, 1979, *19*, 169–174.

Sieber, S. D. *Fatal remedies: The ironies of social intervention*. New York: Plenum, 1981.

Siegel, J. S. *Prospective trends in the size and structure of the elderly population, impact of mortality trends, and some implications*. U.S. Department of Commerce, Bureau of the Census, Current Population Reports Series P-23, No. 78, January 1979, 22 pp.

Soldo, B. J. *America's elderly in the 1980s*. Washington, D.C.: Population Reference Bureau, 1980.

Sussman, M. B. *Social and economic supports and family environments for the elderly*. Final report to the Administration on Aging, 1979.

U.S. Bureau of the Census. Prospective trends in the size and structure of the elderly population. *Current Population Reports*, Series P-23, No. 79. Washington, D.C.: U.S. Government Printing Office, 1979. (a)

U.S. Bureau of the Census. Social and economic characteristics of the older population: 1978. *Current Population Reports*, Series P-23, No. 85. Washington, D.C.: U.S. Government Printing Office, 1979. (b)

U.S. Bureau of the Census. Household and family characteristics: March 1980. *Current Population Reports*, Series P-20, No. 366. Washington, D.C.: U.S. Government Printing Office, 1981.

U.S. Bureau of the Census. Money income and poverty status of families and persons in the United States: 1981. *Current Population Reports*, Series P-60, No. 34. Washington, D.C.: U.S. Government Printing Office, 1982. (a)

U.S. Bureau of the Census. Population profile of the United States: 1981. *Current Population Reports*, Series P-20, No. 374. Washington, D.C.: U.S. Government Printing Office, 1982. (b)

U.S. Bureau of the Census. Marital status and living arrangements: March 1982. *Current Population Reports,* Series P-20, No. 380. Washington, D.C.: U.S. Government Printing Office, 1983. (a)

U.S. Bureau of the Census. *Statistical Abstract of the United States: 1982–3.* Washington, D.C.: U.S. Government Printing Office, 1983. (b)

U.S. Congress, Senate, *Congressional Record,* June 17, 1981, S 6328.

U.S. Congress, Senate, Special Committee on Aging. *Developments in aging: 1981.* Washington, D.C.: U.S. Government Printing Office, 1982.

U.S. Congress, Senate, Special Committee on Aging. *Aging reports* March 1983.

Verbrugge, L. M. Women and men: Mortality and health of older people. In M. W. Riley, B. B. Hess, & K. Bond (Eds.), *Aging in society: Selected reviews of recent research.* Hillsdale, N.J.: Erlbaum, 1983, pp. 139–174.

18

Women, Men, and the Lengthening Life Course*

MATILDA WHITE RILEY
National Institute on Aging

Introduction

I begin with a quotation:

> Today mature women no longer find a full life in the home, their traditional place. If we are ever to have a good society, wives, as well as every other category within the population, must have a place with ample opportunity for earning the social approbation which humankind so desperately needs.

Authorship? Date? Written by John Riley and me 50 years ago. In a not yet finished book (we put it away until we were older and wiser), we then hoped to exhort the better-educated, middle-aged women of that era to create new leisure roles in society—to recast leisure as not merely "recreation" but as a serious and productive pursuit (as in ancient Athens, the Renaissance, or seventeenth-century England). These women did seize the opportunities to create new roles for themselves, not in leisure, but in paid work. With these women began the dramatic long-term metamorphosis in the process of aging (growing older), from the earlier cohorts in which with aging, decreasing proportions of women engaged in paid work, to the more recent cohorts in which (up to retirement) increasing proportions of women are so engaged. In response to social changes in family formation, education, and the demand for labor, women's lives changed and with them the social structures of work, the family, and education.

*I am grateful for criticisms and suggestions on earlier versions of this chapter to: Ronald Abeles, Paul Baltes, Kathleen Bond, Herman Brotman, Dale Dannefer, Paula Darby, Freya Dittman-Kohli, Manning Feinlieb, Anne Foner, Mathew Greenwald, Leonard Jakubczak, Karen Miller, Marcia G. Ory, Richard M. Sallick, Harris Schrank, Richard Suzman, Joan Waring, and most especially to my long-time collaborator, John W. Riley, Jr.

I cite this example here because it foreshadows the current very real potentials for recasting of roles during the next 50 years, for men as well as for women, and because it illustrates how such recasting can be brought about through the continual dialectical interplay between changes in society and changes in the aging process. That is, as society changes, oncoming cohorts of people age (grow up and grow old) in new ways; and in turn, similar changes in the lives of many members of a cohort produce further structural changes in the society. I have written about this dialectic elsewhere (Riley, 1978, 1982). But with a difference. For here, my theme is the impact on this dialectic of the unprecedented twentieth-century revolution in longevity. I shall examine two ways in which longevity enters the dialectic:

1. Longevity alters the social structure by increasing structural complexity and hence the *option* open to individuals as they age.
2. Longevity alters the aging process by prolonging the opportunity for accumulation of social, psychological, and biological *experiences* as lives lengthen.

Thus, examination of a demographic change brings to attention increases in two sociologically significant but neglected concepts: *Structural options* and *accumulated experience*. Both can have negative consequences, but I shall emphasize the untold positive opportunities for today's cohorts of long-lived individuals, with all their accumulated experiences, not merely to respond to, but also to create, new social structures. These new structures are destined to have forms, meanings, even underlying values quite different from those in any society ever known.

The startling facts about *longevity* are still unfolding, and many are still moot. Not yet answered are questions as to how far the average length of life will be extended, and just how healthy and capable people will be of using their accumulated experience as increasing proportions survive past infancy and middle age and into their eighties and nineties (Manton, 1982). However, two facts stand out clearly. First, as never before in all history, we now live in a society in which most people live to be old.[1] In the United States, life expectancy at birth has risen from less than 50 in 1900 to 70 for males and 78 for females today. Even in the past decade, mortality has been declining at such an unexpectedly high rate that females surviving to age 65 can now expect to live on the average for at least another 18 years, males another 14 (Allan & Brotman, 1981). At the start of the

---

[1]Note that increasing longevity in a society is not necessarily the same as the increasing proportion of old people in the population, a proportion influenced in the long term more by fertility than by mortality. Longevity affects individual lives and family structures, while population composition affects the total society in which individuals are growing older (Preston, 1976). Barring annihilation by nuclear war, longevity will predictably persist late into the twenty-first century even as the baby boom cohorts are replaced in the oldest age strata by the smaller cohorts.

century, most deaths occurred in infancy and young adulthood, but today two-thirds of all deaths occur after age 65 and 30% after age 80 (Brody & Brock, in press). Difficult as it is to comprehend revolutionary change while we are in the midst of it, over two-thirds of the improvement in longevity in the entire world from prehistoric times until the present has taken place in the brief period since 1900 (Preston, 1976).

The second fact: Because longevity has increased faster for women than men, at the oldest ages women are the predominant members of society. In the United States by the year 2000, there will be an estimated 150 women for every 100 men at age 65 and over and at age 85 and over an estimated 254 women for every 100 men (Allan & Brotman, 1981).

What then are the sociological consequences of these two unprecedented demographic facts for the dialectical interplay between social change and aging? The consequences, many of them already swirling around us, are themselves unprecedented. I shall begin with examples from social life, considering how increased longevity affords new options in the social structure for persons who are growing older and adds to the diverse stores of accumulated experience. Then I shall discuss the influence of these new options and this accumulated experience on the multifaceted processes of aging from birth to death, including biological aging. Finally, I shall touch on some possibilities for future structural change, as foreshadowed by the innovative women of half a century ago.

Examples from Social Life

In social life, the increases in longevity, together with other major social changes, are permeating and literally transforming many familiar social structures, their social meanings, and their influence over people's lives.

Family Life

Especially sensitive to changes in longevity is family life, where one resultant transformation in social structure is the dramatic prolongation of the linkages among family members. In married couples a century ago, one or both partners were likely to have died before the children were reared. Today, couples marrying at the customary ages can anticipate surviving together (apart from divorce) as long as 40 or 50 years on the average (Uhlenberg, 1969, 1980). Because the current intricacy of kinship structures transcends even the language available to describe them, it sometimes helps to do thought experiments from one's own life. As marital partners, my husband and I have so far survived together for over 50 years. That means that we share over one-half a century of experiences! Because we were born at approximately the same time (and thus belong to the same cohort), we have shared much the same historical experiences. We have also shared our own personal family experiences: Bearing and raising young children; readjusting to couplehood as our children, by marrying and producing their own offspring, endowed us with added roles as parents-in-law and grand-parents.

Long-lived marriages, such as my own, provide increasing opportunity to accumulate shared historical and personal experiences and perhaps to build from these a solidary relationship (Hagestad, 1981; Turner, 1970). They also present shifting exigencies and role conflicts that require continual mutual accommodation and reaccommodation; and many marriages, not ended by death, are of course ended by divorce.

As lives are prolonged, parent–offspring relationships also take on entirely new forms. For example, my daughter and I have so far survived together for 45 years, of which only 18 were in the traditional relationship of parent with dependent child. Unlike our shorter-lived forebears, she and I as adults have become status equals in the eyes of society, negotiating long-term adult relationships with one another (Hess & Waring, 1978). As adults, we share many common experiences—though at different stages of our respective lives. She shares a major portion of the historical changes that I have experienced. She can also empathize with my earlier experiences with a daughter who asserts her own independence and who moves through the transitions of adult life.

But longevity means more than the prolongation of particular relationships. It also means that four (even five) generations of many families are now alive at the same time. Moreover, each generation becomes increasingly stable in the sense that more of its members survive. Young children born today, compared with those born a century ago, are almost entirely protected against death of a parent or sibling. Orphanages, once omnipresent, have all but disappeared. Fragile as the contemporary family is often thought to be, Peter Uhlenberg (1980) demonstrates the surprising fact that disruptions of marriage up through the completion of childrearing have been *declining* since 1900! Although many marriages have been broken by divorce, still more have remained intact because of fewer deaths.[2] That is, the young family, and also each of the older generations, becomes more stable through survival. Of a child's four grandparents, increasing numbers survive. And among middle-aged couples, back in 1900 more than one-half had no surviving elderly parents; but today one-half have two or more parents still alive (Uhlenberg, 1980).

Of course, as these surviving generations proliferate, spread, and overlap, the process of aging changes. Typically beginning life with both parents, but then often living only with their mothers after divorce and later with their mothers and stepfathers (Cherlin & Furstenberg, 1982), the members of each generation are continually growing older and moving up the generational ladder to replace their predecessors, until ultimately all the members of the oldest generation die.

---

[2]Note that, if divorce rates continue to rise, there could be a future "threshold effect" producing instability in young families, since there is now little room for major decreases in mortality among young parents to offset rising divorce.

Because women are the more longevitous, they are most likely to stand alone at the top of the ladder—expected to develop new relationships that can earn, not demand, from their descendent kin the companionship, advice, and emotional support needed as death approaches (cf. J. Riley, 1983).

Thus, under the compelling influence of longevity, I have come to replace the traditional notion of the "nuclear" family of young parents and their little children with the notion of today's large and complex kinship structure as a "matrix of latent relationships"—father with son, child with great grandparent, sister with sister-in-law, ex-husband with ex-wife, and so on (Riley, 1983a). These relationships form a latent web of continually shifting linkages that provide the *potential* for activating and intensifying close family relationships. These relationships, no longer ascribed, must continually be achieved and reachieved.

I have dwelt on this greatly expanded kinship structure to emphasize the pervasive social consequences of the lengthening life course. Many new options are now open for people at different points in their lives to select and activate those relationships they deem most significant. Deep and diverse shared experiences now accrue to kindred over their long lives. The family structure is not what it used to be, nor is the process of growing old within the family.

Social Life

In similar fashion, longevity operates throughout social life to prolong time spent in roles, to generate varied role sequences, and to create complexes of roles for simultaneous occupancy.

Prolongation of roles. With increases in longevity have come striking extensions of the years spent in roles, not only in the family but also in schooling, work, and retirement. In the United States, where Colonial children rarely went beyond primary school, the percentage of high school graduates in the population (aged 25–29) has been rising steadily from 38% in cohorts entering adulthood early in the century to 86% today (Dearman & Plisko, 1982). Retirement, which scarcely existed early in the century, now accounts for over one-fourth of the adult life course (Torrey, 1982).

This prolonged aging in a role allows diverse experiences to accumulate, with consequences dependent on the rate and quality of interactions involved. In some roles, experience can mean increased skill and wisdom, increased investment of resources, increased commitment of self. People hesitate to lose benefits accrued in a job, to lose a long-time friend, or to move away from a long-familiar community. Early studies of voting behavior have shown that, regardless of age, the longer people have belonged to a political party, the greater their commitment to that party (Campbell, Converse, Miller & Stokes, 1960). Studies of old people have shown that the longer they have lived in a neighborhood, the more neighborhood friends they have and the less willing they are to move away (Riley & Foner, 1968).

In other roles, however, too much experience can mean boredom, "burn-out," lack of challenge. Long duration in an unpleasant role—an unhappy marriage, a hated job, being an "inmate" in an institution—can simply compound the misery. Recent research has shown that "daily hassles" can be more destructive of well-being than can stressful life events (DeLongis, Coyne, Dakof, Folkman, & Lazarus, 1982).

Varied role sequences. Prolongation of roles, whether pleasant or unpleasant, may in itself give impetus to numerous personal or social plans to shorten these roles or to vary the role sequences. Adding time to life gives opportunity at every age for individuals to change jobs, careers, marriages, or educational plans, and for societal manipulation of compulsory ages of schooling or of retirement. Prolonging time spent in a role not only increases the probability of inadvertent changes (Preston, 1976) but also, in Robert Merton's term (1982), the "socially expected duration" may encourage people at every age deliberately to order their lives in new ways (Harris Schrank, personal communication). Thus, through the addition of time, the options for creating new and varied role sequences have expanded.

Complex role sequences mean accumulated experiences in numerous role transitions over a person's life course, transitions that require learning to relinquish the former role and to adopt the new one. Transitions are variously experienced: Sometimes casually; sometimes as a source of new opportunities, challenges, and rewards; sometimes with a sense of failure, hurt, defensiveness, and withdrawal (Riley & Waring, 1976). Women, whose longer and more complex lives give greater opportunity for role transitions, seem on the average to weather them better than men. For example, one study shows that bereavement results in excess deaths for men (unless they remarry) but not for women (Helsing and Szklo, 1981).

Role complexity. Time added to the life course through longevity also encourages simultaneous assumption of multiple roles. Now that most women survive for many years after their children have left home, women seem even more likely than men to combine family roles with varied work, leisure, and community roles. Much has been written about the burden on mature working women who must care for an elderly parent or on young working women who must care for the children—even in planned socialist societies (Croll, 1981). Yet the outcomes of performing multiple roles are not all bad. In one study, Lois Verbrugge (1983) has shown from the Detroit Area sample that the combination of job plus family responsibilities has no simple connections with health, either negative or positive, for either women or men (see also Haynes and Feinlieb, 1980). Several other studies show that multiple roles can enhance role flexibility, social involvement, and the sense of personal achievement, and that learning to cope with compound role difficulties can often bring its own satisfactions (Marks, 1977; Sieber, 1974; Spreitzer, Snyder, & Larson, 1979).

However, the institutionalization of multiple roles has been developing un-
evenly between the sexes. At work, though women seem more durable than men,
their roles are still typically defined and rewarded as inferior. In the family, few
men spend much if any time in caring for home and children. Mathew Greenwald
reports (from unpublished national surveys conducted for the American Council
of Life Insurance) that the public still holds the opinion that a woman's most
important quality is to be "a good cook," a man's to be "a good provider";
although in the popular view, there are incipient declines (from 1968 to 1983) in
such stereotypically manly characteristics as being "physically strong," "keeping feelings under control," "confident when making important decisions," and
"willing to risk his life in the face of danger."

Moreover, for the greatly expanded numbers of people at the oldest ages, too
few new roles have so far been institutionalized. Despite widespread expression
of satisfaction with retirement as it now exists, delays in further structural innovations continue to reduce the challenge that could sustain vigor and functioning
in older people and could foster their continuing contributions to society. Older
women in particular, who are thought to be the affective and nurturant members
of society, are in the end the ones most often left alone to create new roles for
themselves. Thus, longevity has produced unparalleled opportunities in the oldest age strata for recasting the structures and meanings of existing roles.

In social life, then, longevity influences the dialectical interplay between
social change and individual aging in exceptional ways. As members of recent
cohorts grow older within the changing structures, they have unprecedented
opportunity to accumulate experience, to respond in their own lives to social
change, and to influence it.

Implications for the Multifaceted Aging Process

Biological as well as social aging enters the dialectic, of course, and is
interdependent with the changing social structures and accumulated experiences
that accrue from longevity (Riley, in press-b). Biological aging is itself the
template for accumulation over the life course of many physiological assaults,
from the wear and tear on cartilage and joints to the multiple chronic diseases that
often develop in later life. Yet physiological declines in old age are not entirely
universal or immutable, as often believed. Indeed, many presumed aging declines are no more than erroneous interpretations of cross-sectional age differences; and, rather than detracting from health, well-being, and effective
functioning, some physiological changes with aging can improve them. The
essential principle is that aging is not a unitary biological process, completely
determined by "natural laws," but a set of multifaceted processes in which
biological aging—genetic predispositions, biological development and decline—
continually interacts with social and psychological aging (Riley, in press-a).

Thus, biological components of the aging process are influenced by social relationship, social structure, and social change (cf. Rossi, 1980a, 1980b, 1984).

Physiological Functioning

The impact of social change on biological aging and physiological functioning is clearly visible in the differences among successive cohorts over the past century. Not only has each cohort outlived its predecessor, but also—in response to social changes in standard of living, sanitation, and medical science—the burden of illness has shifted from the infectious diseases of early life to the chronic diseases of later life. Moreover, cohorts of people growing up under today's social conditions differ from people in earlier cohorts in physical size, age at onset of menstruation, and numerous other physiological respects. And in future cohorts, many of the current physiological age decrements can be prevented if people accumulate different life-styles from those of earlier cohorts—improved diets, reduced dependence on tobacco and drugs, maintenance of physical and intellectual activity, or societal protections against pollution and accidents.

Cigarette smoking, the most deadly of the health-risk factors, provides one example of how life-preserving behaviors can be responsive to changes in society. Over the past decades, each successive cohort of adult *males* in the United States—presumably responsive to the Surgeon General's warnings—has been less likely than its predecessors to smoke (Riley, 1981). For *women*, however, the proportions who smoked *increased* from cohort to cohort—coordinated with the women's movement—up until the health warnings of the mid-1960s; since then, the most recent cohorts of women are beginning to follow the declining pattern. Thus, predictably, the death rates attributable to smoking, currently increasing for women (Brody & Brock, in press), can be expected to decline as these more recent cohorts grow older.

Another example of cohort differences in health risks (Feinlieb, 1975) comes from the Framingham Heart Study, in which the lives of some 1600 married couples have been traced for many years. Recently, a parallel study has been made of their offspring, comparing the offspring cohorts today with the cohorts of their parents 22 years ago when they were approximately the *same* ages. The differences between these two cohorts in three of the major risk factors in coronary heart disease are striking. The offspring, as compared with their parents, show lower blood pressure, lower serum cholesterol, and less cigarette smoking. Note that these differences are not due to age, since the ages of parents and offspring are the *same* at the time for which measures in these risk factors are compared. What the differences *do* suggest is that the more recent cohorts are responding to increasing cultural emphases on their own future health and the importance of primary prevention of chronic disease. As these cohorts grow old in the future, they may be healthier, at least in certain respects, than cohorts already old today.

For each individual within a cohort, the changing social environment and the added years of life extend the opportunity for interaction between biological predispositions and social experiences. Stressful social situations at work or in the family, if inadequately dealt with, can accumulate over a long life, affecting neural, endocrine, immunologic, and other physiological systems which can, in turn, react upon physical and mental functioning (cf. Elliott & Eisdorfer, 1982). Biological events, if the social circumstances are adverse, can have deleterious social sequelae. In a familiar early-life example, school-age pregnancy can jeopardize the mother's subsequent life course: If her education is interrupted, educational and job opportunities can become closed; if her family relations are threatened, her social and economic functioning as well as her physical and mental well-being may be impaired (Furstenberg, 1976; Presser, 1974). Without appropriate rehabilitative treatment and family support, her infant, too, predictably underweight, may be at risk of developmental defects if not of perinatal death (Menken, 1972; Nortman, 1974).

Yet, like biological predispositions, not all social situations are immutable. And as the interplay between biological and social aging processes begins to be comprehended, signs of new opportunities and increased flexibilities can be glimpsed in the social structuring of jobs, retirement, households, and communities. Even in nursing homes, social interventions allowing for independence and interaction with other people have demonstrated improved physical and mental functioning and lowered risk of death even in the oldest patients (Rodin, 1980). For individuals, too, accumulated experience can count, as awareness of the need to protect one's health increases. In one example (Maradee Davis, personal communication), although elderly men who live alone tend to suffer from malnutrition, the diets of elderly women living alone are just as nutritious as those of married older people (to be sure, one wonders whether this gender difference in experience will continue to accumulate in oncoming cohorts of older people).

Psychological Functioning

Much like biological functioning, the potential for intellectual and sensory functioning in maturity and old age, once thought to be biologically proscribed, is increasingly found to be responsive to social structures that provide challenge, self-direction, and opportunities for continued use, training, and learning of new strategies. Investigations that illustrate how social structures, themselves changing as longevity lengthens and society changes, impinge on the course of psychological development in adulthood include, for example, studies that:

- Demonstrate improvement in intellectual functioning if the work situation is challenging and demands self-direction (Kohn & Schooler, 1983).
- Point to adult-life opportunities to practice and sharpen those types of ("crystallized") cognitive ability that remain stable or even improve in later adulthood (Horn & Donaldson, 1980).

- Demonstrate improvement in older people's performance on intelligence tests if the social environment affords both incentives and opportunities for practicing and learning new strategies (Baltes & Willis, 1982).
- Indicate that even slowed reaction time, long attributed to aging losses in central nervous system functioning, can be markedly improved in social situations that provide training, consistent feedback, and encouragement (Perone & Baron, 1982).

One exciting line of research here points to the use of accumulated social and psychological experience to compensate for biologically based age deficits when they do occur. Consider the example of vision (cf. Hoyer & Plude, 1982) as a perceptual process where persistent structural changes in the eye begin at very early ages. However, as retinal images deteriorate, perceptual and cognitive processes are brought sharply into play, to select and integrate the available cues and to activate these cues in order to construct what older people "see." For example, even though for me the road sign is largely a blur, as long as I can discern the initial letter "D" and that the word is comparatively short, then I can "see" that the sign must say "Detroit." Whence do these perceptual abilities arise? Clearly from the accumulation and mental integration of many selected perceptions of relevant situations in the past. Thus, vision, even though physiologically deteriorating with age, can continue to function as the consequence of accumulated experiences.

Or consider the example of wisdom as a currently undervalued and understudied asset of later life (Riley, 1983b). Like vision, wisdom clearly rests on the accumulation of experience. Wisdom creates a perspective for evaluating alternative actions, setting priorities, knowing what responses a situation requires. Wisdom is apparent through its absence when adolescents combine drinking with driving or when they approach their first sexual encounter. Wisdom does not mean sustaining childhood—Ashley Montague's (1981) "neotony"— but sustaining and extending the strengths of adulthood. Yet, while psychologists have concentrated on those cognitive or neuropsychological variables that develop in early life and may be vulnerable to deterioration in old age, little serious scientific attention has been given to wisdom as a strengthening of intellectual functioning that is unique to later life (cf. Dittman-Kohli & Baltes, in press). Only now are we beginning to reconceptualize and to seek measures for wisdom as it depends on lifetime processes of aging through social roles: Acquisition of styles of thinking, coping, and relating to others; personal approaches to discontinuities and problems of identity; and the development of active, innovative, creative attacks on living.

In short, we now recognize the possibilities of optimizing physical and intellectual functioning in the extended life course through changes in social structures and through utilization of accumulated experience. To be sure, accumulated experience can wreak utter confusion. Minds can become replete with names, faces, facts, ideas, and emotions gathered over the many decades. It is small wonder that the elderly have difficulties of retrieval!

Yet it is possible to bring order into this chaos. There are strategies for integrating and selecting the proper pieces at the proper times—strategies that can be learned and continually practiced. And the broad base of accumulated experience is needed—for wisdom, decision making, human relationships, order, and innovation in our own lengthening lives. Accumulated experience is needed in our collective shaping of new roles that can avoid the limitations and capitalize on the strengths of the past. It is needed if, in the words of Derek Bok, we are to add "to the growth of the economy, the pursuit of culture, or the enhancement of the human spirit" (1983, p. 6); or in the words of Winston White, we "conceive of the ideally good society as one that continually seeks to develop the capacities of all its members and to provide them with the opportunities for exercising these capacities" (1961, p. 211).

Potentials for Structural Change

What, then, is the outlook for the proximate future? As longevity yields wider options in the social structure and extends the lifelong accumulation of experiences, what are the future potentials for shaping these structures and for activating these experiences? Perhaps women and men will work collaboratively in developing these potentials, as men adapt their own identities to the societal changes, and as (with "androgyny") the gender typing of roles becomes blurred in later life once childrearing is over and, with retirement, the distinction between paid and unpaid work is set aside (Gutmann, 1976; McGee & Wells, 1982; Sinnott, 1982). Yet even more than men, women of the future will be coming toward the end of life with greater experience with close relationships, with multiple roles, and with the multiple facets of aging. These future cohorts of older women will have been innovators, adding work to family, practicing flexibility in modifying their own lives, and helping to organize the lives of others. Thus, women, with their longer lives and their fresh approaches to old problems, may predictably set the future pace for humankind.

Since longevity has now surpassed all historical parallels, I can only share with you some of my own visions of this future over the next half century—not as givens, but only as possibles, suggested by fragmentary data:

- Longevity will bring new needs for health care as death is postponed and a substantial minority of the very old become ill and disabled. Women, as the traditional carers (cf. Aiken, 1983), will take the lead in inventing new forms of lay care (social, mental, and spiritual as well as physical) to supplement current high technology cures.
- Longevity will bring new flexibility in the phasing over the life course of education, work, and leisure. Such flexibility, already widely practiced in the lives of women, is beginning to appear throughout the society, as adults return to school, industry relaxes its work schedules, and at last count (*The New York Times,* August 14, 1983) one-fifth of all United States workers (most by choice) work only part-time.

• Longevity will give women a new capacity for self-hood—for independence, personal mastery, assurance. Women can use this capacity to
give new character to outmoded structures: To bulwark humane standards
in political life in face of reaction and militarism; to teach employers to
expect what older workers have long since come to know about their own
competence (cf. Huber & Spitze, 1983); to infuse leisure with their special
expressive and artistic talents and their accumulated experience.

For the foreseeable future, longevity will bring massive problems both for the
elderly and for society. But longevity will also mean continuing transformation
of kinship relations, continuing proliferation of role options, continuing increments of accumulated experience, continuing alteration in the social, psychological, and biological patterns of growing up and growing old. As we all know,
social change does not just happen. All of us can exercise the newly available
options, can make use of the enlarged stores of experience, can enhance health
and effective functioning, and can contribute fresh social meanings to work,
leisure, and human relationships as lives grow longer. We can use the perspective gleaned from long experience to rethink our social assumptions. My husband
and I already have started again on that book on new and more humane leisure
roles, the book we began half a century ago.

References

Aiken, L. H. Nurses. In D. Mechanic (Ed.), *Handbook of health, health care, and the
health professions*. New York: The Free Press, 1983, pp. 407–431.

Allan, C., & Brotman, H. *Chartbook on aging in America. The 1981 White House
conference on aging*. Washington, D.C.: U.S. Government Printing Office, 1981.

Baltes, P. B., & Willis, S. L. Plasticity and enhancement of intellectual functioning in old
age. In F. I. M. Craik & E. E. Trehub (Eds.), *Aging and cognitive processes*. New
York: Plenum Press, 1982, pp. 353–389.

Bok, D.C. *The President's Report 1981–82*. Cambridge, Mass.: Harvard University,
1983.

Brody, J. A., & Brock, D. B. Epidemiological and statistical characteristics of the United
States elderly population. In C. Finch & E. Schneider (Eds.), *Handbook of the
biology of aging*. New York: Van Nostrand Reinhold, in press.

Campbell, A., Converse, P. E., Miller, W. E., & Stokes, D. E. *The American voter*.
New York: John Wiley, 1960.

Cherlin, A. J., & Furstenberg, F. F., Jr. The shape of the American family in the year
2000. *Trend analysis program*. Washington, D.C.: American Council of Life Insurance, 1982.

Croll, E. J., 1981. Women in rural production and reproduction in the Soviet Union,
China, Cuba, and Tanzania: Socialist development experiences. *Signs*, Winter,
1981, *7*, 361–374.

Dearman, N. B., & Plisko, V. W. (Eds.), *The condition of education*. Washington, D.C.:
U.S. Government Printing Office, 1982.

DeLongis, A., Coyne, J. C., Dakof, G., Folkman, S., & Lazarus, R. S. Relationship of daily hassles, uplifts, and major life events to health status. *Health Psychology,* 1982, *1,* 119–136.

Dittman-Kohli, F., & Baltes, P. B. Toward a neofunctionalist conception of adult intellectual development: wisdom as a prototypical case of intellectual growth. In C. Alexander & E. Langer (Eds.), *Beyond formal operations: Alternative endpoints to human development,* in press.

Elliott, G. R., & Eisdorfer, C. (Eds.), *Stress and human health: Analysis and implications of research.* New York: Springer, 1982.

Feinlieb, M. The Framingham Offspring Study: Design and preliminary data. *Preventive Medicine,* 1975, *4,* 518–525.

Furstenberg, F. F., Jr. *Unplanned parenthood: The social consequences of teenage child bearing.* New York: The Free Press, 1976.

Gutmann, D. Individual adaptation in the middle years: Developmental issues in the masculine mid-life crisis. *Psychiatry,* 1976, *9,* 41–59.

Hagestad, G. O. Problems and promises in the social psychology of intergenerational relations. In R. W. Fogel, E. Hatfield, S. B. Kiesler, & E. Shanas (Eds.), *Aging: Stability and change in the family.* New York: Academic Press, pp. 11–46.

Haynes, S. G., & Feinlieb, M. Women, work and coronary heart disease: Prospective findings from the Framingham Heart Study. *American Journal of Public Health,* 1980, *70,* 133–141.

Helsing, K. J., & Szklo, M. Mortality after bereavement. *American Journal of Epidemiology,* 1981, *114,* 41–52.

Hess, B. B., & Waring, J. M. Parent and child in later life: Rethinking the relationship. In R. M. Lerner & G. B. Spanier (Eds.), *Child influences on marital and family interaction.* New York: Academic Press, 1978, pp. 241–273.

Horn, J. L., & Donaldson, G. Cognitive development in adulthood. In O. G. Brim, Jr. & J. Kagan (Eds.), *Constancy and change in human development.* Cambridge, Mass.: Harvard University Press, 1980, pp. 445–529.

Hoyer, W. J., & Plude, D. J. Aging and the allocation of attentional resources in visual information-processing. In R. Sekular, D. Kline, & K. Dismukes (Eds.), *Aging and human visual function.* New York: Alan R. Liss, 1982, pp. 245–263.

Huber, J., & Spitze, G. *Sex stratification: Children, housework, and jobs.* New York: Academic Press, 1983.

Kohn, M., & Schooler, C. *Work and personality: An inquiry into the impact of social stratification.* Norwood, N.J.: Ablex Press, 1983.

McGee, J., & Wells, K. Gender typing and androgyny in later life: New directions for theory and research. *Human Development,* 1982, *25,* 116–139.

Manton, K. G. Changing concepts of morbidity and mortality in the elderly population. *Milbank Memorial Fund Quarterly,* 1982, *60,* 183–244.

Marks, S. R. Multiple roles and role strain: Some notes on human energy, time and commitment. *American Sociological Review,* 1977, *42,* 921–936.

Menken, J. The health and social consequences of teenage child bearing. *Family Planning Perspectives,* 1972, *3,* 54–63.

Merton, R. K. *Socially expected durations: A temporal component of social structure.* Paper presented as the American Sociological Association Career of Distinguished Scholarship Award Lecture, San Francisco, August, 1982.

Montague, A. *Growing young.* New York: McGraw-Hill, 1981.

Nortman, D. Parental age as a factor in pregnancy outcome in child development. *Reports on Population/Family Planning,* 1974, *16,* 1–51.

Perone, M., & Baron, A. Age-related effects of pacing on acquisition and performance of response sequences: An operant analysis. *Journal of Gerontology*, 1982, *37*, 443–449.

Presser, H. Early motherhood: Ignorance or bliss? *Family Planning Perspectives*, 1974, *6*, 8–14.

Preston, S. H. *Mortality patterns in national populations: With special reference to recorded causes of death*. New York: Academic Press, 1976.

Riley, J. W., Jr. Dying and the meanings of death: Sociological inquiries. *Annual Review of Sociology*, 1983, *9*, 191–216.

Riley, M. W. Aging, social change, and the power of ideas. *Daedalus*, 1978, *197*, 39–52.

Riley, M. W. Health behavior of older people: Toward a new paradigm. In D. L. Parron, F. Solomon, & J. Rodin (Eds.), *Health behavior and aging*. Washington, D.C.: National Academy Press, 1981, pp. 25–39.

Riley, M. W. Aging and social change. In M. W. Riley, R. P. Abeles, & M. S. Teitelbaum (Eds.), *Aging from birth to death Volume II: Sociotemporal perspectives* (AAAS Selected Symposium 79), Boulder, Colo.: Westview Press, 1982, pp. 11–26.

Riley, M. W. The family in an aging society: A matrix of latent relationships. *Journal of Family Issues*, 1983, *4*, 439–454. (a)

Riley, M. W. *Aging and society: Notes on the development of new understandings*. Paper presented at the University of Michigan, Ann Arbor, December 12, 1983. (b)

Riley, M. W. Age strata in social systems. In R. H. Binstock & E. Shanas (Eds.), *Handbook on aging and the social sciences*. New York: Van Nostrand Reinhold. 2nd Edition, in press. (a)

Riley, M. W. Aging, health, and social change: An overview. In M. W. Riley, A. S. Baum, & J. D. Matarazzo (Eds.), *Perspectives on behavioral medicine Volume IV: Biomedical and psychosocial dimensions of aging*. New York: Academic Press, in press. (b)

Riley, M. W., & Foner, A. *Aging and society* (Vol. 1). New York: Russell Sage Foundation, 1968.

Riley, M. W., & Waring, J. Age and aging. In R. K. Merton & R. Nisbet (Eds.), *Contemporary social problems*. New York: Harcourt Brace Jovanovich, 1976, pp. 337–410.

Rodin, J. Managing the stress of aging: The role of control and coping. In S. Levine & H. Ursin (Eds.), *Coping and health*. New York: Plenum Press, 1980, pp. 171–202.

Rossi, A. S. Aging and parenthood in the middle years. In P. Baltes, & O. G. Brim (Eds.), *Life-span development and behavior* (Vol. 3). New York: Academic Press, 1980, pp. 137–205. (a)

Rossi, A. S. Life-span theories and women's lives. *Signs: Journal of Women in Culture and Society*, 1980, *6*, 4–32. (b)

Rossi, A. S. Gender and parenthood. *American Sociological Review*, 1984, *49*, 1–19.

Sieber, S. D. Toward a theory of role accumulation. *American Sociological Review*, 1974, *39*, 567–578.

Sinnott, J. D. Correlates of sex roles of older adults. *Journal of Gerontology*, 1982, *37*, 587–594.

Smelser, N.J. *Essays in sociological explanation*. Englewood Cliffs, N.J.: Prentice-Hall, 1968.

Spreitzer, E., Snyder, E. E., & Larson, D. L. Multiple roles and psychological well-being. *Sociological Focus*, 1979, *12*, 141–148.

The New York Times, August 14, 1983.

Torrey, B. B. The lengthening of retirement. In M. W. Riley, R. P. Abeles, and M. S. Teitelbaum (Eds.), *Aging from birth to death Volume II: Sociotemporal perspectives.* Boulder, Colo.: Westview Press, 1982, pp. 181–196.

Turner, R. H. *Family interaction.* New York: John Wiley, 1970.

Uhlenberg, P. R. A study of cohort life cycles: Cohorts of native born Massachusetts women, 1830–1920. *Population Studies,* 1969, *23,* 407–420.

Uhlenberg, P. R. Death and the family. *Journal of Family History,* 1980, *5,* 313–320.

Verbrugge, L. M. Multiple roles and physical health of women and men. *Journal of Health and Social Behavior,* 1983, *24,* 16 30.

White, W. *Beyond conformity.* New York: The Free Press, 1961.

AUTHOR INDEX

349

SUBJECT INDEX